Global Asset Allocation

WILEY FINANCE EDITIONS

CORPORATE FINANCIAL DISTRESS AND BANKRUPTCY, SECOND EDITION
Edward I. Altman

FIXED-INCOME ARBITRAGE
M. Anthony Wong

TRADING APPLICATIONS OF JAPANESE CANDLESTICK CHARTING
Gary S. Wagner and Brad L. Matheny

FRACTAL MARKET ANALYSIS: APPLYING CHAOS THEORY TO INVESTMENT
AND ECONOMICS
Edgar E. Peters

UNDERSTANDING SWAPS
John F. Marshall and Kenneth R. Kapner

GENETIC ALGORITHMS AND INVESTMENT STRATEGIES
Richard J. Bauer, Jr.

TRADER VIC II—PRINCIPLES OF PROFESSIONAL SPECULATION
Victor Sperandeo

THE NEW TECHNICAL TRADER
Tushar S. Chande and Stanley Kroll

FORECASTING FINANCIAL AND ECONOMIC CYCLES
Michael P. Niemira and Philip A. Klein

TRADING ON THE EDGE
Guido J. Deboeck

GLOBAL ASSET ALLOCATION: TECHNIQUES FOR OPTIMIZING PORTFOLIO
MANAGEMENT
Jess Lederman and Robert Klein, Editors

Global Asset Allocation
Techniques for Optimizing
Portfolio Management

Edited by

Jess Lederman
Robert A. Klein

John Wiley & Sons, Inc.
New York • Chichester • Brisbane • Toronto • Singapore

To Monsieur Veselin Djurdjevac

Library of Congress Cataloging-in-Publication Data:

Lederman, Jess.
    Global asset allocation : techniques for optimizing portfolio
management / Jess Lederman, Robert A. Klein.
        p.   cm. — (Wiley finance editions)
    Includes index.
    ISBN 0-471-59373-7 (cloth : acid-free paper)
    1. Asset allocation.   2. Portfolio management.   3. International
finance.   4. Asset allocation—United States.   5. Portfolio
management—United States.   I. Klein, Robert A. (Robert Arnold),
1953-   , II. Title. III. Series.
HG4529.5.L43   1994
332.6—dc20   94-11921

Printed in the United States of America

10 9 8 7 6 5 4 3 2

About the Editors

Jess Lederman, a private investor and the editor and co-author of seventeen books on the financial markets, is one of the pioneers of the trillion dollar market for mortgage-backed securities. Lederman co-founded two of the nation's largest private sector counterparts to Fannie Mae and Freddie Mac, and was the principal architect of several innovative securities. He was formerly chairman of The Asset Backed Capital Group, and earlier held the positions of executive vice president for Bear Stearns Mortgage Capital Corporation and associate director of Bear Stearns & Co., Inc.

Lederman graduated from Columbia College in New York, and received his MBA from the Columbia University Graduate School of Business.

Robert A. Klein is a leading management consultant and the co-editor of six books on the financial markets. Klein assists Fortune 100 clients and smaller firms in the areas of financial analysis and control, systems design and management, organizational design, PC systems development and training, and operations training. He was formerly assistant portfolio manager of both the Weingarten Equity Fund and the Constellation Growth Fund. Prior to joining Weingarten, Klein was a financial analyst for Citibank.

Klein is a graduate of both the Cornell University College of Arts and Sciences, where he received his Bachelor of Arts in Chemistry, and the Stern School of Business Administration at New York University, where he earned his MBA in Finance.

About the Authors

Brian R. Bruce is vice president and portfolio manager with State Street Global Advisors, where he is responsible for managing SSGA's asset allocation and balanced fund portfolios. Prior to joining State Street, he worked eight years for Northern Investment Management Co., where he was director of international equity. Mr. Bruce serves as editor-in-chief of Institutional Investor's Journal of Investing, and has authored and edited five books on investing. He is also adjunct professor teaching international portfolio management at the Brandeis University Graduate School of International Economics and Finance.

Mr. Bruce received a BS from Illinois State University, an MS in Computer Science from DePaul University, and an MBA in Finance from the University of Chicago.

Roger G. Clarke is president and chief investment officer of TSA Capital Management. He was formerly associate professor of finance at Brigham Young University's Graduate School of Management. He is a recipient of the Roger F. Murray Award for investment research from the Institute for Quantitative Research in Finance, and also received the Financial Analysts Federation's prestigious Graham and Dodd Scroll.

Dr. Clarke is the author of numerous books and articles related to corporate finance and the use of options and futures in investment management. He holds BA and MBA degrees from Brigham Young University and a PhD in Finance from Stanford University.

A. Darrell Braswell, CFA, is a managing director of QuantiLogic Asset Management Company, Inc. He was previously portfolio manager with Pacific Telesis Group pension fund, responsible for internally managed tactical asset allocation assets and externally managed fixed income and international assets. Mr. Braswell has also held positions as consultant and general partner with Frank Gordon Associates and vice president with Dean Witter Reynolds.

Mr. Braswell graduated from East Carolina University with a BS in Business Administration in 1977.

Janice L. Deringer is a principal in Wells Fargo Nikko Investment Advisor's Intermarket Strategies Group. She is responsible for the implementation of domestic and non-U.S. tactical asset allocation strategies and for SIGMA. She oversees the implementation of over $15 billion in tactical asset allocation and related strategies, and coordinates research in this area.

Ms. Deringer joined WFNIA in 1987, having received her BS in Economics and Political Science from Wilammette University and an MBA in Finance from the University of California at Berkeley.

Arjun Divecha is currenty a managing director at Grantham, Mayo, Van Otterloo & Company. He was a managing director at BARRA, responsible for setting up a new portfolio management operation in conjunction with Citibank. He has also handled product development, marketing and client support, and recently managed the development of BARRA's new Emerging Markets and Korean models.

Mr. Divecha did his undergraduate work in Aerospace Engineering at the Indian Institute of Technology in Bombay and received an MBA from Cornell University.

Charles J. Freifeld is senior quantitative analyst with the Fixed Income Management Group of The Boston Company, responsible for the design and implementation of quantitative investment strategies, as well as the analysis of structured investment products containing options and derivative-linked payoffs. Previously, he was president of Advanced Algorithms, Inc., a Commodity Trading Advisor and Commodity Pool Operator. Mr. Freifeld has written articles on portfolio management, spoken at industry conferences, and served as an arbitrator for the National Futures Association.

Mr. Freifeld holds a degree in Mathematics from Columbia College in New York and received an MA and PhD in Mathematics from Harvard University.

Geoffrey Gerber is the chief executive officer and chief investment officer of Twin Capital, with ten years experience as an institutional investment manager. Prior to founding the firm he was senior vice president, head of Quantitative Analysis and Systems for Mellon Equity Associates. He was the portfolio manager for several of Mellon Equity's largest institutional clients, and responsible for all research and investment systems used to manage over $15 billion. Mr. Gerber also served as a director at Prudential Asset Management Company.

Mr. Gerber holds a PhD in Finance and Economics from the University of Pennsylvania and a BA in Economics from the State University of New York at Buffalo.

David A. Hammer, CFA, is the president of Curbstone Investment Management, an independent money manager based in Sandy, Utah. He was formerly the trust investments manager at a prominent regional bank in the west and the chief financial officer of a major insurance company in the northeast. He is the author of *Dynamic Asset Allocation: Strategies for Stock, Bond, and Money Markets* (John Wiley & Sons, 1990).

Steve Hardy started Zephyr Associates in 1994. He co-founded the firm of Balch, Hardy Inc. in 1973. For the past twenty years, the firm has pioneered the use of derivatives among tax-exempt funds, and has recently developed several software packages which it licenses to tax-exempt funds for their internal stock and options management, and has also introduced software which measures manager styles and creates customized style benchmarks.

Prior to co-founding Balch, Hardy Inc., Mr. Hardy was vice president of Dean Witter and Company. He received his degree in Business Administration from Whittier College.

Jennifer Hargreaves, investment officer, joined State Street Global Advisors in 1990. Her responsibilities include managing consulting relationships, marketing research, and prospect communication. Ms. Hargreaves graduated from the University of California, Berkeley, with a BA in Economics.

Peter M. Hill is president of the Institutional Group at Bailard, Biehl & Kaiser. He is responsible for the research, portfolio management, and business development activities of the firm's tax-exempt accounts. As a member of Bailard, Biehl & Kaiser's asset allocation team, he determines the final asset allocation for institutional clients. Mr. Hill also serves as chairman of the board for Bailard, Biehl & Kaiser's International Equity and Fixed Income Funds.

Mr. Hill formerly worked in the United Kingdom as the deputy investment manager for the Royal London Mutual Insurance Society, Ltd. He received a BA in 1972 from Leeds University and is a Fellow of the Institute of Actuaries, London.

Michael Keppler is president of Keppler Asset Management, Inc., a firm that specializes in the development of value-oriented integrated portfolio approaches which focus on specific asset allocation as well as market, sector, and stock selection strategies designed to exploit market inefficiencies. Mr. Keppler serves on the board of directors of the Luxembourg equity mutual fund, Global Advantage Funds; and is a member of the investment committee of Graf Lambsdorff Vermogensverwaltung AG in Germany, a leading money management firm.

Previously, Mr. Keppler served in various capacities in the securities business with the third largest German bank, Commerzbank AG, in both Frankfurt and New York. He holds an MBA from the University of Regensburg, has been an active contributor to numerous investment conferences, and has published in leading investment journals both here and in Germany.

Craig J. Lazzara, CFA, is a vice president with Salomon Brothers. Previously, he was president of Vantage Global Advisors, managing $2 billion in quantitatively disciplined equity, tactical asset allocation, and currency management strategies. Mr. Lazarra was previously a managing director of TSA Capital Management, with responsibilities for both applied research and client relations. Earlier, he was a vice president and portfolio manager for Mellon Bank.

Mr. Lazzara is a graduate of Princeton University and the Harvard Business School.

Michael A. Leavy, CFA, joined Citibank Global Asset Management in 1993 to assist in building a multi-strategy fund business. His responsibilities include qualitative and aquantitative analysis of commodity trading advisors and traditional money managers, and of asset allocation decisions. Previously, he was responsible for portfolio management and quantitative analysis for Quantilogic Asset Management Company.

Mr. Leavy graduated from the University of California at Santa Barbara with a BA in Economics.

Scott L. Lummer, PhD, CFA, is a managing director of Ibbotson Associates in charge of the Consulting Services Group. His research has appeared in the *Journal of Financial Economics, Financial Management,* the *Journal of Investing,* the *CFA Digest,* and several other publications. He has conducted lectures in investments and corporate finance for numerous organizations and has served on several committees, including the Association for Investment Management and Research and the Financial Management Association.

Dr. Lummer was a professor at Texas A&M University from 1983 to 1992, and has served as a visiting professor at Johannes Kepler University in Austria. He received his BS in Mathematics and his PhD in Finance from Purdue University.

Larry L. Martin, CFA, is senior vice president for State Street Global Advisors, where he is responsible for overseeing the management of all global passive and active portfolios. Mr. Martin joined Asset Management in 1982 and was instrumental in the development of the stock index futures funds, SPIFF and SPIFF Plus. Specializing in quantitative analysis, he also developed the Cash Plus product, which employs arbitrage trading between stocks and stock index futures. Previously, Mr. Martin was head of the Core Portfolio Services Department, overseeing all U.S. passive equity portfolios. He is a graduate of Cornell University with a degree in Applied Mathematics and holds an MBA from Boston University.

Douglas B. McCalla became first investment officer of the San Diego City Employees' Retirement System after serving as a SDCERS trustee for four years. He is responsible for the administration of a $1.1 billion investment program. Previously, he was first administrator of the City of San Diego's Supplemental Pension Savings Plan, a defined contribution system established to replace participation in Social Security. Mr. McCalla also has 13 years experience as an independent financial consultant.

Mr. McCalla is a graduate of San Diego State University with a BA degree and graduate level studies in Industrial/Personnel Psychology. He has published articles on the subject of the impact of computerized management information systems on both individual decision makers and organizations.

Jack Mosevich is a senior partner with Harris Investment Management, Inc. Previously, he was president of Burns Fry Analytics Inc., and earlier held management positions in operations research and fixed income analytics. Mr. Mosevich was a professor of Computer Science at the University of Waterloo. He holds a PhD in Mathematics from the University of British Columbia.

J. S. Parsons is a vice president with the San Francisco office of Merrill Lynch, where he specializes in equity derivatives. He was previously executive vice president with Leland O'Brien Rubinstein Associates Incorporated.

Mr. Parsons graduated from Claremont Men's College with a degree in Mathematics and Economics, and received an MBA from the University of Chicago.

E. K. Easton Ragsdale, CFA, is a senior vice president and Kidder, Peabody's chief quantitative analyst, responsible for the Kidder, Peabody Asset Allocation Mutual Fund. Prior to joining Kidder in 1989, Mr. Ragsdale was a vice president and senior industry analyst with First National Bank of Chicago, responsible for analyses of economic and industry factors affecting the firm's loan portfolio. From 1982 to 1986, he developed equity investment strategies in the investment management group at American National Bank & Trust Company as research analyst and second vice president. He spent a number of years in academia as an instructor with the Illinois Institute of Technology and the University of Chicago and has been an independent consultant.

He has an AB in History and an MBA with specializations in Statistics and Marketing. Mr. Ragsdale has been a chartered financial analyst since 1989 and has received Certificates of Achievement (1990–1993) from the Institute of Chartered Financial Analysts. He is a member of the Association for Investment Management & Research, New York Society of Security Analysts, and the Society of Quantitative Analysts.

Gita R. Rao, PhD, is vice president and quantitative analyst in Equity Research with Kidder, Peabody & Co. Incorporated. Ms. Rao joined Kidder, Peabody in 1991. She was formerly an assistant professor of Finance at the University of Illinois at Urbana-Champaign.

Ms. Rao graduated with honors in Economics from St. Stephen's College, Delhi University, Delhi, India. She received an MBA degree from the Indian Institute of Management, Ahmedabad, India, and worked in product management for the Indian subsidiary of Nestle Inc. She received her PhD in Finance from the University of Rochester, the topic of her dissertation being the post-offering earnings and stock price performance of IPOs. She is a member of the American Finance Association, the Society of Quantitative Analysts, the National Association of Business Economists, and the New York Society of Security Analysts.

Mark W. Riepe is a vice president with Ibbotson Associates, where he is a member of both the Consulting Services Group and Legal Services Group. He has authored studies on corporate planning, bankruptcy, valuation of a corporate division, the performance of asset classes, money manager evaluation, equity investing styles, global investing, the appropriate return on equity for regulated utilities, and pension fund investment policy.

Prior to joining Ibbotson Associates, Mr. Riepe worked for four years at GNP Commodities specializing in financial futures and options research. He received his BA in Economics and his MBA in Financial Management from the University of Chicago.

Laurence B. Siegel is a managing director of Ibbotson Associates, which he co-founded with Roger G. Ibbotson. He is an author, consultant, and lecturer on cost of capital, investment policy and strategy, asset allocation, capital market history, and other economic issues. Among Mr. Siegel's many accomplishments is the design of a bond index and related futures contract for Moody's Investors Service and the COMEX.

Prior to joining Ibbotson Associates in 1979, Mr. Siegel was a regulatory economist for the Marmon Group and the American Enterprise

Institute. He received his BA in Urban Studies and his MBA in Finance and Economics from the University of Chicago.

Lawrence G. Tint is chief investment officer for the Intermarket Strategies Group of Wells Fargo Nikko Investment Advisors. He rejoined WFNIA in 1990 from Sharpe-Tint, Inc., where he served as president. Prior to Sharpe-Tint, Mr. Tint served in a variety of senior research and product development roles at Trust Company of the West, Wilshire Associates and Merrill Lynch. He has published articles in a number of journals on subjects ranging from performance evaluation to integrated asset allocation, and has been a frequent guest speaker at professional conferences.

Mr. Tint received an AB in Economics from Haverford College, and an MBA in Finance and Operations Research from the Wharton School of Finance of the University of Pennsylvania.

Heydon D. Traub, CFA, is senior vice president and unit head of Non-U.S. Active Strategies for State Street Global Advisors. His responsibilities include portfolio management, currency hedging, and research and development of new investment services. Mr. Traub previously worked with Brandeis University as a financial analyst. He is a graduate of Brandeis University with a BA in Economics and holds an MBA in Finance and Accounting from the University of Chicago Graduate School of Business.

Richard A. Weiss is a senior vice president of SAWWA Trust, responsible for supervising the research and development of global tactical asset allocation and active currency management strategies. Formerly, Mr. Weiss was senior vice president at Vantage Global Advisors and a managing director and senior investment strategist at TSA Capital Management. Earlier, he was an investment strategist at Paine Webber Inc., and a vice president and head of the quantitative and systems area at Mellon Bank in Pittsburgh.

Mr. Weiss has a BS degree in Finance and Statistics from The Wharton School, University of Pennsylvania and an MBA in Finance from the University of Chicago.

Richard Q. Wendt is a principal and director of Asset/Liability Forecasting with Towers Perrin, specializing in providing financial planning services to a variety of clients. He is also responsible for the maintenance and development of the firm's asset/liability models. Previously, Mr. Wendt was pension actuary for a large life insurance company, responsible for group annuity product development and financial reporting. He has been on the faculty of the Society of Actuaries' Pension Forecasting seminar and is a former member of the American Academy of Actuaries' Committee on Pension Accounting.

Mr. Wendt is a Fellow of the Society of Actuaries, a member of the American Academy of Actuaries and an Enrolled Actuary. He holds a BS in Mathematics from the University of Notre Dame and a Master of Actuarial Science degree from the University of Michigan.

Kurt Winkelmann is manager, fixed income at Vestek Systems, a San Francisco based investment technology company. Prior to joining Vestek Systems, he worked at BARRA as manager, fixed income marketing.

Mr. Winkelmann has a PhD in Economics from the University of Minnesota and undergraduate degrees in Mathematics and Economics from Macalester College.

Jeffrey L. Winter, PhD, CFA, is a managing director of QuantiLogic Asset Management Company, Inc. Previously, he was manager of investment planning and strategy and executive director of investment management with the Pacific Telesis Group pension fund, responsible for overall fund strategy and oversight of internal and external asset management. Mr. Winter earlier was senior investment analyst with the Amoco Corp. pension fund, responsible for quantitative investment analysis.

Mr. Winter is chairman of the Council of Examiners of the Institute of Chartered Financial Analysts and a member of the editorial board of the CFA Digest. He graduated from the New Mexico Institute of Mining and Technology with a BS and MS in Mathematics, and graduated from Arizona State University with a PhD in Mathematics.

Preface

Over the past several years, no aspect of portfolio management has attracted more attention—and controversy—than asset allocation. Many analysts have proclaimed asset allocation as the key to investment success, far outweighing the importance of individual security selection. Others complain that faddish asset allocation strategies have proved disastrously counterproductive. Quantitative experts have created complex models to compute optimal asset allocation decisions, but some equally bright minds have pointed out that there are serious problems with many of the input assumptions being used, as well as the techniques for implementing the models' output.

As explained in the Introduction that follows, the topic of asset allocation covers a wide spectrum, from strategic decisions about long-term weightings for different asset classes to short-term adjustments of the asset mix in response to market fluctuations. Several excellent books have been published that cover the basics of asset allocation, but this volume is the most comprehensive source of information ever compiled on state-of-the-art asset allocation techniques. *Global Asset Allocation* explores the latest quantitative analytical techniques and the most successful asset allocation models. Equally important, it offers detailed discussions of critical input assumptions and practical application issues, and it broadens the scope to include consideration of allocations that go far beyond the traditional asset classifications. These chapters are the result of years of research, analysis, and market experience by men and women who are preeminent in their field. Readers will find it to be a working handbook that they can use to solve real-world problems and make portfolio management decisions.

The early chapters offer insight into the strategies, tactics, and analytical tools that will be the fundamentals for investment success as the 21st century approaches. Mean-variance optimization (MVO) is one of the cornerstones of modern asset allocation theory. Chapters 1 through 4 explore different aspects of MVO, including critical implementation issues and input variables such as expected return, volatility, and correlation of return between asset classes.

Synthetic and derivative instruments such as futures and options have greatly increased the ability of portfolio managers to access new asset classes. Chapters 5 and 6 provide an overview of how synthetics and derivatives can be integrated into an asset allocation strategy.

An asset classification such as "stocks" is extremely broad, encompassing everything from risky high-flyers to staid blue-chip issues. Chapters 7 and 8 argue that allocating between styles of equity management can be as important as allocating between asset classes. Chapter 9 turns from the equity market to the bond market, and offers specific techniques for constructing optimal fixed-income portfolios.

The next four chapters deal with various aspects of strategic and tactical asset allocation. Chapter 10 discusses asset/liability forecasting, which is the building block for strategic asset allocation decisions. Chapter 11 analyzes the implications of transaction costs on tactical asset allocation decisions, and Chapters 12 and 13 detail the inner workings and evolution of two of the most successful tactical asset allocation models.

Although its application to finance is as yet unproven, chaos theory, one of the newest and most exciting branches of mathematics, may give 21st-century portfolio managers a critical competitive edge. Chapter 14 provides an overview of chaos theory and examines how it may one day be applied by tactical asset allocators.

Smart investors are constantly searching for new investment frontiers and new asset classes to add to the portfolio mix. The international markets are the ultimate investment frontier, and domestic money managers are increasingly turning their attention overseas. The quantitative and qualitative aspects of global investing and their application in asset allocation strategies are the subject of the remaining chapters.

Chapter 15 begins with a general discussion of global asset allocation, outlines the incremental risks and rewards, and offers a framework for implementation. Chapter 16 then gives a comprehensive overview of global fixed income and currency management. Chapter 17 expands the early chapters' discussion of tactical asset allocation to a global context. The next two chapters deal with country allocation strategies: Chapter 18 demonstrates how traditional risk–return concepts need to be revised in evaluating country allocations, and Chapter 19 explains why investing in "risky" emerging markets can actually reduce overall portfolio volatility. Chapter 20, the final chapter, explores how global passive management can provide a cost-effective way of diversifying into the world marketplace.

Many thanks must be given to each of the contributing authors for the time and energy they took from their hectic schedules to produce this important contribution to the existing body of literature on asset allocation. We are also grateful to the superb staff at John Wiley & Sons, without whose help this project could not have been completed.

JESS LEDERMAN AND ROBERT A. KLEIN

Contents

Introduction

The Role of Asset Allocation in Portfolio Management

Scott L. Lummer, PhD, CFA
Managing Director

Mark W. Riepe
Vice President
Ibbotson Associates, Inc.
Chicago, Illinois

> Tis the part of a wise man to keep himself today for tomorrow, and not venture all his eggs in one basket.
>
> Miguel de Cervantes, *Don Quixote de la Mancha*, 1605.

> Behold, the fool saith, "Put not all thine eggs in the one basket"— which is but a manner of saying, "Scatter your money and attention"; but the wise man saith, "Put all your eggs in the one basket and— WATCH that basket."
>
> Mark Twain, *Pudd'nhead Wilson*, 1894.

Cervantes and Twain were both great writers, but Cervantes would have been the better investor. In fact, diversification has been a key component of asset allocation for some time. A prominent magazine, in 1926, recommended that a portfolio contain 25 percent sound bonds, 25 percent sound preferreds, 25 percent sound common stocks, and 25 percent speculative securities.[1] This may not be an entirely appropriate portfolio today, but the importance of asset allocation remains.

Any security-specific selection decision is preceded, either implicitly or explicitly, by an asset allocation decision. Asset allocation is therefore the most fundamental of investment decisions. Recent

The authors wish to thank Laurence B. Siegel for his helpful comments.

1

research has estimated that the asset allocation decision accounts for 91.5 percent of the variation between returns on different portfolios.[2] With this result, it is not surprising that asset allocation has found its way into the financial spotlight. But the spotlight has not always been focused properly. Until recently, asset allocation was a pedestrian affair. Many institutional investors were advised to allocate 60 percent of their assets to stocks and 40 percent to fixed income. Individual investors would be advised to allocate anywhere from 100 percent stocks to 100 percent bonds, depending on such factors as age, income, number of dependents, and so on. The basis of analysis on which this recommendation was determined could most charitably be described as ad hoc.

Today, asset allocation is a far more rigorous enterprise involving the use of tools that have transformed the process. What follows is a brief survey of these tools.

MEAN-VARIANCE OPTIMIZATION

Mean-variance optimization (MVO) refers to a mathematical process that calculates the security or asset class weights that provide a portfolio with the maximum expected return for a given level of risk; or, conversely, the minimum risk for a given expected return. The inputs needed to conduct MVO are: security expected returns, expected standard deviations, and expected cross-security correlations. For his work in developing this process, Harry Markowitz was awarded a share of the 1990 Nobel Prize in Economics.[3]

When first developed, mean-variance optimization was applied (if at all) only to portfolios of individual stocks. Today, this technique is applied with increasing frequency on an asset class level. This trend is appropriate for two reasons. First, the inputs required by the Markowitz model are more difficult to estimate for individual securities than they are for asset classes. Second, the range of asset classes available to investors is now much larger, especially given the increased willingness of U.S. investors to consider global investing.

Institutional investors are not the only ones to benefit from this development. Retail brokerage houses have traditionally provided only stock selection advice to their individual clients. However, with increasing frequency, they are suggesting a greater degree of passive security selection, and instead are providing asset allocation recommendations to their investors. This is accomplished by using optimization to create allocations that give their individual accounts greater expected return, less risk, or both. In addition, sophisticated techniques derived from utility theory and behavioral economics can be employed to develop questionnaires that more accurately gauge an individual's risk preferences.

Optimization has also found a home with pension fund managers, who consider not just the assets themselves when choosing investment mixes, but the fund liabilities and the interaction between the two. The resulting allocations maximize the expected fund surplus (assets minus liabilities) for a given level of risk.

The consequence of mean-variance optimization is a set of asset class weights that can be used as a long-term guide for investing. This is often described as the portfolio's *strategic asset allocation* plan. The portfolio weights should be updated occasionally to reflect changes in estimates of the long-term parameters or different needs of the portfolio. However, these changes will likely result in only small revisions in the portfolio composition.

DYNAMIC ASSET ALLOCATION

Dynamic asset allocation refers to strategies that continually adjust a portfolio's allocation in response to changing market conditions. The most popular use of these strategies is *portfolio insurance.* Broadly speaking, portfolio insurance is any strategy that attempts to remove the downside risk faced by a portfolio. A popular means of implementing portfolio insurance is to engage in a series of transactions that give the portfolio the return distribution of a call option.

Option replication is based on the work of Fischer Black and Myron Scholes, who showed that, under certain assumptions, the payoff of an option can be duplicated through a continuously revised combination of the underlying asset and a risk-free bond.[4] Hayne Leland and Mark Rubenstein extended this insight by showing that a dynamic strategy that increased (decreased) the stock allocation of a portfolio in rising (falling) markets and reinvested the remaining portion in cash would replicate the payoffs to a call option on an index of stocks.[5]

Through the mid-1980s, the popularity of portfolio insurance programs soared. It has been alleged that the procyclical nature of these strategies contributed to greater market volatility, particularly during the stock market crash of October 19, 1987. Moreover, portfolio insurance proved to be unsuccessful in totally eliminating losses on the day of the crash. Consequently, the use and viability of portfolio insurance are controversial. Nevertheless, portfolio insurance continues to play a significant role in asset allocation.

TACTICAL ASSET ALLOCATION

Tactical asset allocation (also known as market timing or active asset allocation) is the process of diverging from the strategic asset allocation when an investor's short-term forecasts deviate from the long-term forecasts used to formulate the strategic allocation. If the investor can make accurate short-term forecasts, tactical asset allocation has the potential to enhance returns. In practice, tactical asset allocation (TAA) models tend to recommend contrarian trades; that is, they recommend purchasing (selling) an asset as its current market value drops (rises).[6] When viewed in this light, TAA becomes the mirror image of portfolio insurance. In other words, tactical asset allocators are the investors providing portfolio insurance.[7]

One consequence of TAA is that, by overweighting certain assets during certain times and underweighting others, the portfolio is riskier because of its reduced diversification. Therefore, the strategy would need to generate above-market returns as compensation for this added risk. Whether tactical asset allocators have achieved this is a matter of continuing study. It is certain, however, that because the potential returns from successful TAA would be large, researchers will continue their investigations, and investors will continue to listen to their findings.

THE FUTURE OF ASSET ALLOCATION

Most forecasters fall into two camps. Forecasters in the first camp are eager to predict that the future will closely mirror the recent past. Their archetypes are those damnable generals who are always preparing to fight the last war. Forecasters in the second camp rely heavily on the adage that the only constant is change itself. Graduates of this school of thought usually don't know what to expect but are quite sure it will not be like anything that has been seen before. These caricatures are a bit harsh, but they illustrate the problem of forecasting.

We view the future of asset allocation through lenses borrowed from both camps. Certain current aspects of asset allocation will continue to be recognizable for many years; others will be historical curiosities. To be more precise, the goals and importance of asset allocation will not change, but the mechanisms by which investors seek to achieve those goals will be new.

The goal of the asset allocation decision was, is, and will be to select a combination of assets that will generate a return sufficiently high and safe so as to offset some future liability. It is also safe to say that asset allocation decisions will have a continuing large role in explaining portfolio returns.

The mechanisms of implementing the asset allocation decision will be quite different. We see significant progress in at least three areas:

1. The neatly drawn return distributions (e.g., those shown in Figure I.1) in the marketing brochures of portfolio insurers have understandable appeal. Unfortunately, the diagrams assume

FIGURE I.1   Return Distribution for Uninsured and Insured Portfolios

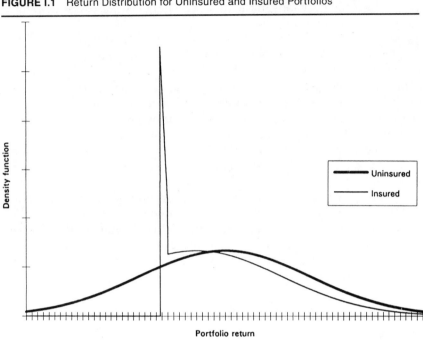

certain market conditions that are not always present. For example, portfolio insurance programs work best when prices do not "jump" and markets have sufficient liquidity.[8] These conditions were not present during the October 1987 crash. In the future, we will see insurance programs that will be more adequately prepared to deal with certain types of market failure.

2. Optimization will continue to play a role in asset allocation, but whether it is the mean-variance optimization practiced today is another question. Using variance as a proxy for risk troubles many investors. Today, numerous researchers are investigating alternative measures of risk (e.g., minimizing the probability of a return below a certain level). Perhaps, in the future, a practical model will be developed that incorporates more intuitive measures of risk. In addition, mean-variance optimization is a one-period model. We expect researchers to develop more robust models that allow investors to enter time-dependent estimates of expected return, risk, and correlation for their assets and then optimize accordingly.

3. Many of the securities investors will use to implement asset allocation decisions in the future do not exist today and will have to be invented.

The asset allocation recommendation for 1926, mentioned earlier, was probably the product of the collective intuition of a writer and some of his acquaintances in the financial community. The process of determining this allocation would probably not be described today as rigorous. We now approach the asset allocation problem more formally, and many advances have been made. Nevertheless, asset allocation remains more art than science and will probably remain so as long as the models used are only approximations of a reality that is in constant flux.

There continues to be a need for investors and researchers to scrutinize the assumptions underlying today's models and evaluate whether the model is a sufficient reflection of reality. Undoubtedly, most of today's approaches will be found wanting in the future, and new advances will be made. Whatever the future holds, it is sure to be interesting. Enjoy the ride!

NOTES

1. *The Magazine of Wall Street*, 1926.
2. Gary P. Brinson, Brian D. Singer, and Gilbert L. Beebower, "Determinants of Portfolio Performance II: An Update," *Financial Analysts Journal* (May/June 1991): 40–48.
3. The original works that set out the principles of mean-variance optimization are: Harry M. Markowitz, "Portfolio Selection," *Journal of Finance* (March 1952): 77–91; and *Portfolio Selection: Efficient Diversification of Investments* (New York: John Wiley & Sons, 1959).
4. Fischer Black and Myron Scholes, "The pricing of Options and Corporate Liabilities," *Journal of Political Economy* (May/June 1973): 637–654.
5. Mark Rubenstein and Hayne E. Leland, "Replicating Options with Positions in Stocks and Cash," *Financial Analysts Journal* (July/August 1981): 63–72.
6. This argument is more fully developed in William F. Sharpe, "Asset Allocation," in John L. Maginn and Donald L. Tuttle, eds., *Managing Investment Portfolios: A Dynamic Process* 2d ed. (Charlottesville, VA: Association for Investment Management and Research, 1990).
7. See William F. Sharpe and André F. Perold, "Dynamic Strategies for Asset Allocation," *Financial Analysts Journal* (January/February 1988): 16–27.
8. A price jump occurs when, for example, a stock trades at $100 per share and then $90 per share, with no opportunity for an investor to transact at an intermediate price. The jump is problematic for dynamic asset allocation because it becomes impossible for the portfolio insurer to gradually sell the stock as it drops from $100 and $90. Liquidity is also necessary because the portfolio insurer, like all traders, requires a counterparty. If the market is illiquid, the series of transactions necessary to replicate the option cannot be undertaken.

1

Taming Your Optimizer:
A Guide through the Pitfalls of
Mean-Variance Optimization

Scott L. Lummer, Ph.D., CFA
Managing Director

Mark W. Riepe
Vice President

Laurence B. Siegel
Managing Director
Ibbotson Associates, Inc.
Chicago, Illinois

Although mean-variance optimization (MVO) is over 40 years old, its use as an applied portfolio management tool has only recently become extensive. Its origins are well-known: Harry Markowitz, a University of Chicago graduate student in search of a dissertation topic, ran into a stockbroker who suggested that he study the stock market.[1] Markowitz took the advice and proceeded to write a pioneering article and book and to receive a share of the 1990 Nobel Prize in Economics.[2] Perhaps the most compelling example of Wall Street's acceptance of this framework is the fact that several PC-based portfolio optimization programs, called *optimizers*, dot the financial product landscape.

The conceptual foundation of optimizers is solid and their use has greatly enhanced the portfolio management process, but they are difficult to use properly. Uncritical acceptance of MVO output can result in portfolios that are unstable, counterintuitive, and sometimes acceptable. This chapter reviews the limitations of MVO (from theoretical and

The authors would like to thank Keith R. Getsinger, Paul D. Kaplan, David Montgomery, and Carmen R. Thompson of Ibbotson Associates for their helpful comments and assistance.

user-oriented perspectives) and provides procedures for estimating the necessary inputs (expected returns, standard deviations, and correlations) for MVO when used as a long-term asset allocation tool.

LIMITATIONS OF MVO

The Beguiling Effects of Estimation Error

An optimizer derives the security or asset class weights for a portfolio that provides the maximum expected return for a given level of risk; or, conversely, the minimum risk for a given expected return. The inputs needed for MVO are security expected returns, expected standard deviations, and expected cross-security correlations. If the inputs are free of estimation error, MVO finds the efficient portfolio weights. However, because the inputs are statistical estimates (typically created by analyzing historical data), they *cannot* be devoid of error. This inaccuracy will lead to overinvestment in some asset classes and underinvestment in others.[3] For example, consider asset classes A and B, which differ only in that A's *true* expected return is slightly lower and its standard deviation slightly higher than B's. The returns to assets A and B have identical correlations with the returns on each of the other assets under consideration for the portfolio. Asset B, the preferable asset of the two, would dominate A without estimation error. However, because of estimation error, asset A might have an *estimated* expected return that is higher and an estimated standard deviation that is lower than B's. In this case, optimizer-generated results will always erroneously select a higher portfolio weight for asset A than for B.

Estimation error can also cause an efficient portfolio to appear inefficient. For example, Figure 1.1 shows a graph of the *efficient frontier* (the set of efficient portfolios for different levels of risk) and a portfolio P. Without estimation error, portfolio P is inefficient because it lies below the frontier; that is, the MVO algorithm has identified other portfolios that can achieve the same expected return with less risk. However, the presence of estimation error renders Figure 1.1 inadequate. Figure 1.2 is a more accurate depiction of reality; the "true" efficient frontier is somewhere within the band. This means that portfolio P may well be efficient.

The width of the band is proportionate to the estimation error of the inputs. For example, the band widens as the expected return increases,[4] a reflection of the fact that portfolios with low expected returns tend to be dominated by short-term fixed income securities for which the MVO inputs are estimated with more confidence.

One approach to limiting the impact of estimation error is to use a *constrained* optimization: the user sets the maximum or minimum

FIGURE 1.1   Efficient Frontier in the Absence of Estimation Error

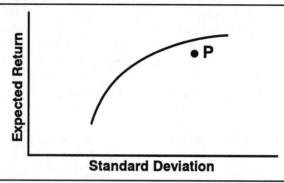

allocation for a single asset or group of assets. Constraints are used to prevent assets with favorable inputs from dominating a portfolio to an extent that violates common sense.

Unstable Solutions

A related problem with MVO is that its results can be *unstable:* small changes in inputs can result in large changes in portfolio contents.[5] Instability inhibits the use of MVO for actual asset allocation policy

FIGURE 1.2   Efficient Frontier with Estimation Error

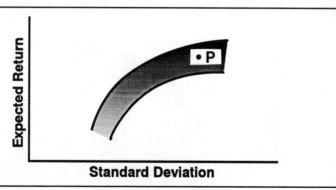

decisions. Assume one uses an optimizer for asset allocation recommendations on a quarterly basis, with revised estimates of inputs prepared each quarter, resulting in new allocation recommendations. Because of instability, an update that leads to a small change in the expected return or standard deviation of an asset class can lead to a radically different portfolio allocation, not only for the asset class with the changed parameters, but for all of the classes under consideration. These potentially large quarterly changes in the portfolio composition will encourage unwarranted turnover and justifiably erode confidence in the quality of the allocations.

In order to minimize dramatic changes in recommended portfolio composition *sensitivity analysis* can be used. This technique involves selecting an efficient portfolio and then altering the MVO inputs and seeing how close to efficient the portfolio is under the new set of inputs. The goal is to identify a set of asset class weights that will be close to efficient under several different sets of plausible inputs.

Reallocation Costs

Two portfolios are indicated in Figure 1.3. Portfolio A is within the band that encompasses the true frontier; portfolio B is below it. Both portfolios have the same expected risk, but A has the higher expected return. It would seem that the manager of portfolio B should alter the portfolio's allocation to match that of A. But is such a policy warranted?

Depending on the asset classes within the two portfolios and the magnitude of the quantities involved, it may be quite costly to implement a reallocation of portfolio B. Before reallocating, managers must make a careful inventory of reallocation costs such as bid-ask spreads,

FIGURE 1.3 Efficient Frontier with Estimation Error

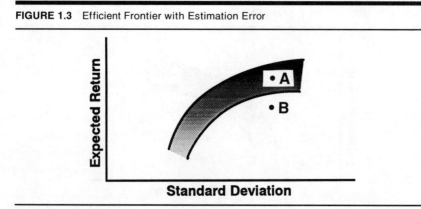

price pressure (market impact) effects, and transaction fees.[6] The correct policy may be to retain the current allocation despite its lack of optimality.[7]

The Skepticism of the Uninitiated

MVO is something of a black box. The box can be opened, but, for many investors, it is filled with impenetrable statistics. Black boxes do have a clientele, but many investors are loath to invest on the basis of trading and allocation systems that they do not understand. MVO is susceptible to this reaction for two reasons:

1. MVO is complex, and prerequisites for understanding it include the formidable trio of statistics, linear programming, and modern portfolio theory.
2. MVO can recommend allocations that are perfectly defensible but counterintuitive.

One of the great insights of MVO is that assets that are risky, when viewed in isolation, can actually reduce portfolio risk if they have low correlations with the other assets in the portfolio. This concept can be proved mathematically, but a surprisingly large number of otherwise intelligent people just don't buy it. For example, because non-U.S. stocks have had historically low correlations with U.S. common stocks and bonds, they typically receive a large weight in efficient portfolios. However, the vast majority of managers underinvest relative to these efficient weights.

Political Fallout

The use of MVO for asset allocation may run counter to the interests of some employees within a money management firm. Consider a scenario in which MVO is to be used by a money manager to allocate client money to particular in-house funds. After creating the inputs for each fund and allowing the optimizer to work its magic, each client (based on the individual degree of risk aversion) is assigned an optimal allocation of the in-house funds. However, particular funds are like to be shut out of most unconstrained allocations. As a practical matter, it is unrealistic for a manager to employ an asset class specialist and not allocate any capital to that asset class. Even if MVO excludes an asset class for reasons other than estimation error, that is little comfort to the managers who are excluded. As a result, optimal allocations are likely to be substantially modified.

DEVELOPING MVO INPUTS FOR MAJOR ASSET CLASSES

Guiding Principles

When developing models to estimate inputs investors should make estimates that are:

- Accurate—within the limits imposed by the state of the art, investor tolerance of complexity, and the amount of effort required to collect and interpret data;
- Timely—amenable to updating with reasonable effort and minimal delay;
- Consistent—reflecting long-run expectations and not fluctuating wildly each time they are updated;
- Comprehensible—within the ability of a knowledgeable person to explain and justify the estimates in easily understandable terms.

On Which Asset Classes Should One Optimize?

Ideally, all assets in the world should be represented in the optimizer. However, many investors cannot or do not want to invest in a particular asset class. MVO can still be of benefit by providing superior allocations among the remaining asset classes. For those investors who have broad latitude in selecting assets, the more relevant question is: What are the major asset classes?

Stated simply, the major asset classes are those that make up the preponderance of world wealth: stocks, bonds, cash, and real estate. However, within these broad categories are subgroups that have exhibited unique behavior and that may deserve to be treated as separate asset classes. Deciding which subgroups qualify is admittedly more art than science, and there is room for reasonable persons to disagree. In our opinion, a group of securities qualifies as an asset class when it meets the following two criteria:

1. Diversification. There must be a broad range of individual securities within the group in question. Without this criterion, every industry, economic sector, or individual stock and bond in the world could be considered an asset class.
2. A degree of independence. Experience with optimizers indicates that the analytical guts of MVO have difficulty handling asset classes that have a correlation of 0.95 or higher. In fact, the inclusion of highly correlated assets is the principal cause of unstable solutions. Also, if two groups of securities are highly correlated, they should not be treated as separate asset classes.

With these criteria in hand, we judge the major asset classes (from the standpoint of a U.S. investor) to be:

U.S. large-capitalization stocks;
U.S. small-capitalization stocks;
 Long-term U.S. Treasury bonds;
 Intermediate-term U.S. Treasury bonds;
 U.S. Treasury bills;
 Long-term U.S. corporate bonds;
U.S. mortgage-backed securities;
U.S. real estate;
Non-U.S. equities.

ESTIMATION PROCEDURES FOR LONG-RUN EXPECTED RETURN AND STANDARD DEVIATION

U.S. Large-Capitalization Stocks

We estimate the long-term expected return (from the perspective of a U.S. investor) on large-cap stocks by using a "long-horizon" form of the capital asset pricing model (CAPM). This variation has the form of the traditional Sharpe-Lintner CAPM:

$$E[r_i] = r_f + \beta(E[r_m] - r_f) \tag{1}$$

where $E[r_i]$ is the expected return of asset i, r_f is the expected return on a risk-free security, β is the measure of the systematic risk of asset i, and $E[r_m] - r_f$ is the equity risk premium.[8] The long-horizon model retains the form of equation (1), but r_f is defined as the current yield (a proxy for expected return) on long-term (20-year) U.S. Treasury bonds.[9] We use a long- rather than a short-maturity bond because we require a default-free security whose maturity matches the time horizon over which one assumes that investors commit their capital; typically, this is a long period.[10] Moreover, long-term bond yields, which are more stable over time than short-term bond yields, produce more stable estimates.

We estimate the equity risk premium by subtracting the arithmetic mean of annual yield (income) returns on long-term Treasury bonds from the arithmetic mean of annual total returns on stocks as proxied by the S&P 500. We use the income return on bonds because it is the completely risk-free portion of the return. In contrast, the total return includes the return that can be attributed to capital gains and losses that result from interest rate changes. In addition, bond yields have risen historically, causing capital losses. There is no evidence that investors expected these capital losses, so the past total return series is biased downward as an indicator of past expectations. The past income return series is unbiased.

On April 25, 1994, the long yield was 7.3 percent[11] and the equity risk premium estimated over the years 1926 to 1993 was 12.3 percent − 5.1 percent = 7.2 percent.[12] Assuming a β of 1.00, this gives an expected return of 7.3 percent + 1.00 × 7.2 percent = 14.5 percent.

Most estimates of expected standard deviation are based on past standard deviations. The question then becomes one of selecting an appropriate historical period. For asset classes that have had accurately measured returns and stable standard deviations, such as stocks, we estimate the expected standard deviation by calculating the actual standard deviation of annual total returns over the entire period for which good quality data are available.[13] Shorter periods are not used because only long-run data capture the full range of possible (and, by inference, expected) return behavior. For example, without an understanding of stock market performance during the 1920s and 1930s, the crash of 1987 would have scarcely been imaginable. For the years 1926 to 1993, the standard deviation of annual total returns for large-cap stocks was 20.5 percent.

U.S. Small-Capitalization Stocks

Small-cap stocks have historically earned higher returns than large-cap stocks. For the years 1926 to 1993, large-cap stocks had a 12.3 percent arithmetic mean total return compared with 17.6 percent for small-cap stocks.[14] We label this 5.3 percent difference the *small stock premium*. Our estimate of the expected return for small-cap stocks is the small stock premium plus our estimate of the expected return on large-cap stocks.

Investors demand a small stock premium because small stocks have greater risk and investors can reasonably expect compensation (in the form of a higher expected return) for bearing this additional risk.[15]

On April 25, 1994, we estimate the expected return on small-cap stocks to be 7.3 percent + 7.2 percent + 5.3 percent = 19.8 percent. As with large-cap stocks, we use the standard deviation of past annual total returns over the longest period for which we have good quality data to estimate the expected standard deviation. Using annual total returns over the period 1926 to 1993, the standard deviation was 34.8 percent.

These estimates for expected return and standard deviation may seem large, but our definition of small stocks includes stocks that are perhaps too small for many investors. In the event that an investor's definition of small stocks includes stocks larger than our definition, it makes sense to reestimate the expected return and standard deviation based on the capitalization range of small stocks under consideration.

U.S. Fixed-Income Assets

We estimate the expected return on each class of U.S. bonds (except mortgage-backed securities) by using the general framework:

$$E[r] = r_f - MP + DP \qquad (2)$$

where $E[r]$ is the expected return on a particular class of bonds, r_f is the current yield on long-term Treasury bonds, MP is the *maturity premium*, and DP is the *default premium*.

The subtraction of a maturity premium accounts for the empirical observation that yield curves typically slope upward. This phenomenon is explained by the liquidity preference hypothesis, which states that the price risk of longer bonds is more burdensome to investors than the reinvestment risk of rolling over short bonds. The higher yields of long bonds are compensation to holders for bearing this risk.

The size of the maturity premium depends on the instrument. For Treasury bills, we estimate the maturity premium as the difference between the arithmetic means of long-term Treasury bond income returns and Treasury bill returns from 1970 to 1993. We select this period because the presence of persistent inflation beginning in the early 1970s and later, the termination of interest rate targeting by the Federal Reserve fundamentally transformed the behavior of the U.S. fixed-income markets. As a result, we consider the data prior to 1970 of limited relevance when used as a forecasting tool.

Using the years 1970 to 1993, the maturity premium is estimated to be 8.6 percent − 7.2 percent = 1.4 percent. The maturity premium for intermediate-term Treasury bonds is estimated as the difference between the arithmetic means of long-term Treasury bond income returns and intermediate-term Treasury bond income returns. For the years 1970 to 1993, the estimated premium is 8.6 percent − 8.3 percent = 0.3 percent.

A bond is a promise to repay a series of cash flows, but, as many a junk bond holder has found, promises are not always kept. To compensate for this risk, bonds with default risk must have yields high enough to cover the expected loss from default and provide additional compensation for being exposed to the risk. We estimate the long-run expected default premium by taking the difference between the arithmetic mean total returns of long-term corporate and long-term Treasury bonds over the 1970 to 1993 period. We use the difference in *total* returns and not *income* returns because only through the total return can an investor get an assessment of how defaults have affected the return on an investment in a pool of corporate bonds. For the years 1970 to 1993, the estimated default premium is 10.5 percent − 10.2 percent = 0.3 percent.

The resulting expected returns (and standard deviations) are summarized in Table 1.1.

We previously mentioned that the historical standard deviation of annual total returns over the longest period for which good data are available is the best estimate of expected standard deviation, provided that the standard deviations have been reasonably stable and the returns are accurately measured. However, the standard deviation of the U.S. fixed income market has not been stable. We believe that a process shift has occurred. Figure 1.4 shows the standard deviation of total returns for rolling 15-year windows from 1926 to 1993. Beginning approximately in 1970, the standard deviations of all fixed income series began to drift sharply upward. Because of this process shift, we estimate the expected standard deviation as the annualized standard deviation of monthly total returns over the January 1970 to March 1994 period.[16]

A more natural choice might be the post-1979 period. We do not use this period because it is too short and this most unusual period should be the sole basis for a long-run projection.

U.S. Mortgage-Backed Securities

When modeling the expected return on a mortgage-backed security (MBS), we are primarily concerned with determining the premium investors require for bearing the *prepayment risk* inherent in an MBS.[17] Unlike straight bonds, which the holder can retain until maturity or a prespecified first-call date, the mortgages that back the security can be prepaid at any time. This poses a risk to the MBS holder. When inter-

TABLE 1.1 Expected Returns and Standard Deviations for U.S. Fixed-Income Asset Classes

Fixed-Income Asset Class	Long-Term Treasury Bond Yield	–	Maturity Premium	+	Default Premium	=	Expected Return	Standard Deviation
Treasury bills	7.3%	–	1.4%	+	0.0%	=	5.9%	0.9%
Intermediate-term Treasury bonds	7.3	–	0.3	+	0.0	=	7.0	6.8
Long-term Treasury bonds	7.3	–	0.0	+	0.0	=	7.3	12.1
Long-term corporate bonds	7.3	–	0.0	+	0.3	=	7.6	10.9

SOURCE: Long-term Treasury bond yield is from *The Wall Street Journal*, April 26, 1994; all other data are from Ibbotson Associates, *Yearbook, op. cit.*

FIGURE 1.4   Standard Deviation of Total Returns over Rolling 15-Year Periods

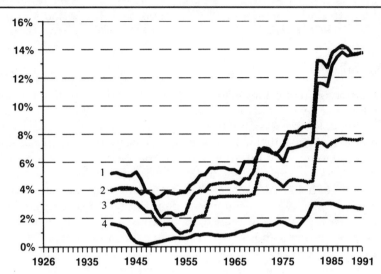

1 Long-Term Government Bonds
2 Corporate Bonds
3 Interm.-Term Government Bonds
4 U.S. T-Bills

est rates fall substantially, homeowners are highly motivated to prepay their current mortgages and refinance at lower rates. Prepayments cause MBS holders to receive their principal early and reinvest it at rates lower than those they originally expected.

We estimate the prepayment premium by subtracting the arithmetic mean of annual income returns for long-term Treasury bonds from the annual income returns from the Lehman Brothers Mortgage-Backed Securities Index. For the years 1976 to 1993 the estimated premium is 10.2 percent − 9.2 percent = 1.0 percent. This is a relatively short time period (necessitated by the fact that the first MBS was created in 1970), but we believe that it adequately captures the market-required compensation for bearing this prepayment risk because the 1976 to 1993 period saw both rapid prepayments (roughly from 1986 to the present) and a dearth of prepayments (in the late 1970s and early 1980s). The expected return is the current yield on long-term Treasury bonds plus the prepayment premium, or 7.3 percent + 1.0 percent = 8.3 percent.

Since the January 1976 to March 1994 period is representative of conditions we expect to hold for the long-run, we use the annualized standard deviation of monthly total returns over this period for our estimate of 9.8 percent.

U.S. Real Estate

The return on real estate is logically and empirically related to inflation. Because real estate prices are a large component of the Consumer Price Index, the most common inflation measure, such a link is almost unavoidable. Primarily for tax reasons, real estate price appreciation exceeded economy-wide inflation rates in the 1960s, 1970s, and much of the 1980s. As the various federal tax reform acts were enacted, the tax motivation to hold real estate eroded in the late 1980s. Real estate prices subsequently fell, while economy-wide inflation rates continued to be positive. Despite this divergence, the historical correspondence of real estate price returns and inflation rates has been reasonably close. For the period 1978 to 1993, semiannual returns on the Frank Russell Property Index and inflation have had a correlation of 0.6.

Our model for estimating the expected total return on real estate is:

$$E[r_{nominal, real estate}] = E[r_{real, real estate}] + E[\pi] \qquad (3)$$

where $E[r_{nominal, real estate}]$ is the expected nominal return to real estate; $E[r_{real, real estate}]$ is the expected real return to real estate; and $E[\pi]$ is the expected inflation rate.

To estimate the expected real total return, we subtract the arithmetic mean annual inflation rate from the arithmetic mean annual total return on the Frank Russell Property Index. For the years 1978 to 1993, this is 2.9 percent. We use this value as our estimate of the real total return on real estate. To arrive at an expected nominal total return for real estate, expected inflation should be added to the 2.9 percent expected real total return. Based on a recent long-run inflation estimate of 4.6 percent,[18] we arrive at an expected nominal total return on real estate of 7.5 percent.

Estimates of the standard deviation of real estate fall in a broad range from a level near that of Treasury bills to one comparable to the stock market. Because most real estate return indexes are appraisal-based and suffer from smoothing of volatile underlying returns, very low risk measures are commonly seen. In optimization, such a measure would allocate almost the entire portfolio to real estate over a broad range of expected portfolio standard deviations. This result defies logic and contradicts observed market behavior.

The other extreme position, that real estate is as risky as the stock market, is also unlikely to be realistic. Investors are likely to require compensation in the form of a higher before-cost expected return in order to bear costs such as illiquidity and high transaction and information costs.[19] If real estate is as risky as the stock market, it would have to beat the stock market by a large margin in order to be held by rational investors. In fact, real estate has had returns that are between those of stocks and bonds. For the years 1978 to 1993, commercial real estate had an estimated compound annual total return of 11.5 percent, compared to 15.1 percent for stocks, 10.8 percent for long-term Treasury bonds, and 10.6 percent for intermediate-term Treasury bonds.

We believe that, like long-run returns, the risk of unleveraged real estate is between that of stocks and bonds. The expected cash flows from real estate are composed of (1) rents, which resemble coupon payments on a bond, and (2) capital gain/loss on sale, which resembles the capital gain/loss on a non-dividend-paying stock. With real estate's cash flow attributes similar to those of both stocks and bonds, real estate investors face both bond-and stocklike risks. This implies that the risk of real estate must logically be between that of a stock and that of a bond.

One way of estimating the volatility of real estate is by using a REIT (Real Estate Investment Trusts) index. REITs are companies or closed-end funds whose assets consist almost exclusively of real estate. These companies are listed on stock exchanges and consequently, their value each day represents the market's assessment of the value of the property holdings. A REIT index therefore has the potential of more accurately representing the volatility of real estate than an appraisal-based series. However, because REITs are traded on an exchange, they may be more volatile than the underlying real estate because of stock market-induced volatility.

A solution to this problem has been suggested by S. Michael Giliberto.[20] In this approach, a portfolio is created that consists of a broad-based REIT index and a short position in the S&P 500. The short position in the S&P 500 will, in effect, subtract the effects of broad stock market movements from the REIT index. The standard deviation of the portfolio should then be a more accurate estimate of the volatility of the underlying real estate.

Applying this approach over the period January 1972 to March 1994 provides an estimate of 13.8 percent for the volatility of real estate.[21]

Global Equities

We estimate expected returns on foreign equity markets by using the global CAPM.[22] Because the United States has a very long data history with which to calculate the equity risk premium, we use it as a baseline.

The world equity risk premium is then determined by dividing the U.S. equity risk premium by the beta of the U.S. equity market on the world equity market, or

$$RP_{World} = \frac{RP_{US}}{\beta_{US}}$$

$$8.1\% = \frac{7.2\%}{0.89}$$

(4)

where RP_{World} is the expected equity risk premium for world equities over the U.S. riskless rate; RP_{US} is the U.S. equity risk premium (estimated previously as 7.2 percent), β_{US} (estimated to be 0.89) is the beta of U.S. equities on a market capitalization-weighted world equity index.[23]

Risk premiums for individual country or regional equity markets can then be estimated by multiplying the country's or region's beta by 8.1 percent. The expected total return for a U.S. investor is obtained by adding the country equity risk premium to the current yield on long-term Treasury bonds. Table 1.2 provides current estimates of the beta, equity risk premium, and expected total return to the U.S. investor for several global regions.

Our calculation of expected return does not involve currencies in any way. The implicit assumption is that currency fluctuations have no expected return over the *long-run*. Currency fluctuations do, however, increase the variability of returns. Therefore, our estimates for expected standard deviations (presented in Table 1.2) are calculated based on returns converted to U.S. dollars.[24]

TABLE 1.2   Global Equities: Estimates of Expected Return and Standard Deviation*

Region	Beta on World Market	World Equity Risk Premium	Expected Equity Total Return	Standard Deviation
MSCI World	1.00	8.1%	15.4%	19.1%
MSCI EAFE	1.04	8.1	15.7	23.4
MSCI Pacific	1.10	8.1	16.2	29.9
MSCI Europe	0.95	8.1	15.0	23.0

* Expected equity total return is calculated by adding the expected return on U.S. long-term Treasury bonds (7.3 percent as of April 25, 1994) to the equity risk premium for each region. The regional equity risk premium is calculated as the world equity risk premium multiplied by the beta of that region.

SOURCE: Returns used to calculate these estimates are from Morgan Stanley Capital International (MSCI).

As stated previously, for asset classes that have had accurately measured returns and stable standard deviations, such as stocks, we estimate the expected standard deviation by calculating the actual standard deviation of annual total returns over the entire period for which good quality data are available. Shorter periods are not used because only over the long run do the data capture the full range of possible (and, by inference, expected) return behavior.

For asset classes such as U.S. large- and small-capitalization stocks, this approach works well because a long time period is available. However, for global equities, high-quality data are available only from 1970 on. Because equities have exhibited lower volatility during this period than during the 1926 to 1993 period as a whole, an estimate based solely on 1970 to 1993 would cause non-U.S. equities to appear to be much more attractive than their U.S. counterparts. To put both sets of equities on more equal footing, we adjust the observed volatility of non-U.S. equities over the 1970 to 1993 period as follows:

$$\sigma_{\text{non-U.S. region, long-term}} = \frac{\sigma_{\text{non-U.S. region, 1970–1993}}}{\sigma_{\text{S\&P 500, 1970–1993}}} \times \sigma_{\text{S\&P 500, 1926–1993}} \tag{5}$$

where $\sigma_{\text{non-U.S. region, long-term}}$ is our estimate of the long term standard deviation for a particular non-U.S. region, $\sigma_{\text{non-U.S. region, 1970–1993}}$ is the actual standard deviation of the region's annualized monthly total returns over the period 1970 to 1993, $\sigma_{\text{S\&P 500, 1970–1993}}$ is the actual standard deviation of the annualized monthly total returns on S&P 500 over the period 1970 to 1993, and $\sigma_{\text{S\&P 500, 1926–1993}}$ is our estimate of the long-term expected standard deviation on the S&P 500 which we calculated using data over the period 1926 to 1993. Our estimates for four regions are given in Table 1.2.

CALCULATING THE CORRELATION MATRIX

The asset class correlation matrix is based on the historical correlation of monthly total returns for each pair of assets. These correlations are shown in Table 1.3. Using a long time period is usually preferable, but there can be process shifts in correlation coefficients. For this reason, our estimate of correlation for every pair of assets does not necessarily use the longest period for which good data are available.

Interestingly, as world capital markets became more integrated, one might suspect that correlations between U.S. and non-U.S. equities would have become higher, but the data suggest otherwise. Table 1.4 illustrates correlations of monthly total returns between non-U.S. stocks and U.S. large- and small-cap stocks for subperiods from January 1970 to June 1992. There is no clear, across-the-board increase in correlations.

TABLE 1.3 Correlation Matrix for Major Asset Classes*

	Stocks			Fixed Income					
	U.S. Large-Cap	U.S. Small-Cap	Non-U.S.	Long-Term Treasury Bonds	Intermediate-Term Treasury Bonds	Treasury Bills	Long-Term Corporate Bonds	Mortgage-Backed Securities	U.S. REITs
Stocks									
U.S. large-cap	1.00								
U.S. small-cap	0.85	1.00							
Non-U.S.	0.51	0.45	1.00						
Fixed income									
U.S. Long-Term Treasury Bonds	0.37	0.22	0.24	1.00					
U.S. Intermediate-Term Treasury Bonds	0.27	0.15	0.17	0.86	1.00				
U.S. Treasury Bills	-0.06	-0.07	-0.11	0.06	0.15	1.00			
U.S. Long-Term Corporate Bonds	0.41	0.27	0.24	0.92	0.85	0.04	1.00		
U.S. Mortgage-Backed Securities	0.32	0.19	0.19	0.89	0.90	0.09	0.93	1.00	
Real estate									
U.S. REITs	0.62	0.75	0.41	0.31	0.26	-0.06	0.38	0.33	1.00

* Correlations are calculated using monthly total returns over the longest period for which relevant data on each pair of assets are available. These periods are: 1926 to 1993 for U.S. large- and small-cap stocks; 1970 to 1993 for U.S. long- and intermediate-term Treasury bonds, Treasury bills, and U. S. long-term corporate bonds; 1970 to 1993 for non-US stocks; 1976 to 1993 for U.S. mortgage-backed securities; and 1972 to 1993 for REITs. The proxy for non-US stocks is the MSCI World (excluding US) Index denominated in U.S. dollars.

SOURCE: Ibbotson Associates, Inc. for U.S. large- and small-cap stocks and U.S. long- and intermediate-term Treasury bonds, Treasury bills, and U.S. long-term corporate bonds. Morgan Stanley Capital International (MSCI) for non-U.S. stocks. Lehman Brothers for mortgage-backed securities. NAREIT for REIT index.

22

TABLE 1.4 Correlation of Non-U.S. Stocks with U.S. Large- and Small-Cap Stocks: Monthly Total Returns*

	U.S. Large-Cap Stocks	U.S. Small-Cap Stocks
1970–1974	0.56	0.58
1975–1979	0.51	0.38
1980–1984	0.59	0.60
1985–1989	0.45	0.41
1990–1992	0.49	0.31

* Non-U.S. stocks proxied by the MSCI World (excluding U.S.).
SOURCE: Morgan Stanley Capital International (MSCI) and Ibbotson Associates, Inc.

SUMMARY

Effective use of mean-variance optimization in a practical setting requires an appreciation of its limitations. As described in this chapter, the procedures for estimating stable, long-term inputs for mean-variance optimization will help to make the inherent limitations of MVO less onerous.

NOTES

1. For this and other financial folklore, see Peter L. Bernstein, *Capital Ideas: The Improbable Origins of Modern Wall Street,* (New York: The Free Press, 1992).
2. Harry M. Markowitz, "Portfolio Selection," *Journal of Finance* (March 1952): 71–91; *Portfolio Selection: Efficient Diversification of Investments* (New York: John Wiley & Sons, 1959).
3. For a more complete development of this argument see Richard O. Michaud, "The Markowitz Optimization Enigma: Is 'Optimized' Optimal?" *Financial Analysts Journal* (January–February 1989): 33–34.
4. For a comprehensive empirical study of estimation error on a portfolio of 100 stocks see Harbans L. Dhingra, "Effects of Estimation Risk on Efficient Portfolios: A Monte Carlo Simulation Study," *Journal of Business Finance & Accounting* (1980): 277–95.
5. See Michaud, *op. cit.,* 35.
6. Higher-quality optimizers mitigate this problem by allowing consideration of reallocation costs.
7. The cost of reallocation is spread out over the time horizon of the investment. Reallocation may then be warranted if the portfolio is intended to be held for a long time.
8. In the Sharpe-Lintner CAPM, the risk-free asset is assumed to have a short maturity. See John Lintner, "The Valuation of Risky Assets and the Selection of Risky Investments in Stock Portfolios and Capital Budgets," *Review of Economics and Statistics* (February 1965): 13–37; and William F. Sharpe, "Capital Asset Prices: A Theory of Market Equilibrium under Conditions of Risk," *Journal of Finance* (September 1964): 425–442.

   β is scaled such that the market portfolio, or portfolio of all risky assets (the S&P 500 has been traditionally used as the proxy for this portfolio), has a β of 1.00.

The equity risk premium is the return in excess of the risk-free rate that investors expect to receive as compensation for their taking the investment risk of a typical stock instead of investing in a risk-free security such as a U.S. Treasury issue.

9. The long-horizon variation was suggested by Roger G. Ibbotson and Stephen A. Ross. It is described in Ibbotson Associates, Inc., *Stocks, Bonds, Bills, and Inflation 1993 Yearbook™* (Chicago: 1993) (annually updates work by Roger G. Ibbotson and Rex A. Sinquefield). In practice, we use the shortest noncallable, current coupon bond with a maturity not less than 20 years. As of April 1994, we used the $7^1/_4$ percent T-bond maturing May 2016.

10. Trading volume suggests that some investors have short time horizons, but most of this activity is the mere substitution of one security for another. Investors typically commit their capital to the *market,* if not a particular security, for the long run.

11. *The Wall Street Journal,* April 26, 1994, p. C26.

12. The source for all historical data on U.S. large- and small-cap stocks, Treasury bonds, and corporate bonds is Ibbotson Associates, *Yearbook, op. cit.*

13. Methods such as ARCH and GARCH have been applied to estimating standard deviation in a capital asset pricing setting (see, for example, Robert F. Engle, "Autoregressive conditional heteroscedasticity with estimates of the variance of United Kingdom inflation," *Econometrica* (July 1982): 987–1008; Tim Bollerslev, "Generalized autoregressive conditional heteroscedasticity," *Journal of Econometrics* (1986); and Tim Bollerslev, Robert F. Engle, and J. Woolridge, "A capital asset pricing model with time-varying covariances," *Journal of Political Economy* (February 1988): 116–31. Although these types of models have garnered much interest in recent years, no consensus as to the means or desirability of applying them in this context has been achieved. Moreover, the inherent complexity and expense of preparing and updating estimates based on these techniques prevents all but the most sophisticated investors from employing them.

14. The returns to small-cap stocks for the period 1926 to 1980 are from Rolf W. Banz, "The Relationship between Market Value and Return of Common Stocks," *Journal of Financial Economics* (November 1981): 3–18. These returns represent a portfolio of stocks that comprise the 9th and 10th deciles of NYSE stocks ranked by market capitalization. For 1981 the return is from Dimensional Fund Advisors (DFA), which calculated the return in a method consistent with that used by Banz. Since 1981, the returns are from the DFA Small Company 9/10 Fund. This fund tracks the 9th and 10th deciles of the NYSE plus stocks listed on the AMEX and NASDAQ with the same or less capitalization as the upper bound of the NYSE 9th decile.

15. Much of the incremental risk of small stocks is captured by their high beta relative to the S&P. Using the regression:

$$r_{small} - r_{T-bill} = \alpha_{small} + \beta_{small} \times (r_{S\&P\ 500} - r_{T-bill}) + \varepsilon$$

we estimate this β_{small} to be 1.30 using monthly returns covering the period January 1926 to March 1994. However, numerous studies (beginning with Banz, *op. cit.*) show a persistent higher return *after* adjusting for beta. We therefore use the difference-of-means approach to estimate the small stock premium, rather than model it in a CAPM framework.

16. Note that for periods less than 30 years in length we use the annualized standard deviation of monthly total returns. Using annual total return to compute a standard deviation would allow the possibility of a single year exerting excessive influence on the estimate.

17. We do not include a default premium because these securities have virtually none. Ginnie Maes have an explicit guarantee by the federal government. MBSs issued by Freddie Mac carry a guarantee of timely payment of interest and eventual payment of principal and those issued by Fannie Mae have a guarantee of the full and timely payment of both principal and interest. Although the federal government has not explicitly done so, the market perception is that the federal government would guarantee the solvency of these organizations if that solvency ever became questionable.

18. Ibbotson Associates derives market consensus forecasts of long-term inflation by subtracting a forecast of the long-term real riskless rate and an estimate of the maturity premium from the observed current 20-year Treasury bond yield. This method is described more fully in Ibbotson Associates, *Yearbook, op. cit.* The most recent estimate is from Ibbotson Associates, *Stocks, Bonds, Bills, and Inflation 1994 Quarterly Market Reports,* 1st quarter (Chicago: 1994).

19. A more complete analysis of the types of compensation investors may require for being exposed to various characteristics of assets can be found in Roger G. Ibbotson, Jeffrey J. Diermeier, and Laurence B. Siegel, "The Demand for Capital Market Returns," *Financial Analysts Journal* (January–February 1984): 22–33.

20. S. Michael Giliberto, "Measuring Real Estate Returns: The Hedged REIT Index," *The Journal of Portfolio Management* (Spring 1993): pp. 94–99.

21. For our REIT index we used the NAREIT-All index prepared by the National Association of Real Estate Investment Trusts. This market capitalization-weighted index is composed of all tax-qualified REITs listed on the NYSE, Amex, and NASDAQ.

22. Solnik first set forth such a model and the corollary three-fund separation theorem. The three-fund separation theorem says that, in an integrated multicurrency world where CAPM assumptions hold, all investors will hold portfolios composed of long and short positions in (1) the unhedged world portfolio of risky assets, (2) the investor's home-country riskless assets, and (3) a currency-hedged portfolio of foreign-country riskless assets. See Bruno Solnik "An Equilibrium Model of the International Capital Market," *Journal of Economic Theory* (July–August 1974).

23. The beta was estimated using the following regression over the period January 1970 to March, 1994:

$$r_{US} - r_{T\text{-bill}} = \alpha_{US} + \beta_{US} \times (r_{MSCI\,World} - r_{T\text{-bill}}) + \varepsilon$$

where r_{US} are monthly returns on the S&P 500, $r_{T\text{-bill}}$ are monthly T-bill returns, and $r_{MSCI\,World}$ are monthly returns on the MSCI World index.

24. For those investors who intend to hedge the exposure of their investments to exchange rate risk, the estimated standard deviations in Table 1.2 are too high. The amount of adjustment is dependent on the degree to which exposure is hedged and the efficacy of the hedge. The cost of the hedge must be deducted from the expected return.

2

Return Distributions and Asset Allocation Decisions

Kurt Winkelmann, PhD
Manager, Fixed Income
Vestek Systems
San Francisco, California

Asset allocation decisions are typically made in the context of a mean-variance framework. An optimal portfolio of securities is selected by combining an efficient frontier (representing the risk and return characteristics of available portfolios) with a specification of the investor's preferences for risk and return.

Central to this procedure is a description of the characteristics of the return distributions for each asset category. As these attributes change, the efficient frontier also changes; consequently, the optimal asset allocation is revised. Thus, measurement of the variances and covariances between asset returns and identification of those factors that might cause these measures to change are relevant issues for the asset allocation decision.

The focus of this chapter is on the implications of changes in return distributions for the asset allocation decision. An asset allocation framework is considered, to show the relationship between the optimal asset allocation and the asset return distributions. A simulation framework is the basis for discussion of sources of estimation error that might occur. International bond returns are used to further explore these issues.

AN ASSET ALLOCATION FRAMEWORK

There are two key specifications for an asset allocation decision: (1) the distributions of asset returns and (2) the investor's preferences regarding risk and return.

The distributions of asset returns provide a specification of the available investment opportunities. In particular, the expected return and variance for each asset must be identified, along with any covariances between asset categories. These attributes show the characteristics of the investment opportunities available in the market.

The specification of investor preferences, or an investor's attitude toward risk and return, is characterized with a *utility function*. This function shows the number of additional basis points of expected return the investor must receive in order to take on an additional unit of risk (as measured by portfolio variance), holding all else equal.

(Investors could also consider the investment horizon. Attitudes regarding risk and return are likely to be dependent on the point the investor has reached in the life cycle: as investors age, their willingness to take on risk decreases. The role of the investment horizon in the asset allocation decision will not be considered here.)

By combining the description of possible investment opportunities with a characterization of investor preferences, an optimal asset allocation can be selected. Revisions in the asset allocation are likely to come from two sources: (1) changes in distributions of asset returns or (2) changes in investor attitudes toward risk.

A simple example will clarify these points. Suppose that three types of assets—stocks, bonds, and cash—were available to an investor. Table 2.1 shows the return distributions for each type of asset, and Table 2.2 shows the correlation matrix for the asset returns. Stock returns were measured using the monthly return to the S&P 500, bond returns were measured using the Lehman Brothers Aggregate Bond

TABLE 2.1   Expected Returns and Volatilities (1989–1991)

Asset	Average	Volatility
Cash	6.02	.46
Bonds	11.76	5.96
Stocks	17.54	18.87

TABLE 2.2   Correlation Matrix: Asset Returns (1989–1991)

Asset	Cash	Bonds	Stocks
Cash	1.00		
Bonds	.31	1.00	
Stocks	.00	.22	1.00

Index, and cash returns were measured as the return to a 30-day Treasury bill. The figures in the table were estimated over the period from January 1989 through December, 1991.

Notice that the average return is highest for stocks, and cash has the lowest expected return. Correspondingly, stocks have the highest variance of expected returns, and cash has the lowest variance. The highest expected return asset category is also the highest risk asset category.

Nine portfolios of the efficient frontier corresponding to these data are shown in Table 2.3. The figures show the maximum expected return portfolio for each level of variance. The portfolios are combinations of the three assets. For example, if the portfolio variance is 7.4 percent, the highest expected return portfolio calls for 0 percent in cash, 73.1 percent in bonds, and 26.9 percent in stocks. This portfolio has an expected return of 13.3 percent. (All figures in Table 2.3 are percentages.)

Table 2.3 is a representation of the investment opportunities available in the market. To determine the optimal allocation of assets, investor preferences must also be represented. Preferences are usually characterized with a utility function that shows mathematically the number of incremental basis points of expected return that an investor must receive to be indifferent between two portfolios with unequal variances. One possible utility function is shown as:

$$\text{Utility} = (\text{Expected Return}) - \text{Parameter}*(\text{Variance}) \qquad (1)$$

To determine the level of utility, the *risk aversion* parameter (labeled Parameter in the equation) must be specified. For example, suppose that the risk aversion parameter is 2. If portfolio A has an expected return of 10 percent and a variance of 2 percent, then the investor's utility would be 6 (10 − 2*2).

Portfolio B has a variance of 3 percent. With a risk aversion parameter of 2, the expected return on portfolio B must be 12 if the investor is

TABLE 2.3 Efficient Frontier (1989–1991)

					Portfolio				
Asset	1	2	3	4	5	6	7	8	9
Cash	0.0	0.0	0.0	0.0	0.0	0.0	0.0	0.0	0.0
Bonds	75.8	73.1	69.7	65.2	58.9	49.4	33.6	1.9	0.0
Stocks	24.2	26.9	30.3	34.8	41.1	50.6	66.4	98.1	100.0
Return	13.2	13.3	13.5	13.8	14.1	14.7	15.6	17.4	17.5
Volatility	7.1	7.4	7.8	8.3	9.2	10.6	13.1	18.5	18.9

to be indifferent between portfolios A and B. Thus, specification of the risk aversion parameter plays an important role in determining the optimal asset allocation.

To find the optimal asset allocation, available investment opportunities (as illustrated in Table 2.3) are combined with investor preferences (as characterized by equation (1)). Using the figures from Table 2.3 and assuming a risk aversion parameter of 1.78 yields an optimal asset allocation of 49.4 percent in bonds and 51.6 percent in stocks.

The efficient frontier is a function of the distributional characteristics of cash, bonds, and stocks, and the utility function depends on the risk aversion parameter. Consequently, it stands to reason and the optimal asset allocation is dependent on these same underlying parameters: changing the distributional characteristics or the risk aversion parameter will change the optimal asset allocation.

Tables 2.4 and 2.5 show alternatives for the return characteristics. The data for Tables 2.4 and 2.5 are taken from the same asset categories, but the sample period is January 1985 through December 1988. Again, stocks have both the highest expected return and the highest variance.

Comparison of Tables 2.1 and 2.2 with Tables 2.4 and 2.5 shows that all asset categories have lower expected returns and variances in the later period. Similarly, the correlation matrix of expected returns shows a lower correlation between returns to bonds and stocks in the later period. As a consequence, the optimal asset allocation can be expected to change.

Table 2.6 shows the efficient frontier obtained by using the data in Tables 2.4 and 2.5. The optimal asset in this case turns out to be 31.7

TABLE 2.4 Expected Returns and Volatilities (1985–1988)

Asset Category	Average	Volatility
Cash	7.15	.36
Bonds	13.12	4.19
Stocks	18.50	15.80

TABLE 2.5 Correlation Matrix (1985–1988)

Asset	Cash	Bonds	Stocks
Cash	1.00		
Bonds	−.01	1.00	
Stocks	−.11	.56	1.00

TABLE 2.6 Efficient Frontier (1985–1988)

Asset	Portfolio								
	1	2	3	4	5	6	7	8	9
Cash	0.0	0.0	0.0	0.0	0.0	0.0	0.0	0.0	0.0
Bonds	75.4	71.0	65.4	57.9	47.4	31.7	5.5	0.0	0.0
Stocks	24.6	29.0	34.6	42.1	52.6	68.3	94.5	100.0	100.0
Return	14.4	14.7	15.0	15.4	15.9	16.8	18.2	18.5	18.5
Volatility	6.2	6.7	7.4	8.3	9.6	11.6	15.1	15.8	15.8

percent in bonds and 68.3 percent in stocks, which stands in contrast with the previous optimal asset allocation.

This simple example illustrates three issues relevant to the asset allocation decision:

1. There is a commonly used procedure for choosing the optimal asset allocation.
2. The optimal asset allocation is a function of both the distributional parameters (i.e., expected returns, variances, and correlations) and investor preferences (i.e., the risk aversion parameter).
3. Proper measurement of expected returns, variances, and covariances is important for asset allocation.

This last point is taken up in more detail in the next section.

VARIATIONS ON A THEME: A SIMULATION

The example given in the previous section illustrated the importance of properly measuring the characteristics of the return distributions for each of the asset categories. As the example demonstrated, changes in the return characteristics imply that revisions must be made to the optimal asset allocation. If the wrong distributional assumptions are made, an inappropriate asset allocation may result.

There are two ways in which an inappropriate distribution can be selected:

1. The general properties of the distribution may be correctly specified but inappropriately measured. For example, one may correctly assume that stock returns are normally distributed but then misestimate the variance of returns. In this example, the general property is the assumption that stock returns are normally distributed.

2. An incorrect general specification may be chosen. For example, stock returns might be assumed to be normally distributed when in fact they are not.

The implications of these issues were explored in the context of a simple simulation.

The simulation was constructed by developing asset return series for fictitious assets X and Y, and simulating their returns under two different distributional assumptions. After simulating the returns, the average and standard deviations of returns were calculated. Similarly, and of importance for the asset allocation decision, the correlation matrix between asset returns was also constructed. The implications for the asset allocation decision were then explored with the simulation results.

In the first case, the returns to asset X were assumed to be normally distributed with a mean of 5.0 and a standard deviation of returns of 2.5; the distribution for asset Y had a mean of 4.0 and a standard deviation of 2.0. The correlation coefficient between the asset return series was assumed to be .65.

It was also assumed that prior information about the return to each asset was irrelevant to the current value, that is, knowledge of the previous value of X was irrelevant for determining the current value of X.

Using a random number generator, the returns to both of these series were simulated over a 144-period time interval. Table 2.7 shows the estimated average returns, standard deviation of returns, and estimated correlation coefficient between the two asset return series. As expected, the simulation statistics come close to the original specification.

The impact of prior information is evident from the correlation between current values of asset X and the previous period's value for asset Y, and vice versa. In both cases, the correlation coefficients are close to zero: for current values of X versus prior values of Y, the correlation is .yy, and for current values of Y versus prior values of X, the correlation is .zz.

Because prior information seems to play a small role in generating asset returns, the estimated standard deviations and correlations can

TABLE 2.7 First Simulation Statistics

Asset	Average	Standard Deviation
X	5.88	1.69
Y	5.03	1.74
	Correlation:	.11

be safely used in an asset allocation framework such as the one out-lined in the preceding section. None of the assumptions regarding asset returns appears to be violated.

The second simulation, however, illustrates a case where the distri-butional assumptions are violated. Let the returns to assets X and Y be generated by:

$$X_t = .6 + .9X_t - 1 + e_t \tag{2}$$

$$Y_t = .5 + .8Y_t - 1 + u_t \tag{3}$$

Let the error terms e_t and u_t each have a mean of zero and variances of 3.0 and 2.5 respectively. Finally, assume that the two error terms have a correlation coefficient of .65 and that the returns on assets X and Y are again simulated for a 144-period horizon.

Table 2.8 summarizes the return characteristics. The standard devi-ations differ substantially from those shown in Table 2.7, and the corre-lation coefficient for contemporaneous movements (i.e., current asset X versus current asset Y) is similar to that shown in Table 2.7.

However, what makes the second simulation different from the first is the degree of correlation across time. The correlation between current movements in asset X and previous movements in asset Y is .55. From the perspective of asset Y, the correlation between move-ments in current values of asset Y and previous movements in asset X is .51.

Tables 2.7 and 2.8 indicate that seemingly minor changes in the dis-tribution of asset returns can result in substantial changes in the sum-mary statistics (e.g., the standard deviation of asset returns). What are the implications for the asset allocation problem?

Suppose that asset returns for X and Y are generated by equations (2) and (3), that the summary data of Table 2.8 are used in the tradi-tional asset allocation framework, and that the information regarding the impact of lagged asset returns is ignored. Now assume that an efficient frontier is developed. Because this frontier is developed without making use of the additional information (i.e., the impact of

TABLE 2.8 Second Simulation Statistics

Asset	Average	Standard Deviation
X	4.74	4.77
Y	1.49	2.90
Correlation:	.70	

lagged information), each portfolio along the frontier will be inefficient. Consequently, the asset allocation chosen using the framework shown in the previous section will not be a minimum variance portfolio. Furthermore, any hedges implemented under these assumptions will also be inefficient: the number of hedging instruments chosen under this framework will be suboptimal.

This example illustrates the importance of correctly specifying the distribution for asset returns and suggests that estimation of the parameters plays a crucial role. The asset allocation decision can be affected by properly specified but improperly estimated return distributions.

The potential for improperly estimating the parameters of a return distribution comes from the choice of a time horizon. The standard deviation of the return to the S&P 500 depends on which time horizon is used. The volatility of the S&P 500 in the 1980s was different from that of the 1950s.

Time horizon is often a mask for more fundamental changes. External changes in the institutional character of financial markets or in the macroeconomic environment can be reflected in structural instability in the asset return distributions. For example, differences in S&P 500 volatility in the 1950s versus the 1980s could reflect differences in both the levels and the volatility of inflation. Consequently, it is important not only to identify potential structural instabilities in the asset return distributions, but also to trace their source to underlying fundamentals.

This section has considered the implications (for the asset allocation decision) of changes in the return distribution and has explored them in the context of two simple simulations. The next section considers these issues using return data for international bond indexes.

AN EXAMPLE: INTERNATIONAL BOND
RETURN DISTRIBUTIONS

The preceding section discussed the importance of structural stability in asset returns. The examples illustrated that changes in asset return distributions imply revisions in the optimal asset allocation, and that changes in the structure of asset return distributions are likely to be a consequence of movements in the underlying economic fundamentals. These movements appear either as differences in estimated parameters across time periods or as changes in the general properties of asset returns.

These movements in underlying parameters and general properties are likely to appear in international asset markets and are explored in this section with international bond data. Monthly return data on six of the countries listed in the Salomon Brothers World Government Bond Index were used to test propositions regarding changes in structure. The six countries chosen were Australia, France, Germany, Japan, the United Kingdom, and the United States. The data covered the period from January 1985 through December 1991. Hedged data (local market returns) were used for all the analyses.

In considering international asset allocation problems, the framework outlined earlier must be modified for currencies. Currencies are included because the domestic return on an international asset can be decomposed into a local market return and a currency return. For example, the dollar return to a U.S. investor in the U.K. gilt market includes the return to U.K. gilts (the local market return) plus a return to movements in the British pound (the currency return).

One standard modification to the asset allocation framework is to include as assets the local market return and the currency return for each of the asset categories under consideration. For the U.S. investor considering the six countries analyzed here, the asset allocation decision would be across 11 assets: the local market returns to each of the six bond markets plus the five currency returns.

A good starting point for analyzing the asset allocation decision is to calculate simple correlation matrices for the local market returns. Table 2.9 shows the correlation matrix of index returns using the entire period. The correlations are shown on the off-diagonal elements, and the local market volatilities are shown along the main diagonal.

Table 2.9 reveals that, as expected, there are different volatilities across countries. For example, the annualized volatility for the U.S. index return is 5.57 percent, whereas in Germany the annualized index return volatility is substantially lower: 3.69 percent.

Table 2.9 also reveals differences in the patterns of correlation across countries. For example, the correlation between index returns in the United States and Australia is .10, but the correlation between the United States and France is .50. Indeed, the correlations between

TABLE 2.9 Correlation Matrix (1985–1991)

			Country			
Country	Australia	France	Germany	Japan	United Kingdom	United States
Australia	5.79					
France	.17	4.63				
Germany	.11	.64	3.69			
Japan	.11	.50	.62	4.94		
United Kingdom	.18	.45	.54	.58	7.41	
United States	.10	.55	.54	.50	.42	5.57

TABLE 2.10 Correlation Matrix (January 1985–June 1988)

	Country					
Country	Australia	France	Germany	Japan	United Kingdom	United States
Australia	6.79					
France	−.16	5.23				
Germany	.05	.54	3.77			
Japan	.02	.48	.76	5.04		
United Kingdom	.08	.47	.57	.55	8.15	
United States	−.04	.58	.54	.52	.33	6.46

Australia and the remaining countries are substantially lower than the correlations for the other countries.

In Tables 2.10 and 2.11, the sample is broken into two pieces. The earlier subperiod runs from January 1985 through June 1988, and the later subperiod includes July 1988 through December 1991. Notice that both the volatilities and the patterns of correlation are different between the two subperiods. Volatilities are almost uniformly higher in the earlier subperiod. The correlations do not show any obvious pattern; they are not noticeably higher in the earlier period for all countries.

The differences across time and across countries can, in part, be accounted for by differences in the distribution of securities. For example, countries with a larger percentage of long-duration bonds will have more volatility in index returns, all else equal.

Security distributions can also affect the pattern of the correlations. Countries where yield movements are highly correlated will have more highly correlated index returns, all else equal. Differences in the distribution of securities across countries can also explain some of the patterns in Tables 2.9 through 2.11. However, the figures suggest that a structural change of some sort occurred in the same period.

TABLE 2.11 Correlation Matrix (July 1989–December 1991)

	Country					
Country	Australia	France	Germany	Japan	United Kingdom	United States
Australia	4.64					
France	.35	3.96				
Germany	.42	.79	3.52			
Japan	.26	.52	.44	4.85		
United Kingdom	.38	.39	.50	.61	6.63	
United States	.40	.49	.55	.48	.58	4.58

TABLE 2.12 Lagged Correlations (1985–1991)

	Country: One Lag					
Current	Australia	France	Germany	Japan	United Kingdom	United States
Australia	.08	.18	.14	.29	.18	.27
Germany	−.08	.17	.14	.24	.28	.23
France	.00	.12	.30	.20	.28	.25
Japan	.00	.17	.12	.15	.11	.10
United Kindom	.10	.15	.06	.24	.22	.09
United States	−.14	−.06	−.05	.00	−.04	.09

The correlations shown in Tables 2.9 through 2.11 also obscure possible effects of correlation across time. Table 2.12 shows the correlation between current values and lagged values for each of the indexes. For example, the correlation between current values of the Australian bond index and lagged values of the German bond market return is .18.

As Table 2.12 indicates, the structure of international bond index returns has some correlation across time. The same conclusion can be drawn from an inspection of the correlation matrices of currency returns, as shown in Table 2.13. The elements in the correlation matrix are the correlations between returns to each of the currencies, from the perspective of the U.S. investor. (Because there are six countries including the United States, there are only five possible currency correlations.) Correlations from the later subperiod (July 1988 through December 1991) are shown in the upper diagonals. The lower diagonal elements show the correlations for the earlier subperiod (January 1985 through June 1988). As the correlations in Table 2.13 show, some changes in structure appear to have occurred, particularly with respect to the Australian dollar.

TABLE 2.13 Currency Return Correlations

	Currency				
Current	Australia	France	Germany	Japan	United Kingdom
Australia	—	−.21	−.20	−.38	.36
France	−.03	—	.99	.66	−.77
Germany	−.02	.96	—	.65	−.76
Japan	−.05	.70	.74	—	−.71
United Kingdom	.03	−.53	−.60	−.48	—

The issue that seems to arise is the identification of the underlying factor driving changes in the structure of the correlation matrices. These are government bond indexes, so it seems reasonable to look at the impact of changes in interest rates as a source of changes in index returns. Had nongovernment securities been included, changes in spreads could also be included as explanatory variables.

To explore the impact of local market interest rates on local market index returns, each local market return was regressed on the changes in the local market one-year and ten-year rates. Each sample period was split in two, and a test for statistical difference between the regression equations estimated on each equation was performed. Data for Germany, Japan, and the United States cover the period from January 1985 through December 1991. Data for the United Kingdom cover the period from August 1986 through December 1991. Data for Australia begin in August 1985 and end in December 1991. France was omitted because of a lack of term structure data.

Table 2.14 summarizes the test results. With the exception of the coefficient on the U.K. ten-year rate in the earlier subperiod and the U.K. one-year rate in the later subperiod, all estimated coefficients are statistically significant at the 5 percent level. (The early U.K. ten-year rate is statistically significant at the 10 percent level.) None of the estimated equations exhibited serial correlation in the residuals.

The estimated coefficients shown in Table 2.14 correspond to intuition regarding the influence of changes in interest rates on bond index returns: as rates drop, index returns increase. However, this result could be a consequence of the distribution of debt.

Furthermore, Table 2.14 suggests that the source for apparent instability in the correlation matrix of index returns is instability in the impact of changes in interest rates on index returns. Such instability could be a consequence of financial liberalization of local markets or of further integration of international financial markets.

TABLE 2.14 Regression Summary

Country	Early Period			Later Period			
	One-Year Rate	Ten-Year Rate	R2	One-Year Rate	Ten-Year Rate	R2	Statistical Difference
Australia	−.31	−3.45	.92	−.86	−2.57	.89	YES
Germany	−.93	−2.98	.85	−1.48	−2.24	.89	YES
Japan	−1.72	−2.02	.80	−.77	−4.44	.88	YES
United Kingdom	−.38	−4.45	.98	−.12	−4.51	.98	YES
United States	−.45	−2.02	.98	−.77	−4.44	.98	YES

What are the implications of these findings for the asset allocation decision? Careful attention must be paid to the correlation matrices used in the asset allocation decision. Instabilities in both the local market returns and the currency returns have the potential for leading to inefficient asset allocations.

Close attention should also be paid to the factors influencing asset return series. Changes in the way the underlying factors drive index returns are likely to lead to revisions in the correlation matrices and, consequently, to an inefficient asset allocation.

CONCLUSION

This chapter has discussed the implications for the asset allocation decision of the structure of asset returns. It has argued that an important consideration in the asset allocation decision is the structure of the correlation matrix of asset returns, because changes in the distributions of asset returns can lead to inefficient asset allocations. However, these changes are likely to reflect changes in the institutional structure of asset markets or other underlying economic fundamentals. Consequently, the asset allocation decision must consider not only the structure of asset return distributions but the impact of possible revisions in the fundamentals. These considerations were explored using international bond index data.

3

The Importance of Time-Horizon

David A. Hammer, CFA
President
Curbstone Investment Management
Auburn, California

INTRODUCTION: COMMON MISUNDERSTANDINGS

Periodically, Wall Street brokerage firms publish their "recommended asset allocation." For what purpose, or for whom, is this recommendation made? Is it for the active trader or the trust account that needs income because the assets may not be liquidated for many years? There is no asset allocation strategy that is good for everybody. Not only do different investors have different risk profiles, but any asset allocation model that is designed to be something other than a market-timing device must take investors' time-horizon into consideration.

Time-horizon, a primary variable, is as important as expected return, volatility, or correlation of returns among the asset classes. In addition, time-horizon should be one of the inputs that *determines* expected return, volatility, and cross-correlation. Therefore, the asset allocation process needs to begin with the determination of the investor's time-horizon. At my firm, every account owns virtually the same individual stock and bond issues, but every account owns them in different proportions.

A major misunderstanding concerning time-horizon can cause an investor's total account to behave differently from what is intended. The source of the misunderstanding is a simplistic belief that time-horizon always can be determined scientifically. Does the investor who will not draw down one penny of an account for ten years really have a ten-year (or longer) time-horizon? Does a defined-benefit plan, which theoretically exists in perpetuity, really have an infinite time-horizon? Does the investor who will be withdrawing all of his or her funds in one year actually have a one-year time-horizon?

CASE STUDIES

Case Study 1: The American Barrick Mercur Goldmine

American Barrick is one of the world's largest gold producers. Its Mercur mine is located southwest of Salt Lake City, Utah, on the western slope of the Oquirrh Mountains. The location of the mine has a lot to do with the way I invest the workers' retirement funds. The mine has a five-year life—the mine literally will cease operations in six years. Many of the workers live in remote towns, like Eureka and Ophir. They have no other nearby place to work, and the employer has few sources from which to attract help. Therefore, the vast majority of the retirement plan participants will be in the plan for exactly five years and will then cash out.

I make allocation decisions for the plan on the basis of a *three-year* time-horizon. These workers are goldminers who know their livelihood is dependent on one employer and the price of gold; they get nervous when their life savings fluctuate in value. In examining what sort of volatility would be psychologically palatable, I determined that a five-year time-horizon would normally produce an allocation that consisted of too much stock. An equity allocation based on a three-year time-horizon is more in keeping with the miners' risk-averse mindset.

Case Study 2: Price Broadcasting Company

This company owned radio and TV stations across the country. Disk jockeys and their coworkers in the entertainment industry tend to be young and move around a lot. A surprising number of retirement plan contributors were in and out of the plan within any one year. I could have managed the asset allocation in accordance with a one-year time-horizon, but following a year or two of give-and-take between the plan's investment committee and myself, it was decided that the plan should be managed on the basis of a five-year time-horizon, even though most of the participants would be gone in five years. The plan participants were young and had an even greater gambling instinct than most young people. The reward–risk utility function was unusual. To the participants, the possibility of an unusually large return was more appealing than the possibility of a large loss was unappealing.

Cast Study 3: "Fast Eddie"

Eddie sold his electrical supply business at the start of his retirement. He wanted to invest his funds for ten years, then cash out and buy property in Hawaii, where he would finish his retirement. A ten-year time-horizon? Forget it! The reason he gave my company trading authority over his funds was because his wife had convinced him that he made emotional investment decisions and could not sleep at night when he managed his own portfolio. He called me several times each week to check on his portfolio. He could not accept portfolio volatility, but neither could he accept the low return of a money-market account. This investor needed to be persuaded to accept an appropriate time-horizon (which, to pacify all concerned, turned out to be two years).

Conclusion

Because they are not hired to create additional stress for their clients, investment advisers should pay a great deal of attention to the "psychological time-horizon." Simultaneously, they should make an effort to educate the clients about the importance and significance of the time-horizon, with particular emphasis on how time reduces volatility (risk).

HOW TIME AFFECTS VOLATILITY

The investment marketplace may or may not be efficient or possess the true characteristics of a "random walk." The argument concerning market efficiency may need to continue until some future time when there are more observations (trading periods) to analyze. Most people are surprised by how many series of events must occur to produce a distribution pattern that closely resembles a normal (bell-shaped) curve. Although my own work casts serious doubt on the random walk hypothesis, I believe the distribution of securities returns appears random enough to offer validity to the following paragraphs. Later in the chapter, it will be shown how a nonefficient market would add even more validity to some of the ensuing arguments.

Binomial distribution (which approximates random distribution) occurs when we measure the frequency of possible outcomes that are the result of a series of two equally probable but opposing events. Examples that produce binomial distribution include the results of many series of coin tosses, of cutting black and red cards from a random deck of 52 cards, or of selecting odd and even numbers by throwing darts at pages of a telephone book. The odds of the stock market being up or down various percentages (relative to its secular trend line) over the next hour, day, week, or year can be at least approximated using normal distribution, which, for a large number of observations, approximates binomial distribution.

When we refer to the distribution of these events, we are referring to the relative probabilities of various combinations of events, such as the relative probability of tossing four heads versus three heads plus one tail; or cutting ten black and five red cards versus eight black plus seven red; or having six up-days in the stock market versus two down-days plus four up-days. Consider plotting a graph showing the results of 1,000 sets of coin-tosses, with 30 tosses per set. Let x represent the number of heads-minus-tails per set (+30 to −30) and let y represent the frequency of each of the possible outcomes. The resulting graph line would look like the familiar bell-shaped curve. Similarly, we could plot the net 30-day percentage changes for 1,000 30-day periods for the Dow Jones Industrial Average ("the Dow Jones") versus their frequency of occurrence. The resulting graph would look very similar to the classic bell-shaped curve, except that most historical periods contain slightly more than the "normal" number of large percentage moves (which creates some doubt about the validity of a truly random market). The curve will be skewed to the right (approximating a log-normal curve), as it should be, to reflect the fact that the curve is depicting the relative frequencies of *percentage* changes. (A stock with a $90 mean price, where the price regularly moves back and forth between $80 and $100, would move up 25 percent, from $80 to $100, with the same frequency that it would move down 20 percent, from $100 to $80.)

If we compared distribution curves for sets of 30 random events per set versus sets of 60 random events per set, the 60-event sets would have a range of possible outcomes twice as wide as the 30-event sets, but the average deviation from the mean outcome would not be twice as wide. The odds of tossing, say, four more heads than tails is not *twice* as great when 60 flips are made rather than 30 flips. Neither is the probability twice as great that the Dow Jones will be 5 percent or more above (or below) its secular trend line after 60 days than after 30 days.

As an example, if the Dow Jones has a 20 percent chance of being up more than 5 percent after 30 trading days, it does not have a 20 percent chance of being up 10 percent after 60 trading days. In fact, it has a 20 percent chance of being up only 7 percent or more after 60 trading days because, in a normal distribution scenario, *volatility is a function of the square root of time*, not a linear function of time. The market cannot move twice as much in two weeks as it can in one week, with the same degree of probability. In two weeks, it can move 1.4 (the square root of 2) times its movement in one week. If the market has a 33 percent probability of moving up or down more than 1 percent in one day, then it has a 33 percent probability of moving up or down more than 2 percent in four days.

Let's carry this example a step further. Assume the market has a 10 percent annualized expected return so that, after five years, the total expected return is 61 percent (10 percent compounded for five years). Assume also that the volatility of the market is such that, over five years, there is a 10 percent chance the return could be 40 percentage points higher or lower than 61 percent. Over 20 years, the expected return would be 573 percent (10 percent compounded for 20 years). Using the square-root-of-time algorithm, the range of possible returns would be 80 percentage points above or below 573 percent (with a 10 percent chance of a move greater than 80 percentage points). In this example, the annualized volatility over five years is 7 percent (40 percent compounded for five years) and the annualized volatility over 20 years is only 3 percent (the annualization of an 80 percent volatility over 20 years). Thus, the range of possible annualized returns for five years is 10 percent plus or minus 7 percent; for 20 years, the range is 10 percent plus or minus 3 percent; and for one year, the range is 10 percent plus or minus 18 percent (all with the same 90 percent degree of probability).

In a very real sense, then, *volatility (risk) decreases with the passage of time*. Risky investments become effectively less risky over time. Therefore, the longer the expected holding period for a security (or class of securities), the more the tolerable periodic risk. Figure 3.1 graphically depicts this outcome.

Let's carry this point to an extreme. Because stocks may have an annualized volatility of return of less than 3 percent for holding periods of 20 years or more, they are barely more risky, over the long term, than certificates of deposit (CDs) or Treasury bills (T-bills). The *average* CD return over the next 20 years very possibly could be 3 percent more (or less) than the average return today. Returns for cash equivalents are not normally distributed. In reality, over any 30-year time-horizon, both stocks and T-bills have shown (approximately 67 percent of the time) actual average rates of return that are within 2 percent of the annualized rates of return for other 30-year periods.

Armed with these data, one could certainly make a case that, for an investor with a 30-year time-horizon, an all-T-bill portfolio is imprudent! Such a portfolio normally offers less than half the expected return, but virtually no less risk (annualized volatility of return over the 30-year time-horizon) than an all-stock portfolio. For a 15-year time-horizon, stocks versus cash equivalents represents a fiduciary trade-off for even the most risk-averse investors. The same is true for bonds versus stocks: empirical evidence shows that, over most 15-year holding periods, bonds offer less than half the return of stocks with about half the risk.

In the real world, many investors are willing to assume more than double the risk for a doubling of their return. If we utilize a single graph to plot points, with each point representing volatility of return (x) versus average return (y) for each of the various classes of investments, we would find that the line that best fits the points has a slope of less than 0.5 (45 degrees). In my opinion, the marketplace (empirical evidence) has

FIGURE 3.1 Range of Annualized Returns over Time (Years)

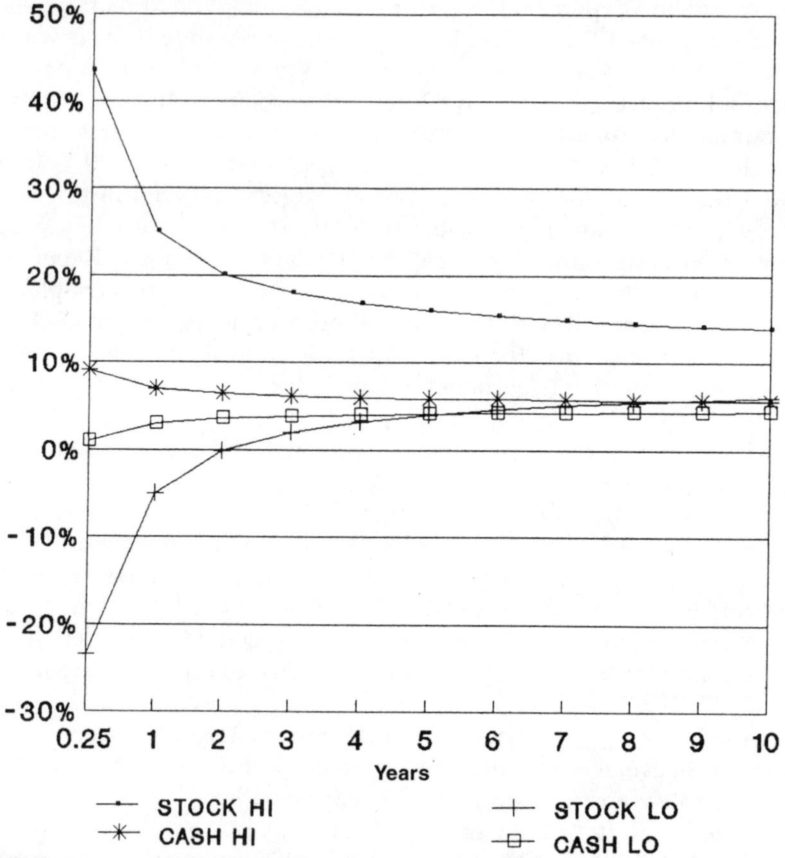

generally deemed it proper to receive 1 percent in additional annual re-turn for each 3 percent (approximate) of additional one-year volatility!

This means that the market itself accepts the idea that equities and zero-coupon bonds offer very attractive reward–risk ratios for longer time-horizons, but, for time-horizons of five years or less, they are only marginally more attractive than bonds or cash equivalents on a reward–risk basis. The proper percentage of equities and zero-coupon bonds that should be held in a portfolio with a short-term time-horizon is very sen-sitive to the investor's level of risk aversion. For investors with long time-horizons, however, we must question the prudence of cash equivalents (and maybe high coupon bonds) just as much as we would question the prudence of high-risk securities.

Conclusion

There is no ideal asset allocation that is suitable for everyone. Asset allocation should be as much a function of time-horizon as it is a function of comparative expected returns and volatility.

HOW TIME AFFECTS CROSS-CORRELATION OF RETURNS

There are three basic types of asset allocation models: (1) efficient frontier models, (2) probability optimizers, and (3) risk-premium models. The combined effects of time-horizon on these types of models will be shown in the next section. Only one of these types—the efficient frontier—utilizes the cross-correlation of returns as a primary input. Accordingly, cross-correlation (in terms of its relationship to time) will be dealt with briefly.

If we were to plot the risk (x) versus the return (y) for various securities or, more appropriately, for various combinations of classes of securities, we would have a graph similar to Figure 3.2. The points in the upper region of the graph are commonly believed to represent the best combinations of investments, because all other corresponding points (relative to the x-axis) below the upper margin offer less return for the same amount of risk. Also, most investment professionals feel the

FIGURE 3.2 Efficient Frontier

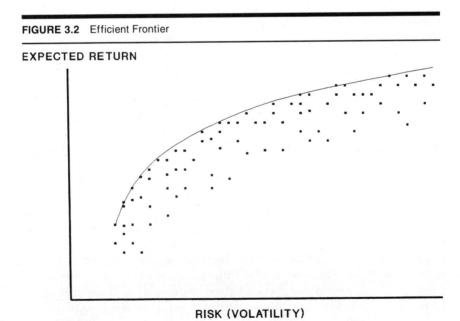

EXPECTED RETURN

RISK (VOLATILITY)

upper-left portion of the graph is especially attractive because points in the upper right region offer less incremental return per unit of incremental risk.

For those who try to fine-tune this process for asset allocation purposes, there are several methods for picking one precise optimal point along the efficient frontier (the upper-left margin). These methods include defining the intersection of the efficient frontier (1) with a straight line drawn from the T-bill rate on the y-axis, (2) with a line drawn from a hypothetical zero-risk stock return on the y-axis, or (3) with a nonlinear representation of the investor's risk profile.

No matter what version of the efficient frontier is used, the position of each of the points on the graph, including the "margin of efficiency," is a function of the *expected* correlation of returns between the various combinations of investments each point represents. If the correlation of returns inherent to any point turns out to be lower than expected, then the point was originally plotted too far to the right, and vice versa. The lower the correlation between the returns of any particular combination of asset classes, the lower the volatility of that combination. For example, assume the following volatility (standard deviation of return): stocks, 15 percent, and bonds, 5 percent. If the returns between the two are highly correlated (that is, the returns tend to increase and decrease simultaneously), a combination of 50 percent stocks and 50 percent bonds might have a volatility of return of, say, 8 percent. This might be no higher than the volatility of a combination of 70 percent stock and 30 percent bonds if the correlation of returns had been low (if stock and bond prices often moved in opposition directions).

How does one determine the expected correlation of future returns of the various asset classes? Unfortunately, past correlation is not very indicative of future correlation. This is in contrast to historic volatility (variance of return), which is relatively stable over the years. Correlation between stock and bond returns (which describes how much stock and bond prices tend to move together, or, in effect, how much stock prices are affected by interest rates) varies significantly from one period to the next. This is true even if the measurement periods span several years.

One thing is certain: the longer the time-horizon, the higher the correlation. Consider an extreme. For very long periods of measurement, the cross-correlation of returns between stocks and bonds approaches unity. That occurs because, over a long-term horizon (say, 30 years), both returns are always positive and they differ by a fairly constant amount (always in favor of equities). On the other hand, between 1 P.M. and 2 P.M. on a particular day, there is probably a 50–50 chance of stocks and bonds moving in the same direction. There have been recent two-year periods when the correlation of stock and bond returns (based on weekly performance statistics) has been as high as 50 percent and as low as zero.

Conclusion

The cross-correlation between the returns of classes of securities, although difficult to predict, *is* a direct function of time. Therefore, an efficient-frontier-based asset allocation model must make an assumption as to time-horizon.

HOW TIME AFFECTS EXPECTED RETURN

The effect of time on volatility and cross-correlation is quite straightforward, as shown in the previous sections. The effect of time on expected return is a little more difficult for many investors to grasp. One might legitimately ask, "Is the expected return for the various classes of securities actually dependent on how far out in time we look?"

I believe expected return (or internal rate of return, IRR) is very dependent on time. Take the expected return for cash as the simplest example. For a one-year time-horizon, the expected returns for T-bills, CDs, commercial paper, or money-market funds would all approximate the going rate. But what about the expected return for cash equivalents for the next five or ten years? One is forced to make some future interest rate assumption.

A similar but more complex situation arises with the expected return for bonds. Most allocation models assume that, for instance, the five-year or ten-year expected return for bonds is what bonds with five- or ten-year maturities happen to yield at the moment. This may not be realistic. How many portfolios actually buy *and hold* bonds that mature at the end of the time-horizon? Even if they did, what is the reinvestment rate assumption? In practice, portfolio managers are more apt to maintain a bond portfolio that has a constant maturity range or duration range. For a five-year time-horizon, for example, it may be more realistic to compute the expected return for a constant duration portfolio (using an index such as the Lehman Brothers Government/Corporate Bond Index) than simply to use the yield-to-maturity of a five-year bond. Once again, this requires assumptions about future interest rates.

Because it would be appropriate to utilize future rates to determine the expected returns for the cash-equivalent and bond portions of a portfolio, it follows that we need to do the same for the stock market expected return. The easiest way to accomplish this is to assume a terminal equity

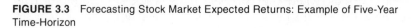

FIGURE 3.3 Forecasting Stock Market Expected Returns: Example of Five-Year Time-Horizon

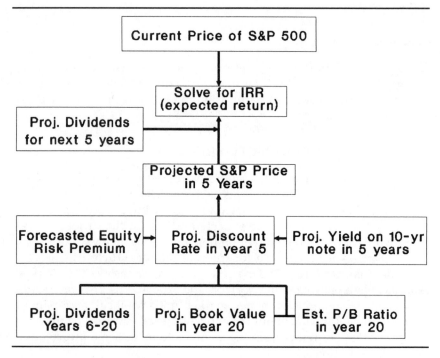

value at the end of the time-horizon, where the terminal discount rate is a function of the expected interest rate at that future point in time. Figure 3.3 illustrates such a system.

What does all this accomplish? A much more realistic and better performing asset allocation process. For instance, assume the yield curve was very steep, investor confidence was extremely high, and the economy was booming. It could make a lot of sense, more often than not, to project the following:

1. Money-market rates will be higher in the future; therefore, the expected return for cash equivalents will be higher for longer-term time-horizons than for shorter ones.
2. Reinvestment rates for interest on bonds will be higher, but bond prices might be lower. The net effect on the bond market expected return will depend on the time-horizon and the assumed portfolio maturity and duration.
3. The stock market's discount rate (the rate of interest that discounts future earnings, dividends, or cash flows) will be higher

for longer-term horizons than for shorter ones, which will reduce the longer-term expected returns for stocks by varying degrees, depending on the time-horizon.

Although the purpose here is not to demonstrate how to determine future rates, the following observations may be helpful. I have never found any meaningful correlation between the shape of the Treasury yield curve and future rates. In other words, forward rate theory, in its raw form, is no better at forecasting rates than is an assumption of an unchanging yield curve.

However, if the analyst were to factor in (or, more literally, factor *out*) the effect of investor confidence on the slope of the yield curve, a high degree of predictability would result. The term confidence refers to the forces affecting and demand for liquidity and quality. Confidence can be quantified by measuring the spread between CD rates or commercial paper rates and the T-bill yield, or between the yields on high-quality versus medium-quality bonds. So, for example, when the yield curve is steep, it may not be because of a higher rate expectation. Instead, confidence may be low and investors may be uncertain and will pay a big premium for liquidity. The effects of any Federal Reserve (Fed) actions must also be taken into consideration. The yield curve can be steep because the Fed is driving down the short end, which should actually result in lower future rates, even though the curve is steepening.

Forecasting future reinvestment rates, discount rates, and equity risk premiums requires a high level of sophistication in the development of asset allocation model algorithms. But investor confidence (and therefore equity risk premiums) and yield-curve slopes have trends; they do not move at random. It is also true that changes in bond yields usually precede similar changes in equity discount rates, all else being equal. Therefore, it is quite possible to make some forecast of future stock and bond discount factors that will be more profitable than no forecast at all.

Conclusion

Comparing the long-term expected return for stocks to the yield on a specific maturity bond and to the current risk-free (or other short-term) rate is mixing apples and oranges with a banana thrown in. When determining an asset mix, the same time-horizon should be used in calculating the expected return for each of the appropriate asset classes. Also, the stock, bond, and money-market portfolios for which the expected returns are computed should be rolling (index-type) portfolios. The use of buy-and-hold portfolios is not conceptually wrong (except for cash equivalents), but the use of realistic future-portfolio proxies produces better results. (The particular asset allocation model I favor has outperformed a static 60–40 stock–bond mix by 4 percent over the past 15 years, compared to 2 percent for its buy-and-hold, constant-rates-assumption counterpart.)

THE SIGNIFICANCE OF THE DISTRIBUTION OF RETURNS

We do not know with complete certainty whether securities returns are randomly distributed; but it seems doubtful. The Efficient Market Hypothesis, which developed roots in the 1950s, made a wonderful contribution to the field of portfolio management by introducing the quantitative methodologies that eventually led to the utilization of probability calculus in the determination of the optimal asset mix. It should be made clear, however, that any accurate calculation of probability or of expected portfolio volatility must assume a normal or log-normal (random) distribution of returns. Without normal or log-normal distribution, there are no "variances" (in a true statistical sense) and therefore no standard deviations and no measurable areas of probability.

An efficient market implies some sort of supply–demand created equilibrium. Yet, it is difficult to believe that equilibrium is the normal state of the marketplace anymore than equilibrium is the normal state of the universe or of the human mind. A random-walk market implies that tomorrow's return has nothing to do with yesterday's return. If this were the case, the market would reverse direction 50 percent of the time, which it does not. Similarly, the number and the lengths of positive and negative return "strings" (consecutive moves in the same direction) would be "normal," which they are not. For example, the number of times that the market goes up three, four, and five days in a row during a period of 10,000 trading days should equal the number of times that a person would flip three, four, and five heads over the course of 10,000 coin-tosses. Such an equivalence does not exist.

In addition to testing for percentage of reversals and number of strings, another very good test for randomness is the Hurst Exponent. This nonlinear analysis was originally developed to forecast the annual rise and fall of a natural body of water; but it can be used to test any number series for trend persistence versus mean reversion. The investment marketplace exhibits persistence; that is, the odds for a positive return increase if the last return was positive, and vice versa (particularly over very short and very long periods of time).

The manifestation of a random distribution requires (1) sampling in the thousands and (2) statistically, thousands of events that have an equal probability of two opposing possible outcomes.

Interest rates, logically, would have to be one of those random events that affect stock returns under an efficient market scenario. But each of the above tests for randomness suggests that interest rates (as well as the value of the dollar, certain commodity prices, investor confidence, and so on) move in trends. If all the factors that cause the stock market to be at its particular level are not random, then how can stock market returns themselves be random phenomena?

One possibility is that the market moves in a secular trend comprised of changing intermediate-term secondary trends around which there exists random "noise." Interestingly, if a graph is plotted that measures the energy dissipation of a pendulum versus time, the resulting curve often looks more like the distribution of equity returns than a normal distribution curve does. Perhaps new information (random, or predicted by only a few) entering the market is equivalent to giving a moving pendulum a big shove and watching it oscillate down toward a resting state, only to receive another shove along the way. Other investment mathematicians are attempting to employ the "bifurcations" of "chaos theory" to explain the apparent (but not actual) randomness of the securities markets.

If the market were efficient, then one could make a case that the expected return for a security or group of securities would be the same for all time-horizons. Under a nonefficient scenario, however, the series of expected prices would not necessarily lie along a straight line projected into the distant future. Therefore, annualized expected returns would vary, depending on the time-horizon. Let us make the plausible assumption that the biggest factors affecting stock market returns, in the short and intermediate term, are interest rates and investor confidence. These factors move in trends that approximate (but often precede) the business cycle. Therefore, for example, if the expected annualized return for the stock market is eight percent for the next two years, it could certainly be 10 percent for the next four years or 7 percent for the next 12 months.

Table 3.1 shows the various allocations by time-horizon (according to a successful, probability-based allocation system) at the January 15 low point in the 1991 stock market. Notice how each investor, regardless of time-horizon, was virtually equally and fully invested at the market trough because the higher expected returns for the shorter time-horizons compensated for the lower annualized volatilities for the longer time-horizons. By comparison, Table 3.2 shows "normal" allocations (using the same model) when stocks, bonds, and cash equivalents are "fairly valued" relative to each other. Here, the model calls for an equity apportionment of 46 percent for an investor with a one-year horizon and 75 percent for an investor with a ten-year horizon. The reason is that the expected returns, in a fairly valued (or efficient) market, would be the same regardless of time-horizon, but the riskier securities (equities) effectively become less risky (therefore, more attractive) as the time-horizon is extended.

TABLE 3.1 Portfolio Optimizer

1/15/91

S&P 500	312.49	Stock Portfolio Standard Deviation	15.97%
Ten-Year Note	8.28%	Bond Portfolio Standard Deviation	7.07%
T-Bill	6.33%	Stock–Bond Correlation	34.9%

	Time Horizon (Years)			
Geometric Means	*1*	*3*	*5*	*10*
Expected Return:				
Stock	17.66%	15.47%	13.01%	10.79%
Bonds	13.09	11.88	10.32	8.95
Cash	5.08	5.33	5.82	6.12
Standard Deviation:				
Stock	15.97%	8.48%	6.30%	4.17%
Bonds	7.07	3.93	2.98	2.04
Optimal Portfolio:				
Stocks	57%	64%	64%	64%
Bonds	40	35	35	36
Cash	3	1	1	0
Total return	15.42%	14.15%	12.01%	10.12%
Volatility (standard deviation)	9.83%	10.86%	10.86%	10.83%
Expected return	17.53%	16.43%	14.29%	12.40%
$1.00 in 20 years	$25.28	$20.96	$14.46	$10.36
Raw Probabilities:				
Bonds vs. cash	87%	95%	93%	92%
Stocks vs. bonds	61	66	67	67
Stocks vs. cash	78	88	87	87
Bonds vs. stocks	26	18	18	18
Raw Combinations:				
Stocks vs. bonds and cash	48%	59%	58%	58%
Bonds vs. stocks and cash	34	32	31	32
Cash vs. stocks and bonds	3	1	1	0
Equity–Cash Portfolio:				
Stocks	78%	88%	87%	87%
Cash	22	12	13	13
Stock–Bond Portfolio:				
Stocks	61%	66%	67%	67%
Bonds	39	34	33	33

The mathematical reason for riskier securities' becoming more attractive over time involves probability calculus. As time increases, the range of possible annualized returns decreases for each asset class, thus increasing the odds that the classes with the highest expected returns will outperform a bogey of a lower magnitude. This outcome can be seen by comparing Figure 3.4 to Figure 3.5.

TABLE 3.2 Portfolio Optimizer: "Normal" Case

S&P 500	380.00	Stock Portfolio Standard Deviation		15.60%
Ten-Year Note	7.00%	Bond Portfolio Standard Deviation		5.24%
T-Bill	5.40%	Stock–Bond Correlation		33.0%

	Time Horizon (Years)			
Geometric Means	1	3	5	10
Expected Return:				
Stock	10.00%	10.00%	10.00%	10.00%
Bonds	7.00	7.00	7.00	7.00
Cash	5.40	5.40	5.40	5.40
Standard Deviation:				
Stock	15.60%	8.30%	6.17%	4.09%
Bonds	5.24	2.94	2.24	1.55
Optimal Portfolio:				
Stocks	46%	57%	64%	75%
Bonds	34	32	29	24
Cash	19	11	7	1
Total return	8.09%	8.55%	8.83%	9.23%
Volatility (standard deviation)	7.66%	9.28%	10.32%	11.89%
Expected return	9.83%	10.59%	11.05%	11.72%
$1.00 in 20 years	$6.52	$7.49	$8.13	$9.17
Raw Probabilities:				
Bonds vs. cash	62%	71%	76%	85%
Stocks vs. bonds	58	64	69	77
Stocks vs. cash	62	71	77	87
Bonds vs. stocks	28	15	9	3
Raw Combinations:				
Stocks vs. bonds and cash	35%	46%	53%	67%
Bonds vs. stocks and cash	26	25	24	21
Cash vs. stocks and bonds	15	8	5	1
Equity–Cash Portfolio:				
Stocks	62%	71%	77%	87%
Cash	38	29	23	13
Stock–Bond Portfolio:				
Stocks	58%	64%	69%	77%
Bonds	42	36	31	23

CONCLUSION

The time-horizon invariably affects risk; under a nonefficient market assumption, it also affects expected return. Therefore, for several reasons, the assumed time-horizon is an extremely important variable in the asset-mix optimization process. Accordingly, the employment of an asset allocation system that minimizes or even nullifies the importance of time is of questionable value.

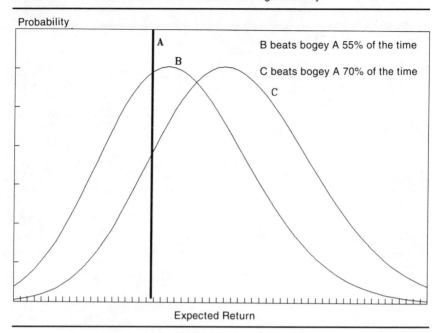

FIGURE 3.4 Possible Returns for Securities with High Volatility

Probability

A

B

C

B beats bogey A 55% of the time

C beats bogey A 70% of the time

Expected Return

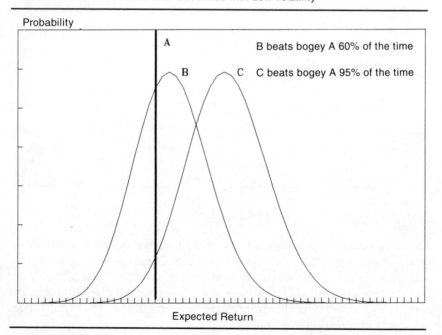

FIGURE 3.5 Possible Returns for Securities with Low Volatility

Probability

A

B

C

B beats bogey A 60% of the time

C beats bogey A 95% of the time

Expected Return

4

Enhancing Asset Allocation Performance with a Volatility-Based Rebalancing Process

Douglas McCalla
First Investment Officer
San Diego City Employees' Retirement System

This chapter reviews the resulting value-added of various traditional methods of rebalancing investment portfolios to their long-term strategic asset allocation targets. The development and implementation of a sophisticated volatility-based portfolio rebalancing process are described. This powerful process was specifically tailored to the risk–return profile of one pension plan's portfolio. Proprietary modeling techniques are being refined that will allow this methodology to be applied to other complex asset allocation structures having multiple allocations.

BACKGROUND

It would be fair to state that modern portfolio theory has validated the importance of asset allocation. The asset allocation decision is now well accepted as the major factor in determining long-term investment performance. The utilization of a Markowitz mean-variance optimization process has been shown to enhance significantly the process of achieving desired long-term investment goals in an efficient, low-volatility manner.

The employment of a sophisticated statistical asset allocation technique such as mean-variance optimization relies on a complex underlying computational process. Additionally, an asset allocation modeling process requires some form of expert technical assistance to provide reasonable capital-market input assumptions. These assumptions concern the expected returns, volatilities, and correlations for the various asset classes to be utilized. Without supporting tools such as computer software, the asset allocation modeling process can also require the same expert assistance to perform the calculations and review the results for reasonableness. Once the asset allocation optimization study is done, however, it is fairly simple to implement: invest x percent in one asset class, y percent in another, z percent in a third, and so on.

Typically, after this point of implementation, the reliance on sophisticated analysis and modeling techniques dramatically decreases. Nevertheless, several salient follow-through questions remain to be addressed. For example, how closely should the asset allocation structure be followed over time? What guidelines or expectations should be established to control the frequency and magnitude of the rebalancing actions necessary to maintain the long-term strategic asset allocation mix?

Compared to the depth of analysis performed to construct optimal asset allocation strategies, the evaluation and implementation of ongoing asset allocation rebalancing techniques are approached with significantly less thought and less precise definition. Conventional advice to pension plan sponsors concerning asset allocation portfolio rebalancing strategies lacks the rigor and intensity of analysis, explanation, and understanding found in the process of establishing optimal target asset allocations.

This situation may be considered analogous to normal human decision-making behavior. Individuals seem more confident and decisive when making an initial, rationally analyzed investment allocation decision. On the other hand, they seem indecisive and less confident in the emotionally clouded situations that confront them when they are trying to choose the appropriate time to sell the winners and buy the underperformers. This indecision has often been attributed to the normal human feelings of avarice and fear—the financial derivatives of the emotions of love and hate.

What methods might be used to minimize the impact of these human emotional responses when making difficult follow-through decisions? Can any of these methods be expected to add value to the long-term performance of the chosen asset allocation mix? To begin to answer these questions, a review of traditional approaches to rebalancing is warranted.

CONVENTIONAL METHODS OF MANAGING ASSET ALLOCATION STATUS

Pension plan investment policy statements usually refer to targeted asset allocation percentages, plus or minus some percentage-of-portfolio range of acceptable variance. Characteristically, this is usually an easily remembered round number. The range of ±5 percent is most frequently presented to plan sponsors as a signal point, when the rebalancing issue should be addressed.

These round percentage numbers have an inherent simplicity and beauty. Percentages are more easily understood by trustees and fiduciaries than standard deviations, variances, geometric means, and other statistical terms. But where do these percentages come from? Are these percentage variance ranges appropriate, given the specific asset allocation mix and the risk tolerance of the plan sponsor? Are other techniques available to more efficiently manage the asset allocation structure?

A number of methods can be employed to control the asset allocation mix. Perold and Sharpe[1] reviewed several rebalancing strategies—buy-and-hold, constant-proportion and option-based portfolio insurance, and constant-mix. They evaluated these strategies for their potential payoff under different market conditions. A buy-and-hold approach is a completely passive strategy where no rebalancing of the portfolio occurs. In constantly declining or rising markets, this strategy will outperform a constant-mix strategy.

A constant-mix strategy keeps the exposure to each asset class at a constant proportion of the total portfolio. This is an active process that usually requires (1) the purchase of an asset class as it drops in relative value and (2) the sale of an asset class as it rises in relative value. These adjustments are usually guided by a decision rule that triggers the point at which rebalancing action is to be taken. The constant-mix strategy tends to outperform the buy-and-hold process in markets that oscillate and show some volatility but do not exhibit a major sustained move in any one direction.

Constant-proportion and option-based portfolio techniques are more complex "portfolio insurance purchase" processes. A detailed explanation of them is beyond the scope of this chapter. The use of a constant-proportion strategy can result in the sale of an asset class as it drops in relative value and the purchase of an asset class as it rises in relative value. An option-based strategy might be summarized as one that uses options to sell an asset class as it drops in relative value, and one in which the effective asset mix can be very calendar-period-dependent because of the expiration characteristics of options. Long-term investors may find this method less desirable because of the additional management required by the option resetting process. The constant-proportion and option-based strategies tend to underperform they buy-and-hold strategy in relatively trendless but volatile markets.

A key point made by Perold and Sharpe was that no one type of rebalancing strategy can be cited as the best for all investors because the asset allocation decision attempts to optimize return relative to risk (volatility). Each investor brings to this process a different "degree of fit" between the investor's risk tolerance and the rebalancing strategy's payoff potential in different types of markets. Therefore, the selection of an appropriate rebalancing strategy requires a clear understanding of who will enjoy the reward of return and who will bear the risk associated with not achieving that return. In defined-benefit pension plans, where the employer has pledged a specific benefit structure to employees, this is a significant issue.

Another interesting analysis concerning portfolio rebalancing was presented by Hurrell,[2] who reviewed eight asset mixes ranging from a blend of 15 percent stocks and 85 percent bonds to a combination of 85 percent stocks and 15 percent bonds. The eight mixes were adjusted in increments of 10 percent. Hurrell used monthly historical return data for stocks and bonds for the 18-year period from January 1973 through December 1990. Transaction costs were taken into consideration at each rebalancing of the investment mix at a rate of two basis points for each buy and sell.

Hurrell evaluated various calendar period and percentage-of-portfolio rebalancing thresholds. The calendar periods were monthly, quarterly, and annually. The percentage ranges were ±3.5 percent, ±5 percent, ±6.5 percent, ±8 percent, ±9.5 percent, ±11 percent, ±12.5 percent, and ±15 percent. The results of Hurrell's study indicated that various methods of rebalancing a portfolio to a constant mix produced superior returns compared to a buy-and-hold strategy. The enhancements to the annualized return ranged between +0.22 percent and +0.51 percent over various rolling ten-year intervals within the 18-year period.

Hurrell's results also indicated that, compared to calendar-date rebalancing methods, percentage-of-portfolio rebalancing methods usually produced superior enhancements to total portfolio return. Of the calendar-based methods, quarterly rebalancing produced the best results.

Another key conclusion of this study was that, although percentage-of-portfolio rebalancing ranges as wide as ±12.5 percent have maximized portfolio total returns over several specific ten-year periods, the risk of having performance revert to that of a buy-and-hold strategy far outweighed the benefit of using a wider rebalancing range over ten-year periods. Thus, this study suggested that the ideal range for percentage-of-portfolio variance bands around target allocations would range between ±5.0 percent and ±9.5 percent.

To further investigate the potential impact of periodic rebalancing on the long-term performance of portfolios, Hurrell's methodology was utilized to evaluate the historic impact of using calendar periods and percentage thresholds to trigger th rebalancing of a simple two-asset portfolio. With acknowledgment to Hurrell, who shared the earlier analysis format, a 21-year period, from January 1973 through December 1993, was evaluated. This replication again used monthly return data for the Standard and Poors 500 (S&P 500) stock index and the Shearson Lehman Government/Corporate (SL G/C) bond index.

These indexes were used to model the rebalancing outcomes on three different asset mixes of stocks and bonds: 60%/40%, 50%/50%, and 40%/60%. The analysis computed the portfolios' annualized rates of total return over the 21-year period for the two types of portfolio rebalancing strategies: (1) calendar and (2) percentage-of-portfolio. The annualized returns are net of transaction costs, that were computed at five basis points for each sale and purchase transaction.

Table 4.1 presents the results of this review. The results remain consistent with Hurrell's earlier published findings. Of the calendar-period methods, quarterly rebalancing produced the best enhancement to return. The most advantageous percentage thresholds were about ±10 percent to ±11 percent. The maximum annualized rate of total return for each portfolio is underlined in the table. These percentage rebalancing thresholds added value over that achieved by quarterly rebalancing.

The optimal portfolio returns associated with using a wide rebalancing range such as ±10 percent to ±11 percent were accomplished with only three adjustment moves during the 21-year period. These adjustments occurred during September 1974, January 1980, and August 1987. Thus, the use of wide adjustment thresholds will provide a very low probability of recognizing any rebalancing benefit on a year-to-year basis.

A review of the narrower percentage rebalancing ranges of ±3 percent to ±5 percent suggests that portfolio returns can achieve enhancement beyond that gained by using any of the calendar-period methods. The number of adjustments necessary to achieve these results ranged from 9 to 19, when the average period between actions was one to two years. Thus, using a narrower variance range provides a higher probability of enhancing total return during shorter intervals. Another benefit of using narrower ranges is the periodic realization and booking of gains.

A RISK-AVERSE PLAN'S APPROACH

With this background in mind, this section reviews a specific instance by which a risk-averse pension plan set up a sophisticated volatility-based asset allocation rebalancing strategy. In the rebalancing strategy described here, the trustees had a low risk tolerance—primarily the result of the pension plan's 95 percent actuarial funding status. The

TABLE 4.1 Annualized Percentage Total Return Rates and Number of Adjustments for Calendar and Percentage Rebalancing Methods during a 21-Year Period (January 1973 through December 1993)

Rebalancing Method	Asset Mixes (S&P 500 & SL G/C Indexes)					
	60/40 Mix Returns (%)	No. of Adjustments	50/50 Mix Returns (%)	No. of Adjustments	40/60 Mix Returns (%)	No. of Adjustments
None	10.651	0	10.485	0	10.314	0
Monthly	10.876	252	10.716	252	10.532	252
Quarterly	10.906	84	10.747	84	10.562	84
Annually	10.819	21	10.657	21	10.477	21
+/– Percentages:						
3.0%	10.902	19	10.738	19	10.538	17
4.0%	10.963	16	10.801	16	10.517	12
5.0%	10.954	9	10.839	11	10.620	10
6.0%	10.841	5	10.650	5	10.404	3
7.0%	10.775	3	10.614	3	10.437	3
8.0%	10.974	4	10.662	3	10.483	3
9.0%	11.014	4	10.862	4	10.601	3
10.0%	11.047	3	10.868	3	10.681	3
11.0%	11.003	2	10.897	3	10.711	3
12.0%	11.003	2	10.851	2	10.314	0
13.0%	11.021	2	10.485	0	10.314	0
14.0%	10.651	0	10.485	0	10.314	0

trustees' risk profile was most consistent with the payoff potential of a constant-mix rebalancing strategy.

From the perspective of the plan's trustees, a constant-mix strategy was (1) the simplest method to understand, implement, and use, and (2) the method most consistent with the plan's underlying asset allocation assumptions and long-term time-horizon. Also, the consistent adherence to a constant-mix strategy imposed a discipline that forced decisions to sell high and buy low.

It was understood by the trustees that portfolio adjustment sell signals would not necessarily be at the top of a market cycle, and buy signals would not necessarily occur at the bottom of a cycle. It was also expected that the utilization of the strategy would force transactions that would occur on the desirable portions of the trend lines. Given the risk profile, the strategy was more desirable than one of selling low and buying high, which would occur using some of the other rebalancing techniques described by Perold and Sharpe.

Initially, the plan had a policy that the target allocations would be allowed to vary by no more than ±5 percent of the portfolio. Thus, the plan's 35 percent allocation to stocks would have to fall below 30 percent or rise above 40 percent of the portfolio before the trustees had to consider taking any action. Similarly, allocations of 55 percent to fixed income and 10 percent to real estate each had a ±5 percent deviation range.

The entire asset allocation structure, however, was more complex than just having three asset classes. Within the 35 percent equity allocation were manager-style and company capitalization suballocations. These consisted of 15 percent each to large-cap growth and large-cap value stocks, and 2.5 percent each to small-cap growth and small-cap value stocks. Within the 55 percent fixed-income allocation were duration suballocations consisting of 27.5 percent to shorter-duration defensive bonds and 27.5 percent to aggregate-duration bonds.

These various suballocations, although strongly correlated, were periodically observed to diverge in performance, but these occasional divergences were not significant enough to cause one asset class to outperform another to the extent that rebalancing became appropriate under the ±5 percent decision rule. This prompted a review and analysis of the plan structure's historic fluctuations in the total returns of asset classes and suballocations within asset classes.

From this review, it was evident that using a percentage-of-portfolio variance range around the target asset class allocations was not resulting in rebalancing actions that enhanced the total return of the portfolio. The review also highlighted the need to develop some method to capitalize on the occasional divergence in performance at the suballocation level within the overall asset allocation structure.

An analysis of the plan's asset mix and the volatility exhibited by each of the investment advisers' management styles indicated that the percentage-of-portfolio variance ranges were set somewhat too wide to result in optimal rebalancing actions. In other words, given the additional volatility reduction associated with the suballocation structure, the asset class rebalancing trigger points were set broad enough that they were more frequently functioning as a buy-and-hold strategy.

A MORE EFFICIENT PROCESS

The foregoing analysis of the effectiveness of percentage-of-portfolio rebalancing thresholds in complex asset allocation structures suggested a fundamental conceptual shortcoming in using percentage measures to define rebalancing actions. Different asset classes and suballocations within asset classes have different levels of associated volatility. Consequently, a percentage-of-portfolio variance range such as ±5 percent assigned to an equity allocation can mean something entirely different in terms of the probability of occurrence than the same ±5 percent range assigned to a fixed-income allocation. This assumes that the portfolio has more than two asset classes. For example, given equal dollar allocations to stocks and bonds, the probability of a 5 percent change in valuation is much more likely to result from the performance characteristics of the stocks than from those of the bonds. (The stocks have higher expected return and higher volatility.)

Because an asset allocation strategy is based on expected return, volatility (standard deviation), and correlation, it would appear conceptually more appropriate to define the rebalancing decision points in terms of the expected volatility of the asset classes and suballocations—in other words, to establish rebalancing trigger points so that there would be an equal probability of having to adjust among the liquid asset classes or suballocations. This would provide any liquid investment category—whatever its size, expected return, or volatility—an equal potential of being sold for current gain and/or added to for future gain. The most suitable measure on which to base this volatility-oriented rebalancing method would be the statistical measure called standard deviation.

Standard deviation (s.d.) is a measure of the total variability of a group of occurrences (for example, historic investment returns). This measure of variability assumes a "normal" symmetrical distribution of occurrences around an average or mean value (see Figure 4.1). Because this measurement is "standardized," it can be translated into a statement of the probability with which the occurrence can be expected to be observed. For example, a standard deviation measurement ranging between −1 and +1 would be expected to occur 67 percent of the time. Measurements falling within ±2 s.d. would be expected to occur 95

FIGURE 4.1 Normal Distribution, Standard Deviation, and Probability

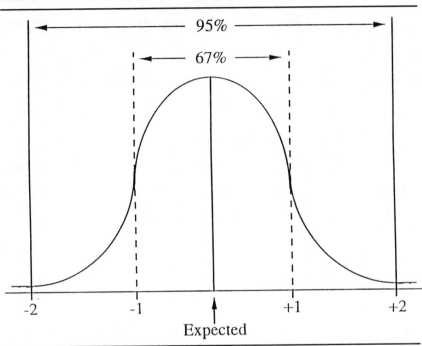

percent of the time. Often, these probabilities are displayed as the area under a bell-shaped, normal distribution curve such as the one shown in Figure 4.1. Table 4.2 shows recent historic s.d. measurements associated with various asset classes and style subcategories.

A NEW VOLATILITY BASED METHOD

In a manner similar to Table 4.1's replication of Hurrell's study of percentage-of-portfolio rebalancing thresholds, Table 4.3 provides a comparative analysis for an equal-probability volatility-based adjustment technique. Table 4.3 displays the annualized total returns and number of adjustments for various s.d.-determined rebalancing thresholds for a simple two-asset class portfolio structure. The results are again compared to various calendar-period rebalancing methods.

The time period used in the volatility-based rebalancing analysis was the same 21-year period (January 1973 through December 1993). The same stock and bond indexes were used to model the rebalancing outcomes, and the asset mixes of 60–40, 50–50, and 40–60 stocks and bonds were again evaluted. As with the earlier review, the annualized

TABLE 4.2 Historic Volatilities: Ten Years Ended June 30, 1992

Asset Category	Standard Deviation (%)
Equity:	
Callan Broad Index	17.22%
Callan Large Cap Index	15.83
Callan Medium Cap Index	18.45
Callan Small Cap Index	21.24
Callan Micro Cap Index	25.05
Callan Value Style	15.08
Callan Growth Style	18.94
Callan Small Cap Value Style	18.95
Callan Small Cap Growth Style	25.04
Brinson Venture Capital Index	17.40
Fixed Income:	
Lehman Aggregate Index	7.14%
Lehman Government Index	6.62
Lehman Corporate Index	8.47
Lehman Mortgage Index	8.11
Callan Short-Term Style	0.89
Callan Defensive Style	4.90
Callan Intermediate Style	6.15
Callan Extended Maturity Style	9.83
International:	
Morgan Stanley (Europe, Australia, Far East)	21.48%
Salomon World Government	9.46
Real Estate:	
NCREIF (National Council of Real Estate Investment Fiduciaries) Index	3.41%

SOURCE: Callan Associates Inc.

returns are net of transaction costs computed at five basis points for each sale and purchase transaction (ten basis points "round trip").

By using appropriate s.d. variance ranges, it is possible to enhance total portfolio return over time in comparison to the best of the calendar-based rebalancing methods. The maximum annualized rate of return for each portfolio is underlined in Table 4.3. It should be noted that, for simple two-asset class mixes, the maximum annualized rate of return achievable in each portfolio mix as a result of rebalancing is identical for both s.d.-based and percentage-of-portfolio-based techniques.

In a simple two-asset class portfolio, these identical results occur because the percentage-of-portfolio method effectively performs as an equal probability volatility-based method. This is the result of perfect negative correlation between one asset's and another's change in proportion of the portfolio. This correlation occurs in a two-asset class portfolio despite which asset class is the cause of any rebalancing

TABLE 4.3 Annualized Percentage Total Return Rates and Number of Adjustments for Calendar and Standard Deviation Rebalancing Methods during a 21-Year Period (January 1973 through December 1993)

Rebalancing Method	Asset Mixes (S&P 500 & SL G/C Indexes)					
	60/40 Mix Returns (%)	No. of Adjustments	50/50 Mix Returns (%)	No. of Adjustments	40/60 Mix Returns (%)	No. of Adjustments
None	10.651	0	10.485	0	10.314	0
Monthly	10.876	252	10.705	252	10.532	252
Quarterly	10.906	84	10.747	84	10.562	84
Annually	10.819	21	10.654	21	10.477	21
+/– Standard deviations:						
0.4	10.866	76	10.731	61	10.543	47
0.6	10.892	50	10.711	37	10.520	28
0.8	10.926	38	10.750	25	10.517	16
1.0	10.928	24	10.727	18	10.517	12
1.2	10.942	20	10.801	16	10.623	10
1.4	10.932	16	10.739	10	10.466	5
1.6	10.881	10	10.795	9	10.404	3
1.8	10.992	11	10.650	3	10.471	3
2.0	10.942	9	10.589	3	10.483	3
2.2	10.810	5	10.614	3	10.601	3
2.4	10.882	5	10.662	3	10.622	3
2.6	10.775	3	10.705	3	<u>10.711</u>	3
2.8	10.909	4	10.731	3	10.711	3
3.1	11.014	3	<u>10.897</u>	3	10.314	0
3.6	<u>11.047</u>	3	10.851	2	10.314	0
4.0	10.990	2	10.485	0	10.314	0
5.0	10.651	0	10.485	0	10.314	0

action. For example, if one asset increases from 50 percent to 55 percent of the portfolio, the other asset must decrease by the same proportion, from 50 percent to 45 percent of the portfolio. Thus, in a two-asset class portfolio, there is always a perfect negative correlation in the magnitude of change in proportions, and there is always an identical probability of change in both of the asset classes because the change in one class dictates the relative change in the other.

With three or more allocations within a portfolio, this is not the case. In more complex asset allocation structures, the fact that one allocation's proportion changes does not dictate that the proportion of each of the other allocations has moved in the opposite direction. Also, the occurrence of change in one asset class does not dictate an equal probability of change in each of the other classes.

It is evident from reviewing the data in Table 4.3 that, compared to the percentage-of-portfolio method, the volatility-based rebalancing technique displays sensitivity to the size of the allocation assigned to each asset class. Although the optimal percentage adjustment ranges are tightly clustered around ±10 percent to ±11 percent, the optimal standard deviation thresholds range from ±2.6 to ±3.6 s.d. Also, as with percentage-of-portfolio rebalancing methods, using narrower s.d. variance ranges increases the frequency of adjustment actions, and, in turn, increases the probability of enhancing portfolio total return during shorter intervals.

Figure 4.2 shows the excess cumulative portfolio return resulting from both quarterly rebalancing and from ±1.2 s.d. rebalancing on a 50–50 asset mix during the 21-year study period. The excess performance is compared to a passive buy-and-hold strategy, which is represented by the 0.00% horizontal line. Figure 4.2 shows the significance, over time, of compounding the modest annualized gains in incremental total portfolio return resulting from following a disciplined rebalancing strategy.

Figure 4.2 indicates the cumulative return advantage to be expected from using a constant-mix rebalancing strategy (±1.2 s.d.) rather than the best calendar-period method (quarterly). The standard deviation of each method's excess incremental quarterly return over that of a buy-and-hold strategy was lower for the ±1.2 s.d. adjustment method than for the quarterly adjustment method. Thus, the volatility-based rebalancing process added more incremental return at a lower level of risk in comparison to the best calendar-period method.

Table 4.4 shows the volatility of the excess incremental returns associated with a number of rebalancing thresholds. Displayed for three different portfolio mixes are the compounded quarterly return rates (geometric means) and the standard deviations of the excess incremental

FIGURE 4.2 Excess Cumulative Portfolio Return Compared to No-Rebalancing: 50/50 Asset Mix (S&P 500 & SL G/C)

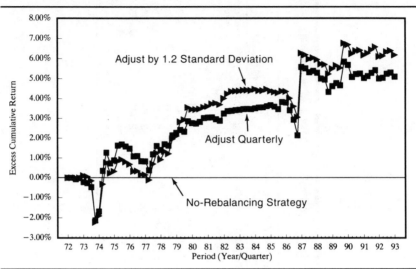

quarterly returns over those of a no rebalancing strategy. The s.d.-based rebalancing thresholds displayed are those that have a higher probability of adding value during shorter time periods.

THE IMPLEMENTATION OF A VOLATILITY-BASED REBALANCING PROCESS

The previously described pension plan's constant-mix rebalancing policy was reevaluated using standard deviation measures as trigger points rather than percentage-of-portfolio thresholds. The historic standard deviations of the liquid asset classes (stocks and bonds) and the individual investment advisers/styles were reviewed to determine whether wider or narrower equal-probability target allocation ranges had more potential to add value to the investment program over time. The results of this plan's review suggested that narrower equal-probability constraints on the allocation ranges had a greater potential to enhance the gains associated with rebalancing the portfolio to the target allocations.

This more sophisticated volatility-based rebalancing approach has been implemented on a customized basis because of analysis of the specific investment structure of the plan. Therefore, the results of this

TABLE 4.4 Compounded Quarterly Rates of Return and Standard Deviations of Excess Returns Compared to a No-Rebalancing Strategy during a 21-Year Period (January 1973 through December 1993)

| Rebalancing Method | Asset Mixes (S&P 500 & SL G/C Indexes) | | | | | |
| | 60/40 Mix | | 50/50 Mix | | 40/60 Mix | |
	Compounded Quarterly Return (%)	Standard Deviation of Excess Return (%)	Compounded Quarterly Return (%)	Standard Deviation of Excess Return (%)	Compounded Quarterly Return (%)	Standard Deviation of Excess Return (%)
None	2.563	NA	2.524	NA	2.484	NA
Quarterly	2.622	0.54625	2.585	0.56591	2.542	0.54082
+/− 0.8 s.d.	2.626	0.53772	2.586	0.56875	2.531	0.49857
+/− 1.0 s.d.	2.627	0.54880	2.580	0.51974	2.532	0.49902
+/− 1.2 s.d.	2.630	0.53031	2.597	0.54975	2.556	0.53824
+/− 1.4 s.d.	2.628	0.53334	2.583	0.51398	2.520	0.47500
+/− 1.6 s.d.	2.616	0.49515	2.596	0.52706	2.505	0.40061
+/− 1.8 s.d.	2.642	0.52281	2.562	0.50983	2.521	0.45892

effort to optimize rebalancing decision points are specific to the particular low-volatility asset mix of this plan. The process is influenced by the correlations between each allocation and the risk-adjusted return profiles of the managers selected. The asset mixes and investment manager risk–return profiles of other plans will likely result in a different volatility range that would have more potential to add value to the rebalancing process. Like the development of the asset allocation strategy, the effort to optimize rebalancing thresholds will be specific to each plan.

As a result of this review, the system's investment policy was amended to define the allowable variance range around target allocations in terms of standard deviation measures. The standard deviation factor adopted in this case resulted in approximately a 40 percent probability of having to perform any rebalancing of the portfolio's liquid allocations. Alternatively, it would be expected that, for about 60 percent of the time, no action would be necessary. In recognition of liquidity constraints, the allowable variance range around the fund's real estate allocation was set much wider than for the liquid asset classes and suballocations.

The plan's investment policy now stipulates that the fund's asset allocation status must be evaluated at least quarterly, or in response to extraordinary market volatility. When a rebalancing action is signaled, the policy also provides for a hierarchy of preferred methods to carry out any adjustments in order to minimize transaction costs. The trustees now have a clear understanding of how frequently rebalancing action might occur and how it will be accomplished. The plan's investment policy now delegates to staff the responsibility to initiate rebalancing actions in a timely manner. Any actions taken are reported to the trustees during subsequent board meetings.

COMMUNICATING ASSET ALLOCATION STATUS TO TRUSTEES

A key component to the effective operation of a portfolio rebalancing strategy is the clear and effective communication of the strategy's status to the plan's trustees. Table 4.5 shows the summary output of the computer model used to track this plan's asset allocation status and rebalancing trigger points. The printout displays an overwhelming amount of numerical data concerning such things as: current market values; actual percentages of the portfolio represented by the current market values; target allocations in terms of both dollars and percentages; minimum and maximum allocations based on the current total portfolio value; and any signaled amount of adjustment required in any allocation not currently falling within the allowable variance range.

TABLE 4.5 Target Asset Mix: 35 Percent Stocks/55 Percent Bonds/10 Percent Real Estate Actual Portfolio Rebalancing Analysis Based on Equal Probability Thresholds (Market Values as of November 1991)

Selected Probability of Not Having to Rebalance Portfolio = = >	60%
& Resultant +/− Adjustment Factor in Standard Deviations = >	0.84

CATEGORY / STYLE	Market Value	Actual Percent of Portfolio	ACCEPTABLE ALLOCATION RANGES						Signaled Rebalancing Adjustment	Expected Standard Deviation
			Target Amount & Target %		Min. Amount & Min. %		Max. Amount & Max. %			
Large Cap Growth	$179,744,000	17.16%	$157,085,250	15.0%	$134,429,159	12.8%	$179,741,341	17.2%	($22,658,750)	17.17%
Large Cap Value	$179,673,000	17.16%	$157,085,250	15.0%	$138,664,805	13.2%	$175,505,695	16.8%	($22,587,750)	13.96%
Small Cap Growth	$18,425,000	1.76%	$26,180,875	2.5%	$20,674,094	2.0%	$31,687,656	3.0%	$7,755,875	25.04%
Small Cap Value	$13,934,000	1.33%	$26,180,875	2.5%	$22,013,403	2.1%	$30,348,347	2.9%	$12,246,875	18.95%
Subtotal US Equities	$391,776,000	37.41%	$366,532,250	35.0%	$315,792,458	30.2%	$417,272,042	39.8%	$0	16.48%
Defensive Bonds	$279,810,000	26.72%	$287,989,625	27.50%	$274,684,504	26.2%	$301,294,746	28.8%	$0	5.50%
Aggregate Bonds	$295,318,000	28.20%	$287,989,625	27.50%	$268,999,589	25.7%	$306,979,661	29.3%	$0	7.85%
Subtotal US Fixed Income	$575,128,000	54.92%	$575,979,250	55.0%	$543,708,285	51.9%	$608,250,215	58.1%	$0	6.67%
Cash	$18,484,000	1.77%	$0	0.0%	$0	0.0%	$0	0.0%	($18,484,000)	0.89%
Real Estate *	$61,847,000	5.91%	$104,723,500	10.0%	$80,725,901	7.7%	$128,721,099	12.3%	$42,876,500	3.41%
*Allocation range expanded 8X due to illiquidity										
TOTAL PORTFOLIO VALUE	$1,047,235,000	100.0%								

The numerical information in Table 4.5 is graphically represented in Figure 4.3. The rectangles for each allocation represent the allowable standard deviation variance range as defined by policy. The crossbars represent the current market values of the allocations. If a crossbar falls within the rectangle, no action is required. If the crossbar falls outside the rectangle, rebalancing is signaled.

The positions displayed in Table 4.5 and Figure 4.3 occurred in November 1991 and resulted in a reduction to target (via sale) in the large-cap equity allocations. Proceeds of these sales were redistributed according to the overall asset allocation strategy: small-cap equities were purchased, and funds were moved to the defensive fixed-income allocation and reserved for pending real estate commitments.

Table 4.6 and Figure 4.4 show the same fund's status at the end of September 1992, ten months after the rebalancing in November 1991. The aggregate duration bond allocation reached a rebalancing trigger point very near the peak of the 1992 bond market rally.

The postimplementation success achieved by the introduction of this volatility-based portfolio rebalancing discipline has stimulated the

FIGURE 4.3 Example of Actual Portfolio Rebalancing

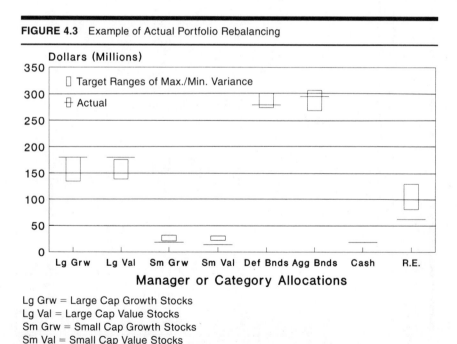

Lg Grw = Large Cap Growth Stocks
Lg Val = Large Cap Value Stocks
Sm Grw = Small Cap Growth Stocks
Sm Val = Small Cap Value Stocks
Def Bnds = Shorter Duration Defensive Bonds (1 to 5 Yr Maturities)
Agg Bnds = Lehman Aggregate Duration Bonds
RE = Real Estate

TABLE 4.6 Target Asset Mix: 35 Percent Stocks/55 Percent Bonds/10 Percent Real Estate Portfolio Status Ten Months after Rebalancing of November 1991 (Market Values as of September 1992)

Selected Probability of Not Having to Rebalance Portfolio = = >	60%
& Resultant +/− Adjustment Factor in Standard Deviations = = >	0.84

CATEGORY / STYLE	Market Value	Actual Percent of Portfolio	ACCEPTABLE ALLOCATION RANGES						Signaled Rebalancing Adjustment	Expected Standard Deviation
			Target Amount & Target %		Min. Amount & Min. %		Max. Amount & Max. %			
Large Cap Growth	$171,518,000	14.92%	$172,387,200	15.0%	$147,524,139	12.8%	$197,250,261	17.2%	$0	17.17%
Large Cap Value	$172,571,000	15.02%	$172,387,200	15.0%	$152,172,387	13.2%	$192,602,013	16.8%	$0	13.96%
Small Cap Growth	$27,360,000	2.38%	$28,731,200	2.5%	$22,687,994	2.0%	$34,774,406	3.0%	$0	25.04%
Small Cap Value	$29,602,000	2.58%	$28,731,200	2.5%	$24,157,768	2.1%	$33,304,632	2.9%	$0	18.95%
Subtotal US Equities	$401,051,000	34.90%	$402,236,800	35.0%	$346,554,355	30.2%	$457,919,245	39.8%	$0	16.48%
Defensive Bonds	$323,782,000	28.17%	$316,043,200	27.50%	$301,442,004	26.2%	$330,644,396	28.8%	$0	5.50%
Aggregate Bonds	$338,093,000	29.42%	$316,043,200	27.50%	$295,203,311	25.7%	$336,883,089	29.3%	($22,049,800)	7.85%
Subtotal US Fixed Income	$661,875,000	57.59%	$632,086,400	55.0%	$596,671,863	51.9%	$667,500,937	58.1%	$0	6.67%
Cash	$5,655,000	0.49%	$0	0.0%	$0	0.0%	$0	0.0%	($5,655,000)	0.89%
Real Estate *	$80,667,000	7.02%	$114,924,800	10.0%	$88,589,552	7.7%	$141,260,048	12.3%	$34,257,800	3.41%
* Allocation range expanded 8X due to illiquidity										
TOTAL PORTFOLIO VALUE	$1,149,248,000	100.0%								

FIGURE 4.4 Portfolio 10 Months after Rebalancing

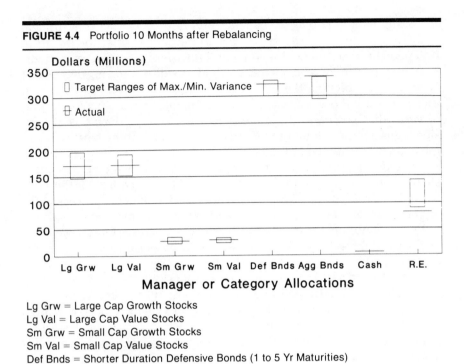

Lg Grw = Large Cap Growth Stocks
Lg Val = Large Cap Value Stocks
Sm Grw = Small Cap Growth Stocks
Sm Val = Small Cap Value Stocks
Def Bnds = Shorter Duration Defensive Bonds (1 to 5 Yr Maturities)
Agg Bnds = Lehman Aggregate Duration Bonds
RE = Real Estate

further development and refinement of proprietary computer modeling techniques. These models are being improved to facilitate the analysis and identification of optimal volatility-based rebalancing decision rules for other complex asset allocation structures having three or more allocations.

CONCLUSION

The development and implementation of an asset allocation strategy creates only an entrance process to conducting a structured and disciplined investment program. To maintain and optimize an asset allocation structure over time, a rebalancing strategy should be adhered to on a systematic basis. Studies that have reviewed the historic volatility of returns of investment classes used in asset allocation strategies indicate that periodic rebalancing of portfolios to their long-range target allocations will result in the addition of incremental return over that resulting from a buy-and-hold strategy.

Systematic portfolio rebalancing processes based on conventional constant-mix techniques have demonstrated a potential to add up to 0.45 percent of annualized incremental return over long-term periods. Different portfolio rebalancing methods exhibit varying degrees of volatility in achieving their value-added results. Efficient rebalancing disciplines are those that maximize incremental return at a lower level of variability compared to less efficient methods. Fiduciaries of pension plans should attempt to identify and implement the most efficient rebalancing technique available.

The development and implementation of a rebalancing discipline should ideally occur in times of nonduress. This will allow for thoughtful and careful study and development of the rebalancing process without clouding asset class issues with either manager performance issues or human emotional responses such as fear and greed. Once developed and set up, the rebalancing process should be periodically communicated to and reviewed by trustees. This approach will result in fewer surprises at crucial times, when it is appropriate to take action.

The more complex or diverse the investment structure, the more powerful a rebalancing maintenance structure needs to be to optimize the value added from the rebalancing process. A two-asset class portfolio can be managed at an optimal level with a percentage-of-portfolio adjustment process. However, the introduction of additional asset categories and diversifying suballocations requires a more sophisticated technique such as a volatility-based process. An optimal rebalancing process for complex, multiallocation portfolios must be sensitive to the relative volatilities of the various allocations, the correlations among the various allocations, and the amounts of assets committed to the various allocations.

NOTES

1. Andre F. Perold and William F. Sharpe, "Dynamic Strategies for Asset Allocation," *Financial Analysts Journal* (January–February, 1988).
2. Mark A. Hurrell, *Measuring Up*, 3 (2, 3) (Yanni-Bilkey Investment Consulting, 1991).

5

Understanding and Implementing Overlay Strategies

Jeffrey L. Winter, PhD, CFA

A. Darrell Braswell, CFA

Michael A. Leavy, CFA
QuantiLogic Asset Management Company, Inc.
San Francisco, California

INTRODUCTION

This chapter provides an introduction to the use of overlay strategies. The concept of overlays is defined and the key issues regarding the implementation of overlays are identified. The following specific applications are then described and discussed:

- Indexing with derivative securities;
- Securitizing cash exposure;
- Rebalancing to target asset allocation;
- Tactical asset allocation;
- Portfolio insurance and dynamic hedging;
- Currency management;
- Option overwriting.

The chapter introduces the issues, and the bibliography suggests some references for further study. Implementation of any specific overlay strategy will require additional, more detailed research by the reader.

A FRAMEWORK FOR OVERLAYS

An overlay strategy uses derivative securities such as futures, forward contracts, and options to change a portfolio's exposure to various assets

75

and broad asset classes. The portfolio can include actively or passively managed domestic and international stocks and bonds, cash equivalents, currencies, or any other asset class on which derivative securities are available.

Exposure to broad asset classes can be controlled in an efficient, timely, and low-cost manner. In addition, the investor is able to separate various investment decisions from each other and from administrative decisions affecting the portfolio. The separation of functions can: increase the efficiency of investment decision making and implementation, allow for the centralization of appropriate functions, and allow for the use of specialists to manage and implement certain strategies. Here are some examples:

- "Macro" asset allocation decisions can be separated from security selection decisions, and the macro decisions can be centralized.
- The timing of investment decisions (asset allocation; hiring, termination, and rebalancing of active managers; and so on) can be separated from other investment decisions and from the timing of administrative considerations such as contributions and withdrawals of assets and short-term cash-flow needs.
- Strategies such as tactical asset allocation, currency management, and static or active rebalancing can be employed without incurring the high transaction costs associated with shifting assets between managers.
- Specialist managers can be hired to add value to both the macro decision-making process and the market implementation process. Specialists can add value strategically on the macro side with models, processes, and insights developed specifically for particular strategies. On the implementation side, specialists can add value with derivatives by identifying the least-cost alternative to obtaining the desired market exposure, and by their experience and trading skill. A specialist is likely to apply the decision rules that guide the strategy in a more rigorous and efficient manner than a manager for whom the strategy is merely an add-on or one of many strategies being implemented.
- Opportunistic risk management can be efficiently employed. For example, in periods of temporary upheaval, such as during a war, investors desiring to protect portfolios by decreasing specific asset class exposure may use an overlay rather than shift the assets away from active managers.
- Some strategies, such as exposing frictional cash to the markets, are difficult or impossible to implement without the use of derivatives. Overlays allow these strategies to be centralized and therefore more effectively controlled.

Some additional administrative and investment considerations factor into the decision of whether to employ an overlay strategy. They are:

- Tracking error. Asset class exposure resulting from the overlay derivatives positions will not be perfectly correlated to the active management exposure that the overlay is designed to hedge. This is often a benefit, such as when active management outperforms benchmark indexes over time. However, it is important to understand the implications of imperfect correlations between the assets in the portfolio and the overlay derivatives being used to hedge broad asset class exposure.
- Current expertise of the portfolio back-office administrators, cost of the educational process, and cost of hiring personnel or consultants to administer and monitor the strategy.
- Impact on management fees, custodial fees, administration costs, and so on.
- Cost of systems for portfolio management, market quotations, back-office and trade settlement, accounting, reporting, and analysis.
- Potential regulatory requirements or internal corporate/political problems and biases regarding derivatives.

DEFINITIONS

Because a widely accepted nomenclature has not yet been established with regard to overlay strategies, we define certain terms used in this chapter. These defined terms appear in upper and lower case to the end of the chapter.

Overlay Strategy. The investment management strategy from the perspective of the manager of the overlay (the Overlay Manager). The Overlay Strategy takes a broad view, in contrast to the more specialized perspective of managers that focus on specific components within the portfolio, such as actively managed stocks and bonds.

Overlay Portfolio. A portfolio of assets that will incorporate an Overlay Strategy as part of the investment process.

Derivatives Reserves. The portion of the Overlay Portfolio used by the Overlay Manager as liquidity reserves to implement the necessary derivatives positions. The Derivatives Reserves remain part of the Overlay Portfolio for the purpose of implementing the proper overall market exposure.

Overlaid Assets. The portion of the Overlay Portfolio other than that used by the Overlay Manager as Derivatives Reserves. Typically, the Overlaid Assets are actively or passively managed by an investment manager other than the Overlay Manager.

Derivatives Reserves Account. The real or conceptual account with cash equivalents, derivative securities, and any other assets held as the Derivatives Reserves in implementing the Overlay Strategy.

THE STRUCTURE OF AN OVERLAY PORTFOLIO: "OVERLAID ASSETS" AND "DERIVATIVES RESERVES"

Assets in an Overlay Strategy are made up of Overlaid Assets and Derivatives Reserves. The combination of Overlaid Assets and Derivatives Reserves represents the total assets subject to the Overlay Strategy and will be referred to in this chapter as the Overlay Portfolio.

The Derivatives Reserves Account holds derivatives positions and assets (usually cash equivalents) necessary to finance the use of the derivatives. The necessary size of the Derivatives Reserves Account depends on the specific objectives of the Overlay Strategy, the specific derivatives used and their respective margin or collateral requirements, and the availability of additional cash on short notice.

Derivative securities are used to change ("hedge") market exposure in the portfolio. The use of derivatives requires an understanding of such issues as fair value, margin, beta adjustment, basis and basis risk, tracking error, and option pricing theory. (The bibliography offers references on these subjects.)

A basic concept is gaining exposure to an asset by using derivative securities. To illustrate, assume an investor has $10 million in cash and buys stock index futures that have $10 million of market exposure. The investor now has effectively zero exposure to cash and $10 million exposure to stocks. The position is not leveraged and is a true hedge, because the market exposure is identical to the total assets of $10 million. A nonleveraged hedge position is the most common use of derivatives in Overlay Strategies, although there may be exceptions.

The basic structure of an Overlay Strategy is illustrated in Example 5.1.

When the Overlay Strategy has been implemented, the accounts will be invested as shown in Table 5.1.

Most of the tables in this chapter represent theoretical scenarios. For illustrative purposes, market exposure shown in these tables is represented to two decimal places. This precision is not obtainable in the real derivatives markets. For example, with the S&P 500 index at 400, one S&P future contract represents $200,000 of S&P 500 market exposure. This means that the exposure "round-off error" of using

_____ **EXAMPLE 5.1** _____

SCENARIO

An investor has a $100 million portfolio currently 100 percent invested with active stock managers. These assets will constitute the total Overlay Portfolio.

The benchmark for the active stock managers is the S&P 500. It is therefore reasonable to assume that the active managers' portfolios will have a beta that is a near match to the S&P 500.

The investor wishes to employ an Overlay Strategy to change the exposure of the Overlay Portfolio from 100 percent stocks to 70 percent stocks and 30 percent long-term Treasury bonds.

Derivative positions will be designed to track the respective "markets": for this example, stock positions will be designed to track the S&P 500; bonds will be designed to track a long-term Treasury bond index (such as the Shearson Lehman 20-Year+ Maturity Treasury Index).

First, the investor liquidates $10 million (10 percent) of the actively managed stocks to raise cash for the Derivatives Reserves Account. This leaves the Overlay Portfolio invested at 90 percent stocks and 10 percent cash.

Next, the investor sells short stock index futures with $20 million market exposure (20 percent of the total Overlay Portfolio). This leaves the Overlay Portfolio invested 90 percent in stocks and −20 percent in stock derivatives, for a net of 70 percent stock exposure. Ten percent of the Overlay Portfolio is in cash and 20 percent is in fully hedged stocks, for a net of 30 percent exposure to cash.

Finally, the investor buys Treasury bond futures with a market exposure of $30 million (30 percent of the total Overlay Portfolio). This leaves the account invested at the desired 70 percent stock market exposure and 30 percent bond market exposure.

_____

S&P 500 future contracts will vary from $100,000 under to $100,000 over the exact exposure desired. On a $100 million portfolio, this will represent an exposure round-off error of between −0.1 percent and 0.1 percent.

The effect of this round-off error on returns will be minimal in an account of this size. For example, with a 5.0 percent move in the stock market, an exposure round-off error of 0.1 percent will have an effect on returns of 0.005 percent.

Note that the bottom row of Table 5.1 (*Overlay Portfolio value*) represents the market value of assets in the subaccounts of the Overlay

TABLE 5.1 Overlay Strategy Initial Implementation: Resulting Value of Accounts, and Portfolio Exposure

($ = millions; % = percent of total Overlay Portfolio)

	Overlaid Assets Account		Derivatives Reserves Account		Overlay Portfolio Exposure	
	$	%	$	%	$	%
Equity exposure:						
Overlaid stocks	90.00	90.00			90.00	90.00
Stock derivatives exposure			(20.00)	−20.00	(20.00)	−20.00
Net equity exposure	90.00	90.00	(20.00)	−20.00	70.00	70.00
Bond exposure:						
Bond derivatives exposure	—	—	30.00	30.00	30.00	30.00
Net bond exposure			30.00	30.00	30.00	30.00
Cash exposure	0.00	0.00	0.00	0.00	0.00	0.00
Overlay Portfolio value	90.00	90.00	10.00	10.00	100.00	100.00

Portfolio. The far right-hand column of Table 5.1 represents a break-down of exposure to each asset class within the Overlay Portfolio (in-cluding exposure to cash). The percentages in the bottom row and in the far right-hand column must each total 100 percent. If the net stock exposure in Example 5.1 was 80 percent and net bond exposure was 30 percent, then cash exposure would be −10 percent, which would be a slightly leveraged position. On the other hand, if net stock exposure was 50 percent and net bond exposure was 30 percent, then cash expo-sure would be +20 percent. In any combination, the sum of the three must be 100 percent.

Table 5.1 has shown how the portfolio will be invested immedi-ately following implementation of the Overlay Strategy. Subsequent to that implementation, however, the markets will undoubtedly move to new price levels. The effect of market returns is illustrated in Example 5.2.

--------------------------------- **EXAMPLE 5.2** ---------------------------------

SCENARIO

After the implementation of the overlay, market returns over a cer-tain period of time are:

S&P 500 return	+5.0 percent
Long Treasury bond return	−2.0 percent

Overlaid Assets are assumed to track the markets. (The effects of assumptions regarding Overlaid Assets are discussed in a later section entitled "Overlaid Asset Information Flows.")

Gains (losses) from the derivatives positions are credited (debited) to the Derivatives Reserves Account.

For simplicity, it is assumed that income is reinvested.

Following these market returns, the account will be invested as de-picted in Table 5.2.

The bottom row of Table 5.2 indicates that the Overlay Portfolio has grown from $100 million in Table 5.1 to $102.90 million, for a total re-turn of 2.90 percent. Note that a portfolio invested 70 percent in the S&P 500 and 30 percent in long-term Treasury bonds would have like-wise returned 2.90 percent (i.e., 70 percent at 5.00 percent plus 30 per-cent at −2.00 percent is 3.50 − 0.60 = 2.90 percent). Thus, the Overlay Portfolio produced returns identical to the intended allocation of 70 percent stocks and 30 percent bonds.

TABLE 5.2 Change in S&P 500 Price Levels: Resulting Value of Accounts, and Portfolio Exposure

($ = millions; % = percent of total Overlay Portfolio)

	Overlaid Assets Account		Derivatives Reserves Account		Overlay Portfolio Exposure	
	$	%	$	%	$	%
Equity exposure						
Overlaid stocks	94.50	91.84			94.50	91.84
Stock derivatives exposure			(21.00)	−20.41	(21.00)	−20.41
Net equity exposure	94.50	91.84	(21.00)	−20.41	73.50	71.43
Bond Exposure						
Bond derivatives exposure	—		29.40	28.57	29.40	28.57
Net bond exposure			29.40	28.57	29.40	28.57
Cash exposure	0.00	0.00	0.00	0.00	0.00	0.00
Overlay Portfolio value	94.50	91.84	8.40	8.16	102.90	100.00

DERIVATIVES RESERVES IN THE OVERLAY PORTFOLIO

Example 5.2 arbitrarily assumed that the investor liquidated 10 percent of Overlay Portfolio to fund the Derivatives Reserves Account. In reality, the optimal size of the Derivatives Reserves Account at any time will depend on the type of Overlay Strategy employed, and strategy's current positions, and the investor's specific circumstances.

In determining the optimal level of Derivatives Reserves, the key questions are:

What causes the need for cash?
How much and how quickly can the needed level of cash change?
How quickly can additional cash be raised from outside the Derivatives Reserves Account?

Cash is usually needed to manage derivatives positions for a number of reasons, depending on the particular derivatives used. In the case of options, cash is needed to pay for the option premium on purchases. For futures, cash may be used for initial margin requirements, although assets outside the Derivatives Reserves Account can also be used for this purpose. However, because futures require daily settlement of the mark-to-market (maintenance margin), cash is still required. Cash may be required for forward contracts or other over-the-counter derivatives in the event that they expire, are exercised, or are unwound at a loss.

Although it is relatively easy to identify why cash is needed, it can be more difficult to anticipate the potential for change in the amount needed. Changes in the level of needed cash are usually associated with a "loss" that requires a cash payment, such as the payment of futures maintenance margin. Such "losses" are usually directly caused by the price performance of the asset underlying the derivative, such as a price decline in the S&P 500 causing a price decline in stock index futures. Thus, estimation of the potential for such "losses" is usually accomplished by consideration of the potential range of returns that might be experienced by the underlying asset.

"Losses" in the Derivatives Reserves Account do not necessarily imply poor performance of the Overlay Strategy. For example, in the scenarios for Tables 5.1 and 5.2, the objective of the Overlay Strategy was to keep the portfolio exposed 70 percent to stocks and 30 percent to bonds. In order to implement this strategy, the Derivatives Reserves Account held a short position in stock derivatives and a long position in bond derivatives. In the scenario for Table 5.2, the Derivatives Reserves Account experienced a $1.6 million decrease (from $10 million down to $8.4 million), yet the Overlay Portfolio successfully matched the return of a portfolio of 70 percent stocks and 30 percent bonds. Although the quotation marks are subsequently dropped from "loss," it is important to recognize that the loss may not be literal. (A later section, entitled "Evaluation of Performance," gives more information.)

The potential magnitude of loss depends on the expected volatility in the Derivatives Reserves Account. The expected volatility, in turn, depends on the exposure incurred by the component assets and asset classes, the potential volatility of each component, and the correlations between the components. The potential volatility in the Derivatives Reserves Account will differ widely between overlays implementing different types of strategies, as well as between overlays with similar strategies but different account structures. It will also vary for a particular Overlay Strategy as the investment position changes.

Table 5.2 illustrated a situation involving a $1.6 million loss in the Derivatives Reserves Account. The scenario does not necessarily call for an instant cash infusion into the Derivatives Reserves Account, but if the markets were to continue this trend, a cash infusion would eventually be necessary.

To avoid sudden needs for cash infusions, many investors with overlay strategies make sure that the cash in the Derivatives Reserves Account at initiation is adequate for most scenarios. The investor systematically adjusts the value of the Derivatives Reserves Account to the predetermined percentage of portfolio value by contributing or withdrawing additional cash. This adjustment is made on a regular basis, such as monthly.

INVESTMENT GUIDELINES

When investment guidelines are established, they should embody the objectives of the overlay as well as the structure within which the manager will operate. Following are some of the primary goals of investment guidelines:

1. Outline the general objectives of the Overlay Strategy.
2. Determine an appropriate "normal" or "benchmark" strategy (typically passive) against which the Overlay Strategy's performance will be measured.
3. Outline the scope of discretion that will be acceptable in the management of the Overlay Strategy, for example, what types of derivatives are acceptable, what types of deviations from the benchmark are allowable, and how much risk should be taken relative to the benchmark.
4. Establish reasonable expectations for performance relative to the benchmark.

OVERLAID ASSET INFORMATION FLOWS

Accurate management of the exposure in an Overlay Portfolio requires timely information regarding the size and composition of the Overlaid Assets. Generally, an actual valuation of the Overlaid Assets (which are not managed by the Overlay Manager) will be communicated to the Overlay Manager on a regular basis, such as monthly, or when an unusual and significant event occurs. Factors that will affect the valuation of the Overlaid Assets are *returns in the markets* and *contributions or withdrawals* of Overlaid Assets.

An accurate knowledge of how the Overlaid Assets are invested will allow the Overlay Manager to estimate changes in their valuation caused by market moves in the periods between receipt of actual valuations. For example, if the Overlay Manager is informed that the Overlaid Assets are well-diversified, actively managed stocks with a beta of 1.2 relative to the S&P 500, the manager can probably assume that their value will fluctuate 1.2 times as much as the S&P 500. During the periods between communication of actual valuations, the Overlay Manager can simply adjust the most recent valuation of the Overlaid Assets for S&P 500 returns adjusted for beta.

The frequency with which information is supplied to the Overlay Manager should balance the need for accurate valuation information against the administrative practicalities of supplying the information. At some point, the benefits of additional exposure accuracy do not justify the resulting administrative difficulties.

Example 5.3 illustrates the effects of this "tracking error" during the periods between information flows.

———————————————— **EXAMPLE 5.3** ————————————————

SCENARIO

After the implementation of the overlay, market returns over a certain period of time are as before:

S&P 500 return	+5.0 percent
Long Treasury bond return	−2.0 percent

Overlaid Assets do not track the S&P 500; instead:

Overlaid Assets total return: +10.0 percent

Table 5.3 shows exposure and value, assuming that the information regarding the outperformance of the Overlaid Assets has been assimilated. Note that stock derivative exposure has grown with the S&P 500,

TABLE 5.3 Resulting Value of Accounts, and Portfolio Exposure

($ = millions; % = percent of total Overlay Portfolio)

	Overlaid Assets Account		Derivatives Reserves Account		Overlay Portfolio Exposure	
	$	%	$	%	$	%
Equity exposure						
Overlaid stocks	99.00	92.18			99.00	92.18
Stock derivatives exposure			(21.00)	−19.55	(21.00)	−19.55
Net equity exposure	99.00	92.18	(21.00)	−19.55	78.00	72.63
Bond exposure						
Bond derivatives exposure	—		29.40	27.37	29.40	27.37
Net bond exposure			29.40	27.37	29.40	27.37
Cash exposure	0.00	0.00	0.00	0.00	0.00	0.00
Overlay Portfolio value	99.00	92.18	8.40	7.82	107.40	100.00

and that Overlaid Asset exposure and value have grown with the actively managed return.

A comparison of Table 5.2 with Table 5.3 illustrates the effects of the "tracking error" caused by inaccurate assumptions regarding the Overlaid Assets. Table 5.2 reflects how the Overlay Manager would think the Overlay Portfolio has been invested when he or she assumes that the actively managed Overlaid Assets have tracked the S&P 500 index. In reality, the Overlay Portfolio is invested as depicted in Table 5.3.

The assumption that the Overlaid Assets tracked the S&P 500 over the period causes the Overlay Manager to assume that the Overlay Portfolio is now invested 71.43 percent in stocks (from Table 5.2), when it is actually invested 72.63 percent in stocks (from Table 5.3).

This difference of 1.20 percent is the invested position of stocks may or may not be critical, depending on the specific Overlay Strategy and the corresponding investment guidelines. If the Overlay Manager is expected to rebalance the Overlay Portfolio back to 70 percent stocks and 30 percent bonds whenever the asset mix is 2.5 percent different, then, in this scenario, the manager's rebalancing will not occur when it should. On the other hand, if the investment guidelines allow the asset mix to vary by 5 percent, the difference is as yet immaterial.

It is important to analyze how well the Overlaid Asset returns are likely to be correlated with their assumed returns (i.e., the index and any beta or duration adjustments used to estimate the returns). The less correlated they are, the more often information regarding differences between Overlaid Asset returns and index returns should be assimilated into the overlay process.

The effects of the inaccurate information will vary (1) depending on the type of overlay and (2) within a particular overlay, depending on the current position being implemented. A careful analysis of likely scenarios is important when designing the information-flow procedures, in order to determine the steps necessary to avoid inaccuracies that may have significant effects.

ACCOUNTING AND PORTFOLIO MANAGEMENT SYSTEMS AND PROCEDURES

Accounting and portfolio management systems for an overlay must allow for the use and analysis of derivative securities, and must address the issue of the Overlaid Assets. Holding derivatives positions involves accounting for margin, collateral, and futures mark-to-market transactions. Administrative procedures must be established to properly settle and maintain derivative positions.

Portfolio management systems must allow the investor to evaluate exposure to the applicable asset classes, taking into account Overlaid

Assets and derivative positions. Because these systems will often be fed by the investment accounting systems, special features in the accounting systems may be necessary to facilitate the process. The exact systems needs will vary with different overlay strategies.

EVALUATION OF PERFORMANCE

Performance evaluation of an Overlay Strategy should be conducted from at least two perspectives:

1. The performance of the total Overlay Portfolio should be evaluated relative to an appropriate benchmark.
2. An attribution of performance should be done on the component pieces.

As an example, suppose the Overlay Portfolio in an Overlay Strategy is consistently achieving a quarterly return that is 100 basis points higher than the return on an appropriate benchmark. This value-added may consist of 50 basis points from active management of the Overlaid Assets and 50 basis points from overlay management. On the other hand, overlay management may be adding 150 basis points per quarter, and Overlaid Asset management may be losing 50 basis points per quarter (or vice versa). It is important to be aware of the source of the value-added.

Evaluation of Value-Added by the Overlay Manager

The goals of the Overlay Manager should be clearly specified in the investment guidelines. The guidelines should specify a benchmark portfolio against which the manager's performance will be compared. The specific components of the management process for which the Overlay Manager is responsible should be embodied by this benchmark, and the performance of the manager relative to the benchmark should be calculated on a regular basis (monthly or quarterly). The investment guidelines should include a discussion of the manager's goals, and, specifically, what is considered to be poor, adequate, or excellent performance.

Specific managerial guidelines, appropriate benchmarks, and accurate attribution of performance will allow for effective evaluation of a manager's performance.

Evaluating Performance of the Overlaid Assets

Management of the Overlaid Assets should be evaluated independently as well as in the context of the Overlay Portfolio. Performance or from management of the Overlaid Assets should be compared to an appropriate benchmark, and deviations from the benchmark return should reflect a level of risk, relative to the benchmark, that is consistent with account guidelines.

APPLICATIONS OF OVERLAYS

This section discusses several strategies that can be implemented using overlays, as listed at the start of the chapter.

Indexing with Derivative Securities

Indexing with derivative securities invests a portfolio in the "market" indexes using derivatives instead of the actual securities. Cash equivalents are held in the portfolio, and derivatives positions are established that have market exposure equal to the amount of cash to be indexed to the markets.

If implemented using an overlay, the Overlaid Assets consist of cash equivalents, and the Overlay Portfolio is intended to perform as the chosen index (such as the S&P 500). The amount of assets held in the Derivatives Reserves Account is generally less important than with some other types of overlays because the Overlaid Assets are usually held in cash, thus providing ample liquidity to meet any potential cash needs.

Advantages to indexing with derivatives are:

- Lower transaction and administrative costs, especially if the amount to be invested in the index is frequently changing;
- Instant availability of cash, because futures require only a small amount of cash for margin;
- Value can be added with successful management of derivative positions;
- Many forms of "enhanced" indexing can be applied; for example, options on individual securities within an index can be used in conjunction with index futures and options to gain optimal exposure to the index, or to otherwise change exposure to specific securities within the index.

Using an overlay to index with derivatives allows the investor to separate derivative management from management of the cash underlying the derivative positions. Specialists can be hired to add value through effective derivative management and/or effective cash management. The separation of functions also allows for increased flexibility in hiring and terminating different managers and in centralizing either the cash management or the indexing functions.

Example 5.4 illustrates indexing using an overlay.

EXAMPLE 5.4

SCENARIO

An investor desires to index a 100 percent cash portfolio to the S&P 500 stock index, using derivatives. The investor chooses to fund the Derivatives Reserves Account with assets representing 20 percent of the total Overlay Portfolio. Table 5.4 illustrates the account structure.

Securitizing Cash Exposure

Securitizing is a form of indexing with derivatives. The key difference is that the term "securitization" implies cash that is unavailable for direct investment in securities because of administrative or practical considerations. Examples of cash unavailable for investment (often termed "frictional cash") are:

- Cash held by active managers for operational purposes (e.g., for buying opportunities, uninvested dividends, and so on);
- Cash required for margin in derivatives accounts;
- Cash held for an impending withdrawal but intended to be exposed to the market;
- Cash received from a recent contribution and as yet uninvested;
- Cash arising from an investment manager change and not yet reinvested by a new manager;
- Cash held to meet operating expenses.

A basic difference between indexing and securitizing is that indexing usually involves a conscious decision to place a certain amount

---

TABLE 5.4 Market Exposure of Indexing Overlay Portfolio (As Percent of Overlay Portfolio)

	Overlaid Assets Account	Derivatives Reserves Account	Overlay Portfolio Exposure
Stock derivatives exposure		100.00%	100.00%
Cash exposure	80.00%	−80.00%	0.00%
Overlay Portfolio value	80.00%	20.00%	100.00%

of assets into an indexed investment, whereas the frictional cash to be securitized is an unconscious by-product of other activities but is nonetheless desired to have market exposure.

Securitization with derivatives is implemented in the same manner as indexing with derivatives. Because the frictional cash is typically held in numerous accounts, the securitization is commonly centralized under an overlay. Futures (or equivalent option positions) are bought with market exposure equal to the level of the cash balances.

Potential advantages of using an overlay to securitize with derivatives are:

- Long-term returns from securitizing frictional cash are likely to be higher than cash equivalent returns;
- Quick adjustments can be made for the changing levels of frictional cash to be securitized;
- Securitization is separated from other asset management;
- Securitization activities are centralized.

Because securitization is simply indexing of frictional cash, Table 5.4 can be used as an example of securitization with derivatives. In Table 5.4, the Overlaid Assets represent frictional cash. An additional amount of cash must be set aside to fund the Derivatives Reserves Account for the overlay. In the example, the frictional cash (Overlaid Assets Account) represents 80 percent of the portfolio, and the Derivatives Reserves Account represents 20 percent of the portfolio.

Rebalancing to Target Asset Allocation

Market returns and active management value-added in different asset classes cause the asset allocation in a portfolio to change over time. Rebalancing refers to the adjustment of the portfolio to a target asset allocation. Portfolios are often rebalanced to a long-term strategic target asset allocation, or to a shorter-term tactical target.

A *passive* approach involves rebalancing at specific deviations (e.g., whenever the asset mix changes by 2 percent) or at specific times (e.g., quarter-end). An *active* approach involves rebalancing based on some set of active decision rules.

Rebalancing with an overlay involves using derivatives to bring the asset mix back to the target allocation, without necessitating trades in the Overlaid Assets themselves.

Using an overlay for rebalancing has the advantages of (1) separating the rebalancing decision from the decision to hire and terminate active managers, and (2) avoiding frequent shifts in assets between active managers. Separating these functions will often lower transaction costs. In addition, rebalancing decisions can be made more quickly and remain independent of the administrative concerns surrounding shifts between active managers. The timing of the rebalancing decision is then more investment-related, rather than affected by active manager-related administrative concerns. Another advantage is that the investor has flexibility to hire a specialist who can add value to the decision and/or implementation functions of the rebalancing process.

An overlay also facilitates centralization of the rebalancing function. This is particularly relevant to strategic rebalancing, where the goal is to control the asset mix of the investor's entire portfolio.

Example 5.5 uses scenarios from earlier in the chapter to illustrate rebalancing with an overlay.

_____ **EXAMPLE 5.5** _____

SCENARIO

As in earlier examples, an investor has a strategic long-term allocation target of 70 percent stocks and 30 percent bonds. At initiation of the account, the portfolio is invested as depicted in Table 5.1. Following specific returns in the stock and bond markets, the portfolio is invested as depicted in Table 5.2. In order to rebalance the account to 70 percent stock exposure and 30 percent bond exposure, additional derivative positions will have to be established.

As a result of the market returns (Table 5.2), the account has become invested at 71.43 percent stocks and 28.57 percent bonds. The total value of the account has risen to $102.90 million. To rebalance the account to 70 percent stocks and 30 percent bonds, the investor requires $72.03 million of stock exposure (i.e., 70 percent of $102.90 million), rather than the existing $73.50 million. Thus, the investor must sell stock derivatives with $1.47 million of market exposure, and needs to buy bond derivatives with $1.47 million market exposure. Table 5.5 shows the account following the appropriate rebalancing trades.

_____

Tactical Asset Allocation

Tactical asset allocation refers to the short- to intermediate-term asset-mix decision. The tactical asset allocation decision is an active decision. Tactical asset allocation can be applied domestically or globally and can include any asset classes.

Tactical asset allocation can be employed with or without an overlay. A tactical process may be implemented alongside other active or passive decision processes, such as active stock and bond management, rebalancing, securitization, or indexing.

TABLE 5.5 Implementation of Rebalancing Trades: Resulting Value of Accounts, and Portfolio Exposure

($ = millions; % = percent of total Overlay Portfolio)

	Overlaid Assets Account		Derivatives Reserves Account		Overlay Portfolio Exposure	
	$	%	$	%	$	%
Equity exposure						
Overlaid stocks	94.50	91.84			94.50	91.84
Stock derivatives exposure			(22.47)	−21.84	(22.47)	−21.84
Net equity exposure	94.50	91.84	(22.47)	−21.84	72.03	70.00
Bond exposure						
Bond derivatives exposure			30.87	30.00	30.87	30.00
Net bond exposure			30.87	30.00	30.87	30.00
Cash exposure	0.00	0.00	0.00	0.00	0.00	0.00
Overlay Portfolio value	94.50	91.84	8.40	8.16	102.90	100.00

Employing tactical asset allocation with an overlay involves using derivatives to make tactical changes in portfolio exposure and to rebalance to the current target tactical allocation. The use of the overlay avoids transacting in the Overlaid Assets themselves.

The advantages of an overlay for tactical asset allocation are much the same as those for strategic rebalancing. An overlay allows tactical asset allocation changes to be implemented quickly, without the transaction costs and administrative difficulties of shifting between active managers. The separation of tactical decisions and implementation from active security selection gives the investor the option to hire a specialist for the decision and implementation functions of the tactical process, and facilitates centralization of the strategy.

The exposure in a tactical asset allocation account is managed and rebalanced in the same manner as described in the previous section, except that the target asset allocation is now determined by an active tactical asset allocation decision process. Example 5.5 is an illustration of the rebalancing process.

Portfolio Insurance and Dynamic Hedging

Portfolio insurance involves purchasing put options to limit the downside risk in the portfolio. This strategy can be implemented by buying actual put options, but is usually implemented with synthetic put options created by dynamic futures hedging. Dynamic futures hedging involves selling futures as the market goes down to replicate the payoff pattern of a put option. (See the bibliography for references that give more detailed discussion of portfolio insurance and dynamic hedging.)

Portfolio insurance, whether gained by buying puts or using dynamic hedging, can be implemented by the manager of the portfolio involved or, more commonly, with an overlay.

When using an overlay to buy protective puts, the manager holds protective puts in the Derivatives Reserves Account, in an amount that matches the size of the Overlaid Assets with the appropriate term to expiration.

Where dynamic hedging is used in the overlay, the operations are very similar to those in Example 5.5, except that the target asset allocation is now determined by the quantitative procedures of dynamic hedging. In effect, the asset allocation target for the Derivatives Reserves Account is the one that would match the hedge ratio (i.e., option delta) of the desired protective put.

The use of an overlay to implement portfolio insurance provides the usual overlay advantages: separation from other asset management activities, centralization of the strategy, and the ability to hire a specialist to implement the strategy.

The use of a specialist may be particularly relevant with dynamic futures hedging, because of the somewhat complicated and continual trading necessary to effectively implement the strategy. In addition, the periods during which portfolio insurance is most useful happen to be the periods during which it is most difficult to implement dynamic hedging in the markets. A primary function of portfolio insurance is to protect the portfolio from loss in times of major downside volatility. As the markets are going down, dynamic hedging calls for continual sales of futures contracts. It is difficult to control transaction costs when selling futures into a down market; experience, trading skill, and continuous focus on the strategy can be valuable, especially during these periods.

Currency Management

A key issue with international portfolios is how (or whether) to hedge currency exposure. The portfolio can be hedged back to the investor's domestic currency, partially hedged in a predetermined manner, or actively hedged.

When assets are denominated in a foreign currency, exposure is incurred to the valuation of that currency relative to the investor's domestic currency. Currency management can be done by the international investment manager (or managers) or by using an overlay. Currency forwards, futures, or options can be bought or sold so as to either eliminate exposure to the foreign currency or change exposure in the desired manner.

Again, an overlay provides the advantages of separation from other asset management activities, centralization of the strategy, and the ability to hire a currency hedging specialist.

Option Overwriting

Option overwriting involves writing covered call options on securities, portfolios of securities, indexes, and so on (often referred to as "covered call writing"). If the price of the underlying asset goes down, losses are reduced by having realized premiums when the options were sold. If the price stays flat, the premiums create an incremental return. However, gains from price appreciation are capped at the option strike prices net of the premium income received. (See the bibliography for sources of more detailed discussion of option overwriting.)

Historically, this strategy has been associated with writing covered call options on individual common stocks. However, the more recent advent of stock index options, bond options, and any number of variants in over-the-counter options considerably expands the potential for option overwriting.

Because the return realized from an option overwriting strategy is closely tied to the performance of the underlying assets, it has been typical for the manager of the underlying assets to also manage the overwriting, especially when overwriting individual common stocks. With the more recently available options, overwriting performance is less linked to the performance of the individual securities in a portfolio and more linked to overall portfolio performance. Consequently, many option overwriting strategies can successfully be managed as overlays.

BIBLIOGRAPHY

Abken, Peter A. "An Introduction to Portfolio Insurance." Federal Reserve Bank of Atlanta: *Economic Review* (November/December, 1989), 2–25.

Bodie, Zvi, Alex Kane, and Alan J. Marcus. *Investments* (pp. 546–692). Homewood, IL: Richard D. Irwin, 1989.

Gastineau, Gary L. *The Options Manual* (3rd ed.). New York; McGraw-Hill Book Co., 1987.

Jarrow, Robert A., PhD, and Andrew Rudd, PhD. *Option Pricing*. Homewood, IL: Richard D. Irwin, 1983.

Morris, Charles S. "Managing Interest Rate Risk with Interest Rate Futures." Federal Reserve Bank of Kansas City: *Economic Review* (March, 1989), 3–21.

Morris, Charles S. "Managing Stock Risk with Stock Index Futures." Federal Reserve Bank of Kansas City: *Economic Review* (June, 1989), 3–16.

Additional sources of information regarding derivative securities and the mechanics of hedging are: the exchanges on which the derivatives are traded, and the major brokerage houses that trade in these securities.

6

Incorporating Options Technology into Asset Allocation

J. S. Parsons
Vice President
Merrill Lynch
San Francisco, California

Asset allocation has always been a key area of the investment process. In the most basic form of pension investing, the main investment decision was to determine the "best" static mix between two or three asset classes. Today, the realm of possibilities has expanded dramatically to include both forecast driven and systematic asset allocation technologies. Perhaps the fastest growing area of systematic asset allocation has been in the application of options theory. Increased interest in options theory began with the publication in 1973, of the seminal article by Fischer Black and Myron Scholes.[1] Since then, extensive work has been done on the application of various option pricing models to a range of problems in finance. This chapter discusses how options technology can be applied to asset allocation.

THE ADVANTAGE OF OPTIONS

How can options technology assist in the asset allocation process? The most basic answer is that options technology—and, more generally, the use of derivative instruments—increases the set of possible outcomes that can be achieved by an investor. Conventional investment techniques, which use a static investment held over some period, can create only a payoff that is a linear function of the returns on the underlying assets held. Imagine a world with only two investment alternatives: (1) stock and (2) cash. Fred, a hapless investor in that world, must invest a portion of his portfolio in stocks and the remainder in cash. Mindful of his ever-approaching retirement, Fred allocates to stocks a percentage equal to his retirement age (60 percent) and to cash a percentage equal to his current age (40 percent). Thankful that these numbers add up to 100 percent, he is able to compute his expected return. Over the period when his investment percentages remain unchanged, his return will be a weighted average of 60 percent of the return of stocks and 40 percent of the return of cash. This asset allocation technique, although functional, is very limiting in that it assumes only linear combinations of assets and, consequently, only linear return patterns. If Fred could include in his world the vast realm of options-related strategies, he could obtain a richer set of payoffs.

Why should Fred consider expanding his world to include options payoffs? Options are contracts that provide the right but not the obligation to buy or to sell something at a set price, at some future time. Because an option is a right but not an obligation, the return to an option holder (or seller) is not a linear function of the return on the underlying asset. The "right" will be exercised only if it is profitable to do so. If the price of the asset moves in the option holder's favor, then the option can increase in value without limit. But if the price of the asset moves against the option holder, he or she can walk away from the option and lose only the premium paid. This nonsymmetric effect of changes in the asset price leads to a much richer set of investment opportunities.

Options thus inherently create a nonlinear payoff, continually adjusting the effective exposure to the underlying asset in reaction to changes in the asset price, interest rates, volatility, time to expiration, and dividend yields. The fact that an option's exposure to the underlying asset changes on an ongoing basis provides investors like Fred with tremendous flexibility to create sculptured payoffs. Options provide the capability to determine how Fred may want his return profile to respond to any of the relevant market forces.

There are two main routes by which Fred can use options and options technology to accomplish asset allocation. The first route is through the actual purchase (or sale) of options, either as a direct investment or as an overlay strategy to an underlying physical investment. In today's marketplace, many institutions stand ready to provide standard and esoteric options payoffs on an over-the-counter (OTC) basis. Fred would have to identify his desired outcome. The institution would endeavor to design the necessary option or set of options and would provide Fred with the price. Upon mutual agreement, the option(s) would be created. A second route would be for Fred to design his desired payoff and then create it himself. In Fred's simple world, this would be accomplished by trading between the stock and cash portfolio to "replicate" the option; in the real world, the replication strategy will use combinations of any or all of the possible investment vehicles: physical assets, cash, exchange-traded and

OTC options, futures, forwards, future options, and so on. This replication technique would allow Fred to have constant control of his investments, facilitating any desired midcourse changes in objective. Further, this technique avoids possible credit risks and the potential for an illiquid secondary market of the OTC option. The replicating technique does, however, require the investor to incur the execution risk of the strategy.

DYNAMIC ASSET ALLOCATION

The first major application of options theory to asset allocation began in 1981. Publication of an article by Mark Rubinstein and Hayne Leland[2] marked the beginning of the portfolio insurance business. Leland O'Brien Rubinstein Associates Incorporated ("LOR") acknowledged the inherent asset allocation applications of all replicating strategies when it named its approach: Dynamic Asset Allocation[sm] or DAA[sm].[3]

In the early 1980s, the main application of DAA was as an overlay strategy on a core portfolio (typically, either an equity or a balanced equity–fixed income portfolio). The strategy adjusted the allocation of the total portfolio between the core portfolio and a cash position. One early selling point of this approach was that a dynamic allocation strategy could increase the expected return of a portfolio when replacing a fixed-allocation strategy. Dynamic strategies that replace fixed-allocation strategies usually allow a portfolio to start with a higher level of exposure to equities and, typically, to maintain a higher average level of equity investment over time. Because equities have a higher expected return, a dynamically run portfolio is expected to have a higher return than a fixed-allocation portfolio of similar downside risk exposure.

As Fred begins to consider using DAA strategies in his investment program, he might use as a benchmark this example of a fixed-allocation portfolio versus one using DAA:

Objective: To maximize expected return and limit losses to 5 percent.

Assumptions	Treasury Bills	Stocks
Expected return	10%	18%
Volatility	2%	20%
Correlation	0.2	

Results	Initial Mix	Average Mix	Expected Return
Fixed allocation	55/45	55/45	14.4%
Dynamic	72/28	78/22	16.2%

Gain from dynamic rebalancing: 1.8%

Although both portfolios in the example are structured so that they are not expected to lose more than 5 percent over a 12-month period, there is a chance that the fixed-allocation portfolio will lose more than 5 percent any time the equity portfolio falls by more than about 17.3 percent. In contrast, the dynamic portfolio is virtually assured of not losing more than 5 percent in one year. When comparing dynamically allocated portfolios with fixed-allocation portfolios of comparable downside risk, the dynamic portfolio will always have a higher expected return. Dynamic rebalancing reduces equity exposure only when necessary to prevent losses; the fixed-allocation strategy reduces equity exposure permanently. Stratified diversification, in a fixed-allocation strategy, does provide insurance against risk, but it is costly in terms of expected return because such diversification is not always needed.

NEW OPTION-BASED STRATEGIES

Portfolio insurance is only one example of how options theory can be applied to asset allocation. Significant work has been done over the past ten years to create new option-based models for asset allocation. A key factor of an option-based allocation strategy is that the rebalancing decisions are systematic, and not the function of a forecast or market "hunch." The bases for the redistribution of assets are: the return experience of the program and current market factors. This systematic approach will avoid the all-too-frequent second-guessing and implementation delays that can result from nonsystematic allocation techniques. Another advantage is that the pricing of these options, and the return they provide, depends on a market that is assumed to be "fair." Therefore, these strategies should represent a good benchmark against which to judge the performance of other nonsystematic models. An investor need only identify the type of return desired and then use packages of options to model it. From the option package, the final cost and expected return would represent the "fair value" of the desired strategy. Any resulting performance above this line would represent either luck or superior market-timing and forecasting ability. Performance below the line would represent either luck or inferior market-timing and forecasting ability.

Let's join Fred as he journeys through various options strategies, learning how to apply them to his asset allocation problems.

BARRIER OPTIONS[4]

Contrary to Fred's belief that the term "barrier option" refers to the difficulty in understanding options, barrier options can be used to design a strategy that will increase or decrease the exposure to an asset class when the underlying asset price reaches a particular level through time and not merely at a specific "horizon" date.

The most basic barrier call option is often referred to as a "down-and-out call." This option is a standard European call until a prespecified barrier is hit. At that point, the option is worthless and expires. The complement to this option is a "down-and-in call"; it does not exist until the prespecified barrier is hit, after which the buyer receives a standard European option. With a very astute mental leap, Fred notes that a standard European option would equal the sum of a down-and-out call and a down-and-in call, assuming equal strikes, expiration, and barriers. Based on this fact, Fred can conclude that each barrier option should be cheaper than the standard European option.

One way for Fred to apply such an apparently esoteric structure as a barrier option in his investment program is to utilize a ratchet strategy: he participates in a given market's appreciation until a certain point is reached, at which point he locks in all or some portion of his gains. The ratchet strategy responds to many investors' concern that large gains (such as those resulting from a market rally) can be lost if the market subsequently falls. However, attempts to value and estimate the cost impact of imposing a ratchet strategy can initially be a daunting exercise. Although the use of a single option produces a payoff whose expected return and expected cost are easily quantified, the same calculations for a ratchet strategy are more difficult. Fred would have to estimate when the lock-in point might occur and evaluate the cost associated with selling the option held before the ratchet and buying the option that will be held afterward. Fortunately, barrier options provide an easy way to quantify, value, and execute this type of strategy.

Let's look at the simple case where Fred wishes to have no loss on his position and still participate in any upside movement in the asset value, up to 15 percent. At that point, Fred wants to raise his protection level by 10 percent. This means that just before the lock-in point he would have been 15 percent above his floor, but afterward he would be only 5 percent above his (new) floor. This ratchet will substantially reduce the amount of the gains he might lose if the market subsequently reverses.

As an example, Fred structured the following scenario. He assumed he held a long stock position plus an up-and-out put combined with an up-and-in put. The up-and-out put has an at-the-money strike and a barrier point of 15 percent, and the up-and-in put has a strike of 10 percent in-the-money and a barrier identical to where the up-and-out put is "knocked out." When one looks at the result of these two barriers, it is easy to see that the required ratchet is created. Fred will hold the European put implied by the up-and-out put as long as the market does not go up by 15 percent. If the market does increase by 15 percent, then Fred will hold the European put created by the up-and-in put. By combining the premiums of these two options, Fred is able to see the cost and potential returns associated with this strategy. Table 6.1 shows the relative return to the ratchet approach versus a simple stock-plus-put strategy. Fred notes that he receives additional protection in the event that the market climbs and then falls back. But this increased protection has a cost: a higher premium for the package of barrier options.

LOOKBACK OPTIONS[5]

Having conquered his fear of nonlinear return patterns, Fred now decides to look for the ideal option—one with perfect hindsight. Lookback options have this characteristic because they provide a payoff that will give the holder the right to exercise a call (put) at a value equal to the lowest (highest) underlying asset price reached during the life of the option. These options have been referred to as "no-regret" options because, at expiration, the holder always receives the most favorable underlying asset value ever experienced.

One very interesting asset allocation strategy with lookback options is to purchase both a put and a call—a lookback spread. This spread would give Fred a payoff that is the difference between the highest and lowest values experienced over the life of the option (regardless of when they occurred). From Fred's viewpoint, this would be like having a portfolio manager who is able to time the market perfectly, entering and exiting the market at exactly the overall peak and valley.

The lookback spread strategy has a high up-front premium; it is most attractive when the underlying asset is expected to have a very large variation in levels. In the example shown in Table 6.2, Fred looked at the percent difference between the high and low values reached by the Japanese Nikkei average over several three-year periods from 1983 to mid-1993. Over these same periods, using reasonable interest rate assumptions and a range of volatilities, Fred estimated that the lookback spread would cost between 40 percent and 70 percent of the Nikkei price level. A comparison of these costs to the realized full three-year spreads of 68 percent to 170.6 percent suggests that the lookback spread could have produced strong returns, even when compared to the large premiums needed to create the option. An interesting feature is that this strategy does not require a particular market direction to pay off; only a large divergence between the high and low values is needed. (Compare, for example, the 130 percent spread in the 1985 to 1987 period (strong increase) with the 133 percent spread in the 1990 to 1992 period (strong decline).)

TABLE 6.1 Ratchet Strategy with Barrier Options

Stock Price	Unhedged Return (%)	Standard Put Return (%)	Barrier Return Conditional on Maximum Stock Price					
			90	100	110	120	130	140
90	−10.0%	−4.6%	−5.09%	−5.09%	−5.09%	4.40%	4.40%	4.40%
100	0.0	−4.6		−5.09	−5.09	4.40	4.40	4.40
110	10.0	4.9			4.40	4.40	4.40	4.40
120	20.0	14.5				13.89	13.89	13.89
130	30.0	24.0					23.38	23.38
140	40.0	33.5						32.87

Premiums:

Standard put	4.84
Up-and-out put	4.73
Up-and-in put	0.64
Barrier package	5.37

Input assumptions:

Stock price	100
Strike (up-and-out)	100
Strike (up-and-in)	110
In-and-out-barrier	115
Volatility	20%
Interest rate	6%
Dividend yield	3%

TABLE 6.2 Analysis of Spread between High and Low Values of Nikkei Index

Three-Year Period Starting	Maximum Value	Minimum Value	Final Value	Ratio (Max to Min)
1983	13,129	7,803	13,083	68.3%
1984	18,936	9,703	18,821	95.2
1985	26,646	11,545	21,564	130.8
1986	30,159	12,882	30,159	134.1
1987	38,915	18,544	38,828	109.9
1988	38,915	20,222	23,849	92.4
1989	38,915	20,222	22,984	92.4
1990	38,713	14,309	16,925	170.6
1991	27,147	14,309	17,417	89.7
*1992	23,801	14,309	19,787	66.3
*1993	21,076	16,287	19,787	29.4
*1994	20,678	17,370	19,787	19.0

* Indicates partial periods beginning on the first trading day of the indicated year and ending on May 9, 1994.

Options to Exchange One Asset for Another[6]

Confused by all the choices, Fred is now demanding to simply own the asset that will produce the best performance over a fixed period. Fortunately, his desire can be satisfied with options to exchange assets. This class of options allows Fred to swap one asset for another at the end of the option period, depending on their relative performance. Most asset allocation programs attempt to select the asset that will, over some horizon, have the highest return. This option class allows Fred to select this highest-return asset with perfect hindsight. These options can be used to provide the better performing of two assets, or the best of two assets and a cash alternative. The key is whether, after the fact, the return will have been of sufficient magnitude to offset the premium charged.

There are two basic ways in which these exchange strategies can be used. First, a program can be trend-following: the model will increase its allocation to an asset as that asset's value increases relative to the other asset—a relative strength strategy. The relative strength allocation technique performs well when there is a divergence of returns that is systematic and persistent. Second, one could allocate less to the asset that performs well—a relative value strategy. A relative value strategy performs best when the assets follow a mean-reversion process.

These two types of allocation programs represent different views of the business cycle. For instance, one might feel that stocks, during a period of low interest rates, will begin to systematically and for an extended amount of time provide increased performance over a bond portfolio. Therefore, as an equity market rally begins, one would want to increase the allocation to equities and continue to increase as the rally builds. Alternatively, an investor could have a view that suggests a consistent risk–return relationship between stocks and bonds. In this case, as an equity market rally begins, one would want to realize systematically the profits accruing to the equity portfolio and increase the investment within the bond portfolio to avoid the expected correction.

Options on Baskets

Fred has noted that most of our examples have dealt with simple one-, two-, or three-asset allocation decisions, but he is concerned that he must maintain an exposure to many assets to satisfy his pension fund's and corporation's diversification requirements. As an example, because his company has sales in many foreign countries, its earnings are exposed to currency fluctuations. For budgeting and planning purposes, the company needs to set a lower limit to the total dollar value of its foreign sales, without losing the opportunity to improve that figure, should the exchange rates move in its favor.

For this type of application, there is a class of "basket options" that deals with a portfolio of assets as opposed to only one or two assets. A basket option assumes that the investor is concerned with the total value of the combined assets and not the separate values of the individual assets, allowing gains in one asset to offset losses in other assets. This offsetting effect leads to a distribution of returns that has a lower effective volatility than the sum of the volatilities of the individual assets considered separately would imply. This lower volatility implies a lower total cost to the option while providing a final payout that is consistent with the company's objective.

TIME INVARIANT STRATEGIES

Finally, Fred observes that all strategies based on options with a fixed horizon date can vary solely as a function of the passage of time. In particular, the sensitivity of Fred's payoff to price changes can increase drastically as the expiration date approaches. This possibility does not seem consistent with Fred's long-term outlook. Fortunately, during the period when fixed-life option strategies were first being broadly applied to investment management, work was also being done on a class of approaches to dynamic trading that addresses this concern. These strategies have the common feature that the shape of the payoff (as a function of the underlying asset's price level) will not vary with time. Examples of such strategies include the Perpetual (a proprietary model of LOR), and the Constant Proportional Portfolio Insurance (CPPI) developed by Fischer Black.

Nikko Securities and Wells Fargo Nikko Investment Advisors have been using LOR's Perpetual model as an asset allocation strategy since

October 1989. The strategy is designed to allocate investments between a Japanese equity portfolio and an S&P 500-based portfolio, both valued in yen. This publicly traded fund was purchased by institutions and retail clients who wished to have an alternative to a straight Japanese equity investment. The fund consistently allocates more assets to the better performing market, and has consequently avoided the dramatic declines that the Japanese market experienced during 1989–1992. Instead, the fund was able to participate in the stronger performance of the U.S. market. By using a time-invariant strategy, the fund is not exposed to changes in the allocation sensitivity with time, which more traditional option-based approaches would face.

Although only a few examples have been shown, they should make it clear that options and the technology that lies beneath them are very efficient tools that offer a stunning array of potential applications. It would be naive to say that everyone should use option-based asset allocation strategies, but it is reasonable to assert that their uses should be both understood and examined to permit a broader range of approaches to realizing many investment objectives. Fred, dizzy with excitement, now recognizes that he was in the twilight zone with his simple strategy. Besides, his birthday is rapidly approaching, which makes current algorithm unworkable. He is beginning to think, "Imagine, if you will, . . ."

NOTES

1. Fischer Black and Myron Scholes, "The Pricing of Options and Corporate Liabilities,"
2. Mark Rubinstein and Hayne Leland, "Replicating Options with Positions in Stock and Cash," *Financial Analysts Journal* (July–August 1981).
3. Dynamic Asset Allocation and DAA are registered service marks of Leland O'Brien Rubinstein Associates Incorporated.
4. Barrier options are also known as down-and-outs, knock-ins or knock-outs, and birth-and-death options. There are eight basic payoff types:

	Payoff at Expiration	Relationship Evaluated during Life of Option	
1. Down-and-out call	max[0, S − K]	if all S > B	else R
2. Down-and-in call	max[0, S − K]	if one S ≤ B	else 0
3. Up-and-out put	max[0, K − S]	if all S < B	else R
4. Up-and-in put	max[0, K − S]	if one S ≥ B	else 0
5. Down-and-out put	max[0, K − S]	if all S > B	else R
6. Down-and-in put	max[0, K − S]	if one S ≤ B	else 0
7. Up-and-out call	max[0, S − K]	if all S < B	else R
8. Up-and-in call	max[0, S − K]	if one S ≥ B	else 0

where: S = underlying asset price at expiration
K = strike of option
B = barrier level
R = rebate amount (an additional ending payment that may be zero).

For a discussion of this type of option, see Cox and Mark Rubinstein, *Options Markets* (pp. 408–411). See also M. Rubinstein and Reiner, "Breaking Down the Barriers," *Risk* (September 1991).

5. For a discussion of this type of option, see Goldman, Sosin, and Gatto, "Path-Dependent Options: Buy at the Low, Sell at the High," *Journal of Finance* (December 1979). See also Garman, "Recollection in Tranquility," *Risk* (March 1989).

6. There are six primary payoff patterns for options to exchange:

1. Zero strike option on min of 2 assets	$\min[S_1, S_2]$
2. Call option on min of 2 assets	$\max[0, \min[S_1, S_2] - K]$
3. Put option on min of 2 assets	$\max[0, K - \min[S_1, S_2]]$
4. Zero strike option on max of 2 assets	$\max[S_1, S_2]$
5. Call option on max of 2 assets	$\max[0, \max[S_1, S_2] - K]$
6. Put option on max of 2 assets	$\max[0, K - \max[S_1, S_2]]$

where: S_1 = Ending price of Asset 1
S_2 = Ending price of Asset 2

For a discussion of this type of option, see Rene Stulz, "Options on the Minimum and the Maximum of Two Risky Assets," *Journal of Financial Economics* (July 1982). See also Mark Rubinstein, "Somewhere over the Rainbow," *Risk* (November 1991).

7

Equity Style Allocations: Timing between Growth and Value

Geoffrey Gerber, PhD
President
Twin Capital Management, Inc.
Pittsburgh, Pennsylvania *

INTRODUCTION: A FRAMEWORK FOR DECISION MAKING

Allocation across asset classes has long been recognized as the greatest single determinant of fund performance. Concurrently, at the other end of the sponsor's decision realm, plenty of attention is devoted to selecting individual managers.

This chapter focuses on a set of decisions falling between the broad policy level and the discrete manager level. At issue is the identification of, and allocation among, domestic equity "styles" (e.g., growth and value, large cap and small cap).

Both long-term and short-term decisions about investment style could have a greater impact on total return than individual manager selections. For this reason, it is prudent to consider style allocation decisions separately and give them a higher priority than manager selection. (The old adage, "If you can find good managers, hire them" still is relevant, but within the context of appropriate style allocation.)

From among the many identifiable styles, the focus herein is predominantly on *growth* and *value*. Later in the chapter, a model is introduced that can be used to allocate between these two broad equity styles. First, we need to establish some common ground for discussion.

---

* Twin Capital Management, Inc. has been applying the Model detailed in this chapter real-time since July 1991.

DEFINITIONS OF STYLE

Two ways for considering the concept of investment style are based on a rate of return approach and a factor model approach.

Rate of Return Approach

Analysis of the components of the rate of return (ROR) on a stock helps us to intuitively define two basic styles—growth and value:

$$ROR = \text{Dividend yield} + \text{Change in Earnings}$$
$$+ \text{Change in price/earnings ratio (P/E)}$$

A growth style can be characterized as an approach focusing on earnings change. A growth manager may focus his or her attention on forecasting future earnings streams, with less attention to current price. As a result, if a growth manager forecasts a large enough positive change in earnings, the stock may be purchased even if the current P/E is already discounting the next one to two years of consensus earnings change.

A value style will focus on dividend yield and/or P/E. A value manager will look for relatively cheap and/or high yielding stocks, while paying less attention to a company's earnings prospects. In the extreme case of a pure contrarian manager, the focus is almost entirely on a depressed price, one that the manager believes represents an overdiscounted position.

These notions may be readily acceptable and somewhat helpful in a conversational way, but we find greater utility in the factor model approach.

Factor Model Approach

An alternative method for defining styles is to use factors, or measurable characteristics of a stock or a portfolio of stocks. For example, one could assign various factors as characteristics that define growth and value:

Growth	Value
High historical earnings	Low price/earnings ratio (P/E)
High expected earnings	High dividend yield
High relative change in expected earnings	High book/price ratio
	Low current P/E relative to historical P/E

These listings are far from exhaustive, but even the simple ones given here illustrate that a factor may be either an absolute measure or a relative measure. Further, we could choose to define a style such as growth or value by a single factor or by some combination.

In any case, it is important to recognize the next trait: Every factor has a return and risk attributable to it. Consideration of large versus small stocks helps illustrate this concept. Historically, small capitalization stocks have outperformed larger capitalization securities over the long term (with greater volatility). However, there have been many subperiods in which larger stocks have significantly outperformed smaller stocks.

As will be shown later in the chapter, analogous statements can be made about the return and risk of growth and value stocks. Yet, regardless of which styles we choose to assess, the critical strength of a factor approach to defining those styles becomes clear: investibility.

This makes the style allocation decision real—something we can systematically implement. First, with returns from portfolios attributable to measurable characteristics (factors), we can derive expectations for return and risk of a style. This helps us establish appropriate long-term allocations to styles. Then we might consider shorter-term predictions with the knowledge that shifting between styles is quite feasible.

With factors as basic building blocks, more complex definitions of style can be suggested. For instance, one might imagine a matrix approach in which four distinct styles are defined:

Large-cap value	Small-cap value
Large-cap growth	Small-cap growth

Such a matrix approach is probably useful in assigning long-term allocations to styles, but it is relatively limiting for shorter-term shifts. If, for example, there are correlations across styles (e.g., growth companies tend to be smaller), then it may be difficult to accurately forecast which segment of the matrix is expected to outperform.[1] Tactical allocation among more than two styles at one time may prove overly ambitious, if not misguided.

In recent years, the advent of various indexes that track specific styles has made these considerations more than just academic. Three consulting organizations maintain indexes that reflect some of the different approaches we have discussed:

1. BARRA's (a financial consulting firm) risk model is often used for screening criteria to determine growth, value, and large- and small-cap styles. Recently, BARRA created the S&P/BARRA Value and Growth indexes, which divide the S&P 500 into two separate index portfolios using the BARRA book/price factor exposure from BARRA's equity risk model.
2. Frank Russell has built factor-based indexes specifically designed to capture the following styles:[2]
   a. Large-growth—measured by the Frank Russell Growth Index, which represents the "growth-oriented" stocks in the Frank Russell 1000;
   b. Large-value—measured by the Frank Russell Value Index, which represents the "value-oriented" stocks in the Frank Russell 1000;
   c. Small-cap—measured by the Frank Russell 2000 Index, which includes both small-cap growth and small-cap value stocks.
3. Wilshire has built four separate index funds consistent with the matrix approach:
   a. Large-cap growth;
   b. Large-cap value;
   c. Small-cap growth;
   d. Small-cap value.

STYLE TIMING INTEREST

Not surprisingly, there has been increased interest in using some of the subindexes mentioned above. *The Wall Street Journal,* in September 1992, introduced two different index-based mutual fund offerings, noting that both Dreyfus Corporation and the Vanguard Group ". . . are separately planning to introduce new index-based mutual funds that will allow investors to bet on two major stock-picking styles: 'growth' (fast-growing earnings) and 'value' (cheap stock prices)."[3] The Vangaurd Group will offer two funds based on the S&P 500/BARRA growth and value portfolios, and Dreyfus will offer four Dreyfus–Wilshire target funds corresponding to Wilshire's matrix approach. (See the itemized listing above.)

The opportunity to use low-cost index funds to systematically effect a style timing decision makes the search for a reliable style timing forecast more significant. The next section introduces a forecasting model based on the Frank Russell Growth and Value indexes. (The same model, incidentally, could be easily applied to the S&P 500/BARRA growth and value portfolios or to the first two Wilshire portfolios listed above: large-cap growth and large-cap value.)

STYLE TIMING MODEL

The objective of this model is to outperform a long-term policy allocation to each style. For our purposes, we selected a passive benchmark of 50 percent growth (as measured by the Frank Russell Growth Index) and 50 percent value (as measured by the Frank Russell Value Index). However, the style timing model can be applied to any reasonable set of long-term allocations. If one believes that style does not matter in the long term, then a 50–50 benchmark makes sense. The greater the expectation of outperformance of one subindex relative to the other, the larger the long-term weight.

The desired output of our style timing model is a forecast of the odds that one subindex will outperform the other. Table 7.1 provides the differential (Russell Value Index ("Value") minus Growth Index ("Growth")) on a quarterly basis since 1979. Of the 57 quarters measured, Value outperformed 28 times, or roughly one half of the time. As Table 7.1 indicates, on both a quarterly and an annual basis, the return differential can be quite large.

In our effort to forecast a probability of return differential, we examined a number of elements that were combined into a logistic regression model. These elements can be broadly categorized into:

1. Long-term trend analysis;
2. Short/Intermediate term "runs";
3. Seasonalities.

TABLE 7.1 Russell Value Index versus Growth Index

Year	Quarterly Return Differential				
	First	Second	Third	Fourth	Annual
1979	2.93	1.80	−0.27	−7.03	−3.36
1980	−0.75	1.03	−7.82	−5.00	−15.16
1981	7.65	5.74	2.17	−2.81	12.57
1982	4.85	−0.42	−0.99	−5.15	−0.42
1983	1.26	−1.68	6.58	4.30	12.31
1984	7.66	−2.48	4.07	1.43	11.05
1985	−0.66	2.79	0.61	−4.26	−1.34
1986	−1.67	−4.42	10.01	−1.29	4.62
1987	−7.68	0.01	−0.91	1.99	−4.81
1988	7.27	2.41	1.68	−0.61	11.89
1989	0.53	−2.25	−4.10	−2.99	−10.75
1990	0.82	−8.42	1.27	−2.80	−7.83
1991	−4.84	1.06	−1.69	−8.44	−16.57
1992	6.06	5.26	−2.32	−1.13	8.81
1993	10.51	N/A	N/A	N/A	10.51
Average	2.26	0.03	0.59	−2.41	0.07

The primary reason for using a logistic regression model is that the desired output is a probability forecast or the predicated odds that Value will outperform Growth. The typical application of least-squares procedures involves a dependent variable measured on a continuous rather than a discrete scale. If, however, the dependent variable is discrete, or relates to proportions, then the application of a logistic, or discrete (Poisson), regression becomes appropriate.

The procedures for logistic regression are based on the theory of generalized linear models.[4] Logistic regression uses an iterative (reweighted least-squares) procedure to obtain maximum likelihood estimates of the probability or odds that Value will outperform Growth.

LONG-TERM TREND ANALYSIS

The long-term trend analysis is based on a log-linear time trend model that estimates the probability of reversion back to a longer-term expected return. Figure 7.1 depicts the cumulative natural log (LN) return of the Frank Russell Index using quarterly data for the period from January 1979 through March 1993. The straight line, or predicted cumulative return, is based on the hypothesis that the index provides a

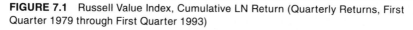

FIGURE 7.1 Russell Value Index, Cumulative LN Return (Quarterly Returns, First Quarter 1979 through First Quarter 1993)

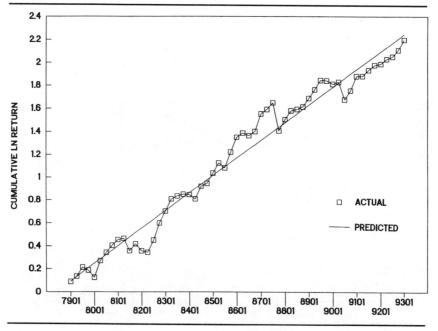

constant long-term positive return equal to the line's slope. Interestingly, the actual cumulative return tracks the expected return quite well: the R^2 lies at 0.97.[5]

If the long-term expected return is to persist, then the application of mean-reversion theory allows for the calculation of a forecast of the direction of future short-/intermediate-term return. The more the actual cumulative (log) return deviates from the trend line, the greater the probability of reversion.

This probability can be estimated using the standardized residual statistic, which is shown in Figure 7.2. The standardized residual is a function of the difference between actual and expected cumulative return and the standard error of the regression. The larger the absolute value of the standardized residual, the greater the probability of reversion to trend. During the period from April 1981 through June 1982, the Russell Value Index ("Value") underperformed its expected return and the standardized residual dropped below −2. This translates into a probability in excess of 95 percent that Value would begin (sometime in the short-to-intermediate term) to outperform its expected return (i.e., have a greater slope) in order to revert back toward trend. Similarly, at

FIGURE 7.2 Russell Value Index, Standardized Residual (Quarterly Returns, First Quarter 1979 through First Quarter 1993)

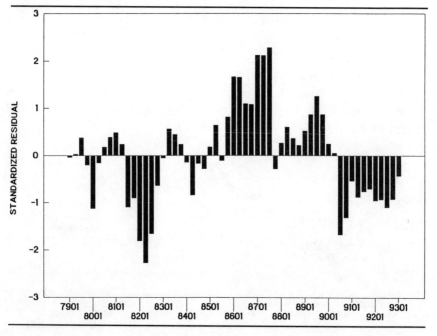

the end of March 1987, the standardized residual peaked above +2, implying that it was timely to underweight the value side of the equity market.

Figures 7.3 and 7.4 show the corresponding analysis for the Frank Russell Growth Index ("Growth"). The R^2 for Growth cumulative return relative to its expected or trend return is 0.96, suggesting again that the application of a standardized residual to forecast short- to intermediate-term direction may be helpful.

The final element of the trend analysis examines any long-term return differential between the two indexes. Figures 7.5 and 7.6 depict the cumulative returns and corresponding standardized residuals for the Value return minus the Growth return. The very small slope of the return differential in Figure 7.5 reflects the fact that, over the entire period, the two subindexes have posted similar cumulative returns. This finding alone would argue strongly for a long-term policy allocation that is relatively close to 50–50 between Value and Growth. However, although the slope and R^2 of this trend model are small compared to the other trends, the standardized residuals shown on Figure 7.6 provide further insight about shorter-term shifts.

FIGURE 7.3 Russell Growth Index, Cumulative LN Return (Quarterly Returns, First Quarter 1979 through First Quarter 1993)

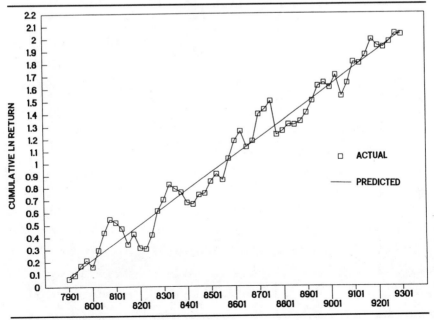

FIGURE 7.4 Russell Growth Index, Standardized Residual (Quarterly Returns, First Quarter 1979 through First Quarter 1993)

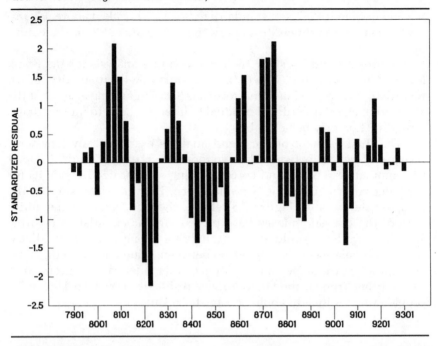

FIGURE 7.5 Russell Value—Growth, Cumulative LN Return (Quarterly Returns, First Quarter 1979 through First Quarter 1993)

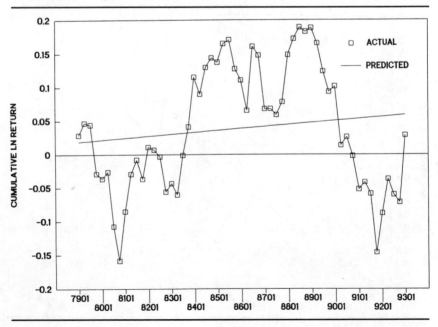

FIGURE 7.6 Russell Value—Growth, Standardized Residual (Quarterly Returns, First Quarter 1979 through First Quarter 1993)

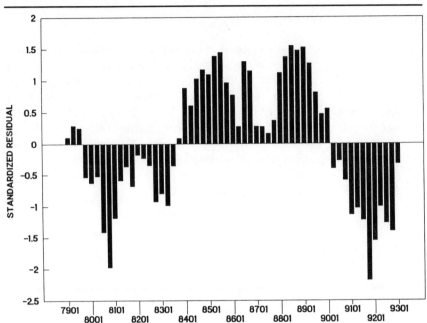

SHORT-/INTERMEDIATE-TERM "RUNS"

In addition to looking at long-term expected returns, we also found it useful to focus on shorter-term "runs" in either index returns or their differentials. For example, when Value outperforms Growth for a given quarter, we can calculate the likelihood that it will outperform again (in direction, not magnitude), based on its probability from a binomial process. The "runs" model applies a value of 1 if Value outperforms Growth, and a 0 value if it underperforms Growth. Given that the historical percentage is 50 percent on a quarterly basis, the probability of a reversal increases as one index continues to outperform the other for multiple consecutive periods.

SEASONALITIES

A quick review of Table 7.1 will lead to a simple conclusion: Value does well in the first calendar quarter, and Growth does well in the fourth quarter. The averages of the first and fourth quarter differentials are significantly different from zero, and those of the second and third quarters are close to zero (and to the annual average differential).

PROBABILITY TO PORTFOLIO MAPPING

The output of the logistic regression model is the probability or odds that Value will outperform Growth. Because the probabilistic insight is focused on direction rather than magnitude, the optimal mapping (or decision rules that translate the probability into an overweight or an underweight relative to the benchmark weight) should be discrete. Figure 7.7 illustrates that the forecast probabilities on a quarterly basis tend to be quite high, quite low, or around 50 percent. Therefore, an optimal mapping is found to include three states of weights:

1. Maximum Value, minimum Growth;
2. Benchmark Value, benchmark Growth;
3. Minimum Value, maximum Growth.

FIGURE 7.7 Twin Equity Style Timing, Probability of Value Outperforming (Quarterly Probabilities, First Quarter 1987 through Second Quarter 1993)

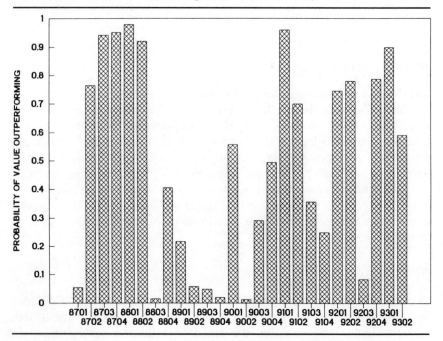

TABLE 7.2   Probability to Allocation Mapping

Current Allocation to Value	Probability Range of Value Outperforming	New Allocation to Value
10	0.0–37.5	10
10	37.6–50.0	10
10	50.1–62.4	50
10	62.5– 100	90
50	0.0–37.5	10
50	37.6–50.0	50
50	50.1–62.4	50
50	62.5– 100	90
90	0.0–37.5	10
90	37.6–50.0	50
90	50.1–62.4	90
90	62.5– 100	90

The reader will note in Figure 7.7 that quarterly probabilities are calculated beginning with January 1987 instead of January 1979. Given the desire to simulate the model out-of-sample, the logistic regression model required eight years (or 32 quarters) of data prior to the first out-of-sample forecast in 1987.

The mapping rules used can be found in Table 7.2. (These weights are to be measured relative to the 50–50 benchmark.) Given the positive long-term trend returns for both indexes, it is advantageous from a risk-minimization perspective to always maintain a minimum weight in each. After analyzing a number of potential weighting schemes, it was determined that the optimal maximum weight for either Value or Growth is 90 percent and the minimum is 10 percent. For example, if, at the end of a quarter in which the current weight was 50 percent Value and 50 percent Growth, the probability of Value outperforming Growth was less than 37.5 percent, then the new weight on Value would be 10 percent. Because the optimal mapping and over- and underweights are symmetrical, this mapping can be translated into active weights for any benchmark, assuming symmetrical moves above and below the passive position.

STYLE TIMING MODEL RESULTS

Applying the mapping of active weights in Table 7.2 to the quarterly probabilities in Figure 7.7, we derive active quarterly allocations to each index. Figure 7.8 details the quarterly active weights from the first quarter of 1987 through the second quarter of 1993.

FIGURE 7.8 Twin Equity Style Timing, Value Allocation (Quarterly Allocations, First Quarter 1987 through Second Quarter 1993)

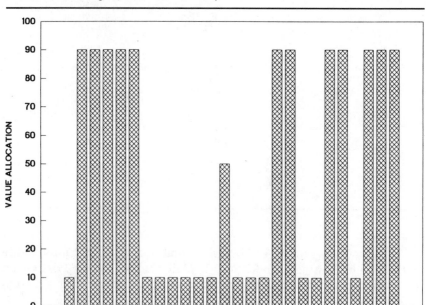

Application of these active quarterly weights to the quarterly index returns has resulted in annualized value-added of 3.41 percent, net of an assumed 1 percent round-trip transactions cost. Given that the index portfolios can be managed passively, or that the strategy could be implemented using no-load mutual funds, the 1 percent round-trip transaction cost assumption is *quite* conservative.

The returns from the style timing model for the period from January 1987 through March 1993 are summarized in Figure 7.9 and Table 7.3. Figure 7.9 provides quarterly returns to both the style timing model (labeled Twinstyle) and the benchmark portfolio. Of the 25 quarters during this period, the style timing model added value (net of estimated transactions costs) 16 times, and underperformed nine times (including the transactions costs associated with moving to a neutral position during the first quarter of 1990). The average quarterly value-added is 0.79 percent; the best quarter added 4.20 percent, and the worst quarter posted a −2.74 percent return relative to the 50–50 passive benchmark.

Table 7.3 lists the annualized returns and standard deviations for the style timing model, the benchmark portfolio, and the two index

FIGURE 7.9 Twin Equity Style Timing, Return (Percent) (Quarterly Returns, First Quarter 1987 through First Quarter 1993)

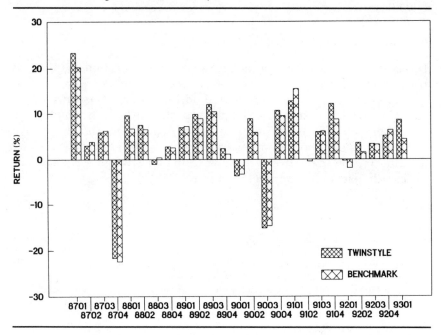

TABLE 7.3 Summary of Results, January 1987 through March 1993

Portfolio	Compound Annual Return	Annual Standard Deviation
Style timing model*	17.56	17.47
Benchmark**	14.15	16.69
Value-added	3.41	
Frank Russell Value Index ("Value")	13.57	15.34
Frank Russell Growth Index ("Growth")	14.53	19.05

* Return is net of assumed 1 percent round-trip transaction cost.
** Benchmark portfolio is 50 percent value, 50 percent growth.

portfolios. The risk of the style timing model is higher than the benchmark by 0.78 percent, but the annualized return is increased by 3.41 percent.

CONCLUSION

Investors should be aware of the impact of style allocation—at the very least, in the determination of long-term policy weights.

Asset allocation decisions should address allocations across asset classes as well as within an asset class (particularly in the equity market, where style return differentials can be quite significant). Active, tactical decisions about overweighting or underweighting a style such as value or growth relative to the long-term policy weights can have significant impact on the aggregate fund return.

NOTES

1. Multiple factor models may be utilized in an attempt to measure the partial effects of each factor's (or each matrix segment's) return. In cases where multicollinearity exists, however, it becomes more difficult to disentangle the effect of each factor as the relationship among the right-side variables increases.
2. The definitions of the Frank Russell growth and value indexes are addressed in the company's publication, "Equity Style Indexes: Tools for Better Performance Evaluation and Plan Management." ·
3. "A New Style of Index Funds Tries to Outperform the Stock Market," *The Wall Street Journal,* September 9, 1992, p. C1.
4. For a broader discussion of these types of models, see D. W. Hosmer and S. Lemeshow, *Applied Logistic Regression* (New York: John Wiley & Sons, Inc., 1989).
5. First-order serial correlation is evident from an examination of the residuals. Autocorrelation may be removed through the use of Box–Jenkins ARIMA (Auto Regressive Integrated Moving Average) models and other time series modeling techniques.

8

Style Analysis, Style Benchmarks, and Custom Core Portfolios

Steve Hardy
President
Zephyr Associates, Inc.
Zephyr Cove, Nevada

INTRODUCTION

This chapter discusses the following concepts:

The importance and impact of style allocation;
Style indexes—a comparison;
Measurement of managers' styles;
Return-based manager style analysis;
Customized manager style benchmarks;
Style analysis for a multimanager fund;
Creation of customized core portfolios with style indexes.

THE IMPORTANCE AND IMPACT OF STYLE ALLOCATION

For years, investors have been told that asset allocation is the most important decision they will ever make. The choice of asset classes has a much greater impact on returns than does the choice of individual managers within those asset classes. Recently, however, sophisticated investors, primarily in the institutional area, have discovered that style allocation among domestic equity managers may be as important as asset allocation. In other words, what kind of equity manager one selects (value, growth, small-cap, and so on) is actually more important than the individual manager selected within that particular style. This has some serious implications for the investor. In the past, the client's job was simply to select a good manager. From that point on, the performance was considered to be the responsibility of the manager. However, the recognition of style allocation has now put an additional burden on the client to select the "right" type of manager. But the manager's responsibility also changes. The manager who professes to be a large-cap growth manager, for example, is responsible for superior stock selection within the large-cap growth universe. If the client hires a large-cap growth manager and, over a period of time, large-cap growth stocks are out of favor and underperform the overall market, a manager can still demonstrate through the use of a proper benchmark that he or she is outperforming the benchmark of large-cap growth stocks. The client is responsible for underperforming the market in this case, because the client chose to bet on that particular style. On the other hand, let's assume (1) that large-cap growth was in favor for a period of time during which the majority of these stocks outperformed the overall market, and (2) that the manager outperformed the market but underperformed his or her universe of large-cap growth stocks. In this case, the client is responsible for the better performance and the manager, to the extent that he or she underperformed the benchmark, is responsible for that underperformance.

To dramatize the return impact of style allocation, in Table 8.1 are listed the annual returns, for 15 years, of four passive style indexes: (1) the Zephyr (Zephyr Associates, Inc.) Large-Growth, (2) Zephyr Large-Value, (3) Zephyr Small-Growth, and (4) Zephyr Small-Value. The next section discusses how these and other style indexes are created and how they differ from one another.

TABLE 8.1   Annual Returns: Four Styles

Year	Large-Growth	Large-Value	Small-Growth	Small-Value	High–Low Spread
1992	2.69	22.70	12.97	39.90	37.21
1991	45.60	43.03	56.11	55.35	13.08
1990	1.78	−15.85	−13.65	−22.52	24.30
1989	38.59	23.39	21.69	10.07	28.52
1988	7.62	26.95	20.75	26.84	19.33
1987	8.99	0.35	−9.84	−5.07	18.83
1986	16.27	24.49	7.19	23.83	17.30
1985	34.08	32.31	31.06	43.42	12.36
1984	−6.28	17.71	−9.00	22.46	31.46
1983	15.13	27.72	25.23	43.92	28.79
1982	24.71	27.21	26.10	39.74	15.03
1981	−10.92	18.03	−4.08	23.37	34.29
1980	42.79	19.83	59.37	21.86	39.54
1979	20.48	17.06	51.50	28.38	34.44
1978	8.21	3.88	16.19	15.68	12.31
Average	16.65	19.25	19.44	24.48	24.45

Table 8.1 shows not only the yearly returns for each of these style indexes, but also the spread between the best (high) and worst (low) performing indexes each year. Notice that the average difference is over 24 percentage points per year. In other words, in any given year, an investor who chose the best style would have outperformed the investor who chose the worst style by an average of 24 percentage points per year. For comparison, we can look at asset class returns for the same period. Table 8.2 compares the yearly returns for stocks, bonds, Treasury bills (T-bills), and real estate.[1] Notice that the difference between the best and worst asset class annually is only 18.86 percent compared to the 24.45 percent in Table 8.1. Figure 8.1 also dramatizes the importance of style allocation. The investment represented began with $100 in 1977. Each year (with the benefit of hindsight), the money was invested in what would be the best performing style. The same thing was done with asset classes. By investing in the best performing styles, the $100 grew to $6,487 in 1992—a 32 percent annualized compound return. The $100 investment in the best asset classes (stocks, bonds, T-bills, and real estate) grew to a much smaller $1,743—an average annual compound return of 21 percent.

One can argue that yearly style differences will smooth out over a longer period of time and that, eventually, the four styles will end up with the same average returns. I would agree, except for the fact that the "long run" may be longer than the period most investors use as a time horizon to judge a manager's performance. To look at the style differences over periods longer than one year, four-year periods were

TABLE 8.2 Annual Returns: Stocks, Bonds, T-Bills, and Real Estate

Year	Stocks	Bonds	T-Bills	Real Estate	High–Low Spread
1992	7.68	9.34	3.25	−4.43	13.77
1991	30.55	20.98	5.13	−5.97	36.52
1990	−3.19	6.48	7.27	1.57	10.46
1989	31.43	15.29	8.18	5.81	25.62
1988	16.50	10.49	6.41	6.95	10.09
1987	5.17	1.47	4.99	5.37	3.90
1986	18.21	18.71	5.54	6.50	13.17
1985	31.57	27.99	6.99	10.05	24.58
1984	6.10	17.66	9.21	13.04	11.56
1983	22.43	8.32	8.60	13.34	14.11
1982	21.58	44.52	10.12	9.44	35.08
1981	−4.91	−0.16	13.98	16.86	21.77
1980	32.42	−2.60	10.97	18.07	35.02
1979	18.44	−4.08	10.03	20.74	24.82
1978	6.56	−0.09	7.31	16.11	16.20
Average	15.03	12.40	7.65	9.19	18.86

FIGURE 8.1 Asset Classes versus Style (1978 to 1992)

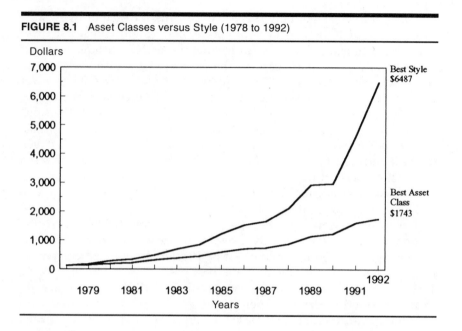

chosen, because four years seems to be accepted as the length of a "full market cycle." If there tended to be very little difference between style returns over rolling four-year periods, then one could ignore the use of style benchmarks and continue to use the more common broadmarket benchmarks such as the S&P 500. However, this was not the case. Table 8.3, which compares rolling four-year periods, shows that, although the style differences smooth out slightly, there is still an average annual difference of 14.56 percent per year. In other words, a skillful manager might significantly underperform the market over a four-year period simply because his or her style was out of favor. By the same token, an unskillful manager could outperform the market over a four-year period simply because his or her style is in favor.

As mentioned earlier, the client, for the most part, is in charge of the style bet, which is determined by the kind of managers the client selects. The dollars involved in these bets are not insignificant. To illustrate, let's look at two fictitious institutional investors, each of whom has $500 million in domestic equity portfolios. In January 1987, one institution decides to hire only large-growth managers and to make no changes in managers or styles for four years. At the end of December 1990, this fund's $500 million has grown to $827.3 million because large-growth investment was up a total of 65.46 percent. During the

TABLE 8.3 Comparative Annualized Rates of Return: Four-Year Periods, January 1979–December 1991

Four-Year Period	Large-Growth	Large-Value	Small-Growth	Small-Value	S&P 500	High–Low Spread
1979–1982	17.58	20.47	30.73	28.15	16.04	14.69
1980–1983	16.25	23.12	24.65	31.86	17.01	15.61
1981–1984	4.64	22.58	8.35	32.03	10.70	27.39
1982–1985	15.90	26.12	17.15	37.09	20.06	21.19
1983–1986	13.88	25.44	12.48	33.01	19.22	20.53
1984–1987	12.33	18.11	3.61	19.87	14.78	16.26
1985–1988	16.29	20.36	11.21	20.93	17.49	9.72
1986–1989	17.25	18.28	9.16	13.18	17.46	9.12
1987–1990	13.42	7.24	3.42	0.66	11.74	12.76
1988–1991	21.93	17.18	18.63	13.85	17.94	8.08
1989–1992	20.52	16.18	16.68	16.68	15.69	4.82
Average	15.45	19.55	14.19	22.43	16.19	14.56

same period, the second institutional investor bet on small-growth, and its $500 million grew to only $571.95 million. The plan sponsor who bet on the successful style saw the fund appreciate by $255 million more than the fund of the plan sponsor who bet on the losing style. Small-value investment did even worse during this period and, compared to large-growth, would have represented an opportunity cost of $314 million. During the four-year period between 1981 and 1984, the opposite result occurred: large-growth investment grew at only 4.64 percent per year and small-value grew at 32.03 percent. The large-growth investor during this period would have seen $500 million grow to just under $600 million; the small-value investor would have seen $500 million grow threefold, to over $1.5 billion. In the above scenarios, the managers selected were assumed to have been average performers. On balance, they neither outperformed nor underperformed their style. Consequently, the investor, who selected the style, was ultimately responsible for the dollar differences in the returns—not the individual money managers.

STYLE INDEXES—A COMPARISON

In Chapter 7, Geoffrey Gerber gave an excellent explanation of the differences between style indexes. I would like to add that there are two different general approaches to creating style indexes. The first approach utilizes an entire universe of stocks and divides that universe equally: half value and half growth. For instance, to obtain the Russell Value Index and the Russell Growth Index, the Frank Russell organization splits the Russell 1000 stocks in half. The advantage of this approach is that the two style indexes add up to the total Russell 1000. The disadvantage is that the two style indexes have reasonably high correlation because they include a number of stocks that are not strongly identified with value or growth; they could be described as somewhat mushy in terms of their style. The Frank Russell Company and the S&P/BARRA use this all-inclusive approach when developing their style indexes.

The second approach to developing style indexes will be referred to here as the "winged" approach. Certain stocks that do not meet strict style criteria are excluded from the broad universe of stocks. In other words, stocks that aren't very "stylish" are eliminated and not placed in any of the style indexes. The purpose of the winged approach is to build style portfolios that capture style effects and thereby differentiate themselves while at the same time making themselves investible. Zephyr uses the winged approach in developing its style indexes. Wilshire also uses the winged approach (but with a slightly different methodology) in the development of the Wilshire style indexes. The advantage of the winged approach is that the style indexes have more distinctive behavior. The disadvantage is that, because of the missing or "nonstyle" stocks, the style indexes are not inclusive and do not add up to an entire index. Table 8.4 is an R-Squared matrix that measures the R-Squared of any two style indexes. Notice that the R^2 between the Russell Value and Russell Growth indexes is 83.02 percent whereas the R^2 between the Zephyr Large-Growth and Zephyr Large-Value portfolios is much lower: 55.17 percent.

MEASUREMENT OF MANAGERS' STYLES

Given the importance of proper style allocation, a reasonable way to determine a manager's style must be developed. The least desirable method is to simply take a manager's word as to what his or her style is. Although time-consuming and expensive, a more desirable method is to perform a detailed analysis of the manager's portfolio. A number of multifactor models are designed to analyze portfolio characteristics and thereby determine to some extent a manager's style, but it is almost impossible to do a style history on a manager with this method. To see how a manager's style has changed over the past 15 years, one would have to obtain monthly, quarterly, or (at the very least) annual portfolios from the manager for the entire 15-year period. Even if it were possible to acquire detailed records of portfolios that existed 15 years ago (for the most part, it is not), it would be extremely labor-intensive because each security in the portfolio would have to be analyzed.

TABLE 8.4 Style Index R² Matrix

	BHSWLG	BHSWLV	BHSWSG	BHSWSV	WILLG	WILLV	WILSG	WILSV	RUSG	RUSV	RUS 2000	S&P 500
BHSWLG	100.00	55.17	81.43	52.59	96.04	67.54	82.98	60.82	98.15	78.85	76.25	92.10
BHSWLV		100.00	50.30	71.75	62.99	89.45	55.14	75.79	59.65	85.30	57.31	73.75
BHSWSG			100.00	66.92	80.11	57.69	98.18	69.68	82.18	70.41	96.32	75.73
BHSWSV				100.00	57.34	66.04	69.09	94.03	56.26	71.47	76.78	62.25
WILLG					100.00	74.75	82.31	64.08	97.98	84.82	76.30	95.14
WILLV						100.00	61.65	73.66	72.24	94.50	62.07	85.86
WILSG							100.00	72.19	83.58	73.99	95.88	78.42
WILSV								100.00	64.17	78.40	77.64	70.06
RUSG									100.00	83.02	77.65	95.15
RUSV										100.00	74.52	94.24
RUS 2000											100.00	75.26
S&P 500												100.00

RETURN-BASED MANAGER STYLE ANALYSIS

Over the past few years, a new method of style analysis, referred to as return-based analysis, has been developed. This method was popularized by William F. Sharpe, a Nobel prize winner and finance professor at Stanford University. Because of its simplicity and accuracy, this method has become very popular recently and is being used by a number of large institutional investors. Sharpe discovered that a great deal can be learned about a manager's style by simply analyzing the manager's monthly or quarterly returns. Sharpe refers to a manager's returns as "tracks in the sand."[2] The returns are compared, to determine how closely they correlate with the returns of a number of style indexes. A very high correlation between a manager's returns and a small-cap growth index would suggest that the manager is a small-cap growth manager. Because most managers have a style that cannot be that easily pigeonholed, a number of indexes must be used to describe the manager's style. The manager's style therefore is configured as a blend of styles defined by a composite of these various indexes. To do this analysis at Zephyr, we use a quadratic optimizer that is part of our Style Advisor, a Windows™-based software program that we developed. Style Advisor, currently being used by a number of pension fund plan sponsors and managers, allows the user to select any desired number of indexes when running this optimization. Typically, for domestic equity managers, we use our four style portfolios plus T-bills. The optimizer then tell us which combination of the four style portfolios plus T-bills would have best tracked the returns of the manager in question. To demonstrate the Style Advisor, we start with the monthly returns from the Magellan Fund from January 1976 through March 1993. Our optimizer tells us which combination of our four style portfolios plus T-bills would have best tracked Magellan's actual returns (the highest possible R^2). This combination is shown in Figure 8.2. In other words, a portfolio that uses only our style portfolios plus T-bills and that would have had the highest correlation to the Magellan Fund's returns over this period would be composed of 16 percent Zephyr Large-Value, 24.2 percent Zephyr Large-Growth, 12 percent Zephyr Small-Value, and 47.8 percent Zephyr Small-Growth, with nothing in T-bills. This composite (or benchmark) can be shown on what we call a management style graph, which consists of four boxes (see Figure 8.3). Clockwise from the upper left corner, they are designated Zephyr Large-Value index, Zephyr Large-Growth index, Zephyr Small-Growth index, and Zephyr Small-Value index. On the horizontal axis, the further a portfolio falls to the left of the graph, the more value the style; the further to the right,

---

* Windows is a trademark of Microsoft.

FIGURE 8.2 Asset Allocation Analysis

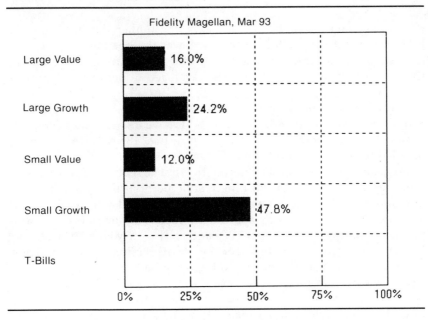

Fidelity Magellan, Mar 93

FIGURE 8.3 Management Style Graph

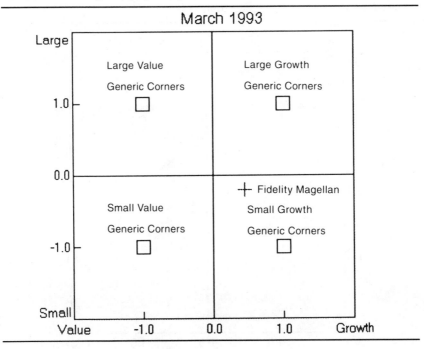

the more growth. On the vertical axis, the higher the portfolio, the larger the portfolio capitalization; the lower the portfolio, the smaller its capitalization. In this example, the Magellan Fund (represented by the "+") has, over the past 17 years, averaged a medium-cap growth portfolio.

Because this analysis covers such a long period of time, it tells little about Magellan's style today versus its style years ago. The style point designated here represents an average style over 18 years. To see a more detailed history of the evolution of Magellan's style, refer to Figure 8.4. These data were generated by taking the first 36 months of returns (beginning in 1976) and determining a style point at the end of that 36-month period. A 36-month window was then moved along each month, and the style analysis was continued. Table 8.5 simulates 177 style points beginning in December 1978 and ending in March 1993. During this 18-year history, there has been a wide dispersion of style in Magellan, ranging from small-growth to large-cap neutral. To see a chronology of these style points, refer back to Table 8.4, which breaks this period down into six equal periods and shows the percentage loadings in each of the style indexes for each of the six periods. By scanning down the large-growth column, one can see that large-growth went

FIGURE 8.4 Management Style Graph: Detailed History

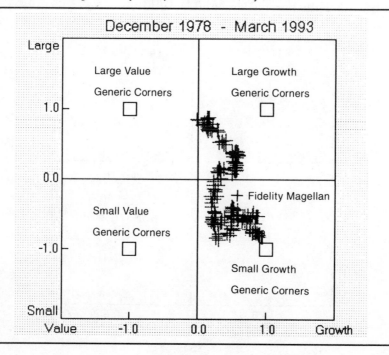

TABLE 8.5 Out-of-Sample Simulation: 36-Month Moving Window; Reoptimized Monthly, December 1978 through March 1993

	Fidelity Magellan
Portfolio Performance (%) . . .	
Annualized return	26.67
Cumulative return	2804.10
Standard deviation	19.25
. . . versus Style Benchmark (%) . . .	
Annualized excess return	6.56
Cumulative excess return	1542.61
Annualized turnover	39.49
Standard deviation of excess return	4.84
Explained variance (Correlation 2)	93.70
. . . versus Beta/SP500 Benchmark (%)	
Annualized excess return	10.49
Cumulative excess return	2056.72
Standard deviation of excess return	7.26
Explained variance (Correlation 2)	87.25

from 7 percent in 1978 to 46 percent in 1993. Small-growth went from 82 percent in 1978 to just over 10 percent in 1993. It becomes obvious from these figures that Magellan began as a small-growth portfolio and has gradually become larger and a little less focused on growth as time has gone by. This style analysis in Table 8.5 was made possible by an optimizer that calculated 177 style points in a matter of seconds. To do this same style analysis with a portfolio-based program, one would have to analyze monthly portfolio holdings for 177 portfolios over a 17-year period—no easy task! The ability to use returns as opposed to portfolios has made the analysis of style and style changes for a large number of managers a practical chore for the sophisticated investor.

CUSTOMIZED MANAGER STYLE BENCHMARKS

A manager can exercise skill and add value in stock selection, market timing, and/or style or sector timing. Most large institutions that hire multiple managers have elected to do their own asset and style allocation internally, which makes them directly responsible for their election to have a certain amount of funds committed to the stock market and to a particular style. Typically, they hire specialty managers within specific style categories. In this case, the manager's value-added is restricted to his or her ability to select stocks within a fairly narrow style range. This contrasts to the practice years ago, when many funds would hire a manager who was expected to make the asset allocation decision (determine whether to invest in stocks, cash, bonds, or whatever), choose the best performing area of the market (style selection), and then select superior stocks within those areas. With this old scenario, it made sense to hold this manager to a broad-based benchmark. Today, with specialty managers who have been selected by the client, this practice is usually not appropriate. What is the purpose of using a benchmark for any particular manager? A benchmark is used to determine the level of a manager's skill and thereby justify the payment of an active management fee. The manager is not paid an active management fee to be in the stock market. One can be in the stock market by owning an index fund (and paying a fraction of an active management fee). The manager is also not paid to simply invest in a particular style (i.e., growth or value). One can do that, again for a fraction of the management fee, by investing in passive style portfolios. The only reason a manager is paid an active management fee is as compensation for his or her ability to select superior stocks within a chosen style. Therefore, an appropriate benchmark should attempt to remove the market and style influences in order to accurately determine the manager's stock selection capabilities. There are still managers who attempt to add value by sector or style rotation. For these managers, the best benchmark is still a large generic benchmark such as the S&P 500 because they are then not being held to working within one particular style.

Many institutional investors and consultants have begun using style indexes as manager benchmarks—certainly a better method than using generic market indexes such as the S&P 500. However, even style indexes alone are inappropriate for most managers, because their individual styles cannot be pigeonholed into such narrow definitions. A more sophisticated approach is to actually build a customized benchmark for each manager, using a blend of investment style indexes designed to specifically replicate that manager's style. The previous section discussed how to identify managers' styles using certain percentages of Zephyr's four style indexes. Those same percentages can be used to develop a composite, which we will call a style benchmark. One of the requirements for an accurate benchmark is that it must be specified in advance.[3] To comply with this requirement, Zephyr creates what are referred to as out-of-sample benchmarks. For instance, we'll take the combination of style indexes that has best tracked a manager's returns over the past 36 months and designate that combination to be the manager's benchmark for the next (37th) month. Each month, this 36-month window is moved forward one month. At the beginning of each month, Style Advisor calculates the benchmark in advance, based on the previous 36-month optimization. When run out-of-sample, the benchmark is actually predicting what the manager's style will be each month, based on the previous 36 months' data. This customized benchmark is dynamic: it constantly reflects the manager's style over the past 36 months and adjusts for any long-term generic changes in that style. For instance, it would be inappropriate to use the same benchmark for Magellan today that was used 17 years ago, when it was a completely different fund with a totally different style. Another qualification for an appropriate benchmark is that it must be investable.[4] The four style indexes that we use to build our benchmark are calculated monthly and are cap-weighted to be investable portfolios. With this in mind, we have constructed a benchmark for the Magellan Fund (see Figure 8.5). It is interesting to note that the style benchmark significantly outperformed the S&P 500. In other words, one could have beaten the market by simply investing in Magellan's benchmark. Nevertheless, Magellan was still able to outperform its style benchmark, which clearly demonstrates superior stock selection. Table 8.5 shows that Magellan had a 6.56 percent annualized excess return over its customized style benchmark.

How do we know that our customized style benchmark is a good benchmark? A good benchmark should capture most of the manager's style and therefore will usually have a high correlation to the manager's actual returns. The left-hand pie chart in Figure 8.6 shows the tracking or the R^2 of the style benchmark to Magellan's actual returns to be 93.7 percent. A good benchmark would typically have an R^2 to the manager's returns of above 80 percent. How do we know that this

FIGURE 8.5 Performance/Cumulative Excess Return (Out-of-Sample Simulation)

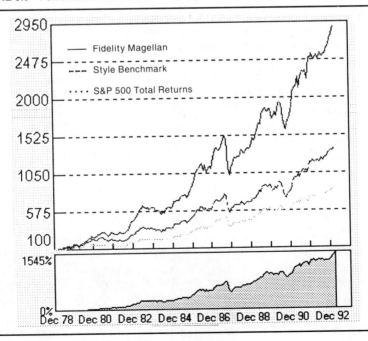

FIGURE 8.6 Performance Attribution Out-of-Sample Simulation

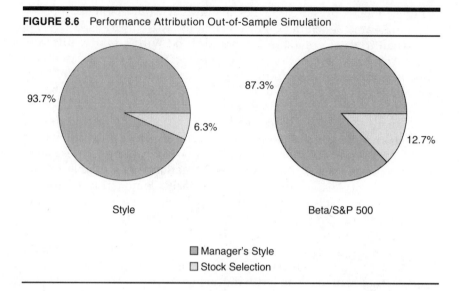

93.7%

6.3%

87.3%

12.7%

Style

Beta/S&P 500

☑ Manager's Style
☐ Stock Selection

benchmark is any better than using a generic benchmark such as the S&P 500? The right-hand pie chart in Figure 8.6 shows the R^2 of Magellan's returns to the S&P 500. As long as the R^2 on the style benchmark is higher than the S&P 500, we know that we have built a better benchmark. The Style Advisor program allows replacement of the S&P 500 with any generic benchmark or index for which data are available. We can then compare our blended style benchmark to any other benchmark we choose. As an example, Figure 8.7 shows what happens when our customized style benchmark is compared to the Russell Growth Index. The index gets a little higher R^2 than the S&P 500 but is still less than what we can achieve with our blended style index. This is not an unusual example. I chose 40 mutual funds at random and created style benchmarks for each of them. I then compared the R^2 of those style benchmarks to the R^2 that was calculated on the S&P 500, Wilshire 5000, and Russell 3000. On average, the blended style benchmarks were able to achieve R^2 ten percentage points higher than the generic market indexes.

How well a style analysis and resulting benchmark are created depends on the indexes to which one compares the managers' returns. For instance, if I select Zephyr's four domestic style indexes plus T-bills and use them to do style analysis and to build a benchmark for an international manager, chances are that I will not build a very good benchmark much less get an accurate style analysis. Poor style analysis and poor benchmark creation are evidenced by a low R^2 figure. Figure 8.8 shows what happens when we try to do a style analysis and

FIGURE 8.7   Performance Attribution In-Sample Simulation

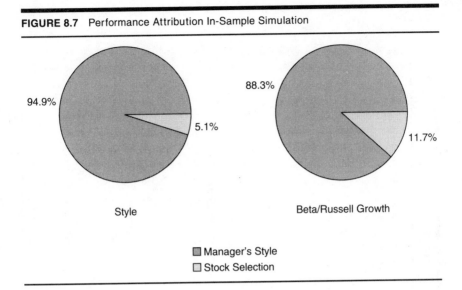

Style

Beta/Russell Growth

■ Manager's Style
□ Stock Selection

build a benchmark for the Templeton Foreign Fund using Zephyr's domestic style indexes. The results can be corrected by changing our palette of indexes. In Figure 8.9, the four Zephyr style portfolios have been replaced with some international indexes (The Financial Times European Index and The Financial Times Pacific Basin Index). With the better indexes, the correlation of the benchmark to the managers' actual returns increases from 55 percent to 80.9 percent. Using the two international indexes, we have created a benchmark that has a considerably higher R^2 to the managers' returns than the EAFE Index.

To do style analysis and build benchmarks, Sharpe uses a 12-index palette that includes international, fixed-income, and domestic style indexes.[5] This approach is useful when the user has no clue as to what type of manager is being analyzed. If we have a general idea of what type of manager is being analyzed (domestic equity, international, global, fixed-income, and so on), we prefer to use a smaller targeted group of indexes. Zephyr's four style indexes, which are used to analyze domestic equity managers, are an example.

STYLE ANALYSIS FOR A MULTIMANAGER FUND

Most individual investors build a portfolio by either making independent stock selections or investing in various mutual funds. Institutions, on the other hand, will typically hire a number of separate account managers to do the same thing. Both the individual investor, who buys mutual funds, and the institutional investor, who hires investment

FIGURE 8.8 One Manager Style Analysis

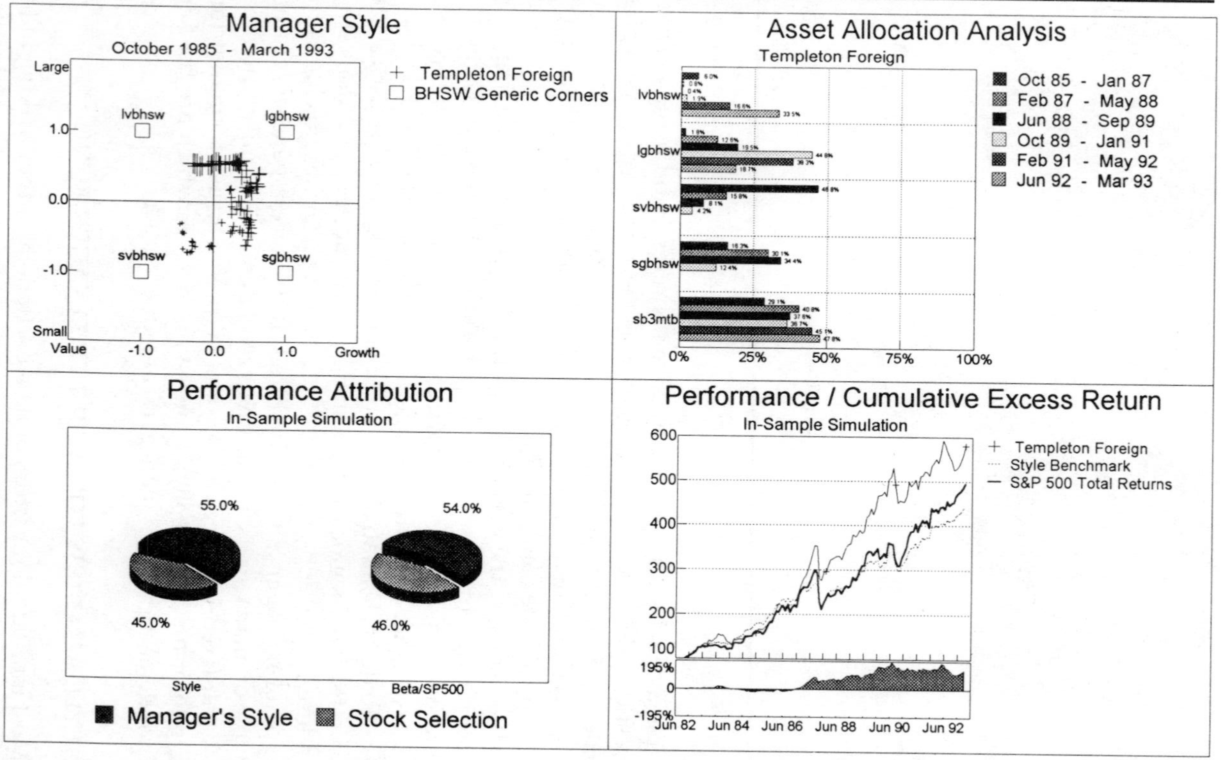

Manager Style
October 1985 - March 1993

+ Templeton Foreign
☐ BHSW Generic Corners

Asset Allocation Analysis
Templeton Foreign

■ Oct 85 - Jan 87
▨ Feb 87 - May 88
■ Jun 88 - Sep 89
☐ Oct 89 - Jan 91
▨ Feb 91 - May 92
▨ Jun 92 - Mar 93

Performance Attribution
In-Sample Simulation

Performance / Cumulative Excess Return
In-Sample Simulation

+ Templeton Foreign
···· Style Benchmark
— S&P 500 Total Returns

■ Manager's Style ▨ Stock Selection

FIGURE 8.9 International Manager Analysis

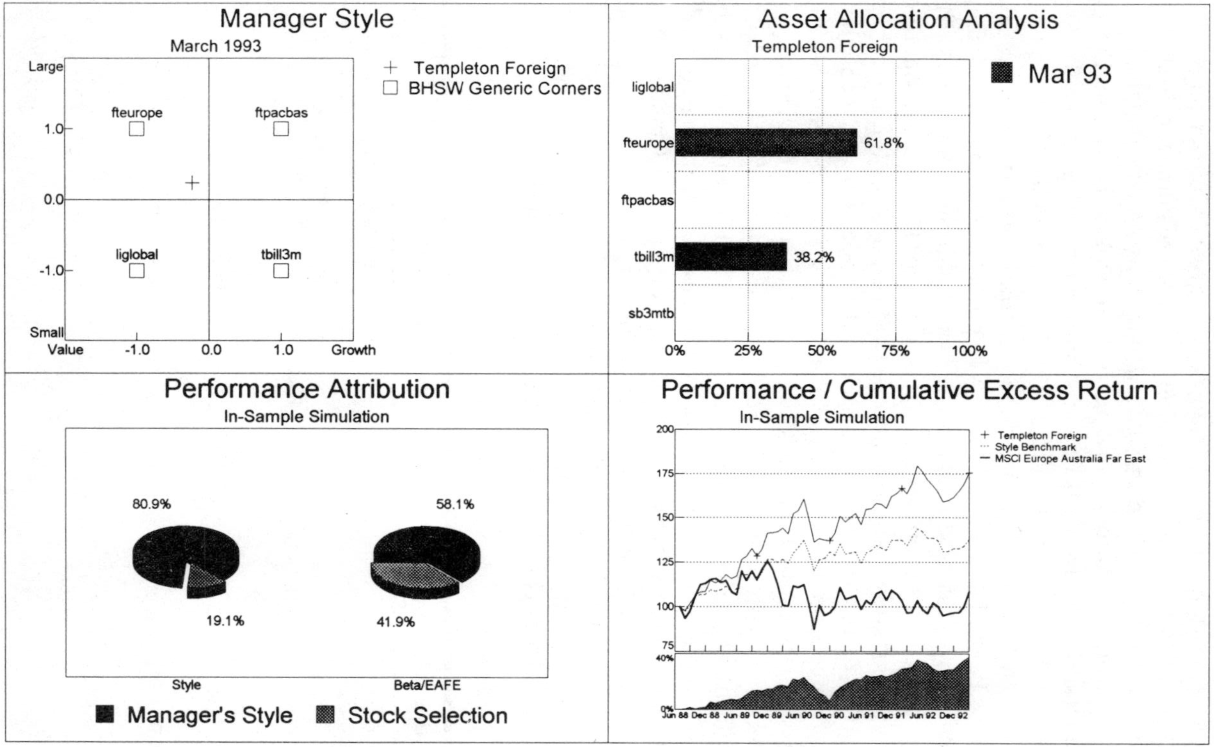

Manager Style
March 1993
Large
Small
1.0
0.0
-1.0
Value
-1.0
0.0
1.0
Growth
fteurope
ftpacbas
liglobal
tbill3m
+ Templeton Foreign
□ BHSW Generic Corners
Asset Allocation Analysis
Templeton Foreign
liglobal
fteurope
ftpacbas
tbill3m
sb3mtb
61.8%
38.2%
0%
25%
50%
75%
100%
Mar 93
Performance Attribution
In-Sample Simulation
80.9%
19.1%
58.1%
41.9%
Style
Beta/EAFE
Manager's Style
Stock Selection
Performance / Cumulative Excess Return
In-Sample Simulation
200
175
150
125
100
75
40%
0%
+ Templeton Foreign
Style Benchmark
MSCI Europe Australia Far East
Jun 88 Dec 88 Jun 89 Dec 89 Jun 90 Dec 90 Jun 91 Dec 91 Jun 92 Dec 92

management firms, make style decisions with regard to what kinds of managers (or funds) they hire. For this reason, the client is really responsible for the overall style allocation. As mentioned earlier, that style allocation will most likely have a greater impact on the total returns of the fund than will the selection of the managers. Just as we can analyze the style of a particular manager, we can also analyze the style of a fund or group of managers that would represent the client's "portfolio." Figure 8.10 demonstrates such an analysis. Three managers' dollar weighted aggregate style is designated by the symbol "0." The client's overall benchmark for his total domestic equity portfolio is the S&P 500, labeled "+." In this hypothetical example, the client has made a significant style bet away from his or her benchmark, the S&P 500. The client bet on smaller size and value. This is a bet that the client should certainly recognize and be held responsible for. It's conceivable that all of the active managers could be skillful and beat their respective benchmarks; but if the client was wrong in his or her bet, it is possible that the total fund would still underperform the overall benchmark—in this case, the S&P 500. The client's bad bet would more than offset the good returns that the individual managers achieved. The reverse could be true as well: the individual managers underperformed their respective benchmarks, but the client made a good bet that more than compensated for the underperformance.

The whole point of this discussion is that the performance comes from two areas: (1) the skill of the manager and (2) the style bet made by the client. The client's big advantage is that he or she can elect to

FIGURE 8.10 Analysis of Manager Style (December 1992)

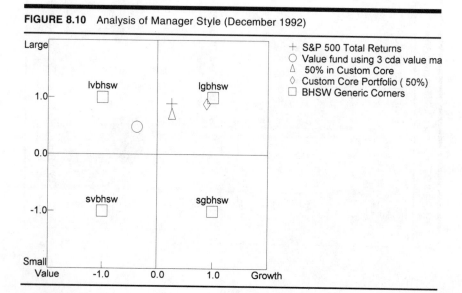

make or not make a style bet. There are several possible ways for the client to eliminate this bet. The client can bring his or her aggregate style point a little closer to the benchmark (S&P 500) by reallocating money among the existing managers. Another alternative is to hire an active manager who has the necessary style. Perhaps the most economical and efficient way to eliminate style bets, make style bets, or change the overall style allocation is with the use of a custom core portfolio.

CREATION OF CUSTOMIZED CORE PORTFOLIOS WITH STYLE INDEXES

Many institutions, over the past ten years, have invested heavily in index funds that are passively managed and designed to track an index such as the S&P 500. In some cases, the rationale for this is that they have not been able to find managers whose performance is superior. In some cases, the funds are so large (in the multibillion-dollar range) that they have almost no choice but to invest a large percentage of their funds into such an index. There has also been an overriding general philosophy, promoted primarily by pension consultants, that promotes the use of index funds. That philosophy suggests that one should put money into an index fund, which becomes the core portfolio, and then hire active managers around the core, to add value. Typically, these specialty managers are selected specifically to be growth, value, small-cap, large-cap, and so on. The problem with this overall philosophy—and perhaps the reason it has performed poorly in terms of adding value—is that it is very difficult to find skillful managers and even more difficult to find skillful managers within specific styles. In fact, the more constraints one uses, the more difficult it becomes to locate truly skillful managers. We believe that a more appropriate philosophy would be for clients to start off by locating good managers before they build their core. They should concentrate on finding managers who can really add value and have demonstrated skill in stock selection. During this initial search, they should place minimum emphasis on the consideration of style. After they have assembled a stable of the best managers they can find, they can build a core portfolio that is customized to complement their particular array of active managers. It is much easier to build a customized core portfolio than it is to find skillful managers in every style category. In this case, an off-the-shelf S&P 500 index fund will do nothing to complement the active managers; it may even aggravate a bias if there was a large-cap growth bias to begin with. The custom core portfolio can now be dynamically managed over time to adjust for any changes in the active managers' styles and for the natural style drift that occurs when one is not rebalancing among the managers. To make these adjustments to a custom core portfolio makes more sense than to constantly reallocate money among managers and/

or change managers strictly for style reasons. A custom core portfolio can also be developed by simply investing in passive style portfolios in a mixture that accomplishes one's objective. In Figure 8.10, as mentioned earlier, the client has taken a sizable small-cap value bet away from the benchmark. If the client wishes to remove the style bet, then the goal is to bring the aggregate style of the managers as close to the style of the client's benchmark (the S&P 500) as possible. To accomplish this, Style Advisor builds a custom core portfolio (diamond) made up of a combination of the four style indexes. How closely the custom core will adjust the aggregate portfolio to the desired level will depend to a large extent on the budget or amount of money that the client is willing to invest in the custom core portfolio. At first blush, one might think that we are converting the client's aggregate portfolio into one big index fund. This is not the case. In fact, each of the active managers is expected to add value to the respective benchmarks. If the managers accomplish this and if the client takes no style bets, then, by definition, the aggregate total fund must outperform the S&P 500. In this simple example, the custom core portfolio can be built by investing in the Zephyr Large-Growth Index. How well the custom core portfolio moves the style bet away from the client's benchmark is demonstrated in Figure 8.11. The left-side pie diagram shows the correlation (87.3 percent) and the tracking error (12.7 percent) of the client's aggregate portfolio ("0") to the benchmark ("+") before any money is invested in a custom core. The right-side pie diagram shows the same statistics as they would appear when the custom core portfolio is included in the client's

FIGURE 8.11   Benchmark Tracking In-Sample Simulation

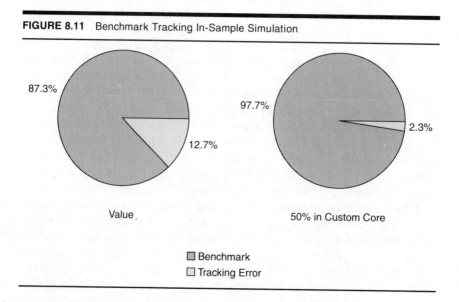

overall aggregate portfolio. In this case, the tracking error measures the "bet" that the client is taking away from the benchmark. By including the custom core portfolio, we have reduced the tracking error substantially and therefore reduced the client's style bet.

If a client actually wanted to make a bet, he or she would pick a point on the style graph to indicate where the aggregate portfolio was to be. This point would be labeled "benchmark for the client." Style Advisor would then build a custom core designed to move the client's aggregate portfolio from its current position to where the client wants it to be (as designated by the benchmark). In this manner, the custom core can be utilized to assist the client in making or changing style bets. Whether the client is making a bet or attempting to eliminate one, the custom core portfolio can be dynamically managed so that the custom core can be adjusted quarterly and any unintentional drift away from the desired style point can be easily corrected.

CONCLUSION

Asset allocation may not be the most important decision an investor will ever make. Style allocation among domestic equity managers may be just as important in terms of its effects on the total rerun of the portfolio. To do style allocation, one must first determine a way to efficiently and accurately measure the style of any manager previously hired or possibly worth considering. Along with measuring the style of the manager, one must also determine the manager's skill by creating a customized style benchmark. The use of such a benchmark should save the investor a significant amount of money because it will eliminate hiring or firing managers for the wrong reasons. The investor must also be aware of the fact that he or she is making a style bet based on the kind of managers hired. If the investor does not wish to make this style bet, he or she can build a custom core portfolio that can be managed dynamically to maintain the style and balance desired for the total fund.

NOTES

1. For stocks, Zephyr uses the total return for the S&P 500; for bonds, the Lehman Brothers Long-Term Corporate Bond Index; T-bills are 30-day U.S. Government Treasury Bills; for real estate, the Russell NCREIF Property Index; and for Styles, the Zephyr indexes.
2. William F. Sharpe, "Determining a Fund's Effective Asset Mix," *Investment Management Review* (November/December 1988): 59–69.
3. David E. Tierney and Kenneth Winston, "Using Generic Benchmarks to Present Manager Style," *The Journal of Portfolio Management* (Summer 1991): 33–36.
4. Id.
5. Id.

9

Implementing Asset Allocation Decisions: Techniques for Constructing Optimal Fixed-Income Portfolios

Kurt Winkelmann
Manager, Fixed Income
Vestek Systems
San Francisco, California

Asset allocation decisions are often reached through a three-step process: (1) the risk and return characteristics of available and relevant investment opportunities are identified; (2) investor risk tolerances are parameterized; (3) the risk–return trade-offs of the investor are combined with those observed in the market to produce an optimal asset allocation, that is, an allocation that maximizes investor preferences for return while accounting for observed levels of risk.

The output from the asset allocation decision is a set of asset categories and dollar amounts (or percentages) invested in each asset category. Should any of the initial assumptions change (e.g., changes in investor risk tolerance), then the amounts invested in each asset category will also change.

By necessity, this three-step process works at the aggregate level: Different investment opportunities are represented in terms of broad aggregates. For example, if the investor wishes to characterize the intermediate component of the fixed-income market, an index such as the Lehman Brothers Intermediate Government Bond Index could be used. Consequently, two questions arise:

1. Do the investment categories used in the asset allocation decision accurately represent the underlying investment problem?
2. What steps are involved in actually implementing the asset allocation decision?

This chapter addresses the second question. It takes as given the description of investor preferences and aggregate level benchmarks, explores sources of risk and return in fixed-income securities, and examines alternative methods of selecting optimal portfolios of these securities.

MEASURING RISK AND RETURN

Implementation of an asset allocation decision requires the purchase of actual securities. Purchasing securities, in turn, requires the identification of factors influencing return (and risk): portfolio decisions are improved as these factors are more accurately identified. Furthermore, performance measurement and performance attribution are enhanced as the influences on return are better understood.

Measurement of the factors affecting bond return can be divided into two phases: (1) the definition of a valuation framework, and (2) an analysis of the pricing residuals obtained from the valuation model. The second phase is necessary because any valuation model will induce pricing errors. The goal of the valuation framework is to make reliable investment decisions on the basis of a well-specified model.

The starting point for fixed-income valuation is the proposition that the underlying value of a security is the discounted value of its cash flows. Using notation, the value of a bond (denoted V) can be written as:

$$V = \sum_{t=1}^{T} d^*_t CF_t \qquad (1)$$

where d^*_t and CF_t are, respectively, the discount factor and cash flow at date t. The discount factor, d^*_t, represents the value at time 0 (today) of a dollar to be received at date t; the cash flow, CF_t, is merely the nominal cash to be received at date t.

Equation (1) suggests three considerations for security valuation:

1. The appropriate discount rates (i.e., the proper set of d^*_t), must be determined;
2. The correct sequence of cash flows, or CF_t, must be found;
3. Any variability in the cash flows must be identified and analyzed.

In particular, the valuation process should account for any correlations between the discounts and the cash flows.

Looking first at the discount factors (or d^*_t), standard fixed-income valuation methods hold that discounts can be broken into a sequence of risk-free discounts and a spread. The spread is a way to account for credit risk inherent in the security. Again using notation, let s_t denote the spread and d_t the risk-free discount. The discount, d^*_t can then be written as:

$$d^*_t = d_t(1/(1 + s_t))^t. \qquad (2)$$

Equation (2) indicates that the discount at any point in time is the product of the risk-free discount and a term that adjusts for credit risk. Identification and estimation of each of these components is necessary for identifying the discount.

Typically, risk-free discounts are taken from the U.S. Treasury term structure. The Treasury term structure can be estimated in several ways, with differences in term structure representations attributable to different estimation algorithms and/or different estimation universes. Possible estimation universes include all traded coupon-bearing bonds, the most recently issued bonds (the "on-the-run" bonds), or Treasury strips. Estimation algorithms range from cubic splines to regression equations. The latter can be specified to include restrictions on the discount factors that may be suggested from finance theory.

An example of an estimated term structure is shown in Table 9.1, which shows the Treasury term structure for January 27, 1992, estimated using all coupon-bearing bonds. The table shows the discount factors, spot rates, forward rates, and current coupon rates.

For bond valuation purposes, the spread (s_t) can be taken from a matrix showing average spreads by each broad economic sector and quality classification. Note, however, that it is unlikely that a particular bond's spread will correspond exactly to the average in the matrix. Consequently, the difference between a particular bond's spread and the spread shown in the matrix represents one source of pricing error.

TABLE 9.1 Treasury Term Structure (Treasury Coupon Term Structure as of 1/27/92)

Maturity (Years)	Discount Function	Spot Rate	Forward Rate	Current Coupon
0.00 to 0.25	0.99045	3.87	3.87	3.87
0.25 to 0.50	0.97996	4.09	4.30	4.09
0.50 to 1.00	0.95828	4.31	4.53	4.31
1.00 to 2.00	0.90300	5.17	6.03	5.14
2.00 to 3.00	0.84386	5.74	6.89	5.69
3.00 to 4.00	0.77906	6.34	8.15	6.24
4.00 to 5.00	0.72050	6.66	7.97	6.54
5.00 to 7.00	0.60726	7.25	8.73	7.05
7.00 to 10.00	0.47367	7.61	8.46	7.36
10.00 to 15.00	0.30429	8.09	9.05	7.71
15.00 to 20.00	0.19910	8.23	8.67	7.82
20.00 to 30.00	0.09692	7.93	7.33	7.77

The implementation of equation (1) illustrated in Table 9.2 has assumed that none of the cash flows varies. However, there are fixed-income securities whose cash flows may vary, depending on certain "states of the world." For example, mortgage-backed securities have variable cash flows: Cash flow projections for these bonds are dependent on the level of prepayment. Consequently, valuation of these securities requires identification of the states of the world, the cash flows associated with these states of the world, and the odds that these events will occur.

A particular case of "state-dependent" cash flows occurs when the cash flows are dependent on the level and anticipated future levels of the discounts. Callable bonds and mortgage-backed securities are examples of this particular case. In these examples, option valuation techniques must be used to value the variable cash flows, and equation (1) must be appropriately modified.

As any of the components in equation (1) change, the bond's value also changes. Hence, the return on a fixed-income security can be attributed to changes in interest rates (the risk-free discounts), changes in spreads, changes in the cash flow structure, or the passage of time itself (e.g., coupon payments).

On the basis of the "no free lunch" principle, it would seem that the sources of value (and return) are also sources of risk. Consequently volatility in interest rates, volatility in spreads, and volatility in cash flows all contribute to volatility in bond returns.

Now that sources of risk have been identified, what remains is a measurement issue: How can fixed-income risk be quantified? Modern asset pricing theory suggests that risk can be expressed in terms of

TABLE 9.2 Security Valuation (Fixed-Income Security Valuation as of 1/27/92)

Cusip: 219327AE			Issuer:	Corning Glass
Coupon: 8.875			Issuer Sector:	Industrials
Maturity Date:	3/15/16		Issue Name:	Deb 8.875%16
Dated Date:	3/15/86		Moody Rating:	A1
Accrued Interest:	3.254		S&P Rating:	A+

	Price	Yld/Sprd
Non-Call Treasury:	111.764	7.785
Econ/Qual Sector:	9.486	0.799
Call Option:	0.000	0.000
Valuation:	102.277	8.647
Current:	103.000	8.577
Difference:	0.723	−0.070

Duration: To Maturity	9.395	Convexity: To Maturity	1.447

variances and covariances, implying that a useful starting point is the variance of return on a fixed-income security.

Equation (1) can be used to relate the return on a fixed-income security to changes in its yield. This is shown in equation (3):

$$dP/P = -D_m(dy) \qquad (3)$$

where dP/P is the percentage change in price, and dy is the change in yield. D_m is the *modified duration* of the bond, and is computed as:

$$D_m = \sum_{t=1}^{T} tCF_t d^*_t / P. \qquad (4)$$

Equation (3) shows that by holding yield changes constant, bonds with higher modified durations also have higher returns.

Because yield changes are rarely (if ever) constant across bonds, equation (3) can be used to analyze volatility in bond returns. Let $sd(dP/P)$ and $sd(dy)$ denote the standard deviation of the bond return and the yield change, respectively. Then, using equation (3), the volatility of the bond return is written as:

$$sd(dP/P) = D_m sd(dy). \qquad (5)$$

It can be concluded from equation (5) that higher-duration bonds have more volatile returns than lower-duration bonds, all else equal.

It is also possible to break dy into changes in its components. If y_r is the risk-free yield and s is the spread, then dy is approximately equal to $y_r + s$. As a result, the standard deviation of the bond's return can be given by:

$$sd(dP/P) = D_m^2 \{var(dy_r) + 2cov(dy_r, ds) + var(ds)\}. \qquad (6)$$

Equation (6) indicates that bond return volatility has three components: (1) volatility in yield changes on the risk-free equivalent bond, (2) volatility in spread changes, and (3) the covariance between the two. Equation (6) also indicates that risk increases as duration increases, all else equal: higher-duration bonds have more volatile returns. Therefore, it can be concluded that modified duration is a measure of risk for fixed-income securities.

Equation (6) asserts that all volatility in bond returns is derived from volatility in interest rates and spreads. Implicit in the derivation of equation (6) is the assumption that cash flows are constant. Should the cash flows themselves be dependent on the level of interest rates, then option pricing methodologies can be used to derive an *option adjusted duration.* The option adjusted duration shows bond return volatility as a function of volatile interest rates, spreads, and cash flows.

The derivation of equation (6) also depends on the assumption that term structure movements are uniform. In other words, equation (6) assumes that all term structure shifts are parallel. An implication of this assumption is that yield changes are equally volatile at all term structure vertices (points), and that the correlation of movements between any two is one. For example, under this assumption, yield changes at the 90-day term structure vertex are as volatile as those at the 30-year term structure vertex, and the correlation between the two is one.

As a practical matter, the assumption of parallel shifts is usually violated. Table 9.3 shows the correlation matrix of excess returns to term structure vertices, with variances (annualized) shown on the main diagonal. (The returns to term structure vertices are calculated by treating each vertex's discount factor as its price.) For example, in Table 9.3, the correlation between the return at the 90-day vertex and the two-year vertex is .55, and the annualized variances of excess returns at these two vertices are .40 and 2.58, respectively. The variances (shown on the main diagonal) indicate that the volatility of yield changes is not independent of the vertex. Furthermore, the correlations of term structure returns are not one, as predicted by the parallel shift assumption. As a result, modifications to the measurement of interest rate risk are warranted. These modifications should account for the empirical regularities as shown in Table 9.3.

Three avenues can be taken. The first is strictly empirical; it breaks term structure volatility into unobservable components, or factors. A second avenue is purely theoretical; and it treats term structure volatility as derivative from two (or more) factors. On the third avenue, empirical models can be used to guide the development of theoretical models.

Table 9.4 shows a principal components analysis of the covariance matrix of term structure returns. This analysis breaks the observed covariance matrix (as shown in Table 9.3) into movements in unobservable components. Each row in Table 9.4 corresponds to a term structure vertex. The entries in each row show the percentage of variance of return at that vertex that can be accounted for by each principal component. For example, at the two-year vertex, one principal component (or factor) accounts for 72 percent of the volatility in excess returns, while three factors explain 97 percent of the variance in excess returns.

As can be seen, on average, two principal components explain 80 percent of the variation in term structure movements. Three principal components explain roughly 86 percent of term structure movements,

TABLE 9.3   Term Structure Volatility

Vertex						Vertices (in years)						
	.25	.50	1.0	2.0	3.0	4.0	5.0	7.0	10.0	15.0	20.0	30.0
.25	.40	.75	.64	.55	.49	.45	.44	.38	.37	.37	.32	.37
.50		.55	.87	.79	.75	.72	.70	.65	.61	.55	.54	.58
1.00			1.18	.95	.93	.90	.88	.81	.76	.67	.66	.72
2.00				2.58	.99	.97	.96	.90	.86	.77	.75	.81
3.00					3.94	.99	.98	.94	.89	.82	.80	.83
4.00						5.37	.99	.96	.92	.85	.83	.85
5.00							6.47	.98	.94	.88	.86	.87
7.00								9.18	.97	.93	.91	.90
10.00									12.32	.95	.95	.92
15.00										19.17	.96	.93
20.00											27.27	.88
30.00												31.18

TABLE 9.4 Principal Components

Vertex	Cumulative	Percentage of Cumulative Explained by:		
		First Factor	Second Factor	Third Factor
90-Day	20.25	67.90	6.37	25.73
180-Day	50.42	69.20	1.09	29.71
1-Year	79.02	66.88	1.59	31.52
2-Year	92.08	73.74	1.02	25.24
3-Year	96.00	70.73	6.75	22.52
4-Year	97.57	80.49	.06	19.45
5-Year	98.81	83.99	.01	16.00
7-Year	98.86	91.00	.21	8.79
10-Year	97.89	96.46	.61	2.93
15.00	96.72	99.36	.60	.04
20.00	99.68	93.33	6.32	.35
30-Year	99.98	94.53	5.27	.20
Average	85.62	82.30	2.49	15.21

again on average. The principal components analysis indicates that theoretical work on term structure movements could reasonably be based on two or three factors.

Theoretical models of term structure movements explain returns to term structure vertices in terms of the dynamics of two (or three) factors. For example, a two-factor model could include as factors the "short rate" and the spread between the long and short rates. In this framework, movements in discount factors are functions of the parameters affecting the two factors. Because bond prices are themselves functions of the discounts, it follows that bond prices are dependent on the movements (or dynamics) of the two factors. Consequently, if the underlying parameters are known, then theoretical bond prices can be determined.

The valuation and risk analysis framework outlined in this section identifies four sources of return: (1) movements in interest rates and the associated effects on cash flows, (2) changes in spreads, (3) the passage of time, and (4) specification/estimation error. As discussed, the last source is a consequence of the modeling procedures used to identify the first two effects.

What bears repeating is that any valuation model, whether it incorporates the simple duration model or a more complicated three-factor model, is an attempt to identify sources of volatility in bond returns. Accurate assessment of return volatility is necessary for both valuation and risk analysis. Implementation of the asset allocation decision requires purchasing securities, implying that risk measurement also has a crucial role in the asset allocation decision. However, full implementation of the asset allocation decision is fundamentally a portfolio decision: portfolios of securities must be picked to satisfy certain characteristics.

PORTFOLIO SELECTION

Portfolio selection has four components:

1. A benchmark must be defined;
2. The risk attributes of the benchmark must be identified;
3. A universe of eligible securities must be compiled;
4. An optimization framework must be used to select securities from the universe.

Benchmark definition is the most straightforward component to handle. In principle and in practice, the benchmark that is used for the asset allocation decision should be used for the portfolio selection problem. The principal reason for this is to maintain the underlying set of assumptions that is used in the asset allocation decision. For example, if the Lehman Brothers Intermediate Government Bond Index is used in the asset allocation decision, then the portfolio selection problem should also be based on this index. Consequently, the underlying issue is not which index should be used for portfolio selection, but how can fixed-income indexes be used in the asset allocation decision.

Index selection in the asset allocation decision should reflect two considerations: (1) the underlying investment problem, for example, the characteristics of a liability stream, and (2) conditional on the first issue, indexes should be chosen to give a broad representation of the fixed-income markets. The second consideration reflects the point that the underlying components of the fixed-income markets have different return distributions.

Table 9.5 illustrates this last point. The table shows the average return and standard deviation of return for the Lehman Brothers Aggregate Bond Index and four of its components: (1) Treasury bonds, (2) agency bonds, (3) corporate bonds, and (4) mortgage-backed securities. Return series for the period January 1985 through December 1991 were used for the index. Averages are arithmetic and annualized. As the table illustrates, the return characteristics of the index components differed considerably from those of the aggregate index.

Once the appropriate benchmark has been selected, its risk exposures must be analyzed. These analyses will consist of exposures to interest rate changes and sectors of the bond markets. These analyses are critical, regardless of whether the underlying investment strategy is passive or active.

TABLE 9.5 Index Returns and Standard Deviations

Index	Average Return	Standard Deviation
Aggregate	12.49	5.25
Government	11.92	5.35
Corporate	13.13	5.61
Mortgage-backed securities	13.35	5.09

Interest rate exposure consists of both single-factor analysis and multiple-factor (e.g., three-factor) exposure. A single-factor analysis shows the yield and duration (and its derivative calculations) of the index. Table 9.6 shows the yield and duration of the indexes illustrated in Table 9.5 (as of December 1991). According to the interpretation of duration given in the previous section, the index least exposed to interest rate changes is the mortgage-backed securities index. The government index is most exposed to interest rate changes.

As discussed in the previous section, duration is at best a first approximation to the interest rate sensitivity of a bond (or portfolio of bonds). For duration to be an accurate representation of portfolio risk, term structure shifts must be parallel, implying that the correlation between returns to term structure vertices must be one. As illustrated in the previous section, the correlations between returns to term structure vertices differ from one, suggesting that the simple duration analysis could be profitably augmented.

A straightforward procedure for augmenting the interest rate risk analysis has its roots in two observations: (1) the value of any bond or portfolio of bonds can be represented in terms of the term structure vertices, and (2) a large proportion of the covariance matrix of returns to term structure vertices can be explained with three factors. Consequently, interest rate risk analysis can be enhanced by first determining the allocation of portfolio cash flows to each of the term structure

TABLE 9.6 Index Yield and Duration

Index	Yield	Duration	Coupon	Maturity
Aggregate	6.70	4.15	8.82	9.02
Government	6.02	4.99	8.54	9.36
Corporate	7.49	4.76	9.08	12.87
Mortgage-backed securities	7.49	2.41	9.21	6.47

TABLE 9.7 Summary Characteristics

Characteristic	Portfolio	Universe
Yield to maturity	6.35	6.35
Duration	4.51	4.51
Coupon	9.25	9.25
Maturity	7.93	7.93
Number of bonds	21	169

vertices and then assessing the impact of movements in each of the three factors.

Tables 9.7 and 9.8 illustrate these points by considering the risk attributes of a universe of 169 Treasury securities versus a portfolio of 21 Treasury bonds. Table 9.7 shows the summary characteristics of the portfolio and the benchmark (i.e., the universe of bonds). Notice that the yield and duration of the portfolio match that of the universe.

In Table 9.8, the cash flows of the bonds in both the universe and the portfolio are allocated to the term structure vertices. Given that the portfolio and the universe have the same duration, one would initially expect that the return responses to term structure movements would be identical. However, because the cash flow allocations to the term structure vertices are different (as shown in Table 9.8), it can be concluded that, for some term structure movements, returns will not be identical.

TABLE 9.8 Cash Flow Distribution

Term Structure Vertex	Percentage of Cash Flow	
	Portfolio	Universe
0 Days	2.61	1.37
90 Days	2.18	2.12
180 Days	2.72	3.08
1 Year	28.15	14.09
2 Years	10.77	18.88
3 Years	9.22	13.77
4 Years	3.95	10.94
5 Years	5.79	11.76
7 Years	12.00	8.75
10 Years	13.19	6.47
15 Years	5.27	4.46
20 Years	3.74	3.32
30 Years	.41	.99

Table 9.9 shows the responses (absolute) of the portfolio and the universe to shocks of one standard deviation to each of the first three principal components. As the table illustrates, the responses are different for all three principal components. A shock of plus or minus one standard deviation will occur 66.66 percent of the time. Consequently, it can be concluded that portfolio and universe returns are unlikely to be identical, even though the summary characteristics are the same.

As Tables 9.7 through 9.9 illustrate, a thorough analysis of interest rate risk for the benchmark will include summary characteristics such as the duration and yield as well as cash flow distributions to the term structure vertices. An additional useful diagnostic tool is the response of the benchmark to shocks in each of the term structure factors.

After the interest rate risk of the benchmark has been analyzed, the next step is to consider its sector exposures. This step is necessary because spreads in different sectors have different distributions. As discussed in the previous section, bond valuation consists of a risk-free component, a sector spread, and an analysis of optionlike characteristics. Consequently, if two bonds are similar in all characteristics except sector, and if the sector spreads behave differently, then the return characteristics of the bonds should also be different.

Table 9.10 shows the average and standard deviations for corporate sector spreads. Each cell in the table has two figures. The upper figure is the average spread; the lower figure (in parentheses) is the standard deviation. Averages and standard deviations are reported in terms of basis points. The table was constructed using month-end data for the period January 1986 through December 1991. AS indicated, average spreads varied across sector and quality, with averages increasing as the quality deteriorated. Furthermore, spreads became more volatile (as indicated by the standard deviation) as quality deteriorated. Consequently, the data in the table seem to corroborate the proposition that analysis of sector distributions is a critical component of benchmark risk analysis.

After completing the risk analysis of the benchmark, a universe of eligible bonds should be constructed. The universe serves as the raw

---

TABLE 9.9 Yield Responses to One Standard Deviation Shock

Factor	Yield Response (in Basis Points)	
	Portfolio	Universe
First	39	37
Second	2	1
Third	8	9

TABLE 9.10 Sector Spread Attributes

Economic Sector	Quality			
	AAA	AA	A	Baa
Industrials	60	86	112	176
	(18)	(24)	(31)	(44)
Utility	67	82	110	154
	(17)	(20)	(29)	(38)
Bank/Finance	71	89	114	161
	(20)	(25)	(31)	(52)
Transportation	66	86	121	176
	(22)	(31)	(33)	(46)
Yankee/Canadian	60	94	116	146
	(16)	(28)	(38)	(43)

material for the optimizer. Bonds should be chosen for the universe on the basis of two considerations: (1) the bonds should be available in the market, and (2) the bonds in the universe should reflect the characteristics of the underlying benchmark. For example, if the benchmark is the Lehman Brothers Government Bond Index, then mortgage-backed securities should not be included in the universe.

Once a universe of eligible securities has been developed and the risk attributes of each of the bonds have been determined, an optimizer can be used to select a final optimal portfolio. An optimizer is an integral part of the security selection process, for two reasons: (1) even the most straightforward portfolio management concept, indexing, is not easy to implement operationally, because full index replication is not feasible, and (2) an optimizer assists the active management process by systematically and quickly considering alternative investment possibilities. Alternatives whose effects would be otherwise difficult to assess can be quickly considered through the use of an optimizer. In either case, use of an optimizer requires the definition of investment objectives that are consistent with the underlying investment policies and the selection of an optimization algorithm.

OPTIMIZATION TECHNIQUES

Different algorithms exist for selecting optimal portfolios. What differentiates one algorithm from the next is the specification of the objective function. Two popular optimization frameworks are the target-penalty and the mean-variance frameworks.

The target-penalty framework works in terms of portfolio and benchmark characteristics. Benchmark risk attributes such as duration, convexity, average quality, average coupon, average yield, and average maturity are determined. Sector weightings such as the proportion of the benchmark that is in each economic sector are also determined. These serve as the targets (or as the base for the targets in the case of a "tilted" portfolio) for the optimal portfolio.

In the next step, each attribute is assigned a penalty. Penalties have two pieces: (1) the (absolute) difference of the portfolio value from its target value, and (2) a weight. A total portfolio penalty is now determined by adding the penalties for each attribute. The objective becomes: choosing a portfolio that minimizes the total penalty.

In notation, this framework can be expressed as follows. Let $C_b(i)$ and $C_p(i)$ denote the value of characteristic i in the benchmark and the portfolio, respectively, and let $W(i)$ denote the weight for characteristic i. The penalty for characteristic i, $(P(i))$, is given as $P(i) = W(i)(C_p(i) - C_b(i))^2$. Consequently, the total penalty (PENALTY) is given as:

$$PENALTY = \Sigma\ W(I)(C_p(i) - C_b(i))^2. \tag{7}$$

Each portfolio characteristic, $C_p(i)$, is a weighted average of the individual securities in the portfolio. As a result, the objective is to pick security weights that minimize the total penalty as given in equation (7).

Table 9.11 illustrates the optimization setup under the target-penalty approach. The first column in the table lists the portfolio level characteristics to be considered in the optimization run, and the second column shows the target values of these attributes. These values serve as the $C_b(i)$ in equation (7). Index values for these attributes are shown in the column labeled "Target Index." (The index in this example

---

TABLE 9.11 Optimization Setup

Optimization Specifications:
  Target Index: Treasury universe
  Universe: Treasury universe
  Portfolio: All cash

Optimization Parameters:

	Target	Target Index	Difference	Penalty
Maturity	7.93	7.93	0.00	4.00
Duration	4.51	4.51	0.00	20.00
Quality	1.00	1.00	0.00	0.00
Coupon	9.25	9.25	0.00	6.00
Yield to maturity	6.35	6.35	0.00	12.00
Convexity	40.47	40.47	0.00	0.25

is the universe of 169 Treasury securities used for Tables 9.7 through 9.9.)

The fourth column shows the difference between the target value and the index value for each characteristic. This information is important if a "tilted" portfolio is to be constructed. Because the differences are zero for all attributes, it can be concluded that the optimizer is to be used to develop an indexed portfolio.

Penalties are shown in the final column of Table 9.11. These are the W(i) of equation (7). The penalties operate in a relative sense in the objective function. For example, because duration has a higher penalty than coupon in the table (20 for duration versus 6 for coupon), it can be concluded that the optimization algorithm will treat duration as relatively more important than coupon.

This optimization framework is not limited to using summary characteristics. Constraint on the sector distribution, weight of each bond in the final portfolio, and so on, can also be incorporated.

With minor modifications, this same framework can be used in active management. Two revisions are necessary: (1) a method for ranking securities must be added, and (2) objective function as shown in equation (7) must be revised to include these rankings.

For example, a valuation model can be used to rank bonds according to mispricing, with the most underpriced bonds having the highest rank. After ranking securities, the objective function can be modified to include a positive term for picking highly ranked securities. Thus, the objective function is to maximize rankings and minimize total penalty.

An alternative approach to selecting portfolios is to use a mean-variance approach. This approach begins with a specification of total portfolio risk relative to a benchmark. Such a specification allows for trade-offs between the various factors affecting portfolio return. Total portfolio risk is defined as the ex ante tracking error of the portfolio against the benchmark. Tracking error, in turn, is defined as the standard deviation of the return differences between the portfolio and the benchmark.

In the second step, investor preferences regarding the risk–return tradeoff are specified. More specifically, a *risk aversion* parameter is chosen. This parameter gives the number of additional basis points of expected return that the investor requires for taking on one additional unit of risk.

Using notation, the mean-variance approach can be expressed as follows. Let var $(R_p - R_b)$ be the variance of the return differences, and let A be the risk aversion parameter. Investor preferences (PREF) regarding risk and return can be expressed as

$$\text{PREF} = (R_p - R_b) + A \sqrt{\text{var}(R_p - R_b)}. \tag{8}$$

In equation (8), the terms involving R_b are fixed, and the terms involving R_p depend on the security weights. Consequently the objective is to pick a set of security weights that maximizes the objective as given by equation (8).

Examination of equations (7) and (8) indicates that the target-penalty and the mean-variance approaches are quite different. To make the target-penalty approach operational, risk attributes must be identified and estimated, and penalties for missing target values must be assigned. To apply the mean-variance technique, a correlation matrix indicating the trade-offs between factors affecting return must be developed. In addition, the risk aversion parameter must be specified.

Even though these are different approaches to selecting optimal portfolios, they share two attributes:

1. Both rely on the estimation of risk attributes, implying a reliance on modeling;
2. Portfolio selection in both cases is predicated on the investor's expressing trade-offs between risk and return, either explicitly (in the case of the mean-variance approach) or implicitly (in the case of the target-penalty approach).

Both optimization frameworks require the use of models to implement. Therefore, a critical step in implementing the asset allocation decision is an ex post analysis of how the portfolio performed relative to the selected benchmark. Performance analysis and attribution will uncover any underlying flaws in the modeling procedure or optimization setup.

CONCLUSION

This chapter has reviewed the techniques used to implement fixed-income asset allocation decisions. It started from the premise that the result of the asset allocation process is broad allocations across asset categories. Consequently, the implementation of an asset allocation decision is the selection of specific securities.

After reviewing methods for valuing and analyzing risk in fixed-income securities, the chapter discussed techniques for selecting bonds. In particular, two portfolio optimization methods were discussed: (1) the target-penalty approach and the mean-variance approach. Each of these techniques was shown to involve assumptions regarding the role of risk.

APPENDIX: FACTOR ANALYSIS

Let P_t denote the price of the bond, CF_n denote the cash flow at term structure vertex n, and d_{nt} represent the discount at term structure vertex n. Equation (A1) shows P_t as:

$$P_t = \sum_{n=1}^{N} d_{nt}CF_n \qquad (A1)$$

where N is the number of term structure vertices.

Denote by R_Δ the return to the bond over holding period $_\Delta$, and let $r_{n\Delta}$ denote the return to term structure vertex n. Equations (A2) and (A3) show the calculation of R_Δ and $r_{n\Delta}$. Thus:

$$R =_\Delta \sum_{n=1}^{N} w_n r_{n\Delta} \qquad (A2)$$

where w_n is the percentage of the present value of the bond's (or portfolio's) cash flows occurring at term structure vertex n. These are the figures in Table 9.10. $r_{n\Delta}$ is calculated as

$$r_{n\Delta} = (d_{n-\Delta\ t-\Delta} - d_{nt})/d_{nt}. \qquad (A3)$$

Let r_f denote the return on a risk-free security (i.e., one with no variance), let R_Δ denote the excess return on the bond, and let er_Δ denote the excess return at each term structure vertex. R_Δ is given in equation (A4) as:

$$R_\Delta = R_\Delta - r_f = \sum_{n=1}^{N} w_n(r_{n\Delta} - r_f) = \sum_{n=1}^{N} w_n\ er_{n\Delta}. \qquad (A4)$$

Equation (A4) can be rewritten in vector notation as:

$$R_\Delta = w'er \qquad (A5)$$

where w' is an $N \times 1$ vector of term structure vertex weights and er is an $N \times 1$ vector of excess returns to term structure vertices.

Notice that the expected value and variance of R are given as:

$$E(R_\Delta) = w'E(er) \qquad (A6)$$

and

$$var(R_\Delta) = w'\Omega w \qquad (A7)$$

where $\Omega = E\{(er_\Delta - E(er_\Delta))(er_\Delta - E(er_\Delta))'\}$. Ω is the underlying covariance matrix for the correlation matrix shown in Table 9.3.

A factor analysis approach assumes that the vector of excess returns can be written as:

$$er = Bf + u \qquad (A8)$$

where B is an N × k matrix of factor loadings, f is a k × 1 vector of factor values, and u is a randomly distributed vector of noise(s). The objective of factor analysis (principal components analysis) is to estimate the unobservable factors, f, and unobservable factor loadings, B, from the sample means and covariances of er.

Ω is estimable from sample data, and can be decomposed as:

$$\Omega = D \wedge D' \qquad (A9)$$

where D is an N × N matrix of eigenvectors and $\wedge$ is an N × N matrix with the eigenvalues on the main diagonal and zeros elsewhere. Hence, let the factor loadings B be given by the eigenvectors of Ω.

Form an N × 3 matrix B_3 from the first three factor loadings. There are two competing objectives in picking the dimension of the matrix (i.e., the "3"). The first objective is to maximize explanatory power, which can always be accomplished by choosing the dimension to be N. The second objective is to minimize the number of factors. The elements of B_3 give rise to the figures in Table 9.4. Using the matrix B_3, the matrix Ω can be written as:

$$\Omega = B_3 \wedge B_3. \qquad (A10)$$

By substituting equation (A10) into equation (A7), the variance of the excess return to the bond can be written as:

$$var(R_{\underset{\sim}{A}}) = w'B_3 \wedge B_3 w. \qquad (A11)$$

10

Strategic Asset Allocation: Asset/Liability Forecasting, from A to Z

Richard Q. Wendt, FSA
Principal
Towers Perrin
Philadelphia, Pennsylvania

INTRODUCTION

Strategic asset allocation refers to the long-term (e.g., ten years or more) asset mix that will best meet a pension plan sponsor's objectives. A number of studies have shown that a pension plan's investment results directly depend on the selected asset strategy. The primary vehicle for making strategic asset allocation decisions is the asset–liability forecast, which uses an integrated model of plan assets, liabilities, and financial results. By testing various asset mixes against the plan's liabilities, the plan sponsor is able to compare the relative advantages and disadvantages of each strategy.

This chapter discusses asset–liability forecasting. Most of the examples focus on salary-related corporate defined-benefit plans, but the same concepts are relevant to other plans as well.

A. WHAT IS A FORECAST?

A pension forecast is a model of the complete financial results of a pension plan, particularly a defined-benefit pension plan. Based on plan liabilities, benefit cash flows, and portfolio returns, among other important factors, the plan model determines contributions for each year, asset progressions, and the accounting requirements specified by FASB Statement No. 87 ("FAS 87" hereinafter).[1] A proper model will determine minimum ERISA (Employee Retirement Income Security Act) contributions and maximum tax-deductible contributions and will allow the user to choose a pattern of contributions between these two extremes. Assets will move forward from year to year based on the net of inflow (portfolio return and contributions) and outflow (benefits and expenses).

A plan model like the one shown in Figure 10.1 will be able to project contributions, expense, funded ratios, and other key financial factors.

B. WHY DO A FORECAST?

Forecasting is as old as or older than the ancient Greek priests' studies of the entrails of sacrificial animals. Seeing the future has been a universal quest of human beings. Pension forecasting is simply the latest high-tech variant.

The financial results of a pension plan are quite complex. The various components are controlled by ERISA, OBRA (Omnibus Budget Reconciliation Act), FAS 87, and intricate government regulations. Decisions made in one year may have unexpected results in subsequent years; decisions that could have been made may have prevented future problems. For example, the contribution policy has a key impact on the plan, in that future assets, contributions, and expense may all be impacted by current contributions.

FIGURE 10.1 Typical Structure of a Pension Forecast Model

LIABILITIES	ECONOMIC DATA
ABO, PBO SERVICE COST PAYROLL BENEFITS	INFLATION INTEREST RATES ASSET RETURNS

FINANCIAL RESULTS
CONTRIBUTIONS PENSION EXPENSE FUNDED STATUS

One of the key uses of a forecast is to ascertain the plan's sensitivity to economic factors. What level of asset return is needed to maintain the plan's funded ratio? What is the impact of changing the liability discount rate? What is the impact of increasing the equity exposure of the portfolio? Each of these questions has a long-term perspective and depends on the complex interaction of all the factors affecting the plan.

Plan sponsors concerned about the volatility of expense or the likelihood of making future contributions can use pension forecasts to evaluate their plan.

C. A DETERMINISTIC FORECAST

A deterministic forecast is the simplest type of forecast. It involves making assumptions about future economic conditions, plan demographics, contribution policy, liability assumptions, and other plan-specific factors. It is "deterministic" in the sense that it is a one-scenario forecast of the plan's financial results.

The results of a deterministic forecast are a 10- to 20-year projection of some or all of the following financial results:

- Payroll;
- Benefits paid out;
- Liabilities for contributions and expense:
- Market value and smoothed value of assets;
- Required and actual contributions;
- FAS 87 expense;
- Funded ratios for accrued and projected benefits.

Figures 10.2 and 10.3 show examples of the financial results of a typical deterministic forecast.

The starting point of a full-blown asset–liability forecast project is normally a forecast of future results, assuming that all future economic factors are based on the best estimate of each factor. For example, if the best estimate of asset returns is 9 percent per year, the "best estimate" forecast would be based on future asset returns of 9 percent.

Another type of forecast is the "no gain or loss" forecast: the future experience is set equal to the actuarial assumptions for valuing the liabilities. For example, if the liabilities are based on 8 percent interest and 6 percent salary scale, the forecast would be based on future asset returns of 8 percent and future salary growth of 6 percent. This approach can have several pitfalls. If the funding and expense liabilities use two different sets of actuarial assumptions, a no gain or loss forecast with respect to one basis will necessarily create gains or losses for the other basis. It is impossible for two dissimilar sets of actuarial assumptions to simultaneously have no gain or loss. Another difficulty

FIGURE 10.2 Model Retirement Plan—Expense and Contribution

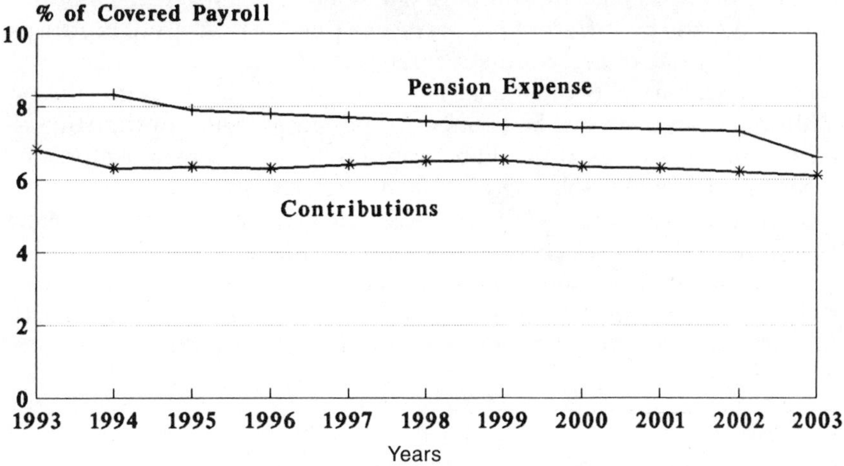

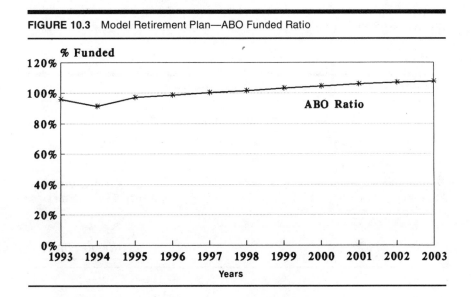

is that the use of an asset smoothing mechanism may complicate the analysis. The normal approach is to assume that the portfolio return is equal to the discount rate; asset smoothing may create year-to-year gains or losses.

It is up to the user to determine the purpose of the forecast and specify the operative assumptions accordingly. Notice that a best

FIGURE 10.3 Model Retirement Plan—ABO Funded Ratio

estimate forecast is identical to a no gain or loss forecast only when the actuarial assumptions are completely consistent with future economic assumptions. This similarity may not exist when the assumptions are made by different people or designed for different purposes.

Another use of deterministic forecasts is to specify a number of alternative scenarios. For instance, in addition to a best estimate forecast, additional forecasts can be created for pessimistic and optimistic scenarios. In some cases, it would be useful to analyze several factors and create scenarios by isolating each factor in turn and also by changing combinations of factors. This process will help to identify the plan's sensitivity to the key economic and actuarial factors.

In an asset allocation context, deterministic forecasts are primarily used as an educational tool or a prelude to performing the stochastic forecast and studying the complete volatility of the plan.

D. A STOCHASTIC FORECAST

On the one hand, a stochastic forecast is one of the most complex calculations that can occur in asset allocation. On the other hand, it can simply be described as a group of multiple deterministic forecasts.

The word "stochastic" is derived from the Greek and means something like "make a guess." A stochastic forecast consists of multiple guesses (perhaps 100 or more) of future plan results. Each guess or scenario is itself a deterministic forecast and all financial results are calculated as if they were true deterministic forecasts.

The stochastic forecast starts with an "asset simulation model," a fancy name for the calculations that create multiple scenarios of interest rates, inflation, and asset returns (see Figure 10.4). The asset model is normally based on a combination of asset assumptions (e.g., expected

FIGURE 10.4 Structure of an Asset Simulation Model

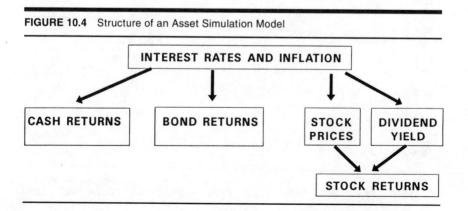

returns, standard deviations) and formulas created by the consultant to produce scenarios that are representative of future possibilities. Each consulting firm has its own asset model, with its unique formulas and assumptions.

In the stochastic forecast, the liabilities are also determined so as to move in accord with the asset scenario. For example, a high inflation scenario will have higher payroll and higher liabilities, because of the impact of higher pay; a high interest rate scenario will have lower liabilities (assuming that the actuarial valuation assumptions change with projected economic conditions). The net result of stochastic assets and stochastic liabilities is a set of financial results, with consistent patterns of expense, contributions, and funded ratio within each scenario.

Because the stochastic forecast involves a great deal of output, the presentation of results must be a condensation of the complete results. The typical presentation format is to show the percentiles of the distribution of results (see Figures 10.5 and 10.6). In such a presentation, the tenth percentile would indicate that 10 percent of the scenarios are below that point and 90 percent of the scenarios are above that point. The range of results for each year or an average of all years' results over the forecast horizon might be shown. Unfortunately, the use of percentiles can make analysis of deeper results more difficult. There is no linkage of percentiles either to other variables or to other years. For instance, the scenario that generates the tenth percentile investment return in

FIGURE 10.5 Employer Pension Expense (%)

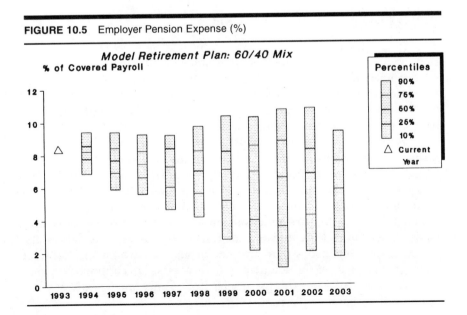

FIGURE 10.6 Employer Contributions (%)

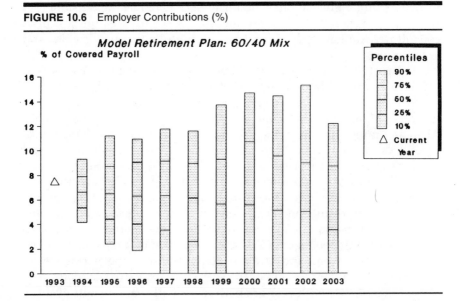

year 4 would probably not generate the tenth percentile contribution in year 4 or the tenth percentile investment return in year 5. Each percentile is determined separately for each variable.

E. WHY DO A STOCHASTIC FORECAST?

The stochastic forecast is very complex, providing much more information than a deterministic forecast. The stochastic forecast simulates the joint movement of assets and liabilities, thereby giving substantial information about the volatility of financial results.

Because the determination of pension expense and contributions is based on quite intricate accounting rules and government regulations, there is no simple relationship between portfolio returns and financial results. For example, if there were two similar plans but each had different actuarial assumptions, the patterns of financial results for the two plans could be quite different. The financial results will also vary with funded ratios, benefit formula, and employee demographics.

All of these factors are quite complex and require a full asset–liability model to determine the trend and volatility of the plan's financial results.

Some plan sponsors may attempt to analyze a plan's investment strategy with a series of deterministic forecasts. This approach is usually motivated to "keep things simple" and is only appropriate as a decision tool for smaller plans.

F. HOW TO CHOOSE ASSUMPTIONS FOR ASSET RETURNS

One prominent asset consultant has stated, "History is not perfect, but it's all we have." The choice of asset assumptions should start with an analysis of historical data but should not stop there.

Assumptions should be chosen by looking to the future rather than to the past. Generally, the key issues in selecting asset assumptions are:

1. Annual expected return;
2. Standard deviation of return;
3. Correlations among asset returns;
4. Compound returns over multiyear periods.

The annual expected return is the arithmetic average of asset returns over time; the standard deviation of return is a measure of the volatility around the expected return. Historical data for these statistics are readily available, but the historical standard deviations are easily misinterpreted. Using excessively long time periods may include trends and cycles and give a higher standard deviation than is appropriate. Using shorter, more recent time periods may not provide enough data for assessment of the standard deviation. Therefore, substantial judgment is required to develop a consistent set of assumptions.

A common approach used by asset consultants is to create consistent risk–return relationships. In other words, an asset category with higher return would have higher risk. Figure 10.7 illustrates a pattern of risk and return assumptions for a number of typical asset categories.

Correlation coefficients determine the relative movement of asset classes. For example, equity categories, such as large capitalization (i.e., S&P 500 stocks) and small capitalization, tend to move in similar patterns. Large-capitalization and small-capitalization stocks would have a relatively high correlation; large-capitalization stocks and, say, T-bills would have a relatively low correlation. In rare cases, two asset classes might have negative correlation: the asset returns would tend to move in opposite directions.

Many pension managers are familiar with the first three issues, but few are aware of the significance of the compound returns over multiyear periods. Many asset models are based on the simplified assumption that asset returns are independent from year to year. This assumption means that the probability of a high, medium, or low return in any year is not related to the return in the prior year. More advanced asset models take account of the linkage of asset returns over time. As a result, these more advanced models may have less volatility of asset growth over time and will show a quite different distribution of financial results over time, even if all other assumptions are similar.

FIGURE 10.7 Asset Risk and Return

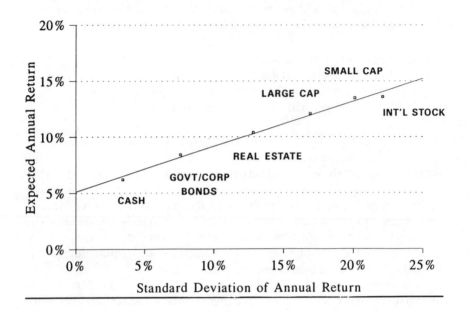

G. QUESTIONS TO ASK THE FORECAST CONSULTANT

A number of questions would be appropriate for any professional consultant, whether legal, financial, actuarial, or in some other field. These questions would request data on education, prior experience in the pension field, experience with studies for clients in the same industry or with similar types of plans, financial stability, cost, and so on.

There are also some important questions specific to asset–liability consultants, particularly regarding the quality of the consultant's models. These questions should address:

1. Access to and understanding of historical economic data;
2. Basic philosophy of the asset simulation model;
3. Features that distinguish the asset simulation model from other consultants' models;
4. Method of calculating liabilities;
5. Any limitations or simplifications of financial calculations;
6. Methodology for analyzing results.

H. THE DIFFERENCE BETWEEN EXPERIENCE AND VALUATION ASSUMPTIONS

There is one concept that many pension managers and even many consultants find difficult: the difference between experience and valuation assumptions in an asset–liability forecast.

Every actuarial valuation report is based on and reports the actuarial assumptions used for valuing the liabilities. Typically, these include demographic assumptions (mortality rates, withdrawal rates, retirement rates) and economic assumptions (discount rates, salary scale, expected return on assets). The valuation report indicates the present value of expected future benefit payments, based on those assumptions and calculated as of the specific valuation date. In other words, the report is like a snapshot of the status of the liabilities.

The liability forecast process attempts to look into the future and project next year's actuarial valuation report. For instance, if it were now one year later and we were receiving the then current report, what would the liabilities be? To make the projection, the consultant's liability model must first project the demographic data for the next year and then calculate the hypothetical liabilities as of that future date. The assumptions used for valuing the liabilities at the initial date are "valuation assumptions"; the assumptions that move the population

TABLE 10.1 Comparison of Valuation and Experience Assumptions

Assumption	Valuation	Experience
Mortality, withdrawal, retirement rates	Yes	Yes; could differ from valuation assumptions
Salary increases	Yes; usually constant for all future years	Yes; may vary from year to year
Population changes	None; closed group method used	Yes; open group method used with future new entrants
New entrants	Not used	Yes; number, age, service, and salary for future new entrants
Liability discount rate	Used to calculate present value of liabilities	Not used
Portfolio return	FAS 87 uses expected rate of return on assets to determine pension expense	Yes; brings assets forward from year to year
Ad hoc cost-of-living increases (COLA)	Usually ignored	Yes; used to update benefit amounts paid

forward from the first to the second year are "experience assumptions." The assumptions used to value the liabilities in the second and subsequent years are also valuation assumptions and may differ from the assumptions used in the first year.

Table 10.1 shows a comparison of the two categories of assumptions.

I. AN ASSET–LIABILITY FORECAST STUDY

Asset–liability studies are usually designed for the specific needs of the client and the consulting approach of the investment consultant, but there are some common elements that can be described.

A "typical" study might follow this sequence

1. An initial meeting is held to discuss objectives, economic assumptions, the investment philosophy of the plan sponsor, and any special concerns of the plan sponsor. It's fairly common for the plan sponsor to either have no knowledge of potential financial concerns or to find that the expressed concerns evolve over time as more information is gained about future possibilities. The asset assumptions are also discussed at this meeting. At this point, the consultant will need to know the current investment policy, asset classes to be included in the study, and constraints (i.e., minimums and maximums) on the allocations for each asset class.

2. The investment consultant creates parameters for a forecast model for the plan, taking into account the benefit formula and any special features of the plan.

3. A second meeting is held, normally starting with a review of deterministic forecasts for a number of scenarios. The purpose is twofold: to illuminate the key trends that might occur and to facilitate the discussion of forecast concepts. The second part of the meeting reviews a stochastic forecast of the current investment policy. This review is designed to illustrate the trends and volatility of financial results and to "diagnose" any issues that may have been unexpected. Based on the results of the stochastic forecast, the plan sponsor may confirm the concerns and objectives for the plan. Finally, there is a discussion of the selection of potential investment policies for further study. This selection is normally based on some form of efficient frontier analysis. The consultant typically selects a "short list" of investment policies and asks the plan sponsor to narrow the list to five or six finalists for further review.

4. After the second meeting, the consultant runs numerous stochastic forecasts and compares the results, not only with

respect to the pattern of portfolio returns, but particularly with respect to the patterns of financial results.

5. At a third, and usually last, meeting, the consultant presents the results of the stochastic forecasts of the selected investment policies. After a discussion of the advantages and disadvantages of each policy, the plan sponsor selects a policy.

6. In some cases, there are continuing activities that follow the basic asset–liability forecast. These include implementation issues, development of a formal investment policy statement, additional scenarios for testing or budgeting, and development of an "in-house" model for the plan sponsor's use.

J. HOW TO PICK THE BEST MIX

There is generally no magic answer as to the best investment policy. An investment policy that has a favorable trend of expected contributions might have more volatility of the projected results. Therefore, even though the average results may be satisfactory, there may be a substantial chance of poor results. Based on the plan's risk-tolerance profile, that investment policy may or may not be better than other alternatives.

Figures 10.8 through 10.10 compare several investment policies with respect to a number of financial statistics. The results are portrayed as percentiles of results over the forecast horizon. For example,

FIGURE 10.8 Average Pension Expense

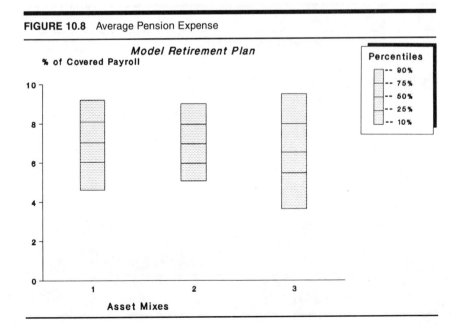

FIGURE 10.9   Average Contributions

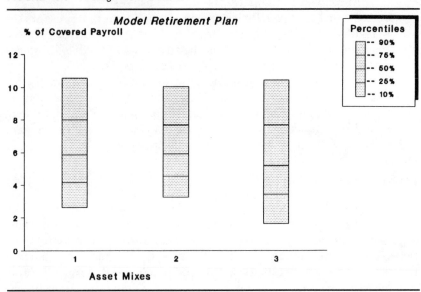

FIGURE 10.10   Final Funded Ratio—ABO

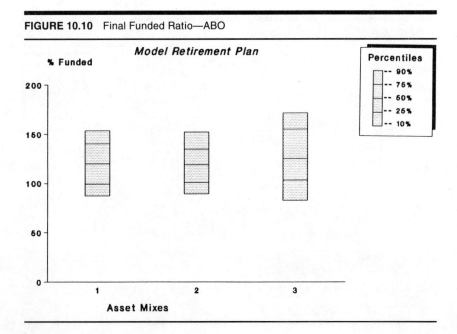

Figure 10.3 shows average contributions (as a percentage of payroll) over ten years for each investment policy. The investment policies with low medians (i.e., the 50th percentile) also tend to have the widest dispersion. In other words, looking only at contributions, there is a trade-off between the desirable aspect of a low-median contribution and the undesirable aspect of high volatility. Based on the plan's risk tolerance with respect to contributions and also with respect to other financial variables, the pension fund manager can choose the investment policy that offers the best pattern of overall results. It is unlikely that any one investment policy will be perfect for all characteristics.

K. HOW FUNDED RATIO AFFECTS THE RESULTS

This is a simple, yet complex issue. Although the funded ratio—the value of assets divided by the value of liabilities—may sound simple, a number of technical issues are involved. The definition of both assets and liabilities could be subject to the particular needs of the plan sponsor.

Normally, the value of assets, the numerator of the ratio, is the current market value of assets. This may or may not include contributions for prior years payable in the next year. Another alternative is that the asset value may be based on a smoothed value, i.e., a method designed to reduce the swings in asset values from year to year.

There are also a number of choices for the definition of liabilities, the denominator of the ratio. The liabilities may be based on accrued benefits (e.g., the FAS 87 accumulated benefit obligation, or ABO) or on projected benefits (projected benefit obligation, or PBO). Another definer of liabilities is whether they are based on FAS 87 assumptions/methodology or funding basis assumptions/methodology—or some completely different basis. Some consultants use the concept of "economic liability," which is a liability amount derived from a market-based value of future benefits. In other words, if the financial markets indicate a current long bond yield of 8 percent, then the economic liability would be based on an 8 percent discount rate.

Given all these options, the pension fund manager needs to be aware of which definition of funded ratio is being used. A higher funded ratio is obviously better than a low funded ratio, for a consistent definition of funded ratio.

The plan's funded ratio may be a key determinant of the plan sponsor's risk tolerance. A plan that is well-funded, with assets exceeding the liability for projected benefits (specifically, the funding basis actuarial liability), is said to be in "full funding" and can eliminate all or part of the required contribution for the current year. It often occurs that a plan stays in a contribution holiday for several years, and the restart of contributions could be a painful event for the plan sponsor.

Therefore, plan sponsors with fully funded plans are often interested in keeping the plan in full funding for as long as possible. This involves synchronizing the investment policy with the liability characteristics of the plan.

At the other end of the spectrum, plans that have lower assets than the FAS 87 accumulated benefit obligation (ABO) have a different type of problem. If the assets were to drop below the ABO, the plan sponsor is required to set up a liability on the sponsor's balance sheets or even an accounting charge against shareholders' equity. Because the values of assets and liabilities may be large relative to the corporation's financial statements, a small change in either assets or liabilities from year to year may generate quite a substantial charge against corporate net worth.

A plan sponsor in this position should consider whether there is corporate concern about potential charges to the corporate net worth. Many plan sponsors in this situation have taken the position that the charge to net worth is only an accounting charge and not a "real" financial issue. Other plan sponsors, perhaps because of loan covenants or other factors, are deeply concerned about such a possibility. A plan sponsor attempting to minimize the possibility of a charge to net worth would generally attempt to adopt an investment policy that closely matches liability movement.

Other plan sponsors, perhaps in the middle of the spectrum, might have critical financial statistics or risk tolerances that are specific to their corporations. These sponsors will set their investment policy so as to be most compatible with their corporations' particular objectives.

L. HOW ASSET SMOOTHING AFFECTS RESULTS

Some pension plans use a smoothed asset value for determining FAS 87 expense or funding requirements. When used for FAS 87, the smoothed value is called the market-related value of assets (MRVA); when used for funding, the smoothed value is called the actuarial value of assets (AVA). The smoothing process attempts to even-out the peaks and valleys of asset movements.

To the extent that the market value of assets fluctuates within a narrow range, smoothing will help to eliminate needless volatility. However, where the actual market value of assets trends either up or down over time, the smoothed value will tend to lag the market value. In a sustained up market, this could result in higher expense or contributions than using unsmoothed asset values. On the other hand, in a sustained down market, expense and contributions may be lower, but the smoothed value may be no more than hypothetical. There's an old saying: "You can't pay benefits with smoothed assets."

The conventional wisdom holds that smoothed asset values reduce a plan's volatility and allow the use of a higher-risk investment policy. However, a poorly designed smoothing method might actually result in higher contributions or expense over extended time periods.

M. THE CONNECTION BETWEEN FUNDING AND EXPENSE

Based on the methodology specified by the FASB for expense calculations and by federal regulations for funding requirements, the expense level has absolutely no direct impact on funding requirements. However, the funding policy definitely affects expense.

The reason for this seeming anomaly is that the expense level has absolutely no effect on asset levels. But, because the funding level directly impacts asset levels, additional contributions in one year will reduce contributions and expense in future years. (If the plan goes into full funding or zero contributions, the contributions cannot be reduced below zero.)

Another interesting difference between expense and funding is that, although contributions can never be negative, it is easily possible for pension expense to be negative, the equivalent of an income item on the corporate income statement. Many corporations have used this fact to make the pension plan a profit center.

N. WHAT SPONSORS SHOULD KNOW ABOUT THE CONSULTANT'S ASSET–LIABILITY MODEL

Some plan sponsors take the consultant's asset–liability model "on faith" and do not feel they need to know the details or inner workings of the model. Other plan sponsors may wish to inspect the model in great detail and understand the underlying formulas and assumptions. There is probably a happy medium between the two extremes.

Of all the components of asset-liability models, many plan sponsors are most comfortable with the asset portion of the model. The asset model generates 100 or more scenarios of future economic conditions. Each scenario includes projections for inflation, bond yields, and returns for each asset class.

The obvious topics to be covered in discussion of the asset model are:

- Expected inflation and the volatility of inflation. Inflation determines future payrolls and is a major component of future liabilities.
- The expected return and standard deviation of return for each asset class. These statistics can be compared to historical data and future expectations as guides for reasonability.

- The correlation among asset classes, which determines the joint movement of asset returns. As is well-known, a correlation coefficient of 1.00 means that the asset classes move in a perfectly coordinated manner, that is, an increase in one asset return is linked to a proportionate increase in the other asset classes.

These topics are reasonably familiar to plan sponsors. But given the increasing complexity in asset models, additional questions need to be asked. These questions should focus on the following two areas:

1. The linkage among bond yields, bond returns, and other asset returns. Prior to the adoption of FAS 87, there was little need to forecast interest rates or bond yields; the convention at that time was to change liability discount rates only rarely. After FAS 87, actuaries and plan sponsors became more aware of the need to vary liability discount rates with economic conditions. Now, because liabilities may vary with interest rates, the connection between interest rates and bond returns becomes much more important. Early models, which used the mean–covariance approach with log-normal distributions of returns, are no longer appropriate: the yields implied by the patterns of bond returns would have too much volatility (e.g., annual yields in excess of 100 percent could be generated). Unfortunately, the joint simulation of bond yields and asset returns causes much more complexity in economic models.

2. The return distributions over time. This question is an outgrowth of the connection of yield and return. Economic models with reasonable yield models and with linkage of the yields to asset returns found that asset returns were not independently distributed from year to year, as earlier models had assumed. The linkage, or serial correlation, between years causes the distribution of compound returns over time to be narrower than if there were no linkage.

These new issues tend to create communication difficulties between the users of the early versus the current models. In my experience, plan sponsors and consultants who are "asset-oriented" seem to be more comfortable with the traditional log-normal/independent model. Because there is a well-recognized formula for the connection between average annual returns and average compound returns, the asset-oriented plan sponsors expect that the simulated returns in the new models will follow the same familiar relationship. The actual relationships of the new models are more complex, and additional discussions of annual and compound results are typically required.

O. AN EFFICIENT FRONTIER AND HOW TO USE IT

Efficient frontiers were originally developed by Harry Markowitz, who won a Nobel prize in economics for his work.[2] An efficient frontier is a form of trade-off analysis. The underlying approach of any trade-off analysis is to compare the advantages and disadvantages of each possible alternative strategy. Normally, the old axiom, "There is no free lunch," holds, and there is rarely a strategy that has better advantages and fewer disadvantages than other strategies.

Markowitz applied this general concept to investment strategies, where the advantage of each asset strategy was represented by the expected return of that strategy. The disadvantage of each strategy was measured by the risk or volatility of that strategy; the risk measure typically used was the standard deviation (or variance) of returns. In other words, an asset strategy with a higher expected return and the same risk level is better than another strategy, and an asset strategy with a higher risk and the same expected return is worse than another strategy. However, if a strategy has both a higher expected return and higher risk, it is not clearly better or worse than another strategy; further analysis is required.

Markowitz's breakthrough, which has been commonly used by asset consultants for many years, was to develop a methodology for finding the exact set of asset strategies that were clearly preferable over all other alternatives. Figure 10.11 shows an example of an "efficient frontier"; for each portfolio on the efficient frontier, the expected return is shown on the Y axis and the risk (standard deviation of return), on the X axis. Each point on the curve is said to be efficient, because it represents an optimal combination of expected return and risk. The curve is also a frontier: it represents the boundary of asset strategies between optimality and lesser strategies. Thus, the term efficient frontier is aptly applied.

The area below the curve contains all the inefficient strategies. For each of these strategies, there is either an efficient strategy with the same risk level and a higher expected return, or an efficient strategy with the same expected return and a lower risk level. The area above the curve is empty; there are no other strategies with the same risk as an efficient portfolio and higher expected return. (This is a little oversimplified; I will explain further in a moment.)

To calculate an efficient frontier, one needs computer software, which is now widely available, and one must develop assumptions for the characteristics of each asset class. These assumptions include (1) the expected return and standard deviation of return of each asset class and (2) the correlation coefficients of the returns among all asset classes. The correlation coefficients are a measure of the joint movement of two asset

FIGURE 10.11 Model Retirement Plan

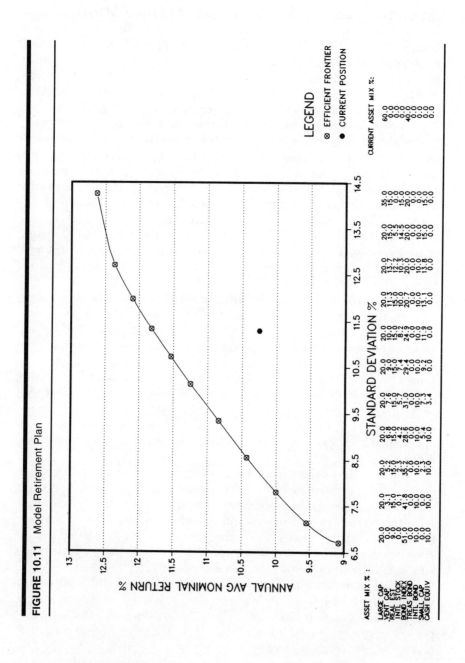

classes and range from −1 to +1. A correlation coefficient close to +1 means that the two asset classes tend to move together; a correlation coefficient close to −1 means that the two asset classes tend to move in opposite directions; a correlation coefficient close to 0.0 means that the movements of the two classes are not linked.

The final data needed for an efficient frontier are "constraints"— limitations on the possible solutions that are imposed by the user. For example, we may consider only portfolios with less than 50 percent in fixed income or more than 40 percent in equity. Some plan sponsors ask, "Why impose constraints? Let's find the best answer that the program can tell us." However, there are a number of reasons to impose constraints on the solution, even though the result will have lower expected return or higher risk than a solution without any constraints.

The primary reason to impose constraints is that the calculation of the solution, the efficient frontier, is purely a mathematical exercise, using only the risk and return of each asset class as input. In many ways, it is a "dumb" result, in that it cannot consider the investment philosophy of the user, fiduciary obligations, the "prudent person" rule, or a host of other subjective but highly important issues. Therefore, to develop sensible, practical, and usable results, the asset consultant will normally include constraints in the efficient frontier input.

Choosing constraints is something of an "art." Novice efficient frontier users usually are content to select minimums and maximums for each asset class; these are "simple" constraints. Much more control can be obtained by using "multiple" constraints, where combinations of asset classes must satisfy a mathematical relationship. For example, my favorite multiple constraint is that the allocation to large-cap stocks should be at least half of the allocation to all equity (i.e., large-cap plus small-cap, international, venture capital, and so on). This constraint eliminates portfolios where the equity component is dominated by the riskier components.

A simple (but interesting) exercise is to create efficient frontiers with varying levels of constraints, to determine the impact of each constraint and decide whether it is cost-justified.

These are the basics of efficient frontiers. The concept has been extended, over the years, to more and more powerful uses. For example, the pension plan sponsor may (and probably should) be more concerned with the plan's surplus than simply with the level of asset returns. To solve this problem, the asset consultant would use a "surplus efficient frontier." This is an extension to the asset efficient frontier; by bringing liabilities into the equation, the surplus efficient frontier finds asset mixes that have optimal combinations of expected surplus and standard deviation of surplus. The resulting portfolios should have good characteristics for managing the total plan finances.

The surplus efficient frontier has itself been extended into additional variations. By focusing on new and more complex financial statistics, a large variety of financial efficient frontiers can be constructed, given sufficient computer power. For example, with the aid of a model of the required calculations, an efficient frontier of contributions could be constructed.

Another recent extension of the efficient frontier has been in the area of the definition of risk. Rather than using the standard deviation, which measures the volatility both above and below the mean, new risk measures have been developed that measure "unfavorable risk," or the volatility of only negative results. This is thought to give solutions that represent a more realistic definition of risk for the plan sponsor.

Another variation of the efficient frontier methodology is to solve for a multiyear efficient frontier. The original Markowitz frontier is premised on expected returns and standard deviations calculated for a single time period. This approach was perfectly adequate for several years, because the single-period answer would also be optimal for multiple years, if the assumption of independence among years is accepted. Consultants and plan sponsors have been very happy to make that assumption. Only with the development of more realistic economic simulation models that include linkage between years has the single-year versus multiyear frontier become an issue. If the asset consultant is using an economic simulation with linkage between years, the single-period optimizer is not likely to provide solutions that will also be optimal over longer time periods.

The plan sponsor should discuss the following issues with the asset consultant:

- Will an efficient frontier be used to identify alternative asset strategies?
- What asset class assumptions will be used?
- What constraints will be used?
- What is the definition of risk and reward?
- Are liabilities or financial results to be included in the frontier?
- What is the time-horizon for the efficient frontier?
- Is the efficient frontier compatible with the consultant's asset simulation model, both for short-term and long-term horizons?

P. AN EFFICIENT FRONTIER USED IN AN ASSET–LIABILITY STUDY

The primary use of an efficient frontier is to identify potential asset mixes to be included in further and more detailed analyses. Because the conventional wisdom is that efficient mixes are "good" and inefficient mixes are "bad," the potential investment policies are typically restricted to efficient portfolios.

However, the efficient frontier is only a tool to assist the consultant and plan sponsor; it is not guaranteed to find the "perfect" investment strategy. First, the perfect strategy usually does not exist; there is typically no asset mix that *simultaneously* provides low contributions, low pension expense, high funded ratio, and good results on other financial measures. The process of selecting the best asset strategy typically involves evaluating the results of each potential mix on a number of dimensions of financial results, and then selecting the mix that best meets the plan sponsor's needs overall.

Second, choosing portfolios from an efficient frontier based on investment return is no guarantee that the portfolios will perform well in the pension fund context, because the frontier has little connection to the financial characteristics of the plan. A liability-based frontier may provide better linkage to the plan's liabilities, but it is still an imperfect proxy of the complex rules governing the determination of the plan's contributions, pension expense, and other financial results.

In fact, any arbitrary portfolio can be included in the detailed stochastic analysis. If chosen well, it might be reasonably close to the true efficient frontier and might very well prove to have superior results on one or more of the dimensions of financial results.

Q. SHOULD FUTURE VALUATION ASSUMPTIONS CHANGE?

Prior to FAS 87, which was adopted by most companies in 1987, the predominant custom among pension sponsors was to use long-term actuarial assumptions. The basic idea was that the actuarial assumptions for future investment return and salary increases should be based on long-run estimates of the future. The time-horizon was considered to be extremely long: the new hire who started at age 20 might still be receiving benefits at age 100, an 80-year span. Therefore, the assumptions would generally be held constant until changes in current economic factors were so dramatic that the view of long-term expectations was clearly different. The result was that actuarial assumptions were usually set on a conservative basis and rarely changed.

With the adoption of FAS 87, a light suddenly blinked on in plan sponsors' and actuaries' minds. FAS 87 introduced the "settlement rate" concept, which required that the discount rate for calculating liabilities be based on the hypothetical rate that would be used to calculate the "market" value of the liabilities, if the benefit obligations could be transferred to another party. The settlement rate was to be representative of current interest rates. Because prevailing interest rates could conceivably change substantially from year to year, liabilities and pension expense would have much higher variability than they previously had. For example, a decrease of 100 basis points in the settlement rate might typically result in a 10–15 percent increase in pension liabilities. An increase of this magnitude, or even higher, could move a plan from surplus funding to a deficit position.

Initially, plan sponsors would adjust the FAS 87 assumptions for each year based on the current level of interest rates, but leave the funding basis assumptions untouched. Although FAS 87 has had no direct impact on plan funding, it has seemed to raise the consciousness of plan sponsors to the issue of variable discount rates. Another factor has been the increase in volatility of long-term interest rates that has occurred since 1979. In today's environment, plan sponsors are much more willing to consider changes in funding assumptions and will tend to change funding assumptions to reflect substantial market changes.

In setting up an asset–liability forecast, the plan sponsor will need to discuss how future valuation assumptions will be determined. I call this the "stochastic actuary" function: conceptually, in each scenario, an actuary is determining the future valuation assumptions, based on whatever factors are thought appropriate. A naive approach would be to simply maintain all current assumptions into the future. However, because simulated market interest rates might typically vary from about 3 percent to 15 percent or more, it would seem hard to justify constant valuation assumptions for all years of every scenario.

Each sponsor can develop methodologies for the stochastic actuary that range from the simple to the complex. A common principle of the methodologies is that the FAS 87 assumptions tend to move fairly quickly, perhaps one-for-one, with market rates, and funding assumptions tend to move more slowly with market rates.

An example of a simple approach would be:

1. FAS 87 discount rates change one-for-one with simulated T-bond yields; the final result is rounded to the nearest 50 basis points.
2. Funding discount rates change 50 percent of the change in simulated T-bond yields; a minimum change of 1.5 percent from the prior discount rate is required before any change is made; the final result is rounded to the nearest 50 basis points.

A more complex approach might include tables of discount rates, based on combinations of factors in the simulation.

One additional issue is the change in salary-scale valuation. The salary scale projects current salaries "forward" for benefit calculations; the discount rate brings the value of the benefits "back" to the valuation date. In fact, the salary scale and discount rate have opposite effects on the liability values. An increase in discount rate reduces liability; an increase in salary scale increases liability. The discount rate operates from the valuation date to the benefit payment date; the salary scale operates only up to termination or retirement. Therefore, the salary scale is generally only half as powerful as the discount rate.

The treatment of salary-scale valuation assumptions typically has several alternatives, each of which has numerous proponents. A number of actuaries argue for no change in salary scale; another group suggests a constant differential between discount rate and salary scale; a third group suggests a proportional change of salary scale to discount rate. Probably a number of additional alternatives have been used; there has been little standardization on the issue of changing salary-scale valuation.

Because salary scale and discount rate have opposite effect on the liabilities (for salary-related plans) a larger change in salary scale will tend to reduce the volatility of liabilities more than a smaller change will, for the same change in discount rate. Therefore, plan sponsors who are concerned with the volatility of pension liabilities need to be aware of the methodology for changing future valuation assumptions and, particularly, the connection between salary scale and discount rate.

R. WHICH IS MORE IMPORTANT: EXPENSE OR CONTRIBUTIONS?

In a survey of a group of plan sponsors about goals for financial results, a strong majority would almost certainly opt for both low expense and low contributions. Furthermore, the majority would probably hope for low volatility in expense and contribution levels, so that there would be little chance of a bad year. It goes without saying that a strong funded ratio would also be desirable.

However, the reality is that these financial results are interrelated in complex ways. For example, there is a "one-way" relationship between contribution and expense. A change in expense levels has absolutely no effect on contributions; however, a decrease in contributions will lower the plan assets and increase future expense.

There is no simple answer to the priority of contribution and expense, because there are many arguments on each side. A number of plan sponsors, such as regulated utilities and defense contractors, are primarily concerned with reimbursements for pension cost and with whatever framework has been decreed by the regulatory body. That framework may vary from industry to industry and even from state to state.

For other plan sponsors, there are circumstances that may dictate a particular choice. For example, a corporation trying to manage cash flow will tend to be most concerned with contributions. Plan sponsors with overfunded plans are usually concerned with keeping the plan in the "contribution holiday" status.

Plan sponsors that consider the pension plan a profit center will tend to focus on pension expense, possibly even attaining a negative expense posture, which is equivalent to generating corporate income.

A minority of plan sponsors have recognized that the long-term health of the plan is not controlled by the arbitrary requirements for expense and contribution. Their view is that they should manage the "true" cost of the plan—a conceptual cost, unconstrained by regulatory restrictions. In this view, the true cost represents the long-term cost of providing plan benefits, and expense and contributions are seen as short-term costs, primarily determined by arbitrary accounting and regulatory requirements. Although everything should balance out in the long run, this group of plan sponsors believes that the specific long-term cost is the priority.

S. THE OUTPUT OF AN ASSET–LIABILITY FORECAST

There are two types of forecasts—(1) deterministic and (2) stochastic—so there are at least two types of output. Because a deterministic forecast is simply the results for one scenario, the output is simply the expense, contribution, and funded ratio over time. This information can be presented in a straightforward manner in two or three graphs. Figures 10.2 and 10.3 presented examples of the results of deterministic forecasts.

A question that commonly arises is whether the expense and contribution should be presented as a dollar amount or as a percentage of pay. Both ways can be used, but additional graphs must then be analyzed. Although dollar amounts would seem to be more meaningful, they are most relevant to the near term and least relevant to a long-term forecast. For example, over the life of a 20-year forecast, the contribution would be heavily impacted by the wage inflation over 20 years. At an annual wage inflation rate of 7 percent, average wages would increase approximately 286 percent over 20 years; yet, a 286 percent increase in the dollar amount of pension expense, viewed by itself, might be seen as a highly unacceptable increase. Expressing expense and contribution as a percentage of pay gives the proper long-term perspective on pension costs.

The output of a stochastic forecast is much more voluminous than the output of a deterministic forecast. Just think of taking the output for one deterministic forecast and repeating it 100 times or more to achieve a stochastic forecast, which is equivalent "in volume" to several hundred deterministic forecasts. Often, an asset–liability study will include stochastic forecasts for ten or more asset mixes, creating output larger by an order of magnitude. The amount of output from a stochastic forecast could be very unwieldy, unless it is simplified in two ways:

1. The stochastic output is almost always presented in graphic form. More numerical results are created than any one person can absorb, and graphs have proved successful in portraying the key points to be learned from the output.
2. Two principal types of graphs are commonly used: one type shows trend and volatility over time for each asset mix, and the other compares the results of several mixes simultaneously.

Figure 10.12 is an example of a graph showing the trend and volatility of pension expense (as a percent of payroll) over 20 years. The first thing to notice is that the distribution of results for each year is shown, based on the percentiles of the simulated results in each year. The 90th percentile means that 90 percent of the results are below that point and 10 percent are above that point. The 50th percentile is the median or midpoint of the distribution. The results of this simulation can be analyzed by checking the pattern of annual medians and the spread of results around the median.

Figure 10.13 is an example of a graph comparing the pension expense percent for ten asset mixes. At first glance, this graph may look similar to Figure 10.12, but it is actually quite different. Rather than show year-by-year results, Figure 10.13 shows the distribution of ten-year average

FIGURE 10.12   Twenty Year Employer Pension Expense (%)

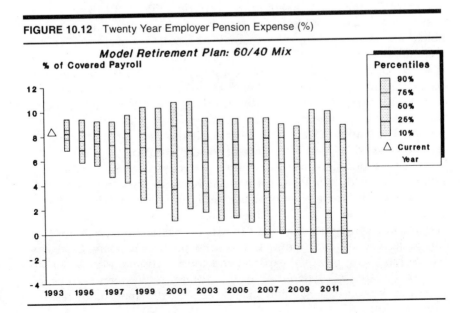

FIGURE 10.13 Average Pension Expense for the Current Asset Mix and Nine Portfolios from an Efficient Frontier

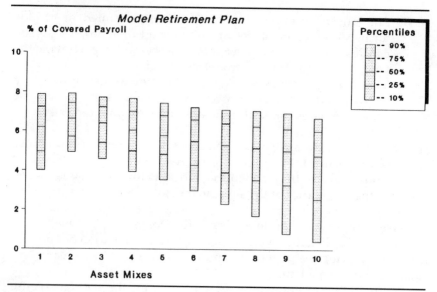

expense. In other words, for each stochastic scenario, the average expense (as a percentage of pay) over ten years is calculated, giving one statistic for each of the 100 or more scenarios. Figure 10.13 shows the distribution of that statistic for each mix and is much more manageable than trying to compare year-by-year results for each mix. This is a common method of selecting a recommended asset mix for the future. By comparing the median results to the positive and negative spread around the median, the plan sponsor can see the effect of different asset mixes on the plan's financial results. A bar graph showing the percentiles of the distribution is more informative than just reporting the standard deviation, because it shows whether the volatility is on the "good" or "bad" side of the distribution.

The final decision on the best asset mix is usually based on an analysis of several dimensions of financial results. These might include comparisons of expense, contribution, and funded ratio. It is also possible to analyze the pattern of changes from year to year, the probability of being in a contribution holiday, or other statistical relationships that can be derived from the simulation results. Some plan sponsors are interested in attaining equal expense and contribution; it's an easy matter to calculate the distribution of the difference between each year's contribution and expense and include that in the analysis of results.

T. THE POTENTIAL FAS 87 BALANCE SHEET AND UNDERFUNDED PLANS

Should the potential FAS 87 balance sheet impact be of concern to underfunded plans? This is a very interesting question, because plan sponsors tend to have different answers, depending on their own point of view and the financial circumstances of their plan and their company.

First, let's describe the issue. Under FAS 87, the accumulated benefit obligation (ABO) must be calculated. This is the actuarial liability for all benefits accrued to date and excludes the effect of future salary increases. If the market value of assets exceeds the ABO on the valuation date, then the plan can completely ignore the issue, at least for that year.

However, if the market value of assets is less than the ABO, then the plan sponsor must establish an additional liability on the *plan sponsor's* balance sheet. Usually, this liability can be offset by an equal intangible asset, but it does reduce the plan sponsor's tangible net worth. (This occurs because the liabilities are increased but the offsetting asset is intangible.) This reduction may be a concern to plan sponsors with loan provisions that require specific levels of tangible net worth.

In some cases, which typically occur when the dollar amount of the deficit is greater than the deficit when the plan adopted FAS 87 (this is not quite correct, but suffices as a simple explanation), then the intangible asset will be less than the additional liability, and the plan sponsor will have a charge to corporate net worth. This is an actual reduction to shareholder equity.

There are a number of subtleties to this calculation. First, because the comparison is based on the dollar amount of the deficit, a plan with growing assets and liabilities must improve its funded ratio to avoid future charges to net worth. Second, because one of the factors is the remaining balance of the original unfunded liability (a detail I hoped to avoid), which decreases over time, the deficit must steadily improve to keep pace with the amortization of the declining balance. Third, because the ABO is based on the current settlement rate, a substantial decline in market interest rates could cause a substantial increase in the ABO; if assets do not also increase, there will be a dramatic increase in the plan's deficit. This gives an additional incentive for liability mimicking assets. Finally, from a stochastic point of view, it turns out that the charge to net worth is like the "tail that wagged the dog." By that I mean, for many plans, the possibility of a charge to net worth is very small (perhaps 5 percent or less), but when it does occur, it tends to take a heavy toll.

Table 10.2 gives an example of the dynamics affecting the charge to net worth. A small change in liabilities and/or a small change in assets

TABLE 10.2 FAS 87 Balance Sheet Impact

	Base Case	2 Percent Decline in Settlement Rate	2 Percent Decline in Asset Value	2 Percent Decline in Settlement Rate and 20 Percent Decline in Asset Value
ABO	104	121	104	121
Less: Assets	−76	−76	−61	−61
Minimum Liability	28	45	43	60
Less: Accrued Expense	−13	−13	−13	−13
Additional Liability	15	32	30	47
Less: Actual Intangible Asset (Max = 20)	−15	−20	−20	−20
Charge to Corporate Net Worth	0	12	10	27

may have a dramatic impact on corporate net worth. A plan with $75 million in assets could conceivably have a "worst case" scenario of a $27 million impact on the corporate balance sheet.

Given all these seemingly dire factors, my experience has been that many plan sponsors who are potentially exposed to this problem are not overly concerned. The most common response seems to be that this is a "paper transaction," only an "accounting issue," and does not reflect economic reality. Financially healthy corporations do not normally manage their plans with the primary objective of minimizing the balance sheet liability.

However, a number of plan sponsors have adjusted their investment policy to have assets that tend to move with the ABO as interest rates change. This strategy requires an investment policy that takes into account the characteristics of the liability, the funded status of the plan, and the future cash flows. Plan sponsors in this situation have typically turned to extremely long-duration assets to help balance the sensitivity of the ABO to current interest rates.

U. INTEGRATING PENSION PLAN FORECAST RESULTS WITH CORPORATE RESULTS

For plan sponsors who model their corporate financial statements or at least do some type of corporate financial forecast, it is fairly easy to include a deterministic pension with the corporate model. The economic scenarios for a corporate model should be easily handled by a pension model.

Stochastic forecasts are quite a different matter. First, very few corporations (except for financial corporations, such as insurance companies) seem to use stochastic forecasting for their corporate financial projections. Second, the corporate model is developed and operated by the corporate staff, but the pension model is typically developed and operated by the plan's actuarial consultant, probably using quite different and incompatible software. It would seem to be a quite challenging project to bring together a stochastic corporate model and a stochastic pension forecast. If any plan sponsors are doing it, they are keeping it secret.

V. LIMITATIONS OF ASSET–LIABILITY FORECASTING

Asset–liability forecasting has a number of important limitations. Consider all the possible future events that are usually ignored, for the purpose of simplicity or "unforeseeability":

- Worldwide nuclear war;
- Prolonged economic depression;
- Catastrophic disease;
- Hyperinflation;
- Extension of the human life span;
- Elimination of all government pension regulations.

This is not to say that the results of a asset-liability forecast are not appropriate for decision making. For example, it would probably not be reasonable to make a strategic investment decision on the basis of the slim possibility that some of the above events might occur. In the 99.9 percent of the time that the event did not occur, the plan would likely have sub-par results; in the .1 percent of time that the event occurred, nobody would care about the pension results.

On a practical level, the plan sponsor should have some awareness of the limitation of the forecast for his or her plan. Although substantial judgment is involved, there are a number of basic issues to be aware of.

Earlier, we discussed the questions that should be asked about the consultant's asset model. The plan sponsor should also be aware of the methodology for projecting future liabilities. Some consultants use a "back-of-the-envelope" method for projecting liabilities; others use a highly sophisticated projection methodology. Surprisingly, the sophisticated methodology is not necessarily better in every case, because it requires a number of assumptions for future experience that may be only rough guesses. A simple liability forecast, from a knowledgeable actuarial consultant who is familiar with the overall plan demographics, may be superior to a sophisticated forecast. Although most plan sponsors do not want to know the details of the liability forecast, it is valuable to ask basic questions about the methodology.

W. THE VALIDITY OF FORECASTS

Don't all forecasts just confirm what the pension manager could have predicted? Quite a few plan sponsors and consultants have made the comment that the asset–liability forecast just "told me what I already knew." In my experience, this is an after-the-fact statement that is made when the results of the study are presented clearly and the decisions are agreeable. The plan sponsor or consultant remembers the recent process leading up to the final recommendations, but has forgotten the meager knowledge available at the start of the study. Armstrong[3] suggests that this is a common occurrence and that if participants are asked to write down their expectations prior to the study, this type of comment will disappear.

Ironically, this type of comment can mean that the study was so clearly and logically presented that the results were absorbed into the plan sponsor's thoughts in the course of the study and taken as his or her own thoughts.

X. AVAILABLE FINANCIAL RESULTS

What types of financial results are available to be analyzed? A sophisticated asset–liability model is able to simulate the full financial results of the pension plan, including the primary financial results of pension expense, contributions, asset values, and funded ratios. In order to more fully understand the patterns of results, the model should also be able to give the full details of any specific scenario in the stochastic forecast. In other words, if someone wants to see why the 90th percentile of pension expense is 9.3 percent of pay, it should be possible to isolate the scenario with the 90th percentile result and fully analyze that scenario in great detail. This "microscopic" view would show the experience assumptions, the valuation actuarial assumptions for each year, minimum and maximum contribution requirements, the calculation of pension expense, and the progression of asset values.

Analyzing some of the outlier scenarios with a "zoom lens" often gives insights into the dynamics of the plan that are not visible in a deterministic forecast.

Y. BASIS OF INVESTMENT POLICY

Should investment policy be asset-based or liability–surplus-based? A number of approaches to determining investment policy involve various levels of sophistication. In general, the simplest approaches (usually asset-based) are more generic, and the more complex approaches (liability–surplus-based) are more specific to the needs and objectives of the plan sponsor.

The absolutely simplest approach would be to pick the average investment policy used by similar pension plans. The average corporate defined-benefit plan tends to have about 60 percent in equity securities and 40 percent in fixed-income securities; the opposite percentages apply for the average public defined-benefit plan. For a plan sponsor who is willing to assume that the plan's characteristics and needs are close to the average, 60/40 (or 40/60) may be a valid answer.

The next level of complexity would be to select an investment policy based only on analysis of asset characteristics. This analysis would probably include the traditional efficient frontier. An experienced investment consultant can usually make an intelligent recommendation as to the degree of risk that the pension fund can reasonably undertake. Once the efficient frontier is narrowed to a small segment, it is fairly easy to make a final selection of an investment policy. The success of this approach is highly dependent on the experience of the consultant. If the plan has some unusual features or special concerns, the answer may not reflect the specific characteristics of the plan.

Although many plan sponsors believe that an asset-only analysis is sufficient, an efficient frontier that ignores the interaction of assets and liabilities may include portfolios with a surprisingly high volatility of financial results. Figure 10.14 shows that the surplus risk and reward for a portfolio with the least asset risk may be substantially inferior to the risk

FIGURE 10.14 Mix with Lowest Asset Risk May Be Very "Surplus Risky"

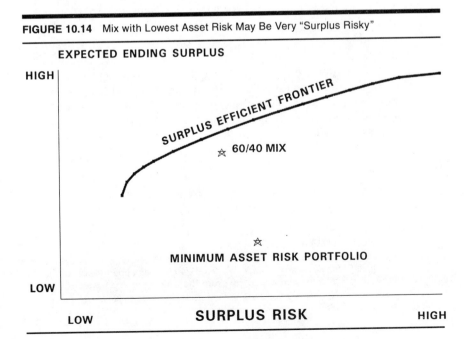

and reward of a surplus efficient frontier. Choosing a seemingly low risk portfolio may actually result in unexpected financial risk.

The highest level of complexity is the full asset–liability study. This takes into account the complete liability and financial characteristics and can specifically model the special features of the plan. Because the output of the asset–liability forecast is in terms of the financial results of the plan, the asset policy can be chosen in the context of the full set of financial results.

There are some instances where it is possible to do a simplified (i.e., asset-only) analysis:

1. Small asset size;
2. No unusual features;
3. Large surplus.

On the other hand, it is almost mandatory for large, underfunded plans with special features to perform a very detailed asset-liability study.

Z. NEW ADVANCES FOR ASSET–LIABILITY FORECASTING

My personal opinion is that asset–liability forecasting will tend to diverge in two directions: (1) simpler, easier-to-use systems and (2) more sophisticated and complex systems for highly theoretical analysis.

Many plan sponsors have expressed a strong desire to have their own system on a personal computer in their office. Although the asset–liability forecast is highly complex, many consultants are developing systems to meet that need. This requires not only a user-friendly system, but development of an educational process to support the plan sponsor.

At the same time, consultants are busy developing advanced techniques with sophisticated asset-simulation models, new types of efficient frontiers, and even dynamic asset rebalancing. Integration of pension (and postretirement welfare) forecasting models with stochastic models of corporate financial results will be an important tool for the CFOs of the future.

NOTES

1. FASB Statement No. 87, "Employers' Accounting for Pensions" (Norwalk, CT: Financial Accounting Foundation, 1985).
2. Interested readers can refer to Harry Markowitz, *Mean-Variance Analysis in Portfolio Choice and Capital Markets.* Oxford: Basil Blackwell, 1987. The appendix of the book contains the source code for a computer program that calculates an efficient frontier.
3. J. Scott Armstrong, *Long-Range Forecasting: From Crystal Ball to Computer* (New York, John Wiley & Sons, 1985).

11

The Information Content of Leading Indicators and Tactical Asset Allocation

Roger G. Clarke
President and Chief Investment Officer
TSA Capital Management
Los Angeles, California

Meir Statman
Professor of Finance
Santa Clara University
Santa Clara, California

Tactical asset allocators who attempt to outperform static asset allocation portfolios face two challenges:

1. They must develop reliable models from variables that are leading indicators of security returns;
2. They must have enough information to overcome the cost of transactions incurred as they shift funds from one class of assets to another.

How much information is needed to beat static benchmarks?

DECISION FRAMEWORK FOR A TACTICAL ASSET ALLOCATOR

Consider an asset allocator who attempts to maximize expected utility by constructing a portfolio of stocks and cash based on a set of leading indicators of stock and cash returns.[1] Leading indicators include measures of value, such as dividend yield; measures of economic activity, such as changes in the GNP; measures of monetary policy, such as changes in the money supply; measures of sentiment, such as the level of short sales; and many others.[2] The expected return and variance of the portfolio, given the set of leading indicators, are:

$$E(R_{t+1}|I_t) = w\ E(S_{t+1}|I_t) + (1 - w)C \tag{1}$$

$$\sigma^2_{R/I} = w^2\sigma^2_{S/I} \tag{2}$$

where

$w =$ the proportion of the portfolio invested in stocks
$E(S_{t+1}|I_t) =$ the expected return on stocks in period $t + 1$, given the set of leading indicators in period t
$C =$ the return on cash
$\sigma^2_{S/I} =$ the variance of the return on stocks, given the set of leading indicators in period t.

The asset allocator attempts to maximize the expected utility:

$$E(U_{t+1}|I_t) = E(R_{t+1}|I_t) - \frac{\sigma^2_{R/I}}{RT} \tag{3}$$

where

$E(U_{t+1}|I_t) =$ the investor's expected utility in period $t + 1$
$RT =$ the investor's risk tolerance.

Maximizing expected utility requires that:

$$\frac{dE(U_{t+1}|I_t)}{dw} = E(S_{t+1}|I_t) - C - \frac{2w\sigma^2_{S/I}}{RT} = 0. \tag{4}$$

Solving for the optimal proportion in stocks gives:

$$w^* = \left(\frac{E(S_{t+1}|I_t) - C}{2\sigma^2_{R/I}}\right)RT. \tag{5}$$

Suppose that the asset allocator knows the return on cash. How does the asset allocator form expectations about the expected return on stocks? The asset allocator begins with the unconditional expected return on stocks—the return expected when an asset allocator has no information other than the long-run average return on stocks. Next, the long-run return is modified by the asset allocator based on knowledge of leading indicators.

To simplify our exposition, we assume that the asset allocator uses a model containing only one leading indicator for stock returns. We write the relationship between the current level of the leading indicator and future stock returns as:

$$S_{t+1} = \overline{S} + \beta I_t + e_{t+1} \tag{6}$$

where

> S_{t+1} = return on stocks in the (coming) period
> $\overline{S}$ = the long-run expected return on stocks
> β = the sensitivity of stock returns to changes in the leading indicator
> I_t = the value of the leading indicator at time t
> e_{t+1} = the residual or error term.

For simplicity, we normalize the leading indicator so that its mean is zero and its standard deviation is one. In addition, we assume that the leading indicator, stock returns, and the error term are normally distributed.[3]

The expected return on stocks for a given value of the leading indicator is:

$$E(S_{t+1}|I_t) = \overline{S} + \beta I_t \tag{7}$$

where

> $\beta = \dfrac{\rho \sigma_s}{\sigma_I}$
> ρ = the correlation coefficient between I_t and next period's stock returns, S_{t+1}
> σ_s = the long-run standard deviation of stock returns
> σ_I = the standard deviation of the leading indicator.

The variance of the return on stocks, given the leading indicator, depends on the variance of the error in the information set in equation (6):[4]

$$\sigma^2_{S/I} = \sigma^2_e$$
$$= \sigma^2_s(1 - \rho^2). \tag{8}$$

When the asset allocator has no information ($\rho = 0$), the variance of the conditional stock returns is equal to the long-run variance of stock returns. When the asset allocator has perfect information ($\rho = 1$), the variance of the conditional stock returns is zero. Using these values in equation (5) yields the optimal proportion of stocks in the portfolio, given the asset allocator's information as:

$$w^* = \frac{(\bar{S} + \rho\sigma_s I_t / \sigma_I - C)RT}{2(1 - \rho^2)\sigma^2_S}. \tag{9}$$

The optimal proportion in stocks for an asset allocator with no information is:

$$w^* = \frac{(\bar{S} - C)RT}{2\sigma^2_t}. \tag{10}$$

We assume in all our examples here that the return on cash, C, is 7.0 percent and that the long-run expected return on stocks, $\bar{S}$, is 15.5 percent, implying a risk premium of 8.5 percent. We use 20.5 percent as the long-run standard deviation of the return on stocks.[5]

The risk tolerance of an asset allocator who splits a portfolio equally between stocks and cash is:

$$RT = \frac{2w^*\sigma^2_s}{(\bar{S} - C)}$$

$$= \frac{2(0.5)(20.5)^2}{(15.5 - 7.0)}$$

$$= 49.44.$$

RISK AND RETURN OF TACTICAL ASSET ALLOCATION

To see the impact of information on performance, we compare the risk and return of an investor choosing a static benchmark portfolio with those received by an asset allocator with the same risk tolerance.

The expected return and standard deviation of a benchmark that is equally split between stocks and cash ($w = 0.5$) is:

$$E(R) = w\bar{S} + (1 - w)C$$

$$= 11.30\%$$

$$\sigma_R = w\sigma_s$$

$$= 10.3\%.$$

The risk and return of the asset allocator's portfolio can be investigated through simulation. For any given level of information in the leading indicator, the asset allocator puts part of the portfolio in stocks and the remainder in cash. For example, consider the case where the correlation between the leading indicator and subsequent stock returns is 0.3. If the leading indicator, drawn randomly from a normal distribution with a mean of zero and a standard deviation of one, is -0.5, the conditional expected return on stocks is:

$$E(S|I) = \overline{S} + \rho\sigma_s I/\sigma_I$$
$$= 15.5 + 0.3(20.5)(-0.5)/(1.0)$$
$$= 12.43$$

and the standard deviation of the conditional stock return is:

$$\sigma_{S/I} = \sigma_s\sqrt{1 - \rho^2}$$
$$= 20.5\sqrt{1 - 0.3^2}$$
$$= 19.56.$$

How should the asset allocator construct the portfolio given these expectations? Equation (5) indicates that the proportion placed in stock is:

$$w^* = \frac{(E(R|I) - C)RT}{2\sigma^2_{S/I}}.$$

An investor with a risk tolerance of 49.44 allocates 35.1 percent to stocks:

$$w^* = \frac{(12.43 - 7.0)49.44}{2(19.56)^2}$$
$$= 35.1\%$$

which is lower than the benchmark position of 50 percent in stocks.

We proceed in the simulation by drawing stock returns from a normal distribution with a mean of 12.43 percent and a standard deviation of 19.56 percent. The return to the asset allocator's portfolio reflects the proportions invested in stocks and cash and their respective returns.

In summary, the simulation proceeds in three stages. The first stage involves the generation of a leading indicator from its assumed distribution. The second stage involves the calculation of an expected return on stocks conditional on the leading indicator. The asset allocator chooses the proportion to invest in stocks based on this expectation.[6] The third stage involves the generation of an actual stock return from a distribution with the conditional expected stock return and standard deviation.

We repeated the three-stage process 3,000 times so that 3,000 returns for the asset allocator's portfolio were generated. The mean return on the portfolio, when the correlation coefficient was 0.2, was 12.4 percent, a 1.1 percent "value-added" over the 11.3 percent mean return of the benchmark. Table 11.1 reveals that an increase in information leads to an increase in the mean return of the asset allocator's portfolio. The mean portfolio return reaches 20.1 percent when the correlation between the leading indicator and future stock returns is a perfect 1.0.

Note that the risk of the portfolio of an asset allocator is higher than that of the benchmark portfolio. The proportion of stock in the benchmark portfolio is 50 percent. However, because stocks outperform cash in 67 percent of all periods, information leads asset allocators to increase the proportion allocated to stocks beyond 50 percent. An asset allocator with perfect information allocates all funds to stocks in 67 percent of all periods and allocates all funds to cash in 33 percent of all periods.[7] An asset allocator with some but not perfect information is more heavily invested in stocks when the expected return on stocks is high, and less heavily invested in stocks when the expected return on stocks is low.

Figure 11.1 shows that the increase in the expected return on an asset allocator's portfolio relative to that of a benchmark portfolio is due to more than a higher average proportion of the portfolio in stocks. The straight line represents the risk and return of a benchmark portfolio where the (constant) proportion in stocks ranges from zero to 100 percent. The curved line represents the risk and return of an asset allocator's portfolio. Note that the asset allocator achieves higher expected

---

TABLE 11.1 Risk and Return of an Asset Allocator's Portfolio (Annual Reallocation)

Information Correlation with Stock Returns	Mean Annual Return on Asset Allocator's Portfolio	Value Added by Asset Allocator Relative to 50–50 Balanced Portfolio	Standard Deviation of Asset Allocator's Portfolio	Mean Proportion Invested in Stocks
0.0	11.3	0.0	10.3	0.50
0.1	11.5	0.2	10.7	0.51
0.2	12.4	1.1	12.2	0.52
0.3	13.5	2.2	13.7	0.54
0.4	14.6	3.3	14.8	0.56
0.5	15.6	4.3	15.5	0.58
0.6	16.6	5.3	15.9	0.60
0.7	17.6	6.3	15.9	0.62
0.8	18.4	7.1	15.8	0.63
0.9	19.3	8.0	15.3	0.65
1.0	20.1	8.8	14.7	0.67

FIGURE 11.1 Risk–Return Trade-Off with Information

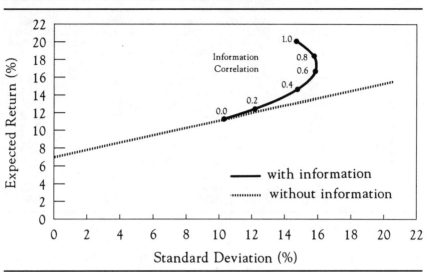

returns for each level of standard deviation. Furthermore, standard deviation is not always a good measure of risk because the distribution of returns on the asset allocator's portfolio becomes skewed to the right as the amount of information increases. The skewed distribution comes from the optionlike characteristics of asset allocation. Indeed, Merton (1981)[8] has compared the price of a call option on stocks to the value of perfect information about future stock returns.[9]

EFFECTS OF A MOVE FROM AN ANNUAL TO A MONTHLY MODEL

Table 11.2 presents the results of a simulation identical to the one presented in Table 11.1, except that monthly rather than annual reallocations are allowed. A 0.2 correlation coefficient brings an asset allocator a value-added of 1.1 percent when only annual reallocations are allowed. However, when monthly reallocations are allowed, a 0.2 correlation brings an expected return of 16.7 percent, a 5.4 percent value-added over the benchmark portfolio.

A comparison of the success of asset allocation with annual reallocation versus asset allocation with monthly reallocation might lead to the conclusion that an increase in the frequency of reallocation (without considering transaction costs) always increases the value added by an asset allocator. This conclusion is not always warranted. We set the

TABLE 11.2 Risk and Return of an Asset Allocator's Portfolio (Monthly Reallocation)

Information Correlation with Stock Returns	Mean Annual Return on Asset Allocator's Portfolio	Value Added by Asset Allocator Relative to 50–50 Balanced Portfolio	Standard Deviation of Asset Allocator's Portfolio	Mean Proportion Invested in Stocks
0.0	11.3	0.0	10.3	0.50
0.1	13.5	2.2	12.4	0.50
0.2	16.7	5.4	13.7	0.51
0.3	19.7	8.4	14.2	0.52
0.4	22.6	11.3	14.4	0.52
0.5	25.5	14.2	14.4	0.53
0.6	28.3	17.0	14.4	0.53
0.7	31.1	19.8	14.1	0.54
0.8	33.9	22.6	13.8	0.54
0.9	36.7	25.4	13.4	0.55
1.0	39.5	28.2	12.8	0.55

parameters for the simulation with monthly reallocation to be identical to the parameters with annual reallocation.[10] In particular, we assumed that the correlation coefficient between the leading indicator and subsequent stock returns does not decline as an asset allocator shifts from a model that allows annual reallocation to a model that allows monthly reallocation.

This assumption might not be justified. We can expect an increase in "noise" and a decrease in availability of data as the length of the period drops from a year to a month; consequently, the correlation coefficient is likely to decline. The decline in correlation does not necessarily eliminate the benefits of the increase in the frequency of reallocation. The optimal period length is the one that maximizes the value added by the asset allocator.

What can we say, then, about the effectiveness of an asset allocation portfolio relative to the benchmark portfolio? We know that the effectiveness of asset allocation increases with the level of information available to the investor. That, by itself, is not surprising. More surprising is the fact that relatively modest amounts of information add considerable value. A 0.2 correlation (R^2 of 0.04) with monthly reallocation brings an expected return that is 5.4 percentage points higher than the expected return available to one who buys and hold the benchmark portfolio.

PROBABILITIES OF SUCCESSFUL TACTICAL ASSET ALLOCATION

An asset allocator's portfolio performs at least as well as the benchmark when:

$$R^* \geq R_B \tag{11}$$

where

R^* = the asset allocator's portfolio return
R_B = the benchmark portfolio's return.

If w^* represents the proportion of stocks in the asset allocator's portfolio and w represents the proportion of stocks in the benchmark, we can rewrite equation (11) as:

$$w^*S + (1 - w^*)C \geq w_BS + (1 - w_B)C \tag{12}$$

or, equivalently,

$$(w^* - w_B)S \geq (w^* - w_B)C. \tag{13}$$

If the asset allocator's portfolio is overweighted in stocks relative to the benchmark ($w^* \geq w_B$), equation (13) is equivalent to requiring that the return on stocks be greater than or equal to the return on cash. If the investor's portfolio is underweighted in stocks relative to the benchmark, equation (13) is equivalent to requiring that the return on stocks be less than or equal to the return on cash.

Consequently, the ex ante probability that the investor's portfolio will do at least as well as the benchmark can be written as:[11]

$$\text{Prob}(R^* > R_B) = \text{Prob}(S \geq C | w^* \geq w_B)\text{Prob}(w^* \geq w_B) \\ + \text{Prob}(S \geq C | w^* < w_B)\text{Prob}(w^* < w_B). \tag{14}$$

Consider the case where the correlation coefficient between the leading indicator and subsequent stock returns is 0.2. Table 11.3 shows that the asset allocator's return is greater than or equal to the benchmark in 72 percent of all periods when stocks are overweighted. Note that stocks are overweighted in 53 percent of all periods. The asset allocator's portfolio return is greater than or equal to the benchmark in 39 percent of all periods when stocks are underweighted. Note that stocks are underweighted in 47 percent of all periods. Combining these probabilities indicates that the asset allocator's return is greater than or equal to the benchmark in 56 percent of all periods. An investor with no information holds the benchmark and adds no value. An asset allocator with information represented by a correlation of 0.2 has an expected value-added of 1.1 percent but runs the risk of underperforming the benchmark portfolio in 44 percent of all periods.

TABLE 11.3 Probability of the Asset Allocator Performing as Well as the Benchmark (Annual Reallocation)

Correlation between Leading Indicator and Stocks	Prob $(R^* \geq R_B \| w^* \geq w_B)$	Prob $(w^* \geq w_B)$	Prob $(R^* \geq R \| w^* < w_B)$	Prob $(w^* < w_B)$	Prob $(R^* \geq R_B)$
0.0	1.00	1.00	—	0.00	1.00
0.1	0.70	0.51	0.37	0.49	0.54
0.2	0.72	0.53	0.39	0.47	0.56
0.3	0.74	0.54	0.42	0.46	0.59
0.4	0.77	0.56	0.47	0.44	0.64
0.5	0.79	0.57	0.52	0.43	0.67
0.6	0.82	0.59	0.56	0.41	0.71
0.7	0.84	0.61	0.64	0.39	0.76
0.8	0.87	0.63	0.71	0.37	0.81
0.9	0.89	0.65	0.81	0.35	0.86
1.0	1.00	0.67	1.00	0.33	1.00

EFFECT OF TRANSACTION COSTS

So far, we have assumed that an asset allocator can switch from stocks to cash and back without incurring transaction costs. Now we remove this assumption.

We estimate the expected return and standard deviation of an asset allocator's portfolio, assuming two levels of transaction costs. The first level, 0.1 percent one-way transaction, represents the range of transaction costs when futures contracts are used to move from one asset class to another. The second level, 1.0 percent, represents the range of transaction costs when physical assets are used. Table 11.4 compares these expected returns with those obtained without transaction costs.

Consider again the case of a 0.2 correlation coefficient. Recall that value added by asset allocation with monthly revisions and without transaction costs is 5.4 percent. The 0.1 percent transaction cost reduces the value-added to 4.8 percent. However, the 1.0 percent transaction cost sends the value-added negative, dropping it from 5.4 to −0.3 percent.

COST OF OVERESTIMATING CORRELATION

Imagine that the true correlation between the leading indicator and subsequent stock returns is 0.2, but the asset allocator concludes, erroneously, that the correlation is higher—say, 0.4. An overestimation of the true correlation might occur if correlations, estimated on the basis of past experience, do not persist in the future. An asset allocator who makes no allowance for such misestimation will make suboptimal

TABLE 11.4 Effect of Transactions Costs on the Value Added by Asset Allocation
(Monthly Reallocation)

Correlation between Leading Indicator and Stock Returns	Value Added when Transactions Costs Are:		
	0.0%	0.1%	1.0%
0.0	0.0	0.0	0.0
0.1	2.2	1.8	−2.4
0.2	5.4	4.8	−0.3
0.3	8.4	7.8	2.5
0.4	11.3	10.7	5.3
0.5	14.2	13.6	8.1
0.6	17.0	16.4	10.9
0.7	19.8	19.2	13.7
0.8	22.6	22.0	16.5
0.9	25.4	24.8	19.3
1.0	28.2	27.6	22.1

decisions. Specifically, he or she will, in some cases, choose to invest in cash or in stocks more than the optimal amounts.

How costly is the error that results from overestimating correlations? Tables 11.5 and 11.6 present the results. For example, the value-added by the asset allocator who estimates a 0.2 correlation correctly is 4.8 percent, assuming a transaction cost of 0.1 percent and monthly reallocation. The value-added actually increases to 5.2 percent when the 0.2 true correlation is overestimated as 0.4. This surprising result occurs because overestimation leads to an increase in the allocation to the higher return stocks on average. However, an overestimation of information is expensive when transaction costs are high. For example, an asset allocator without information who overestimates the information at a correlation of 0.2 can expect to lose −5.6 percent per year when the one-way transaction cost is 1.0 percent.

TABLE 11.5 Effect of Misestimation of Correlation on Value Added by Asset
Allocation (Monthly Reallocation)

True Correlation	Value-Added when Transactions Costs Are 0.1 Percent and Estimated Correlation Is:					
	0.0%	0.1%	0.2%	0.3%	0.4%	0.5%
0.0	0.0	−0.5	−0.5	−0.4	−0.4	−0.4
0.1	0.0	1.8	2.2	2.3	2.5	2.4
0.2	0.0	4.0	4.8	5.1	5.2	5.2
0.3	0.0	6.3	7.5	7.8	7.9	8.0
0.4	0.0	8.5	10.2	10.6	10.7	10.8

TABLE 11.6 Effect of Misestimation of Correlation on Value Added by Asset Allocation (Monthly Reallocation)

True Correlation	Value-Added when Transactions Costs Are 0.1 Percent and Estimated Correlation Is:					
	0.0%	*0.1%*	*0.2%*	*0.3%*	*0.4%*	*0.5%*
0.0	0.0	−4.7	−5.6	−5.7	−5.8	−5.8
0.1	0.0	−2.4	−2.9	−3.0	−3.0	−3.0
0.2	0.0	−0.1	−0.3	−0.2	−0.3	−0.2
0.3	0.0	2.1	2.5	2.5	2.5	2.5
0.4	0.0	4.4	5.0	5.2	5.3	5.3

CONCLUSION

An asset allocator who has the requisite risk tolerance and who follows optimal rules always invests in proportions equal to the benchmark, when he or she has no information beyond the fact that expected long-run stock returns exceed cash returns. In other words, an asset allocator without information acts as a buy-and-hold investor.

An asset allocator with information who follows optimal rules still has to overcome the effect of transactions—costs that are not borne by a buy-and-hold investor. An asset allocator with modest amounts of information who uses futures to switch between stocks and cash can expect to pay 0.1 percent per transaction and outperform a buy-and-hold stock investor. An investor who uses physical securities can expect to pay 1.0 percent per transaction and requires substantial information to outperform a buy-and-hold investor.

NOTES

1. Except that a mean-variance decision rule, instead of an all-or-nothing rule, is used here to choose the proportion of stocks and cash, this framework is similar to that in R. G. Clarke, M. T. FitzGerald, P. Berent, and M. Statman, "Market Timing with Imperfect Information," *Financial Analysts Journal* (November–December 1989): 27–36; and "Required Accuracy for Successful Asset Allocation," *Journal of Portfolio Management* (Fall 1990): 12–19.

2. Many examples of reliable leading indicators exist. See W. E. Ferson and C. R. Harvey, "The Variation of Economic Risk Premiums," *Journal of Political Economy, 99* (April, 1991): 385–415. (dividend yield, the differential between the yields of investment grade and junk bonds, and the differential between yields of one- and three-month Treasury bills are reliable leading indicators of stock and bond prices); D. M. Chance, "Option Volume and Stock Market Performance," *Journal of Portfolio Management* (Summer 1990): 42–51. (the ratio of the volume of put options to calls could be used to forecast stock prices); C. Engel and J. D. Hamilton, "Long Swings in the Dollar: Are They in the Data and Do Markets Know It?," *American Economic Review* (September 1990): 689–713 (evidence of nonlinear serial dependence in changes of

exchange rates, which implies that past changes in exchange rates can be used to forecast future changes).

3. The assumption of normality is not critical for the results. Other distributional assumptions could be used, but normality puts the computations into a familiar framework.

4. The variance of the error term depends on the correlation between stock returns and the leading indicator. This can be seen by taking the variance of stock returns in equation (6) as:

$$\sigma^2_s = \beta^2\sigma^2_I + \sigma^2_e$$
$$= \rho^2\sigma^2_s + \sigma^2_e$$

This follows from the relationship between β and the correlation coefficient between the leading indicator and stock returns $\beta = \rho\sigma_s/\sigma_I$.
Solving for the variance of the error term gives:

$$\sigma^2_e = (1 - \rho^2)\sigma^2_s$$

With imperfect information ($\rho = 1$), the variance of the error term is zero and there is no residual uncertainty. With no information ($\rho = 0$), the variance of the error term is equal to the entire variance of stock returns.

5. The risk premium and standard deviation of stock returns were adopted from the *Stock, Bonds, Bills and Inflation* yearbooks published by Ibbotson Associates, Chicago, Illinois.

6. For purposes of the simulation, we have not allowed the investor to take leveraged positions in stocks if the expected return is high enough. The proportion allowed to be invested in stocks is kept between zero and one.

7. An investor whose risk tolerance normally keeps him or her 100 percent invested in stocks would gradually reduce the average level of stocks in the portfolio to the perfect information level of 67 percent. The value-added for the stock investor with perfect information would only be (20.1 − 15.5) = 4.6 percent compared to 8.8 percent for the more risk-averse investor. The lower value-added is a result of the inability of the stock investor to overweight stocks beyond the benchmark proportion of 1.0. The more risk-tolerant investor can only underweight stocks relative to the benchmark and is constrained from overweighting them in the simulation. As a result, the value-added numbers are correspondingly lower but the variance of returns is smaller than the 100 percent stock benchmark.

8. R. Merton, "On Market Timing and Investment Performance: I. An Equilibrium Theory of Value for Market Forecasts," *Journal of Business* (July 1981): 363–406.

9. Notice that when the annual standard deviation is converted to a monthly number, the probability that stocks outperform cash drops from .67 on an annual basis to .55 on a monthly basis. As a result the investor with perfect information is invested in stocks only 55 percent of the time. This change in probabilities is a result of risk as measured by standard deviation being proportional to the square root of the investment horizon.

10. For a discussion of performance measurement problems associated with options in a portfolio, see R. Bookstaber and R. Clarke, "Problems in Evaluating the Performance of Portfolios with Options," *Financial Analysts Journal* (January 1985): 48–62.

11. The probabilities in equation (14) can be expressed in terms of the parameters of the probability distributions of the random variables I and e. For example, we can write:

$$\text{Prob}(S \geq C|w^*_B) = \text{Prob}(e \geq C - \bar{S} - \beta I|I \geq -\rho(\bar{S} - C)\sigma_I/\sigma_S)$$
$$= \int_{-\rho(\bar{S} - C)\sigma_I/\sigma_s}^{\infty} \text{Prob}(e \geq C - \bar{S} - \beta I)dI$$
$$\text{Prob}(w^* \geq w_B) = \text{Prob}(I \geq -\rho(\bar{S} - C)\sigma_I/\sigma_S)$$

where the error term e is normally distributed with zero mean and variance $\sigma^2_s(1 - \rho^2)$. I is also normally distributed with zero mean and variance σ^2_I.

Tactical Asset Allocation at Kidder, Peabody

E. K. Easton Ragsdale
Chief Quantitative Analyst
Kidder, Peabody & Co. Incorporated
New York, New York

Gita R. Rao*
Quantitative Analyst
Kidder, Peabody & Co. Incorporated
New York, New York

INTRODUCTION

The Kidder, Peabody Quantitative Research Group has developed two tactical asset allocation models. The first model selects between stocks and cash; the second model chooses among stocks, bonds, and cash. This chapter begins with a brief discussion of tactical asset allocation. We then describe our approach to asset allocation. In the final section, we report the investment results for our models.

TACTICAL ASSET ALLOCATION

Asset allocation refers to decisions about the appropriate asset mix in a given portfolio: the asset classes to be included and their relative weightings. All investors engage in asset allocation, whether they intend to or not. Asset allocation decisions can be divided into two broad categories: (1) strategic and (2) tactical. Asset allocation policy, or strategic asset allocation, refers to the establishment of a long-term, or normal, asset mix. Tactical asset allocation, or market timing, involves

---

* Gita R. Rao is now at Fidelity Management & Research Company, Boston, MA 02109.

shifting the asset mix based on predictions of the relative returns offered in the short term by the alternative asset classes. Although the number of asset classes utilized can vary considerably, the most commonly studied classes are stocks, bonds, and cash.

In tactical asset allocation, the central question is: Which asset class will provide superior future returns? Because relative returns are more important than absolute returns in this particular setting, many tactical asset allocators have focused on expected return premiums or spreads. As a practical matter, the most important comparison is that between stocks and fixed income (either bonds or cash), and the forecast on which the most effort is expended is the expected return for stocks. The comparison between stocks and fixed income is crucial because these are the two largest pools of assets in most institutional portfolios. Stock return forecasts are important because, historically, stocks have provided the highest and most volatile investment returns.

These forecasts of future returns may be generated judgmentally or they may be based on quantitative models. For example, a group of experienced investment professionals may meet periodically to generate return forecasts based on their experience and judgment. Alternatively, forecasts may be generated by statistical models that are based on historical relationships.

The forecasts can be generated bottom-up or top-down. In the bottom-up approach, forecasts for individual stocks are combined (typically, using a weighted average) to generate a forecast for the entire stock market (based on a proxy such as the S&P 500). In the top-down approach, forecasts are simply made at the market level. Readers should note that both bottom-up and top-down approaches can combine human judgment (for example, earnings and dividend forecasts) and quantitative models (for example, a dividend discount model or a statistical model).

One bottom-up approach uses the earnings and dividend forecasts for an individual stock as inputs into a dividend discount model, to generate an expected return for that stock. Expected returns for individual stocks are then combined to generate a bottom-up estimate for the expected return for the stock market. In an alternative top-down approach, some combination of economists, market strategists, and quantitative analysts provides earnings and dividend forecasts for the stock market as a whole, and these forecasts are input into the dividend discount model. Simpler approaches calculate expected return as earnings yield or the sum of current dividend yield and a forecast of future dividend growth.

The bottom-up approach to generating the expected return on stocks has at least two advantages over the top-down approach:

1. It reflects the combination or synthesis of information and experience from a large number of industry analysts. In the top-down approach, only a small group of top-down strategists or quantitative analysts is typically involved.
2. The bottom-up approach is based on the current expectations of individuals who are in constant contact with company managements and other industry sources. This is in contrast to the top-down approach, where the analysis is done at a more aggregated level with much less information about individual companies and industries.

The top-down approach also has its attractions:

1. It requires less maintenance and fewer inputs and therefore does not require a large number of expensive analysts.
2. It is easier to ensure consistency of top-down forecasts with the underlying economic assumptions.

Having developed forecasts of future returns for the relevant asset classes, the tactical asset allocator must then turn these forecasts into asset-mix decisions. Once again, the asset-mix recommendations can be generated judgmentally or based on quantitative models. These quantitative models might take the form of a portfolio optimizer or a set of trading rules based on statistical study of the historical record.

At Kidder, Peabody, we have developed a pair of quantitative tactical asset allocation models based on an equity risk premium and a bond risk premium. The first model selects between stocks and cash based only on the equity risk premium; the second model chooses among stocks, bonds, and cash using both risk premiums. The expected return component of the equity risk premium is calculated on a bottom-up basis using forecasts from Kidder, Peabody industry analysts. The recommendations derived from these models are implemented in a disciplined and contrarian manner. For both models, allocations are fully flexible, ranging from 0 percent to 100 percent for each asset class. A more detailed description of our approach is contained in the following section.

THE KIDDER, PEABODY ASSET ALLOCATION MODELS

In this section, we first describe the central concept in our models, the equity risk premium, and the method we use for computing the expected return for stocks. Next, we discuss the bond risk premium. Finally, we describe the trading rules used for setting the asset allocation weights.

Equity Risk Premium

The central concept in the Kidder, Peabody asset allocation models is the equity risk premium—the spread between the expected return for stocks and the risk-free interest rate. A distinguishing feature of the Kidder, Peabody models is the method used to generate the expected return for stocks. Many analysts compute a top-down expected return based on top-down assumptions for earnings growth and dividend payout. Kidder, Peabody's expected return on stocks is based on a bottom-up approach, requiring dividend forecasts from our industry analysts.

Kidder, Peabody industry analysts make specific earnings and dividend forecasts for the next five years for each company they follow. They also forecast the earnings growth rate and dividend payout ratio in a "plateau" period that typically represents a period of above-average earnings growth for a stock. Finally, our analysts forecast the earnings growth rate and dividend payout ratio in a subsequent "steady-state" period that typically represents a period of slower growth.

The analysts' forecasts are made relative to forecasted baseline assumptions for the S&P 500. For example, in early 1994, our baseline assumptions in the plateau period were a 7.5 percent growth rate and a 47 percent payout rate, which implied a 14 percent return on equity. For the steady-state period, our baseline assumptions were a 7.0 percent growth rate and a 45 percent payout ratio, which equated to a 13 percent return on equity.

These assumptions allow us to generate dividend forecasts as far into the future as needed. The dividend forecasts and the current price of the stock are combined in our dividend discount model to calculate the expected return for each stock. Strictly speaking, the expected return is defined as the discount rate that equates the current stock price with the discounted value of the future dividend stream. These individual expected returns are then weighted by their market capitalization to generate a capitalization-weighted average expected return. This is our expected return for the stock market.

Our stock market proxy is defined by those stocks in the S&P 500 that are covered by Kidder, Peabody analysts. Our analysts cover a high percentage of the S&P 500, on a market-capitalization basis.

As explained earlier, we then obtain the equity risk premium by subtracting the bond-equivalent yield on the one-year Treasury Bill from the stock market's expected return. Figure 12.1 shows the equity risk premium calculated at the end of each month since 1967. Figure 12.2 provides a recent history of this variable.

Next, we assume that, over time, the risk premium will return to a long-run "normal" level, based on the concept of reversion to the mean.

FIGURE 12.1 History of the Equity Risk Premium and Market Performance (Using 1-Year Treasury Bill Yield)

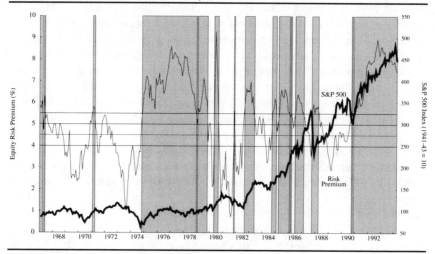

SOURCE: Kidder, Peabody Quantitative Research Group
NOTE: Shaded areas represent equity risk premium greater than or equal to 5.5%.

Thus, when the risk premium becomes very high, we assume stock prices are likely to rise and cause the risk premium to fall toward normal. Conversely, if the risk premium is well below average, we believe stock prices are likely to fall and thus cause the risk premium to rise toward normal. As a practical matter, the market rarely spends much time at "fair value" (see Figure 12.1). Rather, investor psychology tends to push the market to extremes of under- and overvaluation.

FIGURE 12.2 History of the Equity Risk Premium (Using 1-Year Treasury Bill Yield)

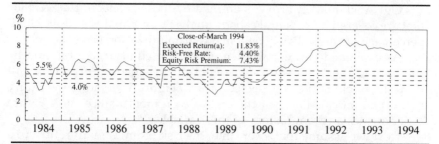

(a) Based on the average expected return on stocks in the S&P 500 covered by Kidder, Peabody analysts.
SOURCE: Kidder, Peabody Quantitative Research Group

TABLE 12.1 Annual Total Returns (a)

| | Kidder, Peabody Quantitative Asset Allocation Models | | Benchmark Portfolio | | | | | |
	Stock/ Cash (%)	Stock/ Bond/Cash (%)	Stock/ Cash (70/03) (%)	Stock/ Bond/Cash (70/20/10) (%)	S&P 500 (%)	Intermediate Treasury Bonds (%)	Treasury Bills (%)	Consumer Price Index (%)
1967	25.7	25.7	17.9	17.1	24.0	1.0	4.2	3.0
1968	10.0	10.0	9.4	9.3	11.1	4.5	5.2	4.7
1969	6.5	8.6	-4.0	-5.4	-8.5	-0.7	6.6	6.1
1970	13.5	22.9	5.2	7.1	4.0	16.9	6.5	5.5
1971	19.0	23.7	11.4	12.4	14.3	8.7	4.4	3.4
1972	10.8	12.0	14.3	14.6	19.0	5.2	3.8	3.4
1973	6.9	5.7	-8.5	-8.8	-14.7	4.6	6.9	8.8
1974	1.4	1.4	-16.9	-17.3	-26.5	5.7	8.0	12.2
1975	37.2	37.2	27.4	27.8	37.2	7.8	5.8	7.0
1976	23.8	23.8	18.1	19.8	23.8	12.9	5.1	4.8
1977	-7.2	-7.2	-3.6	-4.3	-7.2	1.4	5.1	6.8
1978	6.6	6.6	7.0	6.3	6.6	3.5	7.2	9.0
1979	18.7	18.7	16.2	14.8	18.4	4.1	10.4	13.3

(Continued)

213

TABLE 12.1 *(Continued)*

| | Kidder, Peabody Quantitative Asset Allocation Models | | Benchmark Portfolio | | | | | |
	Stock/Cash (%)	Stock/Bond/Cash (%)	Stock/Cash (70/03) (%)	Stock/Bond/Cash (70/20/10) (%)	S&P 500 (%)	Intermediate Treasury Bonds (%)	Treasury Bills (%)	Consumer Price Index (%)
1980	25.3	25.5	26.1	24.6	32.4	3.9	11.2	12.4
1981	10.7	10.7	0.8	-0.2	-4.9	9.5	14.7	8.9
1982	35.4	38.4	18.4	22.1	21.4	29.1	10.5	3.9
1983	23.4	23.8	18.4	18.0	22.5	7.4	8.8	3.8
1984	7.6	11.3	7.5	8.3	6.3	14.0	9.8	4.0
1985	32.8	34.1	24.5	27.3	32.2	20.3	7.7	3.8
1986	16.9	18.6	15.0	16.8	18.5	15.1	6.2	1.1
1987	29.6	29.2	6.4	6.0	5.2	2.9	5.5	4.4
1988	13.9	14.9	13.7	13.6	16.8	6.1	6.3	4.4
1989	13.0	13.0	24.3	25.4	31.5	13.3	8.4	4.6
1990	5.4	7.5	0.3	0.6	-3.2	9.7	7.8	6.1
1991	30.5	30.5	22.8	25.0	30.5	15.5	5.6	3.1
1992	7.7	7.7	6.5	7.2	7.7	7.2	3.5	2.9
1993	10.0	10.0	7.9	9.6	10.0	11.2	2.9	2.7
Geometric Average Annual Returns								
1967–93	15.6	16.7	10.1	10.4	11.0	8.7	6.9	5.7
1970–79	12.5	13.8	6.3	6.4	5.9	7.0	6.3	7.4
1980–89	20.5	21.6	15.2	15.9	17.5	11.9	8.9	5.1
1990–93	13.0	13.5	9.1	10.3	10.6	10.9	4.9	3.7

(a) These unaudited results are before trading costs. Changes in asset allocation were made at the end of each month. These results are presented for information purposes only and should not necessarily be looked upon as a guide to future results.

SOURCE: Kidder, Peabody Quantitative Research Group; Ibbotson Associates.

214

Our tactical asset allocation methodology attempts to recognize and take advantage of this phenomenon of reversion to the mean. Note that this approach often leads to contrarian investment positions, because periods of high equity risk premiums tend to be periods when investors are overly pessimistic and perceive a high level of stock market risk. Conversely, low equity risk premiums are often associated with periods of strong investor optimism about equities.

Overall, our focus is on equities because this is the asset class (among stocks, bonds, and cash) that has provided the highest total returns over time (see Table 12.1). As a result, we first determine what percentage of assets should be allocated to stocks based on the equity risk premium. Assets not committed to stocks are invested in either intermediate-term Treasury bonds ("bonds") or Treasury bills ("cash"), based on the level of the bond risk premium.

Bond Risk Premium

The bond risk premium is the spread between the yield on the five-year Treasury note and the risk-free interest rate, the one-year Treasury bill yield. Figure 12.3 provides a recent history of this variable. When this spread has exceeded 50 basis points, the extra return from investment in intermediate Treasury notes ("bonds") has generally more than compensated investors for the added risk of holding these notes.

A Disciplined Approach

We take a disciplined approach to developing our asset allocation recommendations. Historically, the spread between the expected return on stocks and the bond-equivalent yield on the one-year Treasury Bill

FIGURE 12.3 History of the Bond Risk Premium

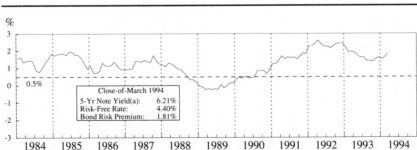

(a) Intermediate-term (five-year) Treasury note.
SOURCE: Kidder, Peabody Quantitative Research Group

has averaged approximately 5.3 percent (see Table 12.6). *When the equity risk premium has been at or above 5.5 percent, stocks have proven inexpensive relative to other asset classes; stocks subsequently have outperformed other asset classes, as well as their own historical average returns.* When the equity risk premium has been below 4.0 percent, stocks have tended to perform poorly until the equity risk premium moved back to 4.0 percent or greater.

For fully flexible accounts, we recommend a fully invested position in the S&P 500 Index ("stocks") when the equity risk premium is at 5.5 percent or higher. The recommendation falls to 75 percent of assets in stocks when the equity risk premium is between 5.0 percent and 5.5 percent; 50 percent of assets in stocks when the equity risk premium is between 4.5 percent and 5.0 percent; 25 percent of assets in stocks when the equity risk premium is between 4.0 percent and 4.5 percent; and no exposure to stocks when the equity risk premium is below 4.0 percent. Assets not allocated to stocks are invested in cash (Treasury bills).

In the case of the fully flexible stock/bond/cash asset allocation model, once the stock allocation is determined, we then use the bond risk premium to determine whether the fixed-income portion of the portfolio will be in intermediate Treasury notes ("bonds") or in Treasury bills ("cash"). *When the bond risk premium is 0.5 percent or greater, we invest in bonds, but when the bond risk premium is less than 0.5 percent, we invest in cash.*

For accounts that are not fully flexible, there are maximum and minimum allocations to stocks, bonds, and cash that represent smaller ranges. For these accounts, we would recommend a minimum allocation to stocks when the equity risk premium is below 4.0 percent and a maximum investment position in stocks when the equity risk premium is 5.5 percent or greater. Because the maximum is less than 100 percent and the minimum is greater than 0 percent, asset shifts should be more modest than the 25 percent increments we use for a fully flexible account.

PERFORMANCE OF THE KIDDER, PEABODY ASSET ALLOCATION MODELS

Table 12.1 shows the historical total return performance of Kidder, Peabody's fully flexible stock/cash and stock/bond/cash asset allocation models over a 27-year period. By "fully flexible" we mean that the allocations to each asset class can range from 0 percent to 100 percent. Table 12.1 also presents performance data for two benchmark portfolios with fixed asset allocations. Finally, performance data are reported for the individual asset classes: S&P 500 ("stocks"), intermediate Treasury notes ("bonds"), and Treasury bills ("cash").

In the case of the stock/cash benchmark portfolio, we assume that 70 percent of assets are allocated to stocks and 30 percent are allocated to cash, with portfolio rebalancing performed at the end of each month. For the stock/bond/cash benchmark portfolio, allocations are assumed to be 70 percent in stocks, 20 percent in bonds, and 10 percent in cash, again with monthly portfolio rebalancing.

Our equity risk premium methodology has added value relative to a buy-and-hold position in stocks alone or the benchmark portfolios with fixed asset allocations (see Table 12.1). Over the 1967–1993 period, the fully flexible stock/cash asset allocation model generated compound average annual returns of 15.6 percent and the stock/cash/bond model provided 16.7 percent. By comparison, the best-performing alternative, stocks, returned only 11.0 percent annually. (All of these returns are reported before transaction costs.)

Table 12.2 shows the average allocations to each asset class for both our asset allocation models. Over the full history from 1967 to 1993, the stock/bond/cash model has a time-weighted average allocation of 60.9 percent to stocks, 14.5 percent to bonds, and 24.6 percent to cash. Note that, although we have used an aggressive 70 percent allocation to stocks in our benchmark portfolios, the long-run average allocation to stocks in our models is considerably lower. If we lowered our benchmark portfolio allocation for stocks to 61 percent in order to more closely match the average allocation of our models, our models' relative performance would be even better.

Although our asset allocation models have underperformed the stock market from time to time, there has been only one year since 1967 in which our asset allocation models turned in a negative performance—1977. In that year, both models matched the performance of the stock market, a negative 7.2 percent total return.

Cumulative Returns

Figure 12.4 shows the cumulative returns since 1967 for our fully flexible stock/cash model versus cumulative returns for stocks, cash, and a benchmark portfolio composed of 70 percent stocks and 30 percent cash. Recall that we have assumed that the benchmark portfolio was rebalanced at the end of each month. An investment of $100 at the end of 1966 in a portfolio based on our fully flexible stock/cash model would have grown to $5,008 by the end of 1993 (before transaction costs). By comparison, similar investments in the S&P 500 and benchmark stock/cash portfolios would have grown to only $1,678 and $1,328, respectively.

For our stock/bond/cash model, Figure 12.5 displays the results versus stocks, bonds, cash, and a benchmark portfolio composed of 70 percent stocks, 20 percent bonds, and 10 percent cash. Again, we have

TABLE 12.2 Average Asset Allocation Weights

	Stock/Cash Model		Stock/Bond/Cash Model		
	Stock Weight (%)	Cash Weight (%)	Stock Weight (%)	Bond Weight (%)	Cash Weight (%)
1967	77.1	22.9	77.1	0.0	22.9
1968	43.8	56.3	43.8	0.0	56.3
1969	4.2	95.8	4.2	12.5	83.3
1970	10.4	89.6	10.4	89.6	0.0
1971	54.2	45.8	54.2	45.8	0.0
1972	43.8	56.3	43.8	56.3	0.0
1973	0.0	100.0	0.0	8.3	91.7
1974	14.6	85.4	14.6	0.0	85.4
1975	100.0	0.0	100.0	0.0	0.0
1976	100.0	0.0	100.0	0.0	0.0
1977	100.0	0.0	100.0	0.0	0.0
1978	100.0	0.0	100.0	0.0	0.0
1979	91.7	8.3	91.7	0.0	8.3
1980	50.0	50.0	50.0	6.3	43.8
1981	8.3	91.7	8.3	0.0	91.7
1982	37.5	62.5	37.5	14.6	47.9
1983	83.3	16.7	83.3	16.7	0.0
1984	41.7	58.3	41.7	58.3	0.0
1985	93.8	6.3	93.8	6.3	0.0
1986	89.6	10.4	89.6	10.4	0.0
1987	66.7	33.3	66.7	33.3	0.0
1988	68.8	31.3	68.8	20.8	10.4
1989	14.6	85.4	14.6	0.0	85.4
1990	50.0	50.0	50.0	12.5	37.5
1991	100.0	0.0	100.0	0.0	0.0
1992	100.0	0.0	100.0	0.0	0.0
1993	100.0	0.0	100.0	0.0	0.0
Average Weights					
1967–93	60.9	39.1	60.9	14.5	24.6
1970–79	61.5	38.5	61.5	20.0	18.5
1980–89	55.4	44.6	55.4	16.7	27.9
1990–93	87.5	12.5	87.5	3.1	9.4

SOURCE: Kidder, Peabody Quantitative Research Group.

assumed that the benchmark portfolio was rebalanced at the end of each month. The degree of outperformance by our stock/bond/cash model is even greater than that of the stock/cash model. *A $100 invest-ment in the fully flexible stock/bond/cash model at the end of 1966 would have grown to $6,428 by the end of 1993 (before transaction costs), compared to only $1,678 for the S&P 500 portfolio and $1,450 for the benchmark stock/bond/cash portfolio.*

FIGURE 12.4 Cumulative Performance of the Kidder, Peabody Tactical Asset Allocation Stock/Cash Model

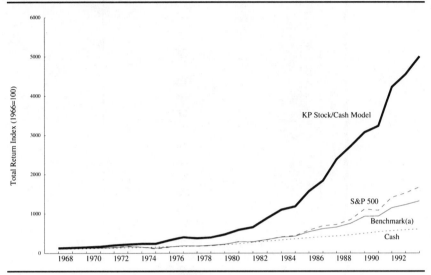

(a) Benchmark portfolio is 70% stocks and 30% cash.
SOURCE: Kidder, Peabody Quantitative Research Group

FIGURE 12.5 Cumulative Performance of the Kidder, Peabody Tactical Asset Allocation Stock/Bond/Cash Model

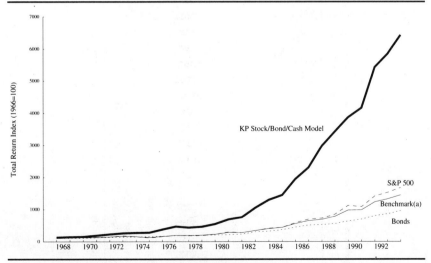

(a) Benchmark portfolio is 70% stocks, 20% bonds and 10% cash.
SOURCE: Kidder, Peabody Quantitative Research Group

TABLE 12.3 Impact of Stock Market Returns on Performance of the Kidder, Peabody Quantitative Asset Allocation Models (1967–93)

	In Years of Positive Returns From the S&P 500				In Years of Negative Returns From the S&P 500			
	KP Models Out-perform	KP Models Under-perform	KP Models Equal Performance	All Years	KP Models Out-perform	KP Models Under-perform	KP Models Equal Performance	All Years
Number of Years								
Stock/Cash Model	9	6	6	21	5	—	1	6
Stock/Bond/Cash Model	10	5	6	21	5	—	1	6
Geometric Average Absolute Return (%)								
Stock/Cash Model	22.5	14.9	18.7	19.2	6.1	—	−7.2	3.8
Stock/Bond/Cash Model	24.4	15.0	18.7	20.5	6.7	—	−7.2	4.3
Geometric Average Relative Return (%)								
Stock/Cash Model	5.5	−5.3	0.0	0.8	20.6	—	0.0	16.9
Stock/Bond/Cash Model	6.9	−5.7	0.0	1.8	21.3	—	0.0	17.4

SOURCE: Kidder, Peabody Quantitative Research Group.

Performance in Good and Bad Years for Stocks

How did the models perform in years of positive and negative returns from the stock market? This analysis is summarized in Table 12.3. Over the 27-year period analyzed, there were 21 years in which the stock market generated positive total returns.

The stock/cash model outperformed the stock market in nine of those 21 positive-return years and matched the stock market in six years. For the stock/cash model, the average outperformance relative to stocks in the 21 good years was 0.8 percent. The stock/bond/cash model performed better in strong stock markets, outperforming the stock market in ten of the 21 years and matching the market in six years. In years when stocks generated positive returns, the stock/bond/cash model outperformed the stock market on average by 1.8 percent.

Table 12.3 clearly indicates that the outperformance of our asset allocation models is concentrated in years when the stock market generated negative total returns. Since 1967, the S&P 500 has experienced negative total returns in six years. Both of our asset allocation models outperformed in five of those years. More importantly, in each of the five years, our models also provided positive returns, with the stock/cash model outperforming on average by 16.9 percent and the stock/bond/cash model outperforming by 17.4 percent. As noted earlier, in 1977, the one down year when our models did not outperform the market, they were able to match it.

Clearly, no system works all the time. However, over the longer term the ability to avoid most bad years in the equity markets has enabled our models to substantially outperform the S&P 500.

Performance and Stock Market Volatility

Our analysis found that the performances of the Kidder, Peabody asset allocation models also have been influenced by stock market volatility. We began by sorting the 27 years based on annual volatility; we found a gap in the distribution resulting in the assignment of 11 years to the low-volatility group and the remaining 16 years to the high-volatility group.

Table 12.4 shows that, for the 11 years of low stock market volatility, both asset allocation models outperformed the S&P 500 in five years and matched the S&P 500 in four years. Over the full 11 years, both models on average outperformed the S&P 500, with the stock/bond/cash model performing slightly better than the stock/cash model.

What about the 16 years of high stock market volatility? Our stock/cash model outperformed the S&P 500 in nine years and matched the

TABLE 12.4 Impact of Stock Market Volatility on Performance of the Kidder, Peabody Quantitative Asset Allocation Models (1967–93)

	In Years of High Volatility for the S&P 500				In Years of Low Volatility for the S&P 500			
	KP Models Out-perform	KP Models Under-perform	KP Models Match Performance	All Years	KP Models Out-perform	KP Models Under-perform	KP Models Match Performance	All Years
Number of Years								
Stock/Cash Model	9	4	3	16	5	2	4	11
Stock Bond/Cash Model	10	3	3	16	5	2	4	11
Geometric Average Absolute Return (%)								
Stock/Cash Model	14.4	17.2	24.0	16.8	20.2	10.4	8.0	13.8
Stock Bond/Cash Model	16.4	17.7	24.0	18.1	21.9	11.0	8.0	14.7
Geometric Average Relative Return (%)								
Stock/Cash Model	14.4	−5.9	0.0	6.2	4.3	−4.0	0.0	1.2
Stock Bond/Cash Model	14.5	−7.1	0.0	7.3	5.8	−3.4	0.0	1.9

SOURCE: Kidder, Peabody Quantitative Research Group.

stock market in three years; our stock/bond/cash model outperformed in ten years and matched the stock market in three years. More importantly, *our asset allocation models exhibited greater relative outperformance during the high-volatility years,* averaging 6.2 percent per year for the stock/cash model and 7.3 percent annually for the stock/bond/cash model. Given the increased uncertainty during periods of high stock market volatility, it is comforting to know that our asset allocation models do well in such an environment.

Risk and Reward

If asset allocation models could be judged only on the basis of returns, the world would be a simpler place. Alas, risk must also enter into the analysis. Risk, or the volatility of returns, is most often measured by the annualized standard deviation of returns. Table 12.5 compares the return and risk levels for our two asset allocation models, the benchmark portfolios, and the individual asset classes. Note that our asset allocation models have experienced considerably less risk than stocks, as measured by the standard deviation of returns. Our stock/cash model's volatility, standard deviation of 11.1 percent, matched that of its benchmark portfolio, and the returns from the stock/bond/cash model were slightly less volatile (standard deviation of 11.3 percent) than those for the benchmark portfolio (standard deviation of 11.6 percent). Only Treasury notes and Treasury bills have experienced lower volatility (standard deviation of 6.7 percent and 2.7 percent, respectively).

Combining risk and reward in a single variable allows us to compare the risk–reward trade-off across portfolios. One simple measure is the return per unit of risk, calculated as the geometric average annual portfolio return divided by the standard deviation of portfolio returns. Because our asset allocation models have better returns and lower volatility, it is not surprising that their returns per unit of risk are higher than any of the alternatives: 1.4 for the stock/cash model and 1.5 for the stock/bond/cash model. Treasury bills have a higher return per unit of risk (2.6), but their returns are quite low.

An alternative measure of risk, the Sharpe ratio, looks at excess return per unit of risk. The Sharpe ratio is the geometric average annual return for the portfolio minus the mean Treasury bill return (a proxy for the risk-free rate), divided by the standard deviation of returns for the portfolio. The Kidder, Peabody models' Sharpe ratios, at 0.8 and 0.9, were much better than those for the stock market or the benchmark portfolios. Note that, by definition, the Sharpe ratio for Treasury bills is zero. (See Table 12.6.)

TABLE 12.5 Risk and Return

| | Kidder, Peabody Quantitative Asset Allocation Models | | Benchmark Portfolios | | | | |
	Stock/ Cash (%)	Stock/ Bond/Cash (%)	Stock/ Cash (70/30) (%)	Stock/ Bond/Cash (70/20/10) (%)	S&P 500 (%)	Intermediate Treasury Bonds (%)	Treasury Bills (%)
Geometric Average Annual Return	15.6	16.7	10.1	10.4	11.0	8.7	6.9
Standard Deviation	11.1	11.3	11.1	11.6	15.8	6.7	2.7
Return per Unit of Risk (a)	1.4	1.5	0.9	0.9	0.7	1.3	2.6
Sharpe Ratio (b)	0.8	0.9	0.3	0.3	0.3	0.3	0.0

(a) Return per unit of risk is the geometric average annual return divided by the standard deviation of returns.
(b) The Sharpe ratio is the geometric average annual return minus the geometric average annual Treasury bill return, divided by the standard deviation of returns.

SOURCE: Kidder, Peabody Quantitative Research Group.

TABLE 12.6 Total Returns to S&P 500 in Periods Following the Rise of the Equity Risk Premium over 5.5%

	Total Returns (%) in Subsequent (a) Periods		
Date	6 Months	12 Months	24 Months
May 67	7.21	14.34	23.61
Feb 71	3.96	13.59	22.46
Nov 74	33.16	36.08	58.26
May 79	16.52	24.49	51.19
Dec 81	−7.8	21.41	48.74
Oct 82	25.71	27.91	36.21
Oct 84	10.63	19.59	59.14
Apr 85	8.09	36.59	72.74
Mar 86	−1.47	26.01	15.71
Oct 87	5.5	14.74	44.92
Oct 90	25.63	33.51	46.77
Average Return	13.04	24.44	40.97
Average Annual Return	27.79	24.44	18.73

(a) These are point-to-point total returns with the base period the level of the S&P 500 at the end of the month in which the equity risk premium first matches or exceeds 5.5%. In many cases the equity risk premium did retreat below 5.5% and even 4.0% during these subsequent periods and, thus, our asset allocation approach did recommend taking profits and reducing holdings. These moves are not captured in the above returns.

SOURCE: Kidder, Peabody Quantitative Research Group.

One final point should be made. To achieve results such as those shown here, one must be willing to apply an asset allocation strategy consistently over an extended period. No approach will always outperform; some periods of underperformance must be expected. Discipline and patience are crucial for success.

13

Development and Implementation of a Tactical Asset Allocation Model at Wells Fargo Nikko Investment Advisors

Janice L. Deringer
Principal

Lawrence G. Tint
Managing Director
Global Portfolio Management
Wells Fargo Nikko Investment Advisors

Wells Fargo introduced the investment management industry's first market expected return model in 1973. The tactical asset allocation (TAA) model was initially used as a consulting tool, and clients committed the first assets for management in late 1977. The model is generally recognized as one of the industry's most successful TAA models, and has not posted a loss in any calendar year since it was funded. The development history of the model and an analysis of its performance characteristics are presented in this chapter.

ORIGIN OF PRODUCT

In the early 1970s, Wells Fargo utilized a dividend discount model with the goal of evaluating opportunities in individual equities. Unlike traditional dividend discount models, in which earnings estimates were coupled with required rates of return to determine the price at which an individual stock should be selling, this model solved for the stock's expected return. Wells Fargo analyst dividend and earnings forecasts were combined with market prices in the following formula:

$$P_0 = D_1/(1 + r)^1 + D_2/(1 + r)^2 + \ldots + D_n/(1 + r)^n + \ldots$$

where

P = price
D = dividend per year
r = discount rate
n = number of periods.

This innovation allowed for better comparison of stock investment opportunities. One could compare the implied or expected returns of stocks with similar risks to determine the most attractive equity investment. Expected returns for groups of stocks, including industry groups, yield groups, and liquidity groups, were also estimated. Finally, the model was used to determine the implied return of the market as a whole (as represented by the S&P 500). The dividend discount model was designed in three stages, allowing for variability of growth rates and payout ratios in the short, intermediate, and long term.

It was observed that the spread between the expected return for equities (from the dividend discount model) and the expected return for bonds (from the long-term yield-to-maturity) varied through time. Wells Fargo determined that the variability in this spread was useful in modeling the stock/bond allocation decision. To determine an optimal trade-off between stocks and bonds, Wells Fargo modeled a risk tolerance function that characterized investors' behavior.

Investors traded off return and risk as a function of the level of expected return. They were very sensitive to underperforming their targeted minimum required return or actuarial rate of return. Consequently, such performance was heavily penalized. Also, because investors obtained little benefit by outperforming the market, returns above the equity expected return were not greatly rewarded. This behavior led to the development of a utility function with three distinctive linear pieces.

The equity market expected return, the bond market yield-to-maturity, and the piece-wise utility function, were used as inputs into an optimization process as described by Markowitz.[1] The resulting recommended stock/bond portfolio allocation, first published as a consulting tool and then used to manage a fund holding the recommended stock/bond mixes, has been produced continuously since that time.

BASIC DESCRIPTION OF PROCESS

Expected returns, risks, and correlations are the primary inputs into the asset allocation optimization process. The expected return for equities is the implied return or discount rate on the S&P 500 from the dividend discount model. The expected return for bonds is the yield-to-maturity of long-term AA industrial bonds.

The standard deviations and correlations used in the model are estimates from long-term historical data. Although these inputs are reviewed regularly, long-term asset class risk and correlation estimates change slowly. Most notably, over the past 20 years, fixed income securities have grown riskier as increasing uncertainty regarding the rate of inflation has led to greater variability of bond returns. Since 1973, the estimated standard deviation of bonds has been raised from 6 percent to 10 percent.

These inputs—expected returns, standard deviations, and correlations—are combined with the utility function in an optimization process that produces the allocation between stocks and bonds that yields the "best" (in terms of utility) mean-variance combination. On a daily basis, the asset allocation model is updated and recommended mixes are recorded.

When the asset allocation model was created, typical "balanced" investment managers of stock/bond portfolios held 60 percent equities and 40 percent bonds as a baseline asset mix. The original asset allocation model was calibrated to produce a "normal" recommended mix of 60/40 (stocks/bonds). Over the history of management, the model has been customized to offer other "normal" positions to meet client preferences.

The tactical asset allocation (TAA) model is calibrated to produce recommended mixes in 10 percent increments. The possible mixes are not constrained; the model allows an investment of 0 percent to 100 percent in any of the asset classes, although actual changes in mix generally occur quite gradually.

REVIEW OF THE IMPLEMENTATION HISTORY AT WELLS FARGO

Following the introduction of the asset allocation model, the paradigm remained essentially unchanged; however, refinements continue to be made to the model and to implementation methods.

Security analysts from Wells Fargo provided the initial earnings and dividend estimates for the S&P 500 equities in the model. Since 1982, in an effort to obtain broad consensus estimates, short-term earnings forecasts have been collected from all security analysts through the Institutional Brokers Estimate System (IBES) service. At the same time, Wells Fargo began conducting a survey of Wall Street equity research departments to determine the intermediate-term earnings and dividend growth rates for the S&P 500. Long-term growth rates were taken from the Blue Chip Economic Indicators' survey of business economists for the long-term level of GDP (gross domestic product) growth in the United States. With these changes, the dividend discount model became a *consensus*-based model of expected returns for the S&P 500.

The original asset allocation model included only stocks and bonds. In 1985, cash was incorporated as a candidate asset class when research indicated that its inclusion improved returns and reduced risk. Cash served as a safe-harbor asset class, and its low correlation with stocks and bonds improved diversification in the fund. Since March 1985, the asset allocation model has been run as a three-way model, allowing for investments of 0 percent to 100 percent in stocks, bonds, and cash.

Initially, the model was updated monthly. Beginning in 1984, the model was updated daily, and changes in the asset mix were implemented at the time of the change, rather than at month-end. Making daily asset allocation shifts is beneficial in volatile markets. For example, on October 5, 1987, the asset allocation strategy was rebalanced to a very defensive mix of 10 percent equities and 90 percent bonds because of the narrow stock/bond expected return spread. Because the markets changed so significantly in value on October 19, the fund was rebalanced on October 20 to a mix of 30 percent equities and 70 percent bonds. In addition, proprietary trading techniques on this day allowed the fund to purchase the additional equities at a significant discount. Opportunities such as October 1987 may occur rarely, but the ability to respond to them daily or intradaily has greatly benefited participants.

The original TAA model was designed as a substitute for funds with a normal mix of 60 percent equities and 40 percent bonds. In 1988, a new version of TAA was produced, with a more risk-tolerant utility function, for investors who desired a more aggressive version of the model. This fund had a normal position of 70 percent stocks and 30 percent bonds. The following year, an even more aggressive fund, with a normal position of 100 percent stocks, was created for clients who wished to use TAA as an equity substitute.

The historical performance of the strategy is shown in Figure 13.1. The point labeled 60/40 TAA represents the original model and is the actual realized return (including transactions costs) for the strategy. Over the 16 years ending in 1992, the 60/40 TAA strategy returned 16.8 percent (on an annualized basis) with a standard deviation of 11.2 percent. TAA posted better returns, by an average of 3.2 percent per year, than a portfolio with a constant mix of 60 percent equities and 40 percent bonds, and had slightly less risk. Over this period, TAA outperformed each of the component asset classes as well. The S&P 500 returned 15.1 percent (annualized) with a standard deviation of 15.4 percent. TAA outperformed equities by about 1.7 percent per year

FIGURE 13.1 TAA Performance History Demonstrates Efficient Risk–Return Trade-Offs (January 1978–December 1992)

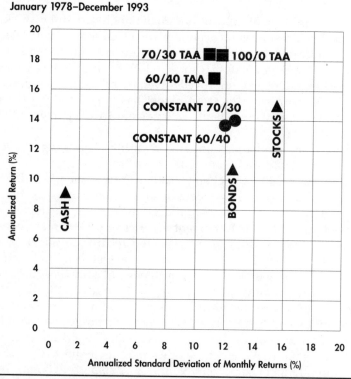

January 1978–December 1993

60/40 TAA: 1978 to 3/31/85: Separate account, combined performance of stocks and bonds. Commingled 3-way TAA fund thereafter.
100/0 TAA: 1978 to 7/31/89: models results; actual results thereafter.
70/30 TAA: 1978 to 3/31/88: model results; actual results thereafter.

while reducing risk by more than one fourth. Bonds and cash returned to 10.8 percent and 9.2 percent, respectively, over this period. The more aggressive asset allocation models, 70/03 TAA and 100/0 TAA, produced similarly attractive performance relative to their benchmarks.

The success of TAA in the United States led to its application in other markets. In 1988, a version was introduced to allocate among Japanese stocks, Japanese government bonds, and Japanese money market instruments. Although a long history of analysts' forecasts was not available to create a dividend discount model, a proxying equation was developed to calculate the expected return of equities based on earnings yield and interest rates. The model was calibrated as an aggressive model to be used as an equity substitute and has enjoyed a very successful track record in a market characterized as difficult to model.

Since the strategy was funded, in September 1988, it has returned (in Yen) 17.8 percent versus −31.3 percent for equities through December 1993, on a cumulative basis. Asset allocation models have been introduced for the U.K. and Canadian markets as well.

In 1989, excellent results were achieved when a similar model was applied to domestic fixed-income markets, to produce optimal allocations among Treasury bonds, Treasury notes, and cash. From inception through 1993, the fixed income model returned 13.5 percent versus 11.7 percent for Treasury bonds, 10.5 percent for Treasury notes, and 5.9 percent for money market instruments on an annualized basis. The ability to apply the TAA model to other markets provides continuing evidence of the power of the original allocation model.

MODEL CHARACTERISTICS

Accuracy of Expected Returns

Wells Fargo's 21-year history of published asset class expected returns is shown in Figure 13.2. With changes in inflation levels, nominal expected return estimates increased throughout the 1970s and fell throughout the 1980s and early 1990s. Although the entire distribution has shifted in the same general pattern, relative opportunities between asset classes varied throughout the period. For instance, the stock/bond expected return spread in 1978 was greater than 6 percent. In 1992, this spread was considerably narrower (below 1.5 percent) for much of the year.

The expected returns are the primary model input. For the model to perform, the expected returns must be extremely accurate forecasts of long-term market returns. The published expected return forecasts versus subsequent ten-year asset class performance are displayed in Figures 13.3 and 13.4, for both stocks and bonds.

In 1973, the Wells Fargo expected return for stocks was 8.5 percent. At that time, this forecast was considered extremely pessimistic, given a recently released Center for Research in Securities Prices (CRSP) study. The study showed long-term average equity returns at 11.8 percent and the most recent ten years at 15 percent. Yet, over the next ten years, the S&P 500 returned only 6.6 percent per year, falling below the "pessimistic" estimate. The highest equity expected return was recorded in 1982: 18.3 percent. This was generally considered unobtainable in those high-inflation, hard economic times, yet the S&P 500 delivered an average return of 17.5 percent over the following ten years. The remaining points have been plotted through 1983, the last period for which we know the ten-year actual result. The expected returns have been a very accurate assessment of long-term value in the

FIGURE 13.2 Wells Fargo's Monthly Expected Returns (1973–1993)

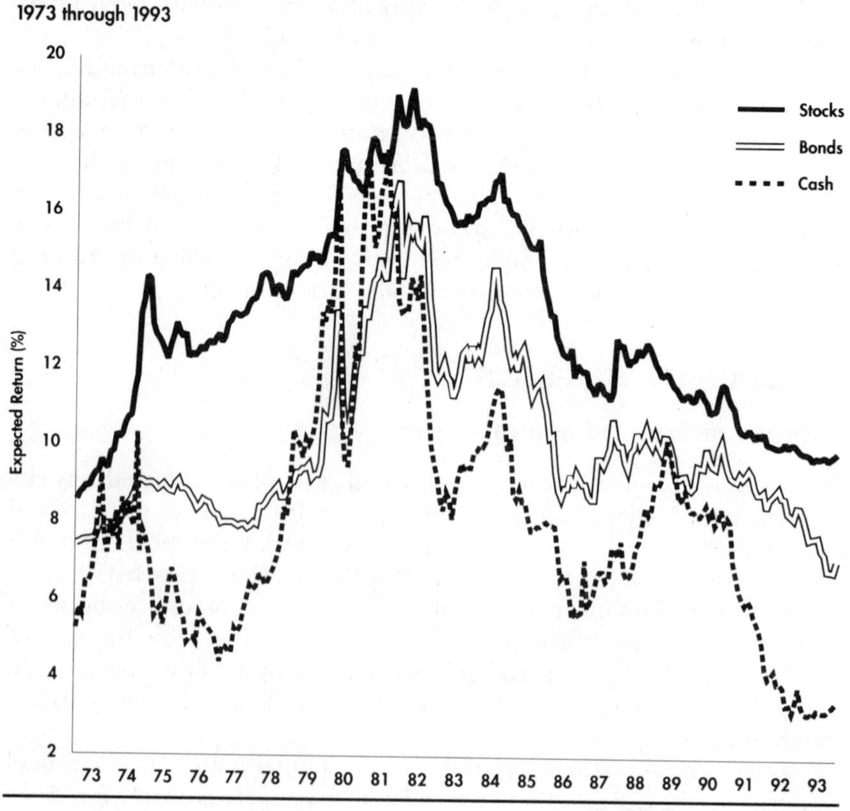

1973 through 1993

equity market. The regression line formed by them lies very close to the 45° perfect forecast line.

A similar pattern of consistent expected returns and long-term realized returns exists for the bond market, as shown in Figure 13.4. This pattern has occurred even with the use of a fairly simple measure for the expected return of bonds—the yield-to-maturity. In spite of reinvestment risk and other complications, it has been a very good predictor of long-term return in the bond market.

If the measurement period is shortened from ten years to five years, the expected returns still are highly correlated with performance, as shown in Figures 13.5 and 13.6. Over the shorter period, the fitted lines are steeper, indicating that low expected returns are followed by even lower actual returns in the shorter term, and high expected returns are followed by even better market performance. This

FIGURE 13.3 Actual Published Forecasts versus Ten-Year Performance, Stocks

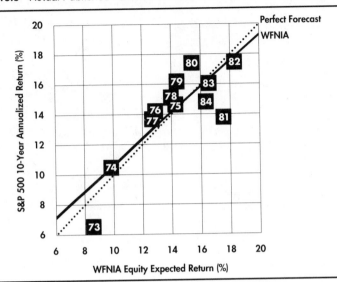

FIGURE 13.4 Actual Published Forecasts versus Ten-Year Performance, Bonds

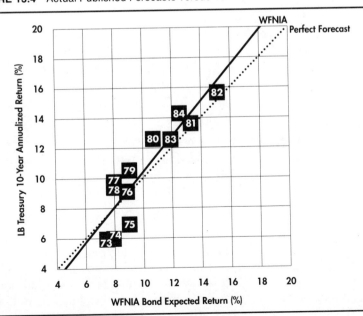

1972 to 1975: Lehman Brothers Long Treasury Index.
1976 to 1993: Lehman Brothers 20+ Treasury Index.

FIGURE 13.5 Actual Published Forecasts versus Five-Year Performance, Stocks

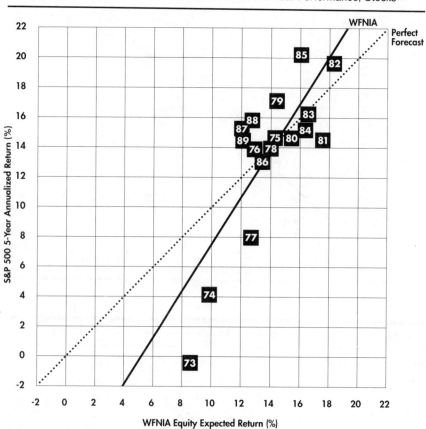

phenomenon is a result of mean reversion. Undervalued or overvalued markets typically provide patterns of very high or very low returns for a short time and more normal returns thereafter, rather than slightly higher or lower returns for longer time periods.

Crystal Ball Models

The expected returns used in the asset allocation model have been very good predictors of the market's long-term value. To demonstrate that even models based on perfect indicators of long-term value do not always provide good short-term performance, a "crystal ball model" was tested. This theoretical model allocates assets monthly to stocks or bonds. The model has perfect foresight; it uses for expected returns the

FIGURE 13.6   Actual Published Forecasts versus Five-Year Performance, Bonds

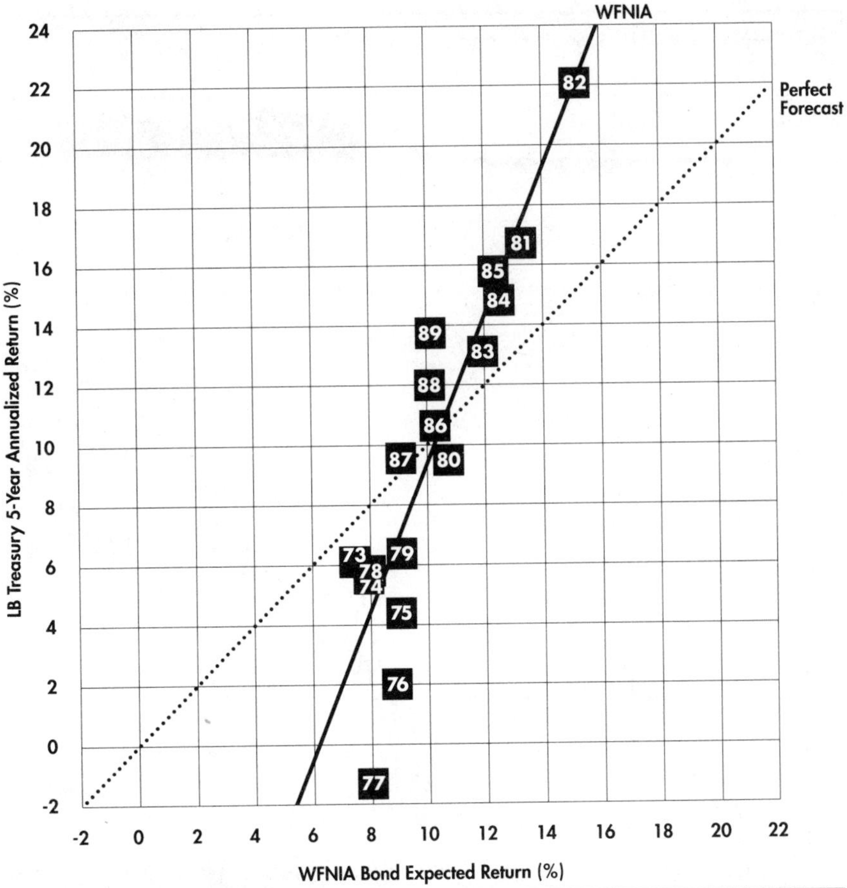

1972 to 1975: Lehman Brothers Long Treasury Index.
1976 to 1993: Lehman Brothers 20+ Treasury Index.

actual future returns that will be earned by each asset over the next five years. Each month, 100 percent of the fund is allocated to the asset that will have the best performance over the next five years.

The model's performance, measured in the cumulative value of a dollar, is shown in Figure 13.7. For every five-year period from July 1970 until September 1974, stocks underperformed bonds and the crystal ball model invested 100 percent in bonds. For every month over the following five-year period, from September 1974 through December 1979, stocks outperformed bonds and the model shifted to all equities. Investing in the crystal ball model for the entire period would

FIGURE 13.7 How Even Perfect Long-Term Market Forecasts Can Produce Imperfect Short-Term Performance

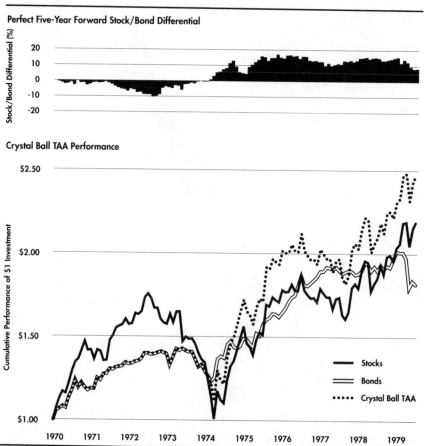

have produced dominant returns, outperforming stocks by 30 percent and bonds by 70 percent.

However, short-term performance was sometimes less attractive. From 1970 through 1972, the model would have invested in bonds in correct anticipation of the poor equity market returns of 1973 and 1974. As a result, the model matched the performance of the bond market and lagged equities by over 30 percent! Although the investment allocation would prove correct, given the coming negative returns in the equity market, this example illustrates an unfortunate consequence of value investing: short-term results can be disappointing as overvalued markets become more overvalued. Investors in these strategies may need a long time-horizon to realize the dominant performance.

Shortening the time-horizon of the perfect forecast improves the crystal ball model's performance. Since 1973, the Wells Fargo TAA model has performed about as well as a two-year perfect-forecast crystal ball model.

PERFORMANCE CHARACTERISTICS OF TAA

Low Downside Risk

Tactical asset allocation's attractive performance history is the result of low downside risk combined with significant participation in upside opportunities. The quarterly results over the 21-year model history are shown in Figure 13.8. Results are also shown for the S&P 500 and for a constant mix benchmark portfolio of 60 percent S&P 500 stocks and 40 percent Lehman Brothers 20+ Treasury bonds. As background, over this period (57 quarters), the S&P 500 earned a positive return 68 percent of the time. In the remaining 27 quarters, the S&P 500 posted losses.

The average quarterly return for TAA was 3.7 percent, better than the 3.1 percent average quarterly return for the S&P 500 and the 2.8 percent average for the 60/40 constant mix portfolio. The return pattern in Figure 13.8 shows that negative TAA returns are smaller in magnitude than those of stocks or the constant 60/40 mix. In the 21-year history of the strategy, TAA delivered only three quarterly losses greater than 5 percent. Over the same 21 years, the S&P 500 had quarterly losses greater than 5 percent in 11 quarters. A diversified investment in the constant 60/40 portfolio had eight such quarterly losses.

TAA posted its worst quarterly loss, −7.9 percent, in the third quarter of 1981. The S&P 500 had losses three times as large—up to −25 percent—in the fourth quarter of 1987 and the third quarter of 1974. Holding bonds as part of a constant mix reduced the magnitude of the losses, but the 60/40 constant mix portfolio lost 16.1 percent in its worst quarter—more than twice the largest TAA loss.

The quarterly mean return of the S&P 500 in the 27 down quarters was −6.3 percent. In its 27 worst quarters, the TAA quarterly mean return was only −2.4 percent. TAA significantly reduced the exposure to these losses. The 60/40 constant mix portfolio experienced average quarterly losses of −4.5 percent. TAA was able to reduce this exposure by almost half.

Examination of the 57 best quarters for each of the strategies indicates performance characteristics in up markets. The average quarterly TAA return in these quarters was 6.6 percent. The S&P 500 earned an average of 7.5 percent per quarter. Therefore, the TAA strategy participated in almost 90 percent of the upside opportunity in the equity market. The 60/40 portfolio returned only 6.3 percent on average.

FIGURE 13.8   Quarterly Returns over a 20-Year Model History

TAA Quarterly Returns 1973–December 1993*

Average Quarterly Return	**3.7%**	Quarterly Losses Greater than 5%	**3**
Standard Deviation	5.9%	Worst Quarter	–7.9%
57 Best Quarters		**27 Worst Quarters**	
Quarterly Mean	6.6%	Quarterly Mean	–2.4%
Standard Deviation	4.7%	Standard Deviation	2.5%

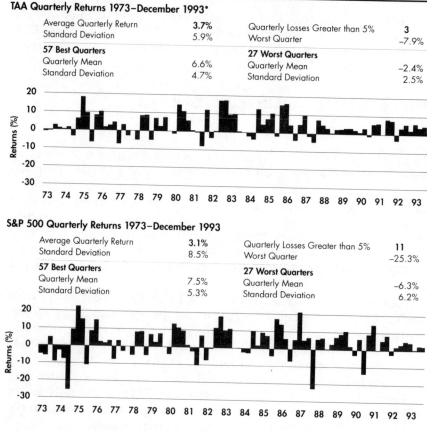

S&P 500 Quarterly Returns 1973–December 1993

Average Quarterly Return	**3.1%**	Quarterly Losses Greater than 5%	**11**
Standard Deviation	8.5%	Worst Quarter	–25.3%
57 Best Quarters		**27 Worst Quarters**	
Quarterly Mean	7.5%	Quarterly Mean	–6.3%
Standard Deviation	5.3%	Standard Deviation	6.2%

60/40 Constant Mix 1973–December 1993**

Average Quarterly Return	**2.8%**	Quarterly Losses Greater than 5%	**8**
Standard Deviation	6.6%	Worst Quarter	–16.1%
57 Best Quarters		**27 Worst Quarters**	
Quarterly Mean	6.3%	Quarterly Mean	–4.5%
Standard Deviation	4.5%	Standard Deviation	3.6%

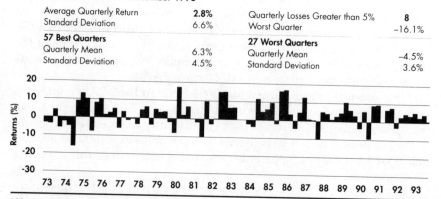

* Model performance prior to 7/1/77. Actual returns from 7/77 to 12/93.
** Model performance of 60% S&P 500 Index and 40% Lehman Brothers 20+ Treasury Index rebalanced monthly.

Examination of the performance of TAA in both positive and negative markets gives insights into the performance pattern of the strategy. TAA was able to earn approximately 90 percent of the equity market's positive returns while reducing its losses by over 60 percent. By participating in most of the upside opportunity while avoiding significant losses, TAA has been able to outperform equities over the long term.

TAA adds similarly, relative to the 60/40 constant mix portfolio. TAA earns more than the 60/40 constant mix portfolio in positive markets. The positive performance is accompanied by better control of downside risks as well. TAA's defensive positioning reduced exposure to losses incurred in the 60/40 constant mix portfolio by almost one half.

Performance Time-Horizon

To realize dominant performance, an asset allocation strategy may require a long-term investment horizon. Relative TAA performance in short versus long time periods is examined in this section. Performance rankings of stocks, bonds, cash, and TAA were created for each period. Figure 13.9 displays a frequency distribution (scaled in percentage terms) of the rankings for each month's performance from 1973 through 1993 (252 monthly periods). Over these very short periods, TAA performance generally ranks second or third, with 92 percent of the outcomes in those positions. Stocks most often rank first or fourth, and fixed income investment rankings are fairly evenly distributed.

When the time period for analysis was extended to rolling one-year periods, as shown in Figure 13.10, TAA ranked second most often—55 percent of the time. TAA ranked fourth only 1 percent of the time. Stocks most often ranked first; however, a full 27 percent of the equity outcomes were fourth-place finishers. In these one-year time periods, investments in bonds and cash generally rank third or fourth.

When the investment horizon is a long-term one—in this case, five years—TAA consistently ranks first or second, as shown in Figure 13.11. In 62 percent of all possible five-year windows, TAA ranked first; in the remaining cases, it ranked second. There were absolutely no occurrences of fourth-place rankings. Given the diversity of market environments in the past 21 years, an investment record with such characteristics is extremely compelling. Stocks most often ranked second; however, stocks ranked fourth in almost 10 percent of the cases and third or fourth in 27 percent of the cases. The number of poor outcomes from equities is counterintuitive, given the longer measurement period.

As the performance rankings demonstrate, a long-term time-horizon may be required to realize asset allocation's dominant first- or second-

FIGURE 13.9 Performance Rankings of all One-Month Results since 1973

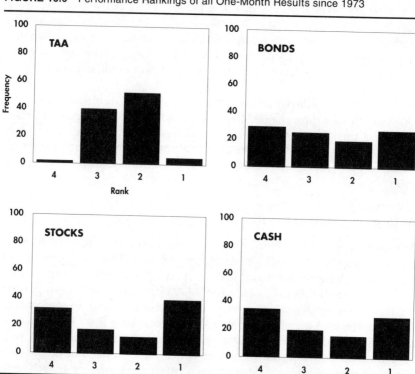

TAA: Model performance from 1/1/73 through 6/30/77. Actual returns thereafter.
Stocks: S&P 500 Index.
Bonds: 1972 to 1975: Lehman Brothers Treasury Index. 1976 to 1993: Lehman Brothers 20+ Treasury Index.
Cash: Money Market Fund.

place record. This provides time for market revaluations to occur and for various asset mix positions to fully benefit the portfolio. Short-term performance remains good, particularly using risk- adjusted performance measures, but a longer horizon guarantees the full benefit of asset allocation strategies.

Impact of Asset Mix on Performance

The performance of the Wells Fargo TAA model has varied as a function of the initial equity allocation. Figure 13.12 shows average realized one-year absolute and relative performance (versus a 60 percent equity and 40 percent bond portfolio) for each possible equity allocation. When markets have been in equilibrium, and the asset allocation model's proportion held in equities has been near the long-term normal

FIGURE 13.10 Performance Rankings of Rolling One-Year Results since 1973

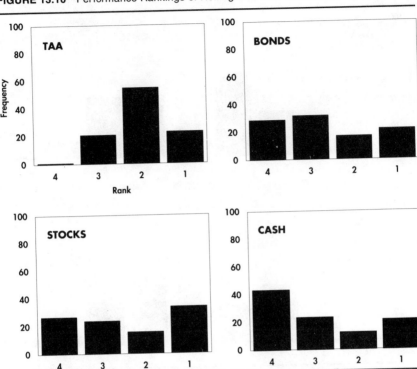

TAA: Model performance from 1/1/73 through 6/30/77. Actual returns thereafter.
Stocks: S&P 500 Index.
Bonds: 1972 to 1975: Lehman Brothers Treasury Index. 1976 to 1993: Lehman Brothers 20+ Treasury Index.
Cash: Money Market Fund.

allocation of 60 percent equities, the absolute or pure performance of TAA has been best. When markets have been in disequilibrium and equity percentages have been either high or low, absolute performance over the next year has been lower.

However, for relative performance, defined as the excess performance of TAA over its 60/40 (stock/bond) benchmark, the opposite is true. The TAA model is able to add the most relative value or alpha when the allocation to equities is extreme—either significantly above or below normal. Such extreme equity allocations occur in response to larger market misvaluations, and the subsequent market corrections provide the TAA model with its best relative performance.

When the time period is extended to five years, the absolute performance of the TAA model is virtually unrelated to asset mix, as

FIGURE 13.11 Performance Rankings of Rolling Five-Year Results since 1973

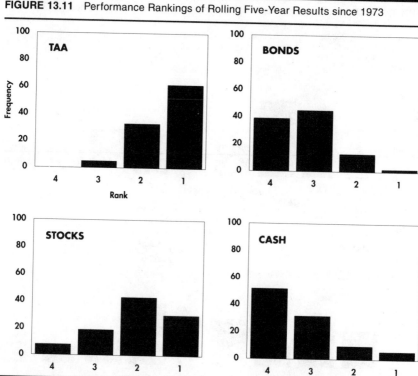

TAA: Model performance from 1/1/73 through 6/30/77. Actual returns thereafter.
Stocks: S&P 500 Index.
Bonds: 1972 to 1975: Lehman Brothers Treasury Index. 1976 to 1993: Lehman Brothers 20+ Treasury Index.
Cash: Money Market Fund.

shown in Figure 13.13. However, even over long time periods, the performance of the TAA model relative to the benchmark is best when the initial investment is made at times of market disequilibrium. Therefore, the best long-term alpha or relative track record will accrue to investors who make or increase commitments to TAA when the model's allocation to equities is extreme—either very high or very low. This is precisely the time when the asset mix is most contrarian and it is most difficult to take advantage of the opportunity.

IMPLEMENTATION CHARACTERISTICS

Comments on Implementation

The performance of any TAA strategy depends not only on the structure of the model generating asset mixes, but, equally as important, on

FIGURE 13.12 Short-Term Absolute and Relative TAA Performance, Given Varying Equity Allocations

TAA Performance

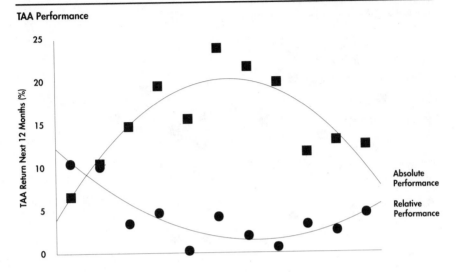

TAA Allocation to Equities

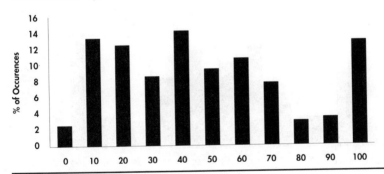

Absolute performance: TAA model returns.
Relative performance: TAA model return—return of 60% S&P 500 and 40% LB 20+ Treasury Index.

the quality of its implementation. If recommended mixes cannot be achieved cost-effectively and asset class returns cannot be reproduced precisely, model results will be far less attractive. Because TAA adds value through a series of mix changes, it is necessary to drive the trading costs toward zero.

Wells Fargo implements TAA with index-replicating portfolios and futures. These vehicles provide precise, low-cost access to returns and allow the strategy to benefit from innovative trading techniques designed to accommodate passive funds. Equity exposure is achieved using the S&P 500, and bonds are implemented with a portfolio replicating

FIGURE 13.13 Longer-Term Absolute and Relative TAA Performance, Given Varying Equity Allocations

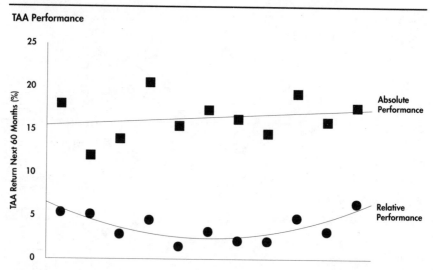

TAA Performance

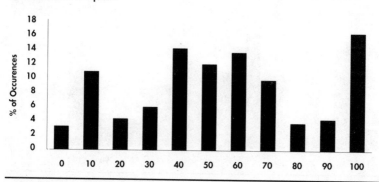

TAA Allocation to Equities

Absolute performance: TAA model returns.
Relative performance: TAA model return—return of 60% S&P 500 and 40% LB 20+ Treasury Index.

Lehman Brothers 20+ Treasury Index. The money market basket is a diversified array of highly rated, liquid money market investments with maturities less than one year.

Before initiating a trade in the marketplace, Wells Fargo aggressively seeks internal and external crossing opportunities to fulfill the asset allocation trade. Crossing allows for the exchange of funds or assets at closing prices, without trading in the marketplace. This trading method eliminates market impact and reduces or eliminates trading costs. Additionally, some funds allow for the use of futures. Even in funds where futures are not allowed, Wells Fargo has developed trading techniques to access the liquidity of the futures markets even though physical securities are delivered or received.

Value of Asset-Mix Changes

The performance record of Wells Fargo's TAA strategy has been documented in academic studies. For example, Evnine and Henriksson[2] applied a statistical timing model to measure the value of asset allocation. In their measures of the value of free options produced by the asset allocation strategy, they found statistically significant value. Additionally, they calculated the probability that such a performance record was produced solely by chance as virtually zero impossible.

TAA's Place in the Strategic Decision

An important discussion issue in TAA over the past year or so has been how the *tactical* nature of TAA harmonizes with the *strategic* nature of plan asset-mix management over time. Some have expressed concern that, by permitting a strategy such as TAA to alter the long-term target asset allocation established by policy, the policy intent may be undermined. For example, if asset allocation policy establishes that a 60 percent exposure to equities will meet a plan's return targets best over the long run, then what is gained by allocating assets to a strategy that can significantly alter the target over the short-to-intermediate run?

Including TAA in a portfolio improves the returns of the fund while maintaining or reducing risk. The result is shown in Figure 13.14. In this case, for a balanced fund with a strategic mix of 60 percent equities and 40 percent bonds, importing the risk reduction characteristics of TAA permits a slight increase in the strategic equity commitment. A 30 percent allocation to TAA, with the remainder of the portfolio invested 50 percent in equities and 20 percent in bonds, improves annual returns by 138 basis points per year, yet keeps risk at the original desired level. TAA's inclusion in the strategic portfolio mix increases the average equity exposure to 68 percent, allows the portfolio to capture the improved return and lower risk of TAA, and significantly improves the reward-to-risk characteristics of the fund.

We have learned much about the true nature of market valuation cycles: They can be much longer than the three-five-year periods we would like them to be! Holding the right asset mix at the right time in the market cycle, perhaps only a few critical times in each decade, nonetheless turns out to explain the success or failure of overall investment results for many years. Tactical asset allocations' role in integrating the *tactical* with the *strategic* is to ensure that, over the long run, the

---

FIGURE 13.14 Why TAA Belongs in a Portfolio's Strategic Decision

1973–1993

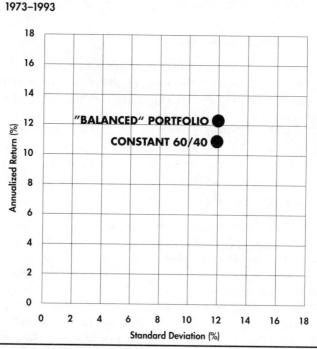

Balanced portfolio = 50% S&P 500 Index, 20% LB 20+ Treasury Index, and 30% 3-Way TAA, rebalanced monthly.
60/40 = 60% S&P 500 Index, 40% LB 20+ Treasury Index, rebalanced monthly.

---

plan's policy asset-mix target is achieved and exceeded. TAA keeps a disciplined, value-based eye on the short-to-intermediate term valuation cycles that critically explain long-run market performance.

NOTES

1. Harry Markowitz, "Portfolio Selection," *Journal of Finance* (Volume 7, no. 1, March 1952): pp. 77–79.
2. Jeremy Evnine and Roy Henriksson, "Asset Allocation and Options," *Journal of Portfolio Management* (Fall, 1987).

14

Chaos Theory

Jack Mosevich, PhD
Partner
Harris Investment Management, Inc.
Chicago, Illinois

"God does not play dice with the Universe."

Albert Einstein

INTRODUCTION

Chaos theory has recently been receiving a great deal of attention in both the scientific and the public press. Many claims are being made that it is a "new science"—one that holds the promise of bringing new insights into the physical, financial, and biological sciences. The purpose of this chapter is to explain what chaos theory is all about and what its potential appears to be for applications in investment decision making and, in particular, for tactical asset allocation. At the very least, chaos theory is a promising approach for analyzing phenomena that have defied analysis by standard methods.

The important message here is: We must change how we mentally and mathematically view some processes, and chaos theory provides the language and framework for such a change.

There are two fundamental lessons to be learned as we analyze phenomena using the ideas surrounding chaos theory. One lesson is that complicated processes can only be modeled properly by using nonlinear dynamical analysis. In the past, when complex systems were analyzed and either we did not understand the underlying mechanisms or we knew the laws but the behavior was still random looking, what was our approach? We applied statistical methods, usually linear regression or models assuming certain statistical distributions. We did this because we could then solve such problems, even if only crudely. Now, with this new approach and with increasing computational power, we can make the jump to nonlinear analysis and not impossible statistical constraints on our models.

The second lesson is: What is important is often not only what we are observing but also how we are looking at it. What appears random is often not random at all; it just appears that way because we are viewing only a part of the process, from the wrong perspective.

We shall have examples of these two lessons throughout the chapter. Before we begin, let us explore a simple example that entails some of the ideas inherent in chaos theory.

Consider a fast-flowing river into which we place two very small spherical corks that are touching each other. Even if the river is flowing through an extremely smooth canal, it will not be long before the corks are separated. It is unlikely that anyone can model the corks' behavior well enough to predict their relative positions after ten minutes. Now suppose the river flows through a twisting, rocky area. If the corks are extremely close to each other and enter a back-eddy, they will be in what is called a "chaotic attractor": once in, they follow orbits that they may never leave; their paths deviate so much that, after only a few seconds, no one would be able to say that they entered simultaneously. Once in the back-eddy, they may stay in there indefinitely or they may exit at some unpredictable time. Note that no external random elements are affecting the corks. In the context of economics and finance, the term chaotic attractor is being applied to price and index series. We shall now explain these concepts and how they may indeed be applied to explain some market behavior.

NONLINEAR DETERMINISTIC PROCESSES

Technically speaking, this chapter should be entitled "Deterministic Nonlinear Dynamical Analysis." Chaos theory is really a special case of this broader subject, and many of the important results we will be examining are not specific to chaos theory at all. The term dynamical means that all of the processes under consideration change through time.

The first profound component of this whole subject area is that there are many phenomena that appear random but, when subjected to normal statistical analysis, they pass all tests fitting them into a known distribution (normal, Poisson, and so on). An example can be found by measuring the motion of a pendulum and plotting its angular speed against its angular position. A pendulum is clearly not a random physical system, to which the millions of clock and watch owners will attest. Yet, Figure 14.1, which shows the plot of angular speed against angle, certainly looks like a random series of observations.

FIGURE 14.1 Chaotic Time Series for a Pendulum, Shown as a Plot of Angular Velocity versus Angle

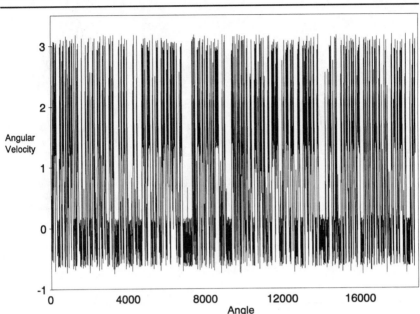

If we observe the angle of the pendulum versus time, we see a smoother graph that will eventually show patterns, as in Figure 14.2.

The point is: Even a simple, smooth, mechanical system can appear like white noise when viewed from a particular perspective.

Deterministic versus Stochastic Phenomena

Many phenomena and their mathematical models have been treated as being one of two basic types: (1) deterministic or (2) stochastic. Deterministic phenomena are phenomena that are governed by laws that possess no randomness; the analyst knows all the forces involved, and the future of these phenomena can be predicted with reasonable certainty. Stochastic phenomena involve known or unknown forces but, in any case, they are governed by random factors that render them impossible to predict. The two examples above (corks and pendulums) are deterministic. Another simple example is the flight of a football: If we know its initial direction and speed, we can predict its trajectory (parabolic); but once it hits the ground, it can bounce just about anywhere. Its

FIGURE 14.2 Plot of Angular Velocity versus Time

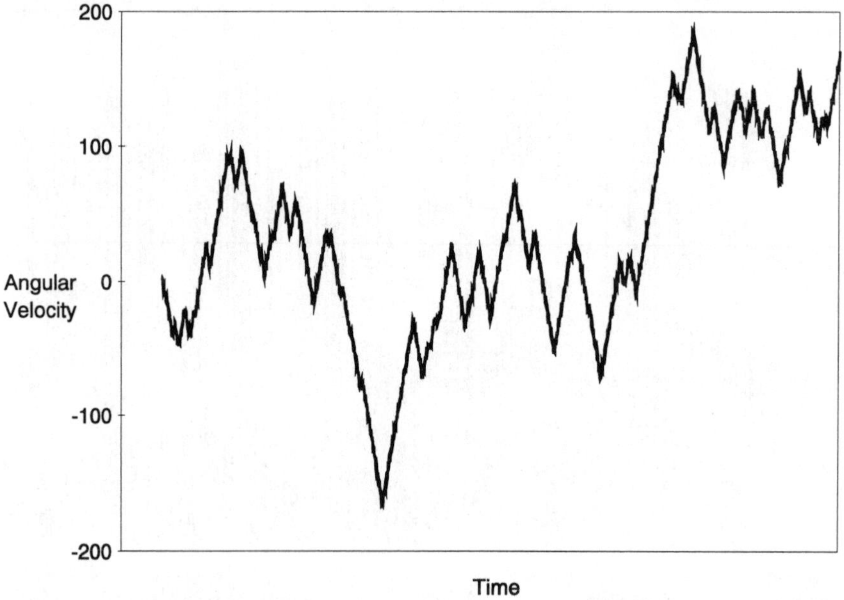

initial flight is deterministic; its motion once it hits the ground is stochastic. No process is completely deterministic or completely stochastic, but Albert Einstein and some others have believed that, within reason, everything is ultimately deterministic.

Following is a short list of phenomena, classified as deterministic or stochastic:

Deterministic	Stochastic
Newtonian laws of motion	Turbulence
Relativity theory	Subatomic particles
Laws of heat transfer	Radioactive decay
Price elasticity	Molecular motion
Law of supply and demand	Interest rates
Nonturbulent fluid flow	Financial prices

A well-documented case of assuming stochastic behavior is that of option pricing. In the case of a non-dividend paying stock, it is assumed that its price is randomly distributed with a "log-normal" distribution. This is represented as follows:

$$P_{i+1} = P_i e^{(r - \frac{\sigma^2}{2})\Delta T + Z\sigma\sqrt{\Delta T}}$$

where P_{i+1} is the price at time $i + t$, r is the risk-free rate, ΔT is the time increment, σ is volatility, and Z is a random number. Such a model can be used to generate possible future price paths to price options, but it is not for predictions; it is valuable only as a statistical tool. A deterministic model, if one exists, would be able (in theory) to predict a specific value of price at some future time.

Linear versus Nonlinear Phenomena

The other major aspect of modeling and explaining complex systems is that of *linear* versus *nonlinear* behavior. A linear relationship exists whenever quantities are related to each other in direct proportions. In a nonlinear relationship, quantities are complicated functions of each other, and behavior can be difficult or impossible to describe or predict. An example of a linear system is a thermostat, which measures temperature to control a furnace or an air conditioner. If the temperature rises three degrees, the indicator will move three times as far as it will in a rise of one degree. A nonlinear example is the price–yield relationship for bonds. The effect of doubling the yield can only be measured using a calculator; it is not possible to use one case to estimate the same result for another case. The same is true of coupon rates and maturity.

It turns out that even the simplest nonlinear models or physical systems can produce incredibly complicated behavior. This is attributable to the feedback characteristics of such systems: a minuscule change in one quantity may be magnified out of all proportion to what one might expect.

The excitement about chaos theory has centered on the fact that simple nonlinear deterministic mathematical models can produce exceedingly complicated results. Let us step back and analyze a complicated reality, using a simple model. In fact, this type of analysis has been accomplished already. For centuries, the observed paths of planets against the stellar background were modeled by crystal spheres and wheels within wheels—with poor results. Along came Newton, with $F = MA$ and $F_G = M_1 M_2 / R^2$ and *"Voila!"* The problem was solved with excellent accuracy. It took a nonlinear model to express the underlying laws. (The latter relationship is simple but nonlinear.)

Can Newton's laws of motion solve any problem in a truly deterministic sense? Consider the case of a simple pendulum. If the only forces involved are gravity and friction, then Newton's (nonlinear) equations of motion work quite well. Future positions, even in the presence of external forces, are predictable. But, if we add one extra simple component, we still have a technically deterministic system but this system is not at all predictable. You can try this yourself: let the "bob" of the pendulum be a bar magnet with its positive end pointing down and just clearing a stationary magnet with its positive end pointing up. The path of this pendulum is totally erratic and unpredictable, and yet we know with great precision all the laws of motion. There are no random factors at all, but minuscule quantities, such as the angle at which the "bob" approaches the other magnet, are magnified tremendously.

This example brings to light the fact that there are actually two meanings to the word *random,* the technicalities of which we will not deal with here. Basically, one meaning is studied in probability theory, with its precise mathematical definition; the other is any process that appears to lack pattern or predictability but may still be the result of a deterministic process.

A question naturally arises as to financial data: they appear to be random, but which type of randomness do they have? We will return to this later.

One last topic of significance concerns the technical subject of "correlation dimension." It is easy to explain this with an example.

FIGURE 14.3 $P_1(i)$ versus Time

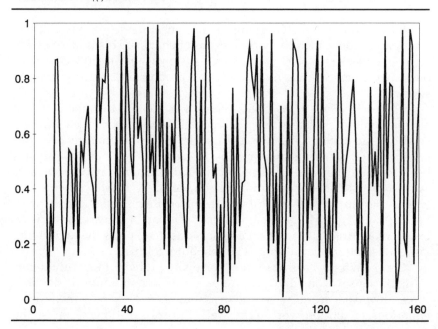

Consider Figures 14.3 and 14.4. Pretend that they represent price series $P_1(T)$ and $P_2(T)$, plotted in time.

Both appear jagged, trendless, and random. Trying to predict the next one or two values of each is fruitless.

We have plotted price versus time. Now, instead, plot $P_1(T + 1)$ versus $P_1(T)$ and $P_2(T + 1)$ versus $P_2(T)$—or, successive values of each price. The results are shown in Figures 14.5 and 14.6.

As is evident, P_1 was a truly random series, generated with a random number generator. Series 2 was 100 percent deterministic; $P_2(n + 1) = 4 \times P_2(n) \times (1 - P_2(n - 1))$. A cursory analysis of both series ($P_i(T)$ versus T) with any statistical package would result in the conclusion that they are uniformly random. The pattern in Series 2 would not be perceived. Thus, to find a deterministic relationship that is perfectly predictable, we needed to analyze autocorrelation rather than time series.

This example demonstrates the concept of correlation dimension. In order to discover the true relationship inherent in Series 2, we were required to consider a two-dimensional view of successive prices. Thus *two* is the correlation dimension. If, for example, $P(T + 1)$ is a function of $P(T)$, $P(T - 1)$, and $P(T - 2)$, then the correlation dimension

FIGURE 14.4 $P_2(i)$ versus Time

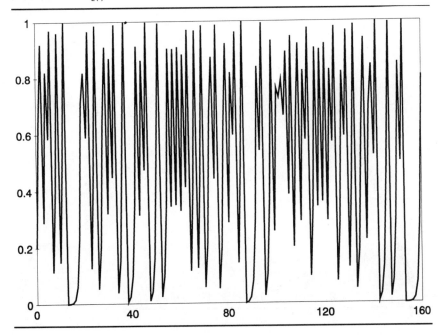

FIGURE 14.5 $P_1 (T + 1)$ versus $P_1 (T)$

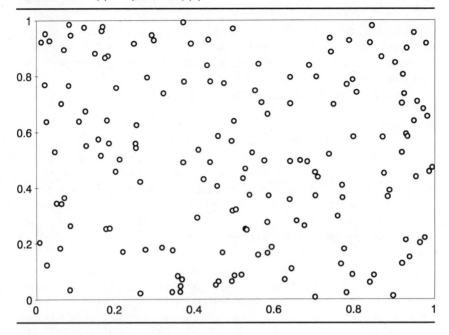

FIGURE 14.6 $P_2 (T + 1)$ versus $P_2 (T)$

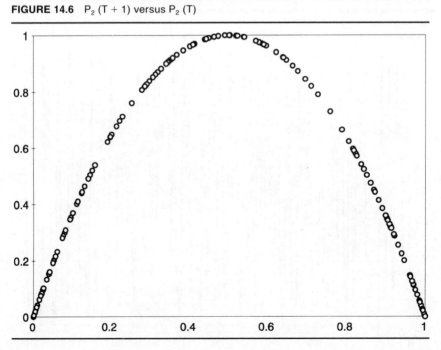

is four. The random sequence $P_1(T)$ does not have a finite correlation dimension.

This concept is critical if one hopes to find a deterministic relationship in a series of data. Current research suggests that some financial data possess deterministic nonlinear structure in seven or eight dimensions. Unfortunately, truly random features are also present, making it difficult, if not impossible, to predict. Actually, there are two problems to tackle:

1. If there is a relationship, what is the correlation dimension?
2. What form does the relationship take?

At the time of writing, there is no known methodology for fully answering these questions in general. However, some researchers are making good progress, especially for the first problem.

CHAOS

The concepts of chaos theory can now be defined. Chaos is any nonlinear deterministic process that satisfies the following properties:

1. It appears random (according to statistical tests);
2. It has extreme sensitivity to initial conditions and is therefore unpredictable;
3. There are points that repeat themselves (periodic) and the whole range of possible values is covered.

A physical example of chaos is the turbulent back-eddy described previously. Motion of corks appears random and is unpredictable. Every location is attainable and many corks will repeat their positions (after several circuits). Also, even if we cannot predict the location of a cork, we can say with certainty that it will stay in a certain area or exit the back-eddy. It will not suddenly shoot back upstream.

A purer example of chaos is offered by the above price series $P_2(T)$. Figures 14.7 through 14.11 are graphs of the time series generated by the formula $P(T + 1) = A \cdot P(T)(1 - P(T))$ for various values of A.

These results demonstrate how a simple nonlinear function can result in diverse, complicated behavior. As the value of A increases, we get series with fixed and periodic points and then more random-looking values. When A = 4, we get true chaos. To see this result, we have plotted P for $P(0) = 1/6$ and $P(0) = 1/6 + 0.000001$ in Figure 14.12. Note that after only five steps, the two series are totally out of synchronization and one can imagine that values between 0 and 1 will be sampled.

FIGURE 14.7 Case 1: A = 2.9

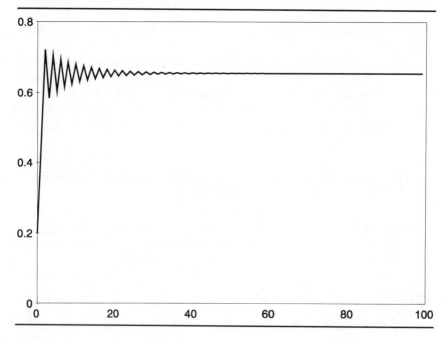

FIGURE 14.8 Case 2: A = 3.0

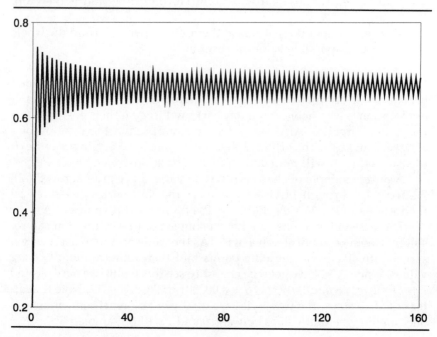

FIGURE 14.9   Case 3: A = 3.5

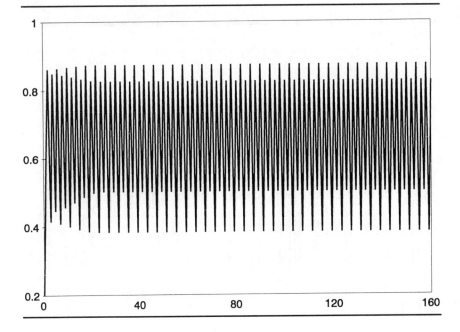

FIGURE 14.10   Case 4: A = 3.6

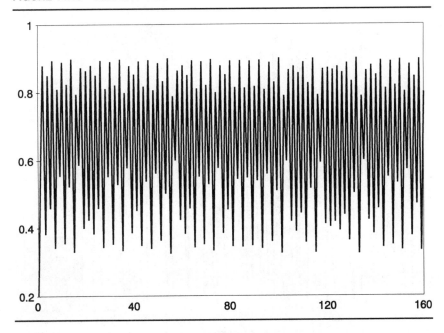

FIGURE 14.11 Case 5: A = 3.7

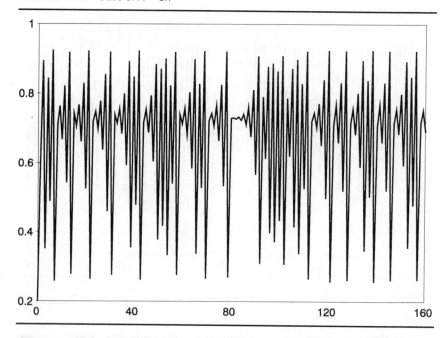

FIGURE 14.12 P(i) versus Time: Two Different Starting Values

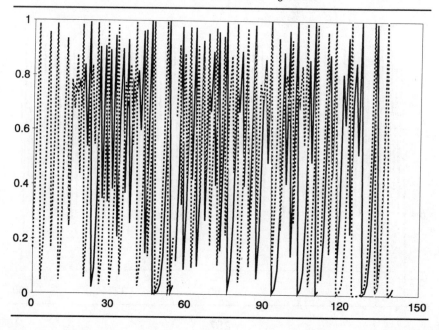

The example with A = 4 demonstrates how unpredictable a very simple nonlinear deterministic mechanism can be. Recall that there are two elements to this problem: (1) because of the feedback mechanism present in such systems, small deviations lead to drastically different results (the "butterfly effect"); and (2) our discovery of the deterministic nature of the process depends on getting the right correlation dimension. These concepts summarize one part of chaos theory.

Attractors

Another concept relating to chaos theory was briefly mentioned in the definition of chaos. It is a property of many nonlinear systems to possess equilibrium states called *attractors;* once an equilibrium state is entered, the system stays in that state either forever or for a finite unpredictable period of time. We have seen previous examples of attractors: the corks in a back-eddy, the final position of a normal pendulum (at rest), the periodic points of the price series P(T) with various values of A. There are many examples of attractors in nature; the most spectacular is a black hole, which is a fatal attractor! The value of 100 (PAR) is an attractor for a bond's price as it approaches maturity or is called.

Attractors are important because, even if we cannot predict a system quantitatively but we know it has an attractor, then at least we know its qualitative behavior. We can perhaps predict its range or duration but not its values.

Two types of attractors are often referred to in the context of chaos theory. One is the *chaotic attractor,* which satisfies the property of chaotic behavior whereby two very close points very quickly move apart. This implies an unpredictable system, and we have already presented examples.

The other type of attractor is the *strange attractor,* which is best described as exhibiting pathological behavior. Strange attractors are examples of sets known as fractals (defined in the next section). These are often, but not always, chaotic attractors. By pathological we mean that strange attractors cannot be described by normal mathematical constructs; they are very difficult to define or describe.

Fractals

Fractals were first defined by M. Mandelbrot who, while examining decades of weekly and monthly cotton price graphs, noticed that there is no means to distinguish between a weekly or monthly price series. They are qualitatively similar. He also analyzed other problems, such as measuring the lengths of coastlines, and describing snowflakes and clouds. Mandelbrot realized that much of the geometry of the natural world is not described by the normal Euclidean geometry of lines and circles. This led him to define a mathematical object called a *fractal,* which includes natural objects. Included in this universe are financial and economic series.

We cannot present a precise technical definition of fractals here; a description and examples will suffice. Two basic features define a fractal. The first is that it is "self-similar." If we magnify a portion of a fractal, the image will look like the fractal, and this feature is reflected ad infinitum. Examples of self-similar objects are clouds, coastlines, frost crystals, snowflakes, and, of course, price series.

The second distinguishing feature of a fractal is that its defining dimension is not a whole number. For example, a sheet of paper is of dimension two, a ball is of dimension three. A fractal cannot be defined with a whole number of dimensions; it will have a dimension of, say, 2.6. For example, a snowflake, being flat, will fit into a two-dimensional plane, but we cannot measure its perimeter with small rods because it is too choppy. Thus, its dimension is neither one nor two.

The most famous fractal, shown in Figure 14.13, is called a Mandelbrot set. It clearly exhibits the property of self-similarity: magnifying a "bud" results in the picture of the whole set with more and more buds. Hundreds of such sets are now sold as art, all computer-generated and in color. The amazing thing about this very complicated object is that,

FIGURE 14.13 Mandelbrot Set

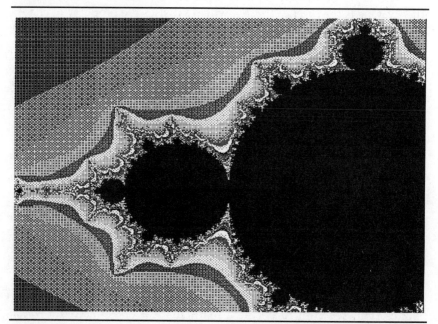

although there is no mathematical formula describing it, to generate it is mathematically very simple:

> Consider the formula $Z^2 + C$, where Z and C are complex numbers $(a + bi, i = \sqrt{-1})$.
>
> If one picks an arbitrary complex number Z_0 and iterates according to $Z_{n+1} = Z^2_n + C$, then one of two things will happen. Either $Z_{n+1} \to \infty$ or to a finite number. The black region is the set of those starting values for which $Z_{n+1} \to \infty$.
>
> Despite the simplicity of the function $Z^2 + C$, the resulting region of divergence is a fractal of incredible complexity.

Why are fractals often discussed in relation to chaos theory? Very often, a chaotic dynamical system possesses strange attractors—attractors that are fractals.

Strange attractors do exist in mathematical models of physical phenomena such as the pendulum. Their importance follows from the fact that, even though they are strange sets and are unpredictable, they do represent an equilibrium situation and one that is bounded.

There is a possible application of these notions to financial markets. If price series are fractals, as implied by Mandelbrot's observations, then their self-similarity may lead to qualitative or quantitative predictability. That is, if a daily price series is congruent to a weekly one, then today's price may be an indication of next week's price. This is still pure speculation, however; if someone has indeed been successful at this theory, it is being kept a secret.

Potential Applications

There are two natural questions that portfolio managers ask regarding nonlinear dynamics and chaos theory. First and foremost is whether nonlinear deterministic relationships exist in financial markets. If the answer is in the affirmative, then the second question is: How are these relationships discovered and exploited? To date, no one has made public anything except allusions to these questions. There have been no announcements of major breakthroughs of super trading systems giving spectacular returns. This is not surprising; if one were to discover such a technique, it would be madness to publish it and give the secret away. However, there are signs that researchers are indeed discovering possible nonlinear relationships with correlation dimensions between 6 and 8. It is our contention that the answer to the first question is, "Yes, nonlinear deterministic relationships do exist in financial markets."

That these relationships exist is perhaps more a matter of faith and intuition than a matter of concrete fact. The evidence leading us to this belief includes the following:

1. There are some researchers reporting such findings using statistical analysis designed to discover such behavior. Naturally, there are others who find no such behavior.
2. Technical analysis, which is more of a linear approach, does have a substantial following; it works better than can be explained by pure randomness. Because it is a linear, low-dimensional approach, however, it cannot perceive relationships in higher dimensions. It is analogous to plotting planetary motion without knowing Newton's laws.
3. If markets are random and follow laws such as those assumed in option pricing models, there would be no gapping and drastic shocks to markets. This is clearly not the case—markets often gap. Chaotic physical systems such as avalanches and turbulent flows can be well-behaved for a long time but suddenly a threshold of sorts is reached and a shock occurs. This means that chaotic systems have instabilities that are inherent in their complex makeup. These cannot be modeled with linear mathematics. The economy at large certainly appears to possess such an inherently unstable character.
4. There are many cycle theories about economics and financial markets. These sound a great deal like strange attractors. Once in a cycle, we stay there for a while until, all of a sudden, we shoot out. All we know for sure is their future ranges, not their actual values.

If we are correct that financial markets are nonlinear deterministic systems, then a new approach to modeling will be required. The implications are:

1. Market behavior will be unpredictable except for short periods.
2. The efficient market hypothesis is incorrect (this is good news because arbitrage opportunities will always be present). Tactical asset allocation will work well.
3. Large-scale quantitative behavior will be predictable; we may not know future values but we will know the slope of attractors. Cycles do exist but they are fractals; they are irregular, but at least we know their ranges.

One major problem is that we are unlikely to discover specific equations for market behavior. This means that approximations based on nonlinear autoregressive functional forms will be used. Perhaps such functions will be as simple as the logistic equation $P_{i+1} = AP_i(1 - P_i)$ but using five or more past values of P_i, not just one.

One thing is certain: If, and when, chaos theory is applied successfully to financial markets, there will be an entirely new vocabulary and viewpoint in our field. As stated above, nonlinear deterministic relationships in an economy imply (1) a negation of the efficient market hypothesis and (2) that value can be added through the techniques of tactical asset allocation.

SOURCES

There is a rich literature available for those interested in chaos theory. The sources listed below are mainly concerned with applications to finance. The work by James Gleick is especially recommended for its broad perspective on the subject. Zhang Shu-yu's book is convincing evidence that chaos theory is not a passing fad: it lists 7,157 technical references on the subject, as of 1991.

Bernd Anders, "Chaos Theory and Market Behaviour," *Technical Analysis of Stocks & Commodities* (November 1989).

Alison Butler, "A Methodological Approach to Chaos: Are Economists Missing the Point?," *Federal Reserve Bank of St. Louis* (March–April 1990).

Murray Frank and Thanasis Stengos, "Chaotic Dynamics in Economic Time-Series," *Journal of Economic Surveys, 2* (February 1988).

James Gleick, *Chaos: Making a New Science* (New York: Viking Penguin Inc., 1987).

Celso Grebogi, Edward Ott, and James A. Yorke, "Chaos, Strange Attractors, and Fractal Basin Boundaries in Nonlinear Dynamics," *Science, 238* (October 1987).

Victor E. Krynicki, "Market Prediction through Fractal Geometry," *Technical Analysis of Stocks & Commodities* (March 1982).

Edgar E. Peters, "A Chaotic Attractor for the S&P 500," *Final Analysts Journal* (March–April 1991).

Edgar E. Peters, *Chaos and Order in the Capital Markets* (New York: John Wiley and Sons, Inc., 1991).

Ilya Prigogine and Isabelle Stengers, *Order Out of Chaos* (New York: Bantam Doubleday Dell Publishing Group, Inc., 1984).

Robert Savit, "Nonlinearities and Chaotic Effects in Options Prices," *The Journal of Futures Markets, 9* (June 1989).

Robert Savit, "When Random Is Not Random: An Introduction to Chaos in Market Prices," *The Journal of Futures Markets, 8* (1988).

Zhang Shu-yu, *Bibliography on Chaos—Directions in Chaos Volume 5* (Singapore: World Publishing Co., 1991).

Lars Tvede, "What 'Chaos' Really Means in Financial Markets," *Futures* (January 1992).

15

Global Asset Allocation

Peter M. Hill
President
Bailard, Biehl & Kaiser

An asset allocator who looks beyond the domestic stock and bond markets will find increased opportunities to improve the return–risk trade-off. Global investing, however, exposes portfolios to increased political and economic risks. Existing quantitative asset allocation techniques may not be sufficient to deal with these risks. A disciplined qualitative approach is needed to analyze risk under conditions of uncertainty. Understanding this dilemma and examining a scenario-based approach to dealing with uncertainty form the heart of this chapter.

WHAT IS GLOBAL ASSET ALLOCATION?

To a global investor, the world does not consist of the United States plus "international" markets. Instead, the United States is viewed as only one of a series of stock and bond markets that provide investment opportunities. The global asset allocator does not just compare the equity markets of the world against one another; he or she compares stocks against bonds within each country and compares the stock and bond markets of each country against others. Asset allocation occurs within countries and across countries.

Global asset allocation can be carried out at a policy, strategic, or tactical level. Policy concerns the very long-run outlook involving a detailed consideration of the liabilities that must be met many years into

Scenario analysis is labor intensive and it would not have been possible to present it in this chapter without drawing upon the efforts of the author's research colleagues at Bailard, Biehl & Kaiser. The author thanks his colleagues but takes full responsibility for any remaining deficiencies in this chapter.

the future. On a strategic level, the time-horizon being considered is usually one year, although it may be longer. On a tactical level, changes in market and country allocation occur much more frequently—for example, on a quarterly, monthly, or weekly basis.

WHY BE A GLOBAL ASSET ALLOCATOR?

Asset allocation techniques have had success in the United States market. The most dramatic example occurred in 1987, when many asset allocation models took investors out of U.S. stocks ahead of the October crash. It is natural for investors to want to apply those same techniques overseas. A glance at Figure 15.1, which displays the familiar return–risk chart for the stock and bond markets of the United States, the United Kingdom, Germany, and Japan, will reveal why the potential prize is worth seeking. The time period covered is 20 years and the returns are annualized; the risk is the standard deviation of the annual returns. Notice that the efficient frontier bounding all eight markets dominates the stock–bond frontier of the United States alone. This implies a superior playing field for the global asset allocator when compared to domestic-only counterparts. Figure 15.1, however, is for "fixed mix" strategies only. Active asset allocation implies an opportunity to achieve even greater returns. Indeed, global allocation implies more opportunities to apply investment skills. Point GAA shows the return

FIGURE 15.1 Risk–Return Analysis (1972–1991)

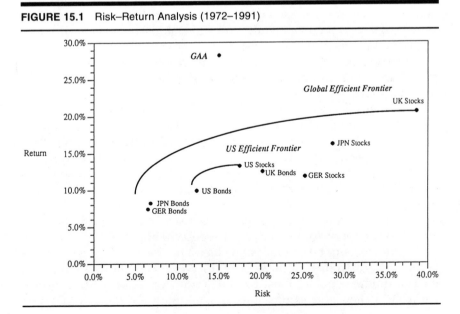

and risk that would have been achieved by a global asset allocator who, each year, successfully picked (and equally weighted in a portfolio) the four best markets. The rewards for demonstrating skill in global asset allocation are potentially very great!

HOW SHOULD GLOBAL ASSET ALLOCATION BE DONE?

Many methods are used for asset allocation, but in the domestic market asset allocation specialists have most often been associated with quantitative techniques. The most widely utilized approach has been mean reversion, or equilibrium theory.

Under the premise of mean reversion, there is an underlying equilibrium valuation of stocks versus bonds (usually expressed as a risk premium). At any point in time, if the relationship has moved to an extreme position, an investor should weight more heavily the undervalued asset in a portfolio. Over time, as reversion to equilibrium occurs, there is relative outperformance from the undervalued asset class.

There are two principal drawbacks to the mean reversion approach: (1) the mechanism and timing of the return to equilibrium are uncertain, and (2) the equilibrium position itself may change over time!

Underlying the mean reversion technique is the assumption that relationships modeled on past data will prove robust in the future. In other words, the risk distribution for key variables is determinable and stable. If this is so, then optimal investment strategies can be developed. Unfortunately, when building models to explain investment markets, care must be exercised to remember that we face not only statistical risk (if there is stability in relationships) but also uncertainty about the future (if the relationships change over time).

Some examples will illustrate the difficulties faced because of simple reliance on mean reversion and the stability of relationships. Figure 15.2 shows equity earnings yield minus long bond yields for the United States between 1960 and 1992. This is a simple expression of the risk premium between bonds and stocks. An investor relying on this relationship's acting in the 1980s as it had in the 1960s and 1970s would have been very surprised! In the most recent decade, only bonds would have been held—unless, of course, the model was changed in recognition of the apparently new relationship between stocks and bonds.

Figure 15.3 shows the relationship between equity earnings yields and ten-year bonds for Germany between 1972 and 1992. The behavior of this relationship before 1975 and since late 1989 would suggest a different pattern from the intervening 14 years. Has the risk premium made a fundamental and lasting shift into new territory? In contrast, Figure 15.4 shows the same equity risk premium for the U.K. between

FIGURE 15.2   Equity Earnings Yield – Long Bond Yields: United States

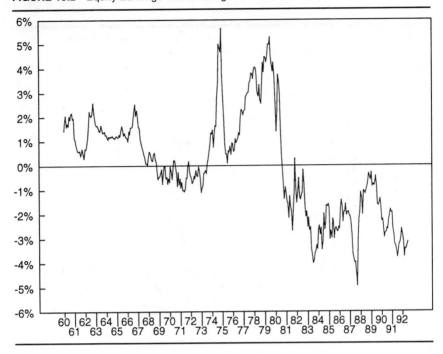

FIGURE 15.3   Equity Earnings Yield – Long Bond Yields: Germany

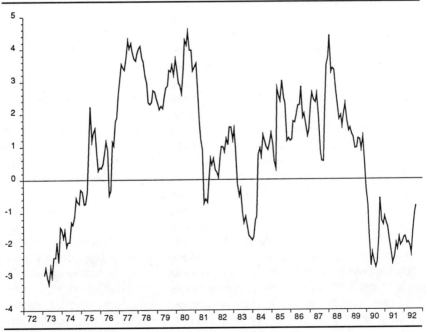

SOURCE: Datastream

FIGURE 15.4 Equity Earnings Yield – Long Bond Yields: United Kingdom

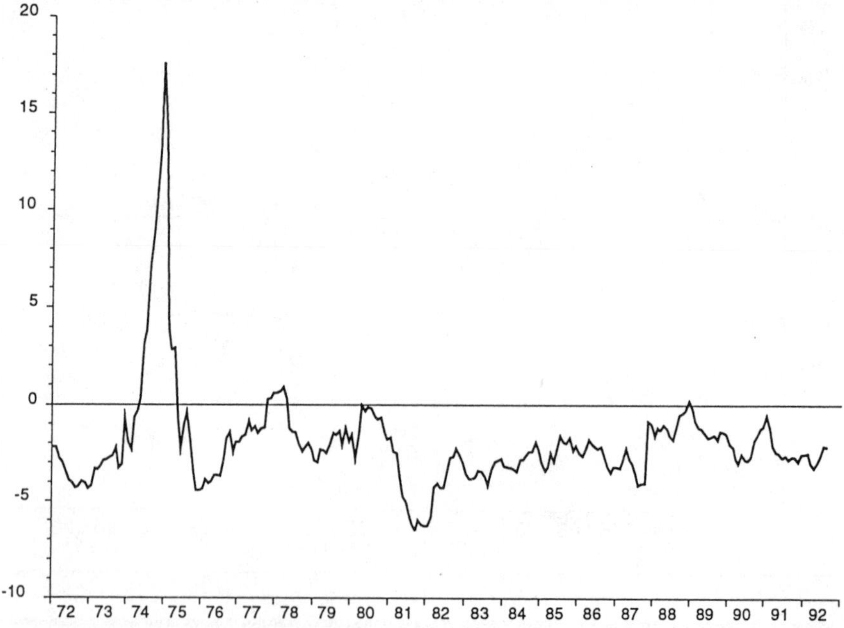

SOURCE: Datastream

1972 and 1992. There is remarkable stability, despite wildly fluctuating economic conditions over the period, and the model still seems to be working in its original form! In Figure 15.5, which shows the equity risk premium for France over the same period, it is hard to see any stability whatsoever in the risk premium relationship.

The future holds uncertainty as well as risk. On a global scale, change means increased uncertainty. Especially on the global stage, there is no sound basis for assuming that investment risk distributions (particularly those relating to mean-reversion techniques) have been adequately mapped out. To invest successfully, it is necessary to look forward and not merely rely on back testing!

What methodology, if any, is there to deal with uncertainty? How can there be disciplined thinking about the future?

One solution is to try to avoid the problem of major changes in relationships by shortening the time-horizon for forecasting and applying factor analysis to the problem. Under factor analysis, market performance is attributed to a series of underlying factors (inflation, real interest rates, and so on), and then attempts are made to predict market behavior by examining the correlation between factors and subsequent

FIGURE 15.5   Equity Earnings Yield − Long Bond Yields: France

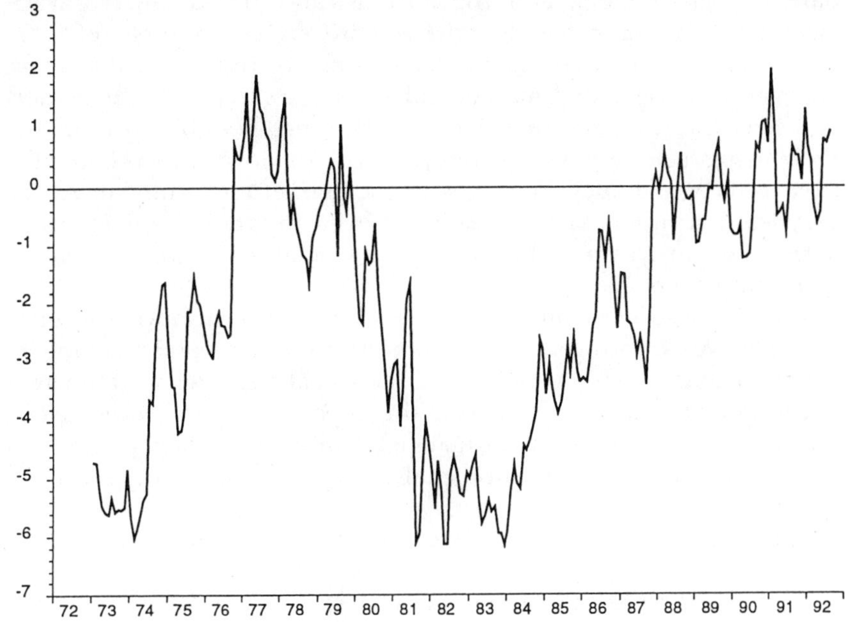

SOURCE: Datastream

market performance. Even a small amount of skill, if exercised over a repeated number of short-term periods (e.g., one or three months), can accumulate to considerable outperformance in the longer term. This is a very promising approach to short-term forecasting and tactical investing, but it still does not address fundamental changes in relationships and future uncertainty.

A second and very promising answer to the dilemma of future uncertainty lies in the field of "scenario analysis." In contrast to factor analysis, this approach usually extends the time period being considered to a year or longer, and admits that the complexity of the investment world needs an approach that can more easily accommodate change. In the remainder of this chapter, a multiple scenario approach to global asset allocation will be outlined and discussed.

MULTIPLE-SCENARIO ANALYSIS

Multiple-scenario analysis can be defined as a disciplined method of applying qualitative analysis to problems of uncertainty. It is a method that combines the learning from experience inherent in the quantitative approach with an intelligent analysis of the future. The greater the uncertainty of the outcome, the better suited is the problem to scenario analysis. On one level, the outcomes and consequences of wars, elections, and economic policy changes are obvious examples of problems that scenario analysis can tackle well. To the extent that these changes are reflected in market and economic variables such as short and long interest rate movements, it becomes possible to integrate them using factor analysis techniques. The key to success is being the first to recognize major changes in the market environment. At the very least, abrupt changes in rules or behavior are more likely to be anticipated in advance through scenario analysis than via existing quantitative models.

Applying scenario analysis to investment problems involves defining objectives, creating scenarios, forecasting returns, and reaching investment conclusions. At first sight, the global stage, with its inherent uncertainties, seems well suited to this type of analysis. Nevertheless, arriving successfully at an optimal global investment strategy involves a complex journey, and scenario analysis must be carried out with discipline and care.

Six important steps are involved in applying scenario analysis:

1. Define global investment objectives;
2. Determine today's starting point;
3. Create future alternative scenarios;
4. Forecast asset returns in each scenario;
5. Assign scenario probabilities;
6. Choose optimal portfolio.

Each is discussed in the following subsections.

Define Global Investment Objectives

What is the time-horizon under consideration? Is it three months, one year, five years? Is the objective to maximize return, minimize risk, or avoid losing money? Are there constraints on the proportions or amounts that may be invested in a particular asset class? Is the aim to outperform a specific benchmark portfolio (perhaps a long-run policy portfolio) that needs improvement during the coming time period? These questions must be formulated at the start of asset allocation so that the process can be designed to provide the right answers. The typical large U.S. institutional investor has a policy or benchmark asset mix, and upper and lower bounds are usually set on the percentage of total assets that can be invested in a single asset category. Table 15.1 gives an example of the plan assets for a typical large company, XYZ.

TABLE 15.1   Company XYZ's Long-Term Policy and Current Mix

	Range (%)	Current Mix (%) (10/9/92)
Equities		
U.S. stocks	50–70%	49.0%
International stocks	0–10	3.5
LBOs	0–10	5.7
	50–70%	58.2%
Fixed Income		
U.S. bonds	20–35%	35.6%
International bonds	0–5	0.0
	20–35%	35.6%
Real Estate	5–10%	5.8%
Cash Equivalents	0–10%	0.4%

SOURCE: Bailard, Biehl & Kaiser (September 1992)

Generally, the scenario approach is best suited to strategic rather than tactical asset allocation, and a one-year (or longer) time-horizon is appropriate.

Determine Today's Starting Point

The global investor has to begin by surveying the starting point for all the key markets of the world. As a practical matter, the most straightforward way to do this is on a country-by-country basis. At this point, the tools and models used will be those that an orthodox quantitative or fundamental analyst might use. Table 15.2 provides starting-point statistics for Germany, France, and the United Kingdom. (This information formed the background starting point to scenario analysis undertaken in September 1992.) The framework for most economic scenarios consists of GNP growth and inflation. The former represents the "goods and services" part of the economy, and the latter represents the "monetary" part of the economy. Short-term and long-term interest rates are also key parameters to scenario construction.

Create Future Alternative Scenarios

This step is very different and more complex. It demands skill, imagination, and openmindedness on the part of the investor.

Scenario analysis needs to be focused. Creating scenarios can be intellectually interesting and stimulating, but the scenarios will only be useful to the problem at hand if they are focused keenly on the question

TABLE 15.2 Starting-Point Data for Three Major European Countries

	RGNP[3]	CPI[3]	Nominal		Real	
			Short Rates[4]	Long Rates[4]	Short Rates[4]	Long Rates[4]
Historical Starting Point: Germany						
1950–1960	7.0%	N.A			—	—
1960–1973	5.3	3.2%	4.7%	7.1%	1.5%	3.9%
1974–1983	1.7	4.8	6.5	8.3	1.7	3.5
1984–1989	2.7	3.8	4.9	6.9	1.1	3.1
1988	3.5	1.3	4.9	6.5	3.2	4.7
1989	3.9	2.8	7.7	7.5	4.5	4.5
1990	4.7	2.7	8.4	8.9	5.7	6.1
1991[3]	0.9	3.5	9.2	8.3	4.8	4.1
1992[1]	1.4 (e)	3.9 (e)	9.5	7.7	3.4	3.6
1993[1]	2.0 (e)	3.5 (e)	8.0	7.5	4.5	4.0
Current[2]	0.6 (Q)	3.5 (July)	9.3 (Sept)	7.3 (Sept)	5.8	3.8
Historical Starting Point: France						
1947–1973	5.3%	4.5%			—	—
1974–1983 (Aug)	1.7	11.2	10.8	12.70	0.3%	1.5%
1984–1989 (Aug)	2.7	4.2	9.1	9.90	4.9	6.1
1988	3.5	2.7	8.2	8.60	5.1	5.6
1989	3.9	3.5	10.5	9.30	6.9	5.8
1990	4.7	3.4	9.7	10.00	6.3	6.6
1991	0.9	3.1	10.1	8.70	7.0	5.6
1992[1]	2.0	3.0	9.5	8.40	7.2	5.4
1993[1]	2.4	2.8	8.5	8.20	5.7	5.4
Current[2]	2.9 (1Q)	2.9 (July)	10.9 (Sept)	8.70 (Sept)	8.0	5.8
Historical Starting Point: United Kingdom						
1950–1973	3.30%	4.8%	5.2%	7.4%	0.4%	2.6%
1974–1983	1.10	13.7	10.1	13.2	3.6	−0.5
1984–1989	3.40	4.1	10.8	9.9	6.7	5.8
1988	4.10	4.9	12.8	9.4	6.0	2.7
1989	2.20	7.8	14.9	10.0	7.2	2.3
1990	1.00	9.5	14.0	10.4	4.7	1.1
1991	−2.10	5.8	10.5	9.6	6.0	5.1
1992[1]	−0.30	4.0	9.6	9.0	5.6	5.0
1993[1]	1.80	3.6	8.5	8.5	4.9	4.9
Current[2]	−0.70 (2Q)	3.7 (July)	9.8 (Sept)	9.1 (Sept)	6.1	5.4

[1] Economist poll.
[2] Trailing 12 months.
[3] Calendar year.
[4] Year-End.
SOURCE: Bailard, Biehl & Kaiser (September 1992)

to be answered: What will be the performance of stock and bond markets? For each of the world's major economies, there are three distinct, financial-market outcomes to consider:

1. Stocks and bonds both rise in price (i.e., favorable financial markets);
2. Stocks and bonds both fall in price (i.e., unfavorable financial markets);
3. There are mixed changes in stock and bond markets (i.e., one asset outperforms significantly, or there is little change in either bond or stock prices).

Scenarios are then constructed that lead to each of these outcomes. Each scenario must contain information regarding the key factors that influence these outcomes. Thus, economic growth, inflation, and interest rate assumptions are essential in defining a scenario. Any changes in the "rules of the game" (e.g., political changes) must also be included if relevant.

Having defined the scenario parameters, it is also important to identify the "driving force(s)" that are likely to determine each scenario's outcome. What will determine whether interest rates are high or low, or economic growth is fast or slow? Ultimately, identifying the right driving forces and betting on their outcome will be at the heart of the success of the multiple-scenario methodology. For example, in 1989–1990, German unification was the driving force behind interest rates in Europe. Correctly assessing the costs and timetable for the integration of East Germany was the key to forecasting the peak in interest rates and how long interest rates would remain high.

Finally, it is important to identify trigger points for confirmation of a particular scenario and to indicate what action should be taken. Trigger points are only useful, however, if they are based on information that is not immediately and universally understood by the markets. For example, waiting for a low inflation number to be announced to confirm the hypothesis that bonds should be bought is too naive to succeed. Conversely, a "bad news" inflation announcement might be sought as a contrarian opportunity by bond investors who have based their investment outlook on a falling interest rate scenario!

Table 15.3 summarizes alternative scenarios for the United States, Japan, Europe as a whole, and Germany, the U.K., and France. (These are simplified versions of scenarios that were actually created and used in September 1992.) The driving force in the U.S. market was determined to be debt. Would excessive debt hinder economic growth and depress earnings-per-share growth? Although no exclusive triggers could firmly define which side of the hypothesis to be on, monitoring

TABLE 15.3 Summary of Scenarios

	Starting Point	Slow Growth	Recession	Strong Recovery
U.S.		Slow Go	Triple Dip	Stronger Growth
RGNP	1.50%	2.00%	1.00%	3.50%
CPI	3.10	2.25	2.00	4.00
Short rates	3.00	2.75	2.25	4.50
Long rates	6.40	6.25	5.75	8.00
Japan		Growth Recession	Recession	Boom
RGNP	2.20%	2.70%	1.00%	4.50%
CPI	1.70	2.00	0.50	3.50
Short rates	3.70	3.25	2.50	5.50
Long rates	4.90	4.50	4.00	6.50
Europe*		Stop/Go	No Ease	Rapid Ease
RGNP	0.30%	2.20%	1.80%	3.25%
CPI	3.40	2.80	3.30	3.50
Short rates	10.00	7.20	10.30	7.00
Long rates	8.20	7.20	8.90	7.00
Germany		Stop/Go	No Ease	Rapid Ease
RGNP	0.60%	2.00%	2.50%	3.00%
CPI	3.50	2.75	4.00	3.00
Short rates	9.30	6.50	10.50	6.25
Long rates	7.30	6.50	8.50	6.25
U.K.		Stop/Go	No Ease	Rapid Ease
RGNP	−0.70%	2.00%	1.00%	3.00%
CPI	3.70	3.50	3.00	4.00
Short rates	9.80	8.25	10.50	8.00
Long rates	9.10	8.25	9.50	8.00
France		Stop/Go	No Ease	Rapid Ease
RGNP	2.90%	2.50%	1.50%	3.50%
CPI	2.90	3.00	2.50	3.50
Short rates	10.90	7.25	10.00	7.00
Long rates	8.70	7.25	9.00	7.00

* GDP-Weighted: Germany 42%, France 32%, United Kingdom 26%
SOURCE: Bailard, Biehl & Kaiser (September 1992)

trends in consumer, corporate, and government borrowing would be important. In Europe, the actions of the Bundesbank were deemed to be the most significant driving force. Monitoring of any discussions or events associated with Bundesbank policy created potential triggers to investment decisions. In Japan, the driving force was market confidence in the Japanese economy. Actions by the government and monetary authorities could be deemed triggers to the direction and timing of the return of confidence. Table 15.3 also aligns the clusters of scenarios that were considered likely to occur together. Thus, global "slow growth" included "growth recession" in Japan and "stop/go" in Germany, the United Kingdom, and France.

Forecast Asset Returns in Each Scenario

Defining the scenarios gives a framework for predicting asset returns within each market. If the scenario has been defined in detail, then it is possible to use rigorous quantitative methods to estimate likely market returns. Given assumptions for inflation, short-term interest rates, and industrial production, it is possible to apply statistical models to predict price–earnings ratios and likely changes in earnings. Figure 15.6, an example of a price–earnings model for the United States, illustrates how far away from "fair value" (measured by standard deviations) the market has been over time. Given short- and long-term interest rates and the inflation rate under each scenario, the model can be used to define the likely price–earnings ratio for each scenario. At a later stage, these price–earnings ratios must be combined with estimates of earnings under each scenario in order to determine the total return from equities.

Beyond forecasts for major stock and bond markets, a crucial step in global scenario analysis is currency forecasting. Once again, all the traditional tools for currency forecasting can be utilized (e.g., purchasing power parity, trade deficit analysis, relative interest rates, and so

FIGURE 15.6 Fair Value Model—Operating Earnings (Deviation from Regression Fit)

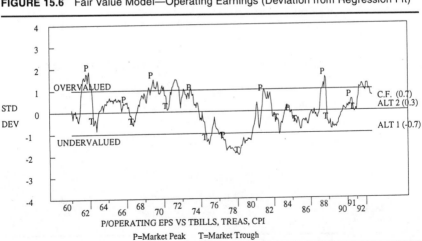

P/OPERATING EPS VS TBILLS, TREAS, CPI

P=Market Peak   T=Market Trough

on). The key difference is that alternate forecasts are made for each global scenario. In the example shown in Table 15.3, when the United States is in slow growth, Japan is considered to be in growth recession. The exchange rate forecast assumes this combination of scenarios will occur.

Table 15.4 shows an example of one-year forecasted returns for global scenarios of slow growth, recession, and strong recovery. Currency forecasts are shown separately, and non-U.S. stock and bond market returns are shown on a local and a hedged basis.

Assign Scenario Probabilities

This step is one of the most controversial aspects of the multiscenario process. How can the probability of occurrence for a given scenario be assigned with any degree of confidence?

Three actions can help here. First, if carried out diligently, the process of creating scenarios itself should shed some light on the likelihood of occurrence. For example, if there are many plausible paths into a

TABLE 15.4 One-Year Forecasted Returns

		Slow Growth	Recession	Strong Recovery
		Stocks		
U.S.		11.4%	−14.2%	4.8%
Europe	Local	18.1%	−23.1%	29.8%
	Unhedged	13.8	−11.6	10.5
	Hedged	13.7	−30.0	25.5
Japan	Local	16.2%	−21.6%	21.0%
	Unhedged	10.0	−32.0	24.5
	Hedged	15.7	−21.7	19.4
		Bonds		
U.S.	10-Year	7.4%	10.8%	−3.8%
	30-Year	17.3	24.1	−3.2
Europe	Local	14.6%	3.9%	16.3%
	Unhedged	10.3	15.4	−3.0
	Hedged	10.2	−3.0	12.0
Japan	Local	8.6%	12.3%	−5.2%
	Unhedged	2.4	1.9	−1.8
	Hedged	8.1	12.1	−6.9
		Currency		
U.S. Cash		2.8%	2.6%	3.8%
D.M./$		4.3	−11.5	19.3
Yen/$		6.2	10.4	−3.5

SOURCE: Bailard, Biehl & Kaiser (September 1992)

given scenario, then that scenario has a relatively high probability of occurring. Extreme difficulty in finding a trail of plausible circumstances that could lead to a particular outcome would suggest a relatively low probability.

Second, it is possible to use historical analyses to examine when similar scenarios have occurred, with what frequency, and under what circumstances. Comparison of today's environment with historical precedents can shed light on the likelihood that a scenario may repeat in some form. Figure 15.7 uses quarterly inflation and GDP rates to show the historical distribution of scenarios for the United States, Europe, and Japan.

Third, quantitative techniques can be utilized to assist in forecasting the key economic parameters that define the scenarios, such as real GDP growth, inflation, and interest rates. This method works better when the time frames for the scenarios are short. The method permits a quantifiable precision of the probabilities.

Choose an Optimal Asset Mix

Given global scenarios, global scenario probabilities, and forecasted returns for each asset (and currency), the stage is set to return to the defined objectives and determine the portfolio of assets that most rationally fulfills those objectives!

By setting the analysis in the form of a matrix, as shown in Table 15.5, the problem can be solved using linear programming techniques. The "objective function" is to maximize returns, subject to the constraints of the assets available, asset class ranges, and the desire to perform better than the benchmark portfolio under all (or some) scenarios.

Across the top of the matrix in Table 15.5 are alternative sets of scenario probabilities. In each case, one of the three scenarios is treated as the most likely and is assigned a 60 percent probability. In conducting the optimization exercise, we begin with the current mix (taken from the XYZ Company example, but excluding the LBO asset category) and then show the optimal portfolios that would be chosen under each set of scenario probabilities (given the constraints of the plan) and the forecasted returns. The bottom section of the table shows the expected return under each set of scenario probabilities, using the optimal mix.

How is "optimal" defined here? Remember that the definition of the optimal mix is driven by the investor's objectives. In the XYZ Company example, the optimal mix was one that—given the scenario probabilities, forecasted returns, and asset range constraints—would have an 80 percent chance of outperforming the current asset mix. The conditions could have been set for equal performance or outperformance

FIGURE 15.7 Economic Scenarios—A Historical Perspective (1970–1991 Quarterly Data)

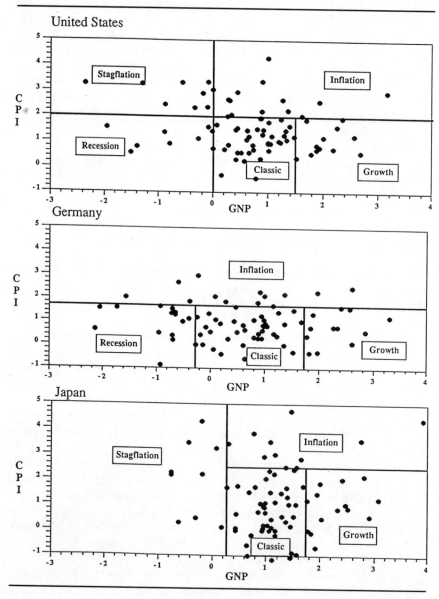

TABLE 15.5 Optimization Results

	Current Mix	I	II	III
Probability				
Slow growth		60%	20%	20%
Recession		20	60	20
Strong recovery		20	20	60
Optimal Portfolio				
U.S. stocks	52%	50%	50%	50%
International stocks	3	10 J(H)	0	3 J(H)
U.S. bonds	38	30	30	30
International bonds	0	5 E(U)	5 E(U)	5 E(U)
Real estate	7	5	10	10
Cash equivalents	0	0	5	2
Expected Return				
Slow Growth	9.7%	10.4%	9.4%	9.8%
Recession	−4.6	−5.7	−3.8	−4.6
Strong recovery	2.5	3.6	2.5	3.0

J(H)—Japan hedged
E(U)—Europe hedged
SOURCE: Bailard, Biehl & Kaiser (September 1992)

100 percent of the time, but the trade-off is that potential returns in the most likely scenario will be curtailed by having to cover the minimum return requirements for an "unlikely" scenario.

This analytical framework provides a convenient format for demonstrating the sensitivity of any of the assumptions, constraints, and/or forecasts that have been used. It is important to focus on assumptions that are key to the optimal portfolios that are being chosen and, where necessary, carefully reconsider those assumptions.

Finally, choosing a single optimal portfolio is a matter of judgment. How great are the investment risks of the "unlikely" scenarios? How confident is the investor about the most "likely" scenario and the associated return forecasts? What are other short-term tactical models suggesting? All of these considerations will play a role in choosing the final strategic asset allocation mix.

GLOBAL SCENARIO ANALYSIS—A CRITIQUE

Scenario analysis is complicated, and a number of arguments have been put forward to declare it unsuitable for asset allocation. Those most frequently heard are:

1. "Too subjective." The construction of scenarios needs creativity but is inevitably subjective. To the extent that judgment is involved, biases may creep into the analysis. These biases could sway the analysis and lead to erroneous conclusions. However, it must be remembered that, under conditions of uncertainty, an extrapolation of historical relationships will be at most risk of misleading the potential investor. Examining the uncertainty in a disciplined but imaginative way is the best method of dealing with uncertainty.

2. "Too labor-intensive." A thorough global scenario analysis requires many work-hours and (ideally) input from a wide variety of experts. It is a cumbersome methodology if the analysis is carried out frequently. However, *the global investment markets are complicated* and there are no shortcuts to examining carefully the and the interrelationships among markets.

3. "Leads to conservative investment style." If a "negative" scenario is presented plausibly, then too much weight may be given (inadvertently) to "safer" investment policies. Over time, this may mean that risks are overestimated. However, this criticism is not so much about scenario analysis as about how it is applied. If investment strategy is based on the single most likely scenario, then the charge of conservatism is inappropriate.

4. "Presents too many links in a complicated chain." Choosing the scenarios, forecasting the returns, and then determining likely probabilities—the many steps involved in the scenario process represent a number of potential sources of error. However, there cannot be fewer steps because the problem of predicting future asset returns is complicated and there are many factors to consider. Breaking the problem down into a series of disciplined steps is a sensible way to handle this complexity.

GLOBAL ASSET ALLOCATION AND SCENARIO ANALYSIS—CONCLUSIONS?

In a changing world of complex interrelationships, the scenario approach provides a useful method for analyzing the possible behavior of asset returns. The method is better suited to longer-term asset strategy than to short-term allocation. New situations or situations where the old order of "rules" may abruptly change (e.g., the breakup of the European Exchange Rate Mechanism) are a better fit for the method. It is a way of expanding the horizon of investment thinking and being prepared for circumstances that may initially be deemed unlikely to occur. It is a tool that equips the investor with greater awareness of opportunities and pitfalls. Indeed, at its most basic level, the scenario approach is a risk-control mechanism—exploring all that might happen to cause investment strategies to go awry, and then stimulating serious forethought to a plan of action. Paradoxically, some of the important strengths of scenario work—the creativity, the ability to imagine new and different investment circumstances—are also its greatest weaknesses. Bias, overconcern with unlikely contingencies, and, ultimately, too much conservatism, are the dangers of the scenario approach.

The best implementation for scenario work therefore is in longer-term analysis, where it can form a backcloth to other tactical approaches that are most sensitive to short-term changes in the markets. To use an analogy from weather forecasting, the scenario approach may reveal that a hurricane exists and could be heading toward land; the short-term analysis waits for the wind speeds to climb before acknowledging that the hurricane exists. For the purposes of planning action, neither piece of knowledge separately is as valuable as knowing both!

─────────── 16 ───────────

Global Bonds and
Currency Management

Charles J. Freifeld
Vice President
Senior Quantitative Analyst
The Boston Company

INTRODUCTION

Institutional investors diversify their investment portfolios to raise returns and lower risk. Domestic investors have therefore allocated increasing portions of their portfolios to foreign stock and bond markets over the past 20 years. The growing liquidity of global markets has further encouraged these trends.

Although the currency markets are the most liquid markets in the world, relatively little institutional money has been assigned to currency management strategies. This is unfortunate for two reasons: (1) currency price volatility can have a substantial effect on the net performance of portfolios of foreign stocks, bonds, and cash; and (2) the returns from currency management are not correlated with those from traditional investment classes.

The purpose of this chapter is to present an overview of the role played by global bonds and currencies in asset allocation strategies. We begin by reviewing the reasons for adding foreign bonds to a domestic fixed-income portfolio. This review is followed by a description of the international bond markets.

Because currency fluctuations can have a significant effect on the return generated by a foreign bond in a domestic portfolio, the domestic

This chapter is an updated and expanded version of an article originally written by Dr. Ulrich S. Moser, Chief Investment Officer, Schröder Münchmeyes Hengst Investment GmbH.

investor who diversifies internationally must take into account the currency markets. The chapter therefore also surveys the currency markets, which can be used for both hedging and investment.

Currency hedging allows the domestic institutional investor to protect foreign bond portfolios against currency losses. The chapter will also show that the dynamics of the currency markets lead naturally to the use of currency investment as an allocation category in diversified portfolios. Currency investment will be shown to be a valuable addition to institutional portfolios for two primary reasons: (1) currency management can generate added returns without increasing risk, and (2) currency management returns are not correlated with returns from investments usually held in institutional portfolios.

GLOBAL BONDS

The goal of investment management is to maximize the compounded rate of growth of capital over the long run. In practice, this goal is pursued by diversifying through asset allocation. The portfolio manager looks for new investment areas that can add return to the overall portfolio. Ideally, the returns from these new investment categories are as uncorrelated as possible with the returns from investments already in the portfolio.

Our purpose here is to examine foreign bonds from this point of view. What are the reasons for investing in foreign bonds?

Through most of the 1980s, yields were high in the United States, in comparison to other countries and to previous decades. The country was emerging from a terrible bout with inflation during the late 1970s, when the prime rate reached 21 percent and yields of long bonds were over 15 percent. Ten years ago, Americans paid little attention to foreign bonds. When American pension plans started to diversify internationally in the early 1980s, they concentrated on stocks.

As inflation subsided in the 1980s, bond yields declined. In 1993, as this chapter is being written, foreign bonds not only look attractive but hold a possibility of becoming even more attractive in the years to come. When allocating or reallocating their assets, American institutional investors will increasingly consider international bonds. Inter-Sec Research, a leading U.S. pension consultant, estimates that the growth rate of international bond investments will reach that of foreign equities investments for the years 1991 through 1994.

Why would anyone buy a 6 percent coupon bond when an 8 percent coupon bond is also available? The purchaser will do so if the price is right, that is, if the total return expected from the lower-coupon bond is equal to or higher than the total return from the higher-coupon bond. Bonds are bought for total return. In the case of foreign bonds,

the total return is a function of the interest rate and redemption proceeds in the foreign currency, and the return of that currency relative
to the home currency of the investor (assumed here to be the U.S. dollar). Over a recent seven-year period, currency contributed 25 percent
of the total return that U.S. investors achieved in international equity
markets (from 1986 to 1992, non-U.S. equities yielded a local currency
return of 9.7 percent annually and a U.S. dollar return of 12.7 percent
annually) as well as 25 percent of the return from holding foreign
bonds. These returns are discussed in later sections.

Throughout the chapter, we will separate the bond-specific aspects
from currency considerations, drawing the reader's attention first to
the fixed-income investment decision. However, this separation is not
possible in practice, and it will become apparent that investment in foreign bonds always requires currency management decisions.

We will use the recent global bond and currency markets to illustrate key points, although the underlying asset class relationships and
currency considerations have not changed over time.

Let us now review in detail the reasons for an investor's decision to
purchase foreign bonds.

REASON 1. RETURN IMPROVEMENT

High-Yielding and Low-Yielding Markets

Historically, low-yielding countries remain low-yielding countries.
The circumstances that permit an easy monetary policy do not change
quickly. The opposite is also true, and high yields persist longer than
most professionals like to believe. Throughout the 1980s, America was
a relatively high-yielding country, but, in spite of high deficits on federal and local levels, yields have recently declined. If it turns out that
America is a relatively low-yielding country in the 1990s, then changing demographics will have been a major reason. The Baby Boomers
are graying, so the savings rate is likely to rise.

The picture has changed dramatically for other countries as well.
Germany, for example, was long considered the country of a super-hard
currency and, therefore, low interest rates. The country had suffered
through two hyperinflations earlier this century, and Germans were
considered to have a strong anti-inflation mindset. As of mid-1993, the
German inflation rate is almost 50 percent above the U.S. inflation rate.
Hence, German yields are above American yields, and many analysts
expect them to stay above for a considerable period to come.

Generally speaking, high yields attract money, at least when they
are not expected to rise much further. This attraction often leads to
international money flows that help to appreciate the high-yielding

currencies. It certainly works in the short-term context (and forms the basis of many central bank policy decisions), but it can also be observed in the longer-term bond markets. Thus, American institutional money flowing into foreign markets will be one of the factors to observe when judging global total returns in the 1990s.

Nominal and Real Yields

Purchasing power considerations are important in the context of retirement planning, for both an individual and a pension fund. The notion is that the prices of "real" assets (stocks, precious metals, and real estate) go up with and therefore protect against monetary inflation. However, these assets can be risky to hold. For planning purposes, bonds offer a more predictable return because they are repaid at their nominal value. Once issued, the inflation risk is with the investor, and borrowers often reap big profits from repaying with inflated money. The bond investor, who is looking for real yields, hopes that the interest received exceeds inflation.

This real-interest aspect takes on a different dimension when investing abroad. If nominal yields in a country are high, inflation in that country is likely to be high, which does not make its markets intuitively attractive. But the purchasing power in that foreign currency is not the investor's primary concern. He or she will ultimately want to spend the money at home. Here is a comparison of the two situations:

Domestic Bonds	Foreign Bonds
Nominal **domestic** yield	Nominal **foreign** yield
− **Domestic** inflation	− **Domestic** inflation
Real yield to investor	Real yield to investor

Looked at in this way, real returns on foreign bonds can be quite staggering. Currency rates are theoretically adjusting for the changes in purchasing power, thereby eliminating the real yield advantage. But, as we will discuss later, the purchasing power parity theory often does not hold in real life. Therefore, international bonds often offer significant opportunities to increase returns, both in nominal and in real terms.

REASON 2. RISK REDUCTION

Most texts on asset allocation concentrate on the risk–return trade-off characteristics. To arrive at a somewhat rational allocation process, they look at past returns and the risks involved therewith, that is, the volatility of such returns. All such numbers are dependent on the time frame selected. The length of the time taken into consideration, the specific ending date and, especially, the time segments (months, quarters, years) all influence the outcome.

Figure 16.1 shows the significant improvement that globalization of bond portfolios brings, as compared to simple domestic investments. The figure also illustrates dramatically the wisdom of diversification. The volatility of most foreign bond markets, looked at individually and expressed in U.S. dollars, is too high for most purposes. But, considered together, the markets smooth out to very attractive levels: "World" has a lower volatility (in U.S. dollars) than any of the foreign markets individually. As shown in Figures 16.2 and 16.3, combinations of domestic bonds with foreign bonds in amounts up to 10 percent of the portfolio improve the risk–return ratio.

Because these risk–return studies look only at the indexes, they underrepresent the good news: active management has proven to be much more successful in global fixed income than their equities counterparts have been in beating the indexes. In the InterSec Research global bond universe as of March 3, 1991, the median manager had outperformed the index over all measured periods, from three months to five years.

FIGURE 16.1 Risk and Return (in U.S. Dollars) of Global Bonds (December 1984 through December 1990)

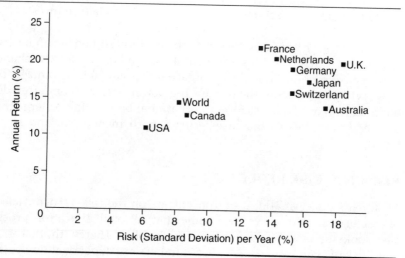

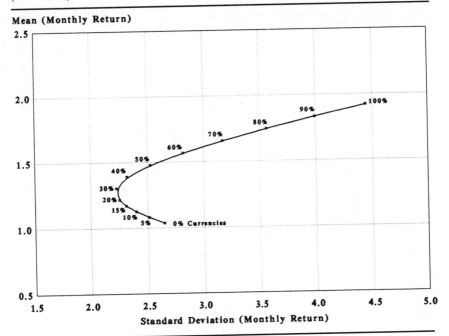

FIGURE 16.2 Efficient Frontier: 50% Bonds/35% S&P/15% EAFE Plus Currencies* (1977–1992)

* For each percentage allocation to currencies, the remaining amount is split 50%/35%/15% among bonds/stocks/EAFE respectively.
EAFE = An index of major stocks of Europe, Australia, and the Far East.

REASON 3. DIVERSIFICATION AMONG MONETARY POLICIES

Every major country today places fighting inflation very high on its national agenda. As a result, global inflation has generally receded, and even countries that have been rather easygoing in the past no longer believe that "a little inflation is a positive thing." The United States is a good example; France is an even better one. Both countries' inflation rates today are below that of Germany.

The current condition of Germany is shedding important light on the simple fact that times change constantly. Germany is considered to be the most inflation-sensitive major country and to have the toughest minded and most independent central bank (Bundesbank). Yet inflation jumped from essentially zero to almost 5 percent in the short period between 1988 and 1992. The reasons were largely outside of the

FIGURE 16.3 Efficient Frontier: Lehman Brothers Government/Corporate Combined with J. P. Morgan Non-U.S. Bond Index (1986–1992)

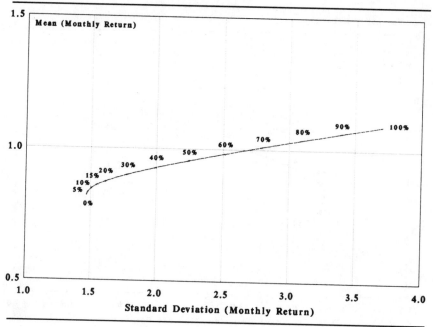

scope of influence of the Bundesbank, which sets the anti-inflationary monetary policy. The lesson to be drawn is that it is unsafe to assume that a current anti-inflationary environment remains in place forever. Eventually, something will happen that will force the U.S. Federal Reserve to tighten monetary policy just as some foreign countries that today are imposing tight money policies will be able to ease their currencies. Because bond investments are typically longer-term decisions, diversification of exposure to monetary policies can add significantly to overall portfolio stability.

A good measure of this diversification effect is the correlation among markets, particularly if looked at in local currency terms, that is, leaving aside the currency impact. Tables 16.1 through 16.3 indicate that some immediately neighboring countries (France, Germany, the Netherlands, and Switzerland) show, as one would expect, a higher correlation, but overall the correlation numbers are surprising low. The tables make a strong case for separating the bond selection from the currency decision.

TABLE 16.1 Correlations of Returns for the Salomon Bond Index in Local Currency, January 1985–September 1991 (Diagonal = Annualized Standard Deviation of Return)

	Australia	Canada	France	Germany	Japan	Netherlands	Switzerland	U.K.	U.S.
Australia	**5.899**								
Canada	0.015	**6.828**							
France	0.112	0.488	**4.765**						
Germany	0.209	0.536	0.631	**3.699**					
Japan	0.103	0.461	0.489	0.617	**4.994**				
Netherlands	0.211	0.545	0.655	0.904	0.561	**3.177**			
Switzerland	0.170	0.376	0.417	0.592	0.485	0.654	**2.702**		
U.K.	0.188	0.477	0.439	0.540	0.568	0.436	0.367	**7.509**	
U.S.	0.063	0.817	0.533	0.525	0.485	0.526	0.451	0.418	**5.549**

SOURCE: BARRA.

TABLE 16.2 Correlations of Returns for the Salomon Bond Index (U.S. Perspective), January 1985–September 1991 (Diagonal = Annualized Standard Deviation of Return)

	Australia	Canada	France	Germany	Japan	Netherlands	Switzerland	U.K.	U.S.
Australia	**15.822**								
Canada	0.165	**8.815**							
France	0.123	0.324	**13.543**						
Germany	0.124	0.291	0.956	**14.906**					
Japan	0.097	0.213	0.747	0.751	**15.976**				
Netherlands	0.132	0.294	0.956	0.994	0.743	**14.367**			
Switzerland	0.087	0.220	0.902	0.938	0.760	0.941	**14.883**		
U.K.	0.249	0.362	0.696	0.695	0.680	0.697	0.682	**17.704**	
U.S.	0.040	0.684	0.361	0.314	0.257	0.303	0.259	0.265	**11.098**

SOURCE: BARRA.

TABLE 16.3 Correlations of Long-Term Government Bond Annual Total Returns in Local Currency, 1961–1990

	Australia	Canada	France	Germany	Italy	Japan	Netherlands	Switzerland	U.K.	U.S.
Australia	1.00									
Canada	0.49	1.00								
France	0.52	0.61	1.00							
Germany	0.35	0.50	0.54	1.00						
Italy	0.41	0.39	0.73	0.30	1.00					
Japan	0.22	0.20	0.48	0.64	0.26	1.00				
Netherlands	0.45	0.74	0.62	0.80	0.35	0.55	1.00			
Switzerland	0.33	0.43	0.55	0.74	0.27	0.59	0.67	1.00		
U.K.	0.47	0.49	0.45	0.59	0.34	0.50	0.61	0.55	1.00	
U.S.	0.51	0.89	0.61	0.45	0.41	0.14	0.68	0.41	0.37	1.00

SOURCE: Ibbotson and Siegel, "The World Bond Markets," *The Journal of Fixed Income* (June 1991): ———.

Pension and retirement planners will also want to take note of this. When domestic yields go up and bond prices fall, domestic stocks are likely to be under pressure as well, and the overall pension reserve value drops precipitously. But retirement benefits *must* be paid. In such an environment, companies are very unwilling to increase the funding of the pension fund. A diversification to foreign bonds will limit the impact that the change in monetary policy has on the pension portfolio. In such a difficult environment, the benefits will be particularly rewarding.

REASON 4. DIVERSIFICATION OF DEBTORS

The American bond market offers an abundance of bonds of every quality and flavor. But what if one wants to diversify sovereign debtors beyond the U.S. Federal Government? A host of foreign governments issue U.S. dollar-denominated bonds, all the way to bonds issued or guaranteed by Japan. But what if an investor wants to have Switzerland or Germany in the bond portfolio? These countries have not issued or guaranteed any bonds outside their local markets.

An ability to incur debt only in the local currency is a sign of great strength. Hence, to have such debtors in a bond portfolio should be a very attractive aspect of globalizing the portfolio. Remember, investors turn to their local market not necessarily out of free choice, but for reasons that range from regulation all the way to lack of knowledge. Thus, the domestic markets can act like monopolies and can easily betray investors. Foreign markets always have to compete on their merits. If they attract funds, they must have intrinsic qualities and comparative advantages.

REASON 5. ARBITRAGE OPPORTUNITIES

The most glaring arbitrage opportunities tend to exist between markets of neighboring countries. For several years, Canada offered much higher yields than the United States (and a rising currency on top of that); in Europe, the Netherlands and Austria always had somewhat higher yields than Germany (and very stable currency relations to the Deutsche Mark (DM)). There are investors who doubt the investment quality and the depth of these so-called secondary markets, but, over time, substantial additional monies were to be earned by going this route. Between 1987 and 1991, investing in one-year rolling Canadian Treasuries brought 1.53 percent per year more return than investing in U.S. Treasury securities for the same maturities. When the rise of the Canadian dollar over that period is added in, the difference jumps to 5.83 percent for every year!

REASON 6. YIELD CURVE MANAGEMENT

In spite of the internationalization of trade and of markets, countries run on different cycles. Some are going strong while others are flat or are in recession. Some are pursuing a monetary policy of easing just as others are tightening.

Yield curves can thus be very different from one country to the other, opening interesting opportunities. Short-term money tends to be very interest-rate-sensitive. Consequently, high short-term rates attract money and cushion or even push up the exchange rate. Therefore, global bond money is attracted by short-term investment opportunities. Even a negative currency outlook can be overcome: As explained later, forward foreign exchange rates reflect interest rates differentials. If a one-month rolling deposit is currency hedged by, say, a six-month forward, then the cost of the forward may very well be much lower than the yield pickup. This arbitrage looks risky because of the maturity mismatch, but it often works very well because interest rate trends are rather stable over time and, thus, differentials do not change overnight.

INVESTING IN FOREIGN BONDS

Straight Bonds and Notes

Bonds and notes come in many forms, and the size of the non-U.S. government bond market is over $3 trillion. However, in 1988, the turnover in Tokyo for the Japanese government bond futures contract exceeded that of the U.S. government bond futures in Chicago. Most foreign markets do not yet have the degree of sophistication of the U.S. markets, although many have recently developed new tools for the management of interest rate risk, such as commercial paper markets and interest rate futures and options.

Floating Rate Notes

From 1984 onward, many of the bonds and notes issued in the Euromarket were floating-rate notes (FRNs). Given the positive yield curve structure at that time, issuers got medium- to long-term capital at what appeared to be very attractive interest costs. Investors were often banks who considered FRNs highly liquid interim investments. Borrowing was rather low at that time, and banks were pressed to reinvest the large liquidity overhang that had come with the second oil price explosion. However, when the Eurodollar yield curve in 1986 turned negative, almost everybody wanted to bail out at the same time, which led to a liquidity crisis. Since then, FRNs have been issued only at reduced levels.

Convertible and Warrant Bonds

The globalization of investment banking, the tremendous growth of the Euromarket, and the plentitude of cash available have led to the development of many types of bonds beyond the simple straight bond. Convertible bonds and bonds with warrants are old concepts, but combined with foreign currency aspects, they can become powerful new tools.

For example, Japanese banks issued bonds denominated in Swiss Francs in 1988. The low 0.5 percent coupon was accepted by the market because it was still higher than the equity yield and the bond had warrants attached for the conversion into shares. The issuers normally did not need Swiss Francs; they needed Yen. When they converted the currency on a fully hedged basis, they made a hedge gain of more than the 0.5 percent coupon that they had to pay. In other words, the banks received capital at negative interest rates(!), and if the share prices had not fallen so much lately, probably everybody involved in this transaction would have been happy.

Commodities Bonds

We have also seen bonds that were repayable in gold (such as the Giscard bond that cost the French government rather dearly) and variations in the form of multicurrency bonds. The index-linked bonds issued by the British government also belong to this category.

THE MAJOR MARKETS

The size of the world bond market at the end of June 1993 was $15.545 trillion. Its major components are shown in Table 16.4.

Over the years, issuers and investment bankers have been very innovative in creating new instruments to attract buyers. We will describe here a few aspects of the major markets, hoping to whet the reader's appetite.[1]

The EuroCapital Market

Regulation of financial markets seems to have one sure result: The more regulation there is, the more alternative markets develop. A classic example is the Euromarket, a direct consequence of the stringent restrictions on the domestic offices of U.S. banks. Since the late 1960s, they were increasingly flooded with U.S. dollar balances that ultimately were to be invested outside the United States. To go through the U.S. offices also implied American minimum reserves. Therefore, the

TABLE 16.4 Major Components of the World Bond Market

Bond Market (U.S. $ Billion)	Total Issued	Percentage of All Markets	Central Government*	State & Local Government	Private Sector	International Bonds	Private Place
U.S. Dollar	7289.3	46.9%	4086.9	1153.0	1248.5	800.9	728.9
Japanese Yen	2873.7	18.5	1697.1	69.3	925.9	181.3	435.2
Deutsche Mark	1402.4	9.0	311.6	64.7	556.5	141.1	328.5
Italian Lira	939.0	6.0	771.8	—	148.9	19.5	—
French Franc	682.0	4.4	542.3	3.4	104.4	34.1	—
U.K. Sterling	358.8	2.3	218.1	.2	27.8	112.7	—

* Including Central Government Agencies and Government Guaranteed.
SOURCE: J. P. Morgan.

London offices were increasingly used to book such monies, and from there the Euromarket developed rapidly. In addition, political fears of the Soviet Union prompted keeping large U.S. dollar deposits outside U.S. banks, further fueling the Eurodollar market.

In the 1970s, several oil price explosions led to enormous imbalances between cash on hand in the oil-rich nations and deep balance-of-payments problems in the rest of the world. Investment of the surpluses and financing of the deficits were largely executed in the Euromarket. From the U.S. dollar, the market developed quickly to include first the DM and, later on, virtually all freely convertible currencies. Table 16.5, which looks only at the bonds issued in the Euromarket, gives a graphic description of the growth that occurred.

A number of countries have or have had withholding taxes applied to bond coupon payments. The Euromarkets are, by definition, free of such taxes; the debt instruments often provide for the issuer to assume any withholding taxes should they be levied. An alternative provision often permits immediate repayment without penalty. Investors are flocking to tax-free markets for a variety of reasons, not all of which involve tax avoidance. The recapturing of withheld taxes costs time and money, for example, and some very large investors, such as most OPEC countries, do not have access to double taxation relief agreements for the simple reason that there is no double taxation.

The Euromarket is a self-regulating market whereas, in many countries, monetary authorities are applying limitations of all sorts. Many of these bonds are not listed on any exchange, so the issuing cost can be kept small—at least as far as regulated fees are concerned. By contrast, the margins for the underwriters are habitually larger than in the domestic markets, at least with regard to private investors, who often buy these bonds because of their tax-free characteristics.

In recent years, the Euromarket has become so big that the central banks keep a keen eye on it. The Association for International Bonds

---

TABLE 16.5 Euromarket Bond Growth, 1964–1989 (Selected Years)

	Outstanding (U.S. $ Billion)	U.S. Dollar Portion
1964	$ 0.61	81%
1970	2.70	63
1975	6.60	41
1980	19.66	65
1985	134.26	70
1989	219.00	55

SOURCE: *The Dow Jones-Irwin Guide to Fixed-Income Investing* (Homewood, IL: Dow Jones, 1990).

Dealers (AIBD) has established a fairly extensive set of rules for issuing and dealing in such bonds, giving further comfort to new users of the market.

An interesting aside is that Eurobonds pay annual rather than semiannual coupons. Because the investor gets one coupon six months later, he or she loses interest on that interest. For a 10 percent domestic bond yield, a Eurobond has to yield 10.25 percent to give the investor the same return.

Japanese Yen

Japan is well known for its high savings rate and for how it propelled prices of stocks and real estate to unheard-of levels. (In 1989, the real estate value of Japan was more than 2.5 times that of the whole of the United States.) The money also pushed into government bonds, thereby making the financing of the huge government deficits easy. As in other countries with high income tax rates (for example, Germany), the tax rules provided for an easy avoidance of income tax on interest, thereby again pushing money in the direction of fixed-income investments.

During the 1980s, the Japanese bond market underwent significant changes. City banks, investment trusts, and local banks, which used to be net sellers of bonds, became the most important net buyers. Foreigners have bought and sold Yen bonds largely for currency reasons, and, overall, trading has increased tremendously. The launching of the Japanese bond futures market in October 1985 played an important role. It quickly became the largest bond futures market in the world, surpassing in volume the Chicago Board of Trade and the LIFFE (London International Financial Futures Exchange) Gilt Bond Futures. After 1989, however, trading volume shrank by 50 percent.

In the past, the market was rather heavily regulated by the Minister of Finance. Recently, the Bank of Japan has gained the freedom to set monetary policy and interest rates.

TABLE 16.6 Summary of the Japanese Bond Market

Type of Bonds Outstanding	1980 (¥ Billion)	1990 (¥ Billion)	1990 (U.S. $ Billion)
Government	68,540	159,291	1,185.20
Other public authorities	70,656	117,596	874.97
Bank debentures	26,049	67,572	502.77
Corporate straights	9,818	28,643	213.12
Corporate convertible and warrants	1,199	16,261	120.99

SOURCE: Salomon Brothers.

In all bond markets, it is customary to construct a yield curve and to look for ways to benefit from distortions of this yield curve, as described in previous sections. In Japan, this does not work. Market activity is often concentrated in very few issues, usually in a "benchmark" bond that is one of the latest government issues. One some days, more than 90 percent of the total turnover of Japanese bonds is accounted for by "benchmark" bond trading. Consequently, its price can be quite out of line with other bonds that have essentially the same coupon and maturity characteristics, but lack the liquidity. One can only speculate about the reasons behind this distortion. Futures arbitrage is sometimes an explanation, but quite often the moves of the benchmark issue seem irrational, providing opportunity for the trader but risk to the investor.

As defined by the AIBD, yield is the internal rate of return of an investment. All future cash flows, whether coupon payments or redemptions, are discounted to their present value. The discount rate used is the purchase yield of the bond. In Japan, however, domestic bond yields are calculated by the "simple yield" method. This method ignores the reinvestment of coupons and looks only at the current yield (coupon divided by purchase price) and the difference between the purchase price and the redemption price, amortized (straight line) over the life of the bond. The formula is:

$$\text{Simple yield} = \frac{\text{Coupon} + \dfrac{\text{Redemption} - \text{Price}}{\text{Years to Maturity}}}{\text{Price}} \times 100$$

When comparing the two methods, the simple yield return will be higher if the bond is trading below par. This means that bonds high above par show a relatively lower yield and are therefore shunned by investors.

But no rule is without exception. Because Japanese insurance companies show as portfolio return only the current income, they are sometimes eager to purchase high-coupon bonds. The AIBD method does not differentiate between bonds below and above par. But alongside these apparent advantages, there is a drawback: The method assumes that all future coupon payments can be reinvested at today's yield. This is neither realistic (yields fluctuate over time) nor methodically correct. Yield payments closer to maturity will be reinvested for a shorter period of time and, given the shape of the yield curve, will therefore draw different returns. The future yield curves are not known, so there is no way to overcome this shortfall. Table 16.7 shows the difference between the various yield computation methods for different bond prices.

TABLE 16.7 Comparison of Simple (Japan) and Compound (U.S. and AIBD) Yields on an 8%, Ten-Year Bond with a Par (Redemption) Value of ¥100

		Compound Yield	
Price (¥)	Simple Yield (Japan)	U.S.	AIBD
¥85	11.18	10.45	10.72
90	10.00	9.58	9.81
95	8.95	8.76	8.95
100	8.00	8.00	8.16
105	7.14	7.29	7.42
110	6.36	6.62	6.73
115	5.65	5.99	6.08

SOURCE: Frank J. Fabozzi, ed., *The Japanese Bond Markets*, (Chicago: 1990).

Deutsche Marks

German investors are not known for their love for equities, but they are undisputedly world class in bonds. After suffering high inflation in the 1920s and another erosion of the value of their money in the Third Reich, they continue, against normal logic, to put the overwhelming part of their liquid savings into fixed-income investments, ranging from savings accounts to long-term bonds. Significantly adding to this flow of money are foreign investors who want to invest in Deutsche Marks. The markets believe that Germany has a stauncher anti-inflation mindset than virtually any other country. This makes bond investment an easy decision.

As is the case in most continental European countries, Germany has a universal banking system in which the banks are also the brokers. Not surprisingly, therefore, practically no corporate bonds are outstanding and the only nongovernment bonds are issued by banks. The latter trade mostly over the telephone, but there is a very active market in government bonds at the Frankfurt Stock Exchange. The reason is

TABLE 16.8 Summary of the German Bond Market

Types of Bonds Outstanding	1980 (DM Billion)	1990 (DM Billion)	1990 (U.S. $ Billion)
Government*	118.3	505.9	338.62
Other public authorities	12.5	40.4	27.04
Bank debentures	413.3	901.0	603.10
Corporate bonds, incl. convertibles	4.6	2.6	1.74

* Including the Federal Post Office and the Federal Railway System.
SOURCE: Salomon Brothers.

that the Deutsche Bundesbank acts on the floor as a market maker. This is in contrast to the United States, where the Federal Reserve also buys government bonds for its own account but does not act as a market maker.

Because of the high costs and the need for government approval of issued bonds, a significant market for Schuldscheine (IOUs) developed in the 1970s and 1980s. These fixed-income securities can be compared to commercial paper, except that the maturities tend to be much longer, often exceeding ten years. Again, issuers are overwhelmingly banks and public authorities. Schuldscheine are often tailor-made to the requirements of a single institutional investor. Another advantage of Schuldscheine is that their interest payments are not subject to German withholding tax if paid to foreigners. But as this now applies to all German bonds, interest in the Schuldscheine market has decreased.

In the past, most German institutional investors pursued a "buy-and-hold" strategy. But today, some 10 percent of the German insurance companies trade their bond portfolio actively, and nearly 60 percent trade at least occasionally.[2] The main reason is the need to squeeze more return out of the portfolio. As the European Common Market develops, the insurance business is losing its national boundaries. British insurance companies have the advantage of higher-yielding portfolios, and the German companies are getting ready to fight that competition by enhancing their portfolio management strategies. Furthermore, some German banks, quite committed to developing the German derivatives markets, are approaching the insurance companies with arbitrage proposals.

The yield calculation in Germany differs from the AIBD formula in two ways:

1. Bonds are expected to pay annual coupons, and yields are therefore expressed on that basis.
2. The Braess method, which is most commonly used, computes simple rather than compound interest for broken periods.

Pound Sterling

The British government bond market (there is also a small nongovernment bond market) has been quite innovative. A few years ago, the market seemed doomed to extinction. The government was running high surpluses: in 1987, the surplus reached almost 3 percent of GDP. Consequently, the government was actively repurchasing its bonds in the open market and projections were made to estimate when all outstanding bonds would be bought back. As a consequence of this unusual situation, the British yield curve was steeply negative, with short rates at

TABLE 16.9 Summary of the United Kingdom Bond Market

Types of Bonds Outstanding	1980 (£ Billion)	1990 (£ Billion)	1990 (U.S. $ Billion)
Government	81.7	113.9	22.29
Other public authorities	1.0	.9	1.74
Corporate bonds, incl. convertibles	5.3	14.5	2.17

SOURCE: Salomon Brothers.

15 percent when long bonds yielded less than 10 percent. This made financing a trading position in bonds prohibitively expensive. Fortunately for bond investors and bond traders, the British government more recently has started to run deficits again and the scare seems over.

There are two important innovations in the British bond market:

1. **Undated loans.** Bonds normally have a definite maturity. Some U.K. bonds, such as the $3^1/2$ percent War Loan, do not. They may never be redeemed. Their price is calculated on a current yield basis only.
2. **Index-linked bonds.** When the U.K. suffered rather high inflation in the early 1980s, the government started to issue bonds that had a redemption price linked to inflation in such a manner that the investor was guaranteed the real return of the coupon, which was between 2 percent and $2^1/2$ percent. The half-yearly coupon payments are also inflation-adjusted. In total, some £13 billion of such bonds were issued. These bonds tend to trade at a discount, implying that the market is skeptical about future inflation.

European Currency Units (ECU)

A particularly interesting segment of the international bond market currently is the market for bonds denominated in ECU, the designated future European Currency Unit. What makes them so attractive is the fact that whereas there is very little doubt that the ECU will, in the long term, become the currency for all of Europe, neither the time frame nor, more specifically, important aspects of its definition are cast in stone as yet. Because the European monetary system permits the individual member currencies to fluctuate (if only within narrow limits) around the central rate, the weight of the individual currencies in the ECU is constantly changing. Furthermore, as the events of September 1992 showed, many adjustments to exchange rates will occur before any final stability is established.

Because the ECU unit is composed of several European currencies, there can be arbitrage opportunities in the ECU market. For example, an Italian ECU bond's price will depend on both Italy's economic outlook and the ultimate relationship between Italy and the rest of the European Monetary Union (EMU).

The recent instability of the Lira implies higher yields for the Italian issues, but if Italy joins the EMU system, these Italian issues will be underpriced.

Payment of coupons and redemptions of ECU bonds can normally be effected, according to the bondholder's choice, either in ECU or in the local currency of the recipient. Many banks carry ECU accounts and even though it is still a long way to a European currency that would be legal tender, the progress so far has exceeded expectations.

LIQUIDITY AND MARKET ORGANIZATION

Normally, the liquidity of most global bonds diminishes shortly after they are issued. It is remarkable and commendable, however, to see that market makers continue to keep a decent liquidity in many of these issues.

The overwhelming majority of global bond trading today is in government and supranational bonds such as the many World Bank issues. Many are listed on exchanges, but most of the trades are done over-the-counter. Government bonds issued by the United States, Japan, and Germany enjoy a global market that is comparable to that of their currencies, even though at a smaller daily transaction volume.

Most of the market makers, such as banks and brokers, are regulated by their governments, but their Euromarket activities are regulated only to a limited degree. The best protection for an investor in such an environment is information, and that is available in abundance. All market information services—Reuters and Knight Ridder, for example—carry a plethora of global bond price information, very often from different market makers, so that investors can easily compare prices and trading margins.

Credit Ratings in the International Markets

In the United States, it is customary for bonds to be rated by several rating agencies, such as Standard & Poor's or Moody's. Because the ratings are paid for by the bond issuers, the agencies have a sound business base. Internationally, most bonds are either issued or guaranteed by governments, which have full taxing authority over their people and cannot default. Therefore, they are very reluctant to pay to have their credit rated, notwithstanding the political repercussions of a poor showing.

In the United States, many bond managers apply credit risk arbitrage techniques. If bonds of a specific quality are mispriced, they can sell the overpriced bonds and buy the underpriced bonds. They expect that normal relations will be reestablished, permitting them to unwind their position at a profit. The country risk tools available today do not seem to make such an arbitrage possible on a global scale, at least not in a strictly numerical fashion. Unfortunately, one consequence is that the smaller markets get less than their "fair" share of global bond portfolios. But the credit rating agencies are making progress in this area, and, sometime in the future, systematic credit risk arbitrage may become a part of the portfolio composition process for global bond managers.

DESIGNING AN INTERNATIONAL BOND PORTFOLIO

There is no single "right" way to construct an international bond portfolio. Instead, there are many successful methods of benefiting from international bonds. There is also no proof at all that markets will converge. It is safe to assume that, in the future, some foreign markets will provide excellent opportunities, whereas others will be full of dangers and pitfalls.

Every investment deals with the future. Assessments have to be made about the likelihood of various possible developments and scenarios. In the international bond markets, there is a confluence of internal and external factors. Their importance changes constantly, making overly rigid portfolio composition processes dangerous. When selecting between different bonds in a specific market, the framework of reference is the same. But when trying to decide between, say, a French and an Australian bond, there may be no commonality at all. Still, portfolio decisions have to be made.

Foreign Bonds or Global Bonds

When American pension funds began to look beyond domestic equities in the early 1980s, they were, almost without exception, comparing their current position with the risk–return improvements that an allocation to international (non-American) equities would bring. Nevertheless, today, a decade later, very few have combined foreign and domestic equities into the asset class "global equities." The money management community, incidentally, has done little to entice pension fund officers to think globally; by and large, they were happy to accept the more limited non-American mandates.

In bonds, the process seems to have gone the other way round. Largely domestic bond managers have asked their clients' permission to put a certain percentage of funds into the foreign bond markets. Bond managers want to have the freedom to pull back if foreign bonds and/or foreign currencies look unattractive. Thus, the number of non-American bond mandates is limited; the majority is for global fixed income.

Defining Market Risk–Return Expectations

Most bond managers start the portfolio composition process with an assessment of the various economies, monetary policies, and current yield curves. They are trying to see how those factors will change over whatever time frame they tend to work with. They can then project a yield curve for some future date and calculate the expected total returns for the various maturities.

Because all decisions imply trade-offs (buying one bond, by definition, means not buying another bond), many investors are also trying to calculate the risks involved in such a decision. Very often, expected yields are defined as ranges. it is also common to look at historic volatilities. But the past may not be a good predictor of the future. Today, the derivatives markets (interest rate options and futures) provide valuable information about expected volatilities.

Portfolio Optimization

Foreign bonds can be put into a portfolio either on an opportunistic basis—that is, only when the expected total return is above what is available in the U.S. market—or in a systematic fashion. Without question, the systematic approach is on the rise and will become the dominant way in which U.S. pension money is invested. Almost invariably, a systematic approach includes Markowitz portfolio optimization. On the basis of the bond manager's expectations, the optimizer finds the best combination of the many bonds available. Before an optimizer can run, the following decisions have to be made:

1. Country minima and maxima. There is no systematic requirement for minimum and maximum allocations to a country, but diversification provides very significant risk reduction at little give-up in yield. Therefore, we want the optimizer to create diversified portfolios; hence the need to define country minima.

Country maxima not only serve that purpose but also take liquidity and exposure aspects into account. Finally, if the portfolio is measured against a benchmark, the percentage of permitted variance from that benchmark needs to be decided.

2. Yield curve segments. Depending on the depth of the analytical process, expectations are to be defined for the short, medium, and long segments of at least the major markets. Because many optimizers are limited in the number of variables they can deal with, careful selection of these market segments on a market-by-market basis is necessary.

3. Currency. All foreign bond investments need to be translated ultimately into the home currency of the investor. Therefore, most optimization processes also include expected foreign exchange returns and thus compare the various international bond markets on a U.S. dollar basis. If currencies are managed separately, expected currency returns should not be part of the initial optimization process. Needless to say, even in that case, currency expectations play an important role when defining expected returns. This is because foreign investors often have a significant impact on bond markets.

Quantitative Strategies

As we have implied in the description of the portfolio construction process, almost all portfolio management approaches today include some type of computer assistance. Whether in the preparation and evaluation of data, the portfolio construction process itself, or its implementation and supervision, computers are omnipresent.

Many money managers have developed programs that focus on mispricings. The best known of these is the cash/futures arbitrage. The bond version of this arbitrage involves not only the direct relationship between the futures and the spot markets, but also the relationship among various bonds that can be delivered against a specific futures contract. Whenever some price gets out of line, there will be a computer exploiting the opportunity.

Does this mean the end of such arbitrage programs? Not at all. Mispricings occur because not enough capital is applied to that specific market segment at that specific time. That has not changed and will not change. Capital will always be a limiting factor. Some market segments get overcrowded and arbitrage opportunities become virtually nonexistent, but so far there is no proof whatsoever that the end of arbitrage has come. The application of modern portfolio management techniques to lesser developed markets provides an ongoing fertile field.

Trading and Valuation

Once the desired portfolio has been constructed, it is implemented through the trading desk. Regular updates of the portfolio are relatively easy because the data on most global bonds are available through a variety of market pricing sources. If over-the-counter derivatives such as interest rate swaps are used, then it is important to define in writing the evaluation process and to communicate it to the client and to the custodian bank so that a basis for common understanding is available and questions about performance calculations and similar issues are avoided.

CURRENCY MANAGEMENT

In the previous section, our focus was on the process of bond selection, an important component of global bond portfolio design. Nevertheless, the goal of bond management is to maximize total return, and the total return of a foreign bond is a function of three factors: (1) the initial yield, (2) the change in yield levels, and (3) the appreciation (depreciation) of the currency.

As we noted earlier, currency movement can have a substantial impact on the total return of foreign bond portfolios. Indeed, at the beginning of 1992, yields on U.K. government bonds were considerably higher than yields on Japanese government bonds. Both countries were probably going to experience recessions in 1992, and it would have been reasonable to assume that conditions would be worse in the U.K. than in Japan. Therefore, investors would probably have preferred to buy U.K. bonds rather than Japanese bonds, expecting a better total return as yields dropped more in the U.K.

In fact, in 1992, U.K. government bonds (J. P. Morgan Index) appreciated 18.84 percent and Japanese government bonds appreciated 11.31 percent in their local currencies, respectively. However, in U.S. Dollar terms, the U.K. bonds lost 3.94 percent and the Japanese bonds gained 11.26 percent, because the British Pound depreciated 18.88 percent while the Yen remained stable against the U.S. Dollar.

The above example makes it clear that the global bond investor must take into account currency price movements. We therefore examine currency management in the remainder of the chapter. An overview of the currency markets is followed by a section devoted to currency hedging. Finally, we present a survey of currency management as a separate investment category in asset allocation decisions.

THE CURRENCY MARKETS

It is estimated that over $800 billion are traded every day in the global foreign exchange markets. From early Monday morning Wellington

(New Zealand) time until Friday afternoon on the U.S. West Coast, this is the truly nonstop global market. A significant part of all trading consists of shifting positions from one trader to another, but client orders represent the fundament on which the traders build. Client orders are generated for many reasons: a tourist buys money to spend overseas; a company imports or exports; an investor requires foreign currency to pay for a purchase of securities in a foreign market. These latter capital flows have grown in relative importance and today often exceed the commercial orders that are connected with trade and services.

In the past several years, Dollar/Yen has seen the highest volume of trading; Dollar/DM is second. Pound Sterling/Dollar and Pound Sterling/DM are today about even, particularly while the U.K. was a member of the European Monetary Union (EMU). Compared with these leaders, the other currencies are small as a percentage of total volume; but, for that very reason, they are often more profitable.

In the foreign exchange market, EMS is of major significance. In 1974, when the Western world was reeling from the first oil price shock, Chancellor Schmidt of Germany and President Giscard d'Estaing of France conceived the EMS. The many revaluations and devaluations among the European currencies were seen as a major threat to commerce. There was also a fear of competitive devaluations whereby countries try to gain export markets by artificially undervaluing their currencies. In spite of significant resistance from large segments of their own administrations, the two heads of state prevailed and the EMS was begun. It provides for a "snake," in which the middle is composed of the averages of the participating currencies and the upper and lower bands are set at defined percentages. Within those bands, the currencies can float freely. If any currency is in danger of breaking out of the snake, all central banks participating in the EMS are obligated to intervene.

The system has worked well so long as European economies and monetary policies have converged. In the beginning, adjustments were necessary quite frequently; then almost five years passed before the middle rates changed. It will probably be some time before many European countries can expect their exchange rates to remain stable, because European political turmoil continues to prevent smooth trade relations.

The Interbank Market

By far, the largest amount of foreign exchange trade is done between banks and brokers in the interbank market. Like other nonregulated markets, the interbank market has developed its own set of rules. The most important rule is that, when called by another market participant (a bank or broker regularly participating in the foreign exchange market), a market participant must quote a two-way price, that is, the price at which the participant will buy and sell the usual minimum quantity, such as $1 million. In this way, liquidity is provided and the price risk remains where it should be—with the trader.

Approximately two-thirds of all trades in the foreign exchange markets today are spot trades. One third, or some $250 billion per day, are forwards with maturities between seven days and five years. The bulk of trades are between one and three months. How is this enormous volume possible? Are currency traders so successful at forecasting what rates will be in a month or a year? No. The pricing of forwards bears little, if any, relation to expected future prices.[3] In fact, forward exchange rates are subject to the principle of covered interest rate parity.

Covered Interest Rate Parity

The principle of covered interest rate parity refers to the fact that the price today of the forward exchange rate (or futures contract) for a foreign currency is completely determined by the relative interest-rate levels of the countries.

Why should this be the case?

Suppose that (1) a one-year government note is available in the United States, and it yields $3^1/2$ percent; and (2) a one-year German government note is also available, and it yields $6^1/2$ percent.

The U.S. note will return $103.50 for every $100 invested, over a one-year period. Similarly, the investor can exchange U.S. Dollars for Deutsche Marks (DM) and then invest in the German note, for which the investor will receive 106.5 DM for every 100 DM invested, after one year. Because the U.S. investor must ultimately convert the Deutsche Marks back into U.S. Dollars, the actual return from the German note will depend on the value of the Deutsche Mark in one year.

To avoid this uncertainty, they can enter into a contract today to sell the Deutsche Marks to be received in one year. This is known as "selling the DM forward" (one year). Because both the U.S. Dollar return and the Deutsche Mark return are certain (government-backed notes), the fair market quote today for the future 106.5 DM to be received must equal $103.50, the future quantity of U.S. Dollars to be received. That is, 106.5 times the one-year forward DM rate must equal $103.50. If this were not the case, a riskless arbitrage profit would be available. Therefore, the one-year forward exchange rate (in U.S. Dollars) for the Deutsche Mark must satisfy:

$$\text{1-year forward DM} = 103.5/106.5 \times \text{spot DM.}$$

Thus, today's forward exchange rate is completely determined by the interest rates in the United States and Germany.

Exchange-Listed Markets

The Chicago Mercantile Exchange (CME) has been quite successful in developing its currency futures contracts, which today average over $10 billion per day. The Singapore International Exchange (SIMEX), the London International Financial Futures Exchange (LIFFE), and other foreign futures markets have also grown and show their usefulness daily, especially at times when Chicago is closed. Futures contracts on these exchanges can be offset against each other, making currencies the first global futures. In addition, there are options on currencies and currency futures. The Philadelphia Stock Exchange alone trades approximately $3 billion of such options a day.

Even these large volumes represent only a small percentage of the total daily turnover in currencies. Hence, these markets are mostly suitable for smaller transactions. Although they enjoy the advantage of easy pricing, the daily adjustment of margins makes the administration of futures contracts in an institutional portfolio cumbersome. This burden may outweigh the advantage of having access to profits from trades on a daily basis via the market-to-market mechanism.

In some countries, such as Germany, currencies are also listed at the stock exchange, but the volume is typically rather small. The importance of the listing lies in fixing a daily price at which retail orders are executed.

Settlement Practices

Spot trades are settled two business days[4] after the trade by transferring the currency to the respective accounts. Because the clearing between banks happens only in the home country of the currency, settlement of foreign exchange trades often involves a time gap between, say, the payment of Yen in Japan and the receipt of the U.S. Dollar countervalue on the West Coast. With very few exceptions, such intraday time risk has been deemed acceptable by market participants.

Many forward transactions are closed out by countertrades before they mature. This close-out would, for example, always occur in the case of hedging an international bond or equity portfolio: The sole purpose of the hedging transaction (i.e., the sale of currency in the forward market) is to counterbalance the currency element of an existing underlying securities position. There is no intention to actually deliver the currency sold or receive the currency bought in the hedge. Therefore, the forward transaction is closed before maturity (or rolled over into a new forward position). In the past, it was customary to settle such closed-out forward transactions in full—pay and receive the gross amounts traded. To reduce the trading volume and also to comply with new banking regulations, it has become more and more customary to settle only the net difference between the original forward transaction and the close-out. Legally, this reduction of payments and exposure is accomplished by netting agreements that market makers have their clients sign.

Cost of Trading and Hedging

The foreign exchange market is extremely competitive and, thus, very tightly priced. Spot and at least the most active forward trades are quoted with margins of a few basis points (b.p.). Thus, currency management and hedging programs can be executed at an annual cost of only 12 to 24 b.p. The settlement cost largely consists of fees charged by the custodian bank and may add another 5 to 10 b.p.

As we showed above, forward prices are determined by the interest rate differential between the two currencies. If the currency to be hedged has a lower yield than the currency into which the hedge is executed, then the hedge produces a payout (net of the spot price move over the period of the hedge). Through the 1980s, when the U.S. Dollar was one of the high-yielding currencies, most hedging of foreign assets into the dollar created additional income. In the 1990s, as the dollar became a low-yielding currency, hedging into the U.S. Dollar normally costs yield, and currency managers are eager to find less expensive alternatives, such as hedging into the Canadian Dollar.

CURRENCY HEDGING

Because currency price fluctuations can have a major impact on the total return of a foreign bond, when evaluated in the domestic currency, investors naturally want to look for currency hedging strategies. In this section, we present an introduction to this subject.

In general, the purpose of hedging is to improve the return–risk characteristics of the investment portfolio. Usually, this means finding strategies that will lower the risk (exposure) generated by the foreign currency, while at the same time not giving up too much return. In this sense, hedging is a generalized form of insurance, designed to protect against excessive risk and/or improve the overall return of the portfolios being hedged.

Ideally, a hedging strategy will produce returns that are negatively correlated with the returns of the portfolio being hedged. When the original positions are performing poorly, the hedge will add positive returns; when the original positions are doing well, the hedge will attempt to be neutral or, at least, to not lose too much. In this way, the total returns will be more uniform (lower volatility) and so compound at a higher rate. This is the underlying reason for asset allocation strategies.

Hedging strategies can be broadly divided into three classes: (1) no hedge, (2) full hedge, and (3) dynamic hedge. The first two are examples of "static" strategies: the hedging decision is made once and not changed. A dynamic hedge strategy allows for frequent currency forward transactions, chosen in a tactical way.

The decision not to hedge at all, the no hedge strategy, exposes the portfolio fully to currency price risk. The full hedge strategy eliminates most of the exposure to the foreign currency. The dynamic hedge attempts to eliminate the exposure when the currency is depreciating, and to keep the exposure when the currency is stable or appreciating. No matter which strategy is chosen, its success depends on correct analysis of currency price movement.

There is some evidence that currencies have an expected return of zero over the long run. An investment manager holding this view with a portfolio of foreign bonds or stocks might choose the no hedge strategy, if his or her investment return horizon is long enough. Many international equity managers adopt this strategy by concentrating on choosing foreign stocks with attractive expected returns while assuming that the currency price movement will either have no net effect on their portfolios or will deliver some benefit. This is an illustration of the general tendency toward separating currency decisions from bond and equity investment decisions. We will revisit this issue in the next section.

Even if a manager believes that currencies will have no detrimental effect on a bond portfolio in the long run, he or she might still want to protect against the substantial impact of currency movement over the short run. The full hedge strategy reduces the volatility of the total return by diminishing the exposure to the foreign currency. Reducing the volatility is desirable, so long as returns are not also greatly reduced, because returns compound faster when they are more nearly equal.

If a portfolio is left unhedged, it will achieve large gains when the currencies move in the right direction and large losses when they don't. A dynamic hedging strategy will make the large (unhedged) gains smaller because it will occasionally sell when currency prices are rising; it will also reduce the size of currency losses by selling aggressively when prices decline. The effects are: the average (mean) return will remain approximately unchanged, the variability of the returns will be reduced, and the compounded rate of return will be higher.

Other static strategies, such as those using options, are generally equivalent in outcome to the full hedge strategy. There is also a partial hedge strategy, in which a portion of the currency exposure is hedged. For example, the investor may choose to hedge only those currencies with lower-than-average yields. The less hedge coverage chosen, the greater the exposure to currency volatility.

Although static strategies may sometimes be desirable for institutional portfolios, they have certain shortcomings. With the no hedge choice, the portfolio benefits from favorable changes in the underlying currency prices. However, it is damaged in direct proportion to the size of unfavorable movements in the currency prices. For the full hedge strategy, the portfolio is generally unaffected by adverse movements in the currency prices. Unfortunately, it does not benefit from favorable movements either. Furthermore, the full hedge strategy can be costly, as a comparative analysis later in this section will show.

The ideal hedging strategy would produce compensating gains for the portfolio when the underlying currencies are generating losses, and would have no net effect when those currencies are either unchanged or are delivering profits to the portfolio. This is precisely what an option is designed to do.

Options cost money (a "premium") because some other party is taking on the risk of the adverse price movement. We describe them as a form of full hedge because the premium paid usually offsets any gains from favorable price movements. The ideal hedging strategy would have an optionlike payoff structure and wouldn't cost anything.

Dynamic hedging strategies attempt to approximate this ideal by reproducing an option's payoff structure. For example, suppose that an institutional portfolio is holding bonds denominated in foreign currencies worth $US 100 million today. How can we create an optionlike payoff structure for this portfolio, without knowing what the future holds for the underlying currencies?

The solution is to use a statistically weighted allocation process, that is, sell forward contracts at any given time in proportion to the probability of a downward move in the underlying currency. To do this successfully, we need two things: (1) a method for deciding when a (downward) movement is starting and (2) a way of calculating the weight to be given to that movement (probability of success).

The key is to develop a model of currency price movement based on the nonrandomness of the currency markets. The model must be able to capture the price movement to a degree sufficient to generate profits comparable to the losses from downward movements, and at the same time not produce too much of a loss when the currencies move favorably. One of the authors of this chapter (C.F.) has constructed such a model and uses it for currency hedging of foreign bonds at The Boston Company Asset Management, Inc.

Several recent studies[5] have confirmed our own research showing that autocorrelations in the currency markets are of a size sufficient to permit the design of profitable investment models.[6]

Regarding comparison of the various hedging strategies, our main conclusion is that dynamic hedging strategies can offer a very attractive alternative to the more traditional static strategies. By responding flexibly to currency price movements, dynamic hedging strategies can deliver the excess returns available while simultaneously reducing the risk.

Referring to Table 16.10, we see that, between 1986 and 1992, the foreign bond portfolio (J.P. Morgan Index of Non-U.S. Government Bonds) returned 13.03 percent per year, in U.S. Dollars, using the no hedge strategy. For the last few years of that period, yields in these portfolio countries (excluding Japan) were higher than in the United States. Nevertheless, much of the return was earned in 1987, when currency appreciation outweighed the lower yields on the bonds.

In 1992, the best return was earned by Japanese bonds, which had a lower yield than U.S. bonds, because the Japanese Yen remained stable against the U.S. Dollar, while yields in Japan dropped. In contrast, British bonds yielded much more than U.S. bonds at the start of 1992, but actually had a negative total return for the year, even though British rates dropped during the year, because the British Pound depreciated nearly 20 percent. It is therefore not necessarily rewarding to avoid lower-yielding foreign bonds.

A portfolio of U.S. Dollar bonds represented by the Lehman Government/Corporate Bond Index returned 10.1 percent per year over the same period, 4 percent less than the foreign bonds. However, the foreign bond portfolio had two and one-half times the volatility of the U.S. portfolio. This volatility came from the movement of the underlying currencies rather than the inherent bond volatility. In fact, when these

---

TABLE 16.10 Comparison of Hedging Strategies for Foreign Bond Portfolios (J. P. Morgan Index of Non-U.S. Government Bonds)

1.	No hedge (1986–1992)	
	Monthly mean	1.09%
	Monthly standard deviation	3.70%
	Sharpe ratio	0.30
	Compound annual return	13.03%
2.	Full hedge (1986–1992)	
	Monthly mean	0.62%
	Monthly standard deviation	1.16%
	Sharpe ratio	0.54
	Compound annual return	7.65%
3.	Dynamic hedge (1986–1992)	
	Monthly mean	1.36%
	Monthly standard deviation	3.05%
	Sharpe ratio	0.45
	Compound annual return	17.00%

foreign bonds are viewed in their local currencies, their volatility was no higher than that of U.S. bonds.

The full hedge strategy is to sell one-month currency forwards against the bond positions. Changes in the yield curves of the United States and the foreign country can affect the returns from this strategy.[7] Table 16.10 shows that, for the entire period, the full hedge strategy cost over 5 percent per year in return; the dynamic hedge, based on the model developed by the author, *added* approximately 4 percent per year.

CURRENCY PORTFOLIO MANAGEMENT

In the previous section, we showed how an institutional investor having exposure to foreign currency fluctuations via a foreign bond portfolio could choose among several hedging strategies. As we stated, the purpose of hedging is to improve the portfolio's return–risk characteristics, in most cases without raising the risk.

Now consider an institution holding a diversified portfolio of investments whose currency exposure has been satisfactorily hedged. In the context of asset allocation decisions, we can now ask another question: Is there any value in adding currency investment as another "asset class"?

In traditional diversification strategies, capital is allocated to new investment opportunities when they offer the possibility of added returns. It is preferable for these new investments to be uncorrelated with those already in the portfolio.

Currency returns are usually uncorrelated with those from traditional investments, but it is far from certain that the expected return from holding currencies is positive. Indeed, some argue that the expected return from holding currencies is zero, and, therefore, that currencies do not constitute an asset class and should not be added to institutional portfolios. Others cite empirical studies showing the positive benefits from diversification through currency exposure to an institutional portfolio, arguing that holding currencies is similar to holding claims on a country's GNP. Because the economies of different countries tend to be uncorrelated, this argument rests on the diversification benefits of currency portfolios.

Modern investment practice separates capital allocation decisions from the value added by investment strategies. We can therefore avoid these issues and, instead, approach currency investment by asking whether there are currency investment strategies that produce added value for investment portfolios. Regardless of how an institutional portfolio has allocated its capital, it may use currency management strategies if these strategies improve the return–risk profile of the overall portfolio.

The relevant question therefore is not whether currencies (or any other investment categories) have an inherent return, but whether there are currency management strategies that can be reliably demonstrated to have positive return, and whether these positive returns improve the overall portfolio return–risk.

Furthermore, because the returns from currency management strategies tend to be uncorrelated with those from traditional investment categories, an institutional portfolio can gain increased return and reduced volatility *simultaneously* by adding currency management. To illustrate this, we will use the currency portfolio management model developed by one of the authors, which is being used for client accounts at The Boston Company Asset Management, Inc.[8]

Figure 16.2 shows the effect of adding this currency management system to a diversified portfolio of bonds and U.S. and foreign stocks, having an allocation similar to allocations found in many pension plans and endowment funds.

Note that the Sharpe ratio (return–risk) is improved by the addition of currency management at allocations up to as much as 40 percent of the overall portfolio size. For example, adding currency management at a 30 percent allocation level increases monthly returns by 26 percent (from 1.04 percent to 1.31 percent) and reduces monthly volatility from 2.77 percent to 2.28 percent at the same time.

Simultaneous reduction in risk and increase in return occur at several allocation levels. Other currency management systems would generate similar graphs.

Table 16.11 shows the correlations (monthly returns) among the various investment categories and confirms that our currency management returns are generally not correlated with equity or bond returns.

Many institutional portfolios are raising their allocations to equities. Table 16.12 shows the effect on yearly returns of adding currency management (at varying allocations) to a diversified portfolio of bonds (45 percent) and stocks (55 percent). The result is general: adding currency management has a beneficial effect* allocations of as much as 70 percent.

In summary, we have shown that currency management systems can be a valuable addition to diversified institutional portfolios seeking to increase return and reduce risk in today's dynamic investment environment. It is therefore incumbent on pension fund managers and their consultants to consider adding this investment category to institutional portfolios.

---

* As measured by an improved Sharpe ratio.

TABLE 16.11 Correlations (Monthly Returns)*

	Currency	U.S. Bonds	Foreign Bonds	S&P	EAFE
1977–1992:					
Currency	4.365				
U.S. bonds	−0.113	2.081			
Foreign bonds					
S&P	−0.015	0.335	−0.035	4.433	
EAFE**	−0.015	0.175	0.381	0.396	5.791
1986–1992:					
Currency	4.195				
U.S. bonds	0.047	1.372			
Foreign bonds	0.090	0.379	3.600		
S&P	0.141	0.276	−0.052	4.798	
EAFE	0.034	0.190	0.560	0.457	6.058

* Monthly standard deviations shown on diagonals.
** EAFE = An index of major stocks of Europe, Australia, and the Far East.

TABLE 16.12 Results of Adding Currency Management to a Diversified Portfolio of Stocks and Bonds*

Percentage Allocation Currencies	Yearly Mean	Yearly Standard Deviation	Sharpe Ratio	Compounded Annual Rate of Return
0%	13.1%	9.2%	1.4	12.7%
5	13.7	8.4	1.6	13.4
10	14.3	7.6	1.9	14.0
15	14.9	7.0	2.1	14.7
20	15.5	6.5	2.4	15.3
25	16.1	6.3	2.6	16.0
30	16.8	6.3	2.7	16.6
40	18.1	7.2	2.5	17.9
50	19.4	9.1	2.1	19.1
60	20.7	11.5	1.8	20.3
70	22.1	14.4	1.5	21.4
80	23.5	17.6	1.3	22.6
90	25.0	21.1	1.2	23.7
100	26.5	24.7	1.1	24.8

* For each percentage allocation to currencies, the remaining amount is split as follows: bonds 45 percent, S&P 45 percent, EAFE 10 percent.

Implementation of Currency Management

We conclude our survey of currency management by addressing some practical issues regarding the actual currency investment process and the attendant valuation accounting.

An institutional investor normally establishes a currency management account in the following way. Through mutual discussion, the currency manager and the institution agree on the maximum size of currency positions to be allowed in the currency investment program. The institution then opens a line of credit with a currency dealer, so that the dealer will permit the currency manager to take on currency forward positions for the institution's account. Because these are transactions in the forward market, the institution needs to make the appropriate credit checks on the dealer. Also, the institution must have available cash to pay for any net losses on the forward transactions, when they become due. If net gains develop, no cash will be necessary for these currency transactions.

As we stated earlier, most institutional business will be done in the interbank market, using forward exchange trades, rather than in the exchange-traded futures markets. If the futures markets are used, however, initial margin would have to be posted, usually amounting to a small fraction of the size of the currency positions.

Regardless of the minimal outlay of capital required to participate in currency management programs, portfolios will need to be evaluated, just as any other exposure would be. This valuation is almost always on a daily mark-to-market basis; that is, the portfolio is evaluated at an agreed-on "settling" time each day. (Currency markets are open 24 hours a day.) The settling time is usually established by the custodian or institution involved with the portfolio.

Today, approximately 10 percent of pension assets use currency management. Pension funds' interest in global bonds and currencies will undoubtedly continue to grow, as the benefits of diversification are demonstrated. We will therefore close with some remarks on the question of choosing an appropriate benchmark for these investment areas.

Choice of Benchmark

For foreign bonds, as we have stated previously, we believe the bond investment decision should be separated from the currency management process. After all, the bonds are bought because the yields look attractive and a fall in yields is expected. The currency fluctuations may cause the investment not to perform as predicted. Therefore, the currency hedging program used should have as its goal the elimination of any losses to the bond portfolio resulting from currency price movements.

According to this reasoning, the benchmark for a portfolio of foreign bonds should be the local currency total return, taken as a *U.S. Dollar* return. That is, if the local currency return of U.K. bonds in a given year is 18.8 percent, then the U.S. investor should compare his or her actual U.S. Dollar return with 18.8 percent. If it is less, then the currency hedging program was the reason.

An example will clarify this important point. Suppose an investor bought U.K. bonds at the start of 1992, correctly predicting sharply lower yields in the U.K. Having no particular expertise in predicting currency movement, the investor might have assumed that the currency would remain unchanged, and therefore might have chosen to do nothing about the currency exposure. We recognize this as the no hedge decision, analyzed earlier. We also know that this would have resulted in a loss of more than 3 percent, in U.S. Dollar terms, for 1992.

If, instead, a hedging strategy had been chosen that returned 18.88 percent or more in 1992, then the entire currency depreciation effect would have been avoided, because the British Pound declined by that much against the U.S. Dollar. In this context, we view currency hedging as "insurance" against currency risk.

What if the British Pound had appreciated instead of depreciating? Then a U.S. Dollar return higher than the local currency return of 18.8 percent would have been achieved. So long as the currency hedge did not lose more than the appreciation of the British Pound, the initial goal of achieving the return offered by the U.K. bonds would have been attained.

To summarize: The foreign bond investment decision should be viewed as a fixed-income investment without regard to currency fluctuations; the currency hedging program should be viewed as insurance against the currency exposure; and the benchmark should be the local currency return achieved by the foreign bond index, counted as a U.S. Dollar return.

The investor may reasonably choose a different benchmark, if there are no hedging programs available that can be expected to perform well against this benchmark. In any case, our approach, which separates the hedge return from the bond return, leads naturally to the most appropriate benchmark against which to judge foreign bond investment performance.

For currency management programs used as a separate investment class, the choice of a benchmark is a more complicated problem. Currency management is a special case of the use of derivatives to alter the asset allocation of a portfolio. It does not require the actual allocation of cash out of other investment assets, however, because it uses the forward exchange market. Therefore, one appropriate benchmark is a zero return; that is, if the currency investment program generates a positive return, it has succeeded.

For derivative-based strategies such as currency management, a variety of other benchmarks can also be used. For example, if some cash is set aside against the currency positions, then the appropriate benchmark can be modified to include the interest earned on the cash. Or, if the investor knows of a passive currency investment strategy that has historically yielded a positive return, the benchmark can be the return generated by that passive strategy. Here, the return from the passive strategy is analogous to the expected return from owning bonds or equities used to evaluate active fixed income and equity managers.

NOTES

1. For a more detailed discussion and a good overview, see Jess Lederman and Keith K. H. Park, eds., "The Global Bond Market" (Chicago: publisher?, 1991).
2. Greenwich Associates International Bond Buyers Survey, 1991.
3. Forward prices statistically trend toward the spot prices and not the other way around, as would be expected if forwards provided a major element of price forecasting.
4. U.S. and Canadian dollar spot trades are settled on the next business day.
5. See Stephen J. Taylor: *Modelling Financial Time Series* (New York: John Wiley & Sons, Inc., 1986), and "Rewards Available to Currency Futures Speculators: Compensation for Risk or Evidence of Inefficient Pricing?," *Economic Record: Proceedings of the International Conference on Futures Markets, December 1990* (1991).
6. For details on the design of currency hedging models, see "Derivatives in Currency Management: Theory and Practice," by Charles Freifeld, in *The Handbook of Derivatives and Synthetics*, R. Klein and J. Lederman eds., Probus Publishing, 1994.
7. Id., Appendix A presents an analysis of the relationship between relative yield curve changes and returns from fully hedged foreign bonds.
8. Id., pp. 597–405 and Appendix II describe the design of this model.

17

Tactical Asset Allocation in the Global Context

Craig J. Lazzara
Vice President
Salomon Brothers, Inc.
New York, New York

Richard A. Weiss
Senior Vice President
SAWWA Trust
Los Angeles, California

INTRODUCTION

Tactical asset allocation strategies, whose goal is to tilt the asset mix of a securities portfolio toward asset classes considered to be of above-average attractiveness, have received considerable attention since their generally good performance during the October 1987 market crash. This chapter describes the authors' attempts to globalize a tactical asset allocation process originally designed for use in the United States.

The chapter begins with a discussion of the degree to which international capital markets are integrated, and the diametrically opposite paradigms of complete segmentation and full integration. Although both of these paradigms have adherents among contemporary market commentators, the authors argue that neither is a satisfactory explanation of world capital market behavior. Instead, they propose a more flexible model that explains a national market's behavior in terms of a number of factors. Some of these factors may operate in more than one national market, which would not occur under conditions of complete segmentation. The weights on each factor are selected to maximize the predictive power of each national asset model. This leads to different weights for similar factors in different countries, which would not occur under assumptions of full integration.

This formulation is tested empirically by deriving tactical asset allocation models for the United States, Japan, Germany, and the United Kingdom. Each national model adds value relative to a passive mix equally divided between stocks and bonds. These models differ substantially from country to country (with Japan showing the most distinctive characteristics), although many of the same explanatory variables are important in more than one country. The models' structure therefore does not support assumptions of either full integration or complete segmentation.

The chapter concludes by illustrating how the national models can be used to allocate assets across borders as well as within each country. Investors willing to allocate funds on an opportunistic basis outside their home country can realize active returns that are both higher and more consistent than those obtainable from a purely domestic approach. Although both country selection and asset selection play a role in producing these results, these two sources of value-added are synergistic in a fully global application.

An obvious question for any practitioner of tactical asset allocation is whether the same intellectual disciplines that help to select asset classes in one country also help in other national markets. Moreover, is it possible to use these disciplines to decide whether the U.S. stock market is attractive relative to, say, its Japanese counterpart? This chapter describes our efforts, both theoretical and empirical, to answer these questions.

A THEORETICAL FRAMEWORK

The degree to which world capital markets are integrated is critical to the design of a global asset allocation process. Two competing paradigms are: (1) complete *segmentation* and (2) total *integration*. A belief that markets are segmented implies that each country's markets are driven by factors that are essentially local and may not be directly comparable. For example, a believer in segmented markets might evaluate German equities by monitoring Germany's inflation rate while regarding price momentum as the most important influence on Japanese stocks. If capital markets are completely segmented, investment returns are determined by unique factors in each country. The volatility of each country's market is likewise determined by idiosyncratic national factors, so that different risks are priced in different countries. Investors who diversify internationally in this setting can expect to achieve lower volatility and potentially abnormal returns, provided that they can identify other national markets with more favorable factor pricing than their own.

The opposite paradigm, complete integration, is a view that returns are determined by the same factors in different countries, and that the expected return to these factors is the same across national borders. A believer in completely integrated markets might evaluate the relative merits of U.S. and Japanese stocks by comparing their price–earnings (P–E) ratios, e.g., implicitly assuming that this factor is of equal importance in both countries. If capital markets are completely integrated, cross-border arbitrage will ensure that factor prices are the same in every country. The main benefit of international diversification under these conditions will be risk reduction, not return enhancement.

We can easily formalize these two extreme views of market structure. In the simplest case, returns will be a linear function of factor exposure. Let $E[R_x]$ be the expected return on the equity market of country X and $E[R_y]$ be the expected return on the equity market of country Y. Let F_{xi} represent the ith factor thought to influence returns in country X, and F_{yi} represent the same in country Y. If we believe that markets are nationally segmented, then the factors that influence returns in X and Y are different. Assuming that there is only one such factor in each country, returns in each country can be written as:

$$E[R_x] = \beta_{x1} \cdot F_{x1} \tag{1}$$

$$E[R_y] = \beta_{y1} \cdot F_{y1}. \tag{2}$$

The differential return will be:

$$E[R_x - R_y] = [\beta_{x1} \cdot F_{x1}] - [\beta_{y1} \cdot F_{y1}], \tag{3}$$

where the β terms represent the sensitivity of each market's return to its underlying national factor. In a completely segmented world, the factors will differ across national borders, and the β terms are likely to differ as well. It is not necessary that there be only one factor for each country; if the explanatory variables are scaled alike (say, by normalizing them), we can think of the β values as weights for each factor.

We can use the same notation to specify a model of fully integrated world capital markets. The individual country returns would be given by:

$$E[R_x] = \beta_1 \cdot F_{x1} + \beta_2 \cdot F_{x2} + \ldots + \beta_n \cdot F_{xn} \tag{4}$$

$$E[R_y] = \beta_1 \cdot F_{y1} + \beta_2 \cdot F_{y2} + \ldots + \beta_n \cdot F_{yn} \tag{5}$$

The differential return would be:

$$E[R_x - R_y] = \beta_1[F_{x1} - F_{y1}] + \beta_2[F_{x2} - F_{y2}] + \cdots$$
$$+ \beta_n[F_{xn} - F_{yn}]. \tag{6}$$

Here, the factors are the same in countries X and Y, and the factor sensitivities (the β coefficients) are identical across markets. Expected asset returns will differ only because the values of the explanatory factors may differ in country X and country Y.

Equations (3) and (6) allow us to identify some of the pitfalls of either extreme paradigm. The fully segmented approach runs the risk of focusing on the wrong factors for each national market, a particularly acute problem when (as in equation (3)) the implicit factor weight is 100 percent. The segmented view's concentration on the country level does not capture any common influences across national borders, thus making cross-border comparisons intuitively difficult.

The fully integrated approach is, in some sense, designed to facilitate cross-border comparisons, but has drawbacks of its own. Equation (6) assumes (1) that factors are directly comparable across borders and (2) that their importance is the same in each country. Neither assumption may be justified. This is a particular problem if the fully integrated approach gets adopted by default. For example, a manager domiciled in country X may develop a model such as equation (4) for his or her own country and then attempt to export it to country Y. In doing so, the manager implicitly constrains the β terms in Y to be the same as those in X. If the βs are in fact different, the manager may reach inappropriate allocation decisions even if most or all of the factors that influence country Y's return are the same as those of country X. Moreover, by constraining the β terms to be equal in each national market, the integrated approach does not capture differences among countries, thereby suboptimizing single-country asset allocation decisions.

Constructing working models for active global tactical asset allocation necessarily requires taking a view on the segmentation versus integration dispute. We address the question by empirical means; rather than constraining the selection of factors or factor weights, we let the data tell us what relative weights should be. In this process, we are guided by two precepts. The first of these is "local first": before we attempt to choose between the stock markets of two different countries, we construct domestic models for each country of interest. This task is necessary in order to avoid the assumption that all countries are alike. We believe that it is essential to determine each market's individual sensitivities to key variables before making cross-border comparisons. An important implication of this local-first view is that we will not move assets from the United States into Japanese stocks, for example, unless we believe that Japanese stocks are preferable to Japanese bonds and Japanese cash from a Japanese viewpoint.

Our second precept is that currency and asset decisions are distinct. We believe that it is possible to add value by shifting among countries and assets without assuming currency risk. It is, for instance, possible to like the Japanese stock market without wanting to be exposed to the Yen. In any situation that calls for asset exposure outside an investor's home market, therefore, we assume that the foreign exchange exposure is hedged back to the home currency. (This implies that all positions in cash equivalents, unlike stocks or bonds, are always held in the home country.) The currency decision is independent of the asset decision and calls for independent analysis.

MODEL STRUCTURE

An investor who wants to hold country X's currency will do so by exchanging his or her own currency for currency X, buying country X's Treasury bills, and earning country X's risk-free rate of return. If we predict asset returns net of their risk-free component, therefore, we facilitate the separation of asset and currency decisions. let I_x and I_y represent the risk-free rate in countries X and Y. The excess return for each country's stock or bond market can then be written as:

$$E[R_x - I_x] = \beta_{x1} \cdot F_{x1} + \beta_{x2} \cdot F_{x2} + \ldots + \beta_{xn} \cdot F_{xn} \tag{7}$$

$$E[R_y - I_y] = \beta_{y1} \cdot F_{y1} + \beta_{y2} \cdot F_{y2} + \ldots + \beta_{yn} \cdot F_{yn}. \tag{8}$$

The differential excess return will be:

$$E[(R_x - I_x) - (R_y - I_y)] = [\beta_{x1} \cdot F_{x1} + \ldots + \beta_{xn} \cdot F_{xn}] \\ -[\beta_{y1} \cdot F_{y1} + \ldots + \beta_{yn} \cdot F_{yn}]. \tag{9}$$

Notice that, unlike equation (3) or equation (6), equation (9) does not limit the number of factors we utilize, nor constrain their weights (the β terms) to be the same in country X and country Y. Equations (7) and (8) can be estimated separately to produce the best fit in country X and country Y without international restrictions, conforming to our local-first approach. As we re-estimate the models over time, we expect the β_x and β_y terms to shift in response to changes in the two countries' capital markets.

As suggested above, this framework helps us to sort out the asset and currency decisions. Assume that country X is our domicile and that we want to invest in country Y's stock market without taking the risk that Y's currency will decline during our holding period. We can control that risk by selling Y's currency for forward delivery when we make our initial investment in country Y. We will buy Y's currency at today's spot rate and sell it for today's forward rate. Let:

S = spot exchange rate; price of one unit of currency Y (for immediate delivery) in terms of currency X.

F = forward exchange rate; price of one unit of currency Y (for future delivery) in terms of currency X.

The relationship between F and S is controlled by an arbitrage transaction. Suppose we want to choose between holding the risk-free asset in country X or country Y. For an investor domiciled in country X, making an investment in the Treasury bills of Y fully risk-free will require a forward sale of Y's currency; that is, the investor must buy 1/S units of Y's currency today and simultaneously sell it in the forward market for a total value of [F · (1/S)]. The return in the two countries is equivalent if:

$$(1 + I_x) = \frac{1}{S} \cdot (1 + I_y) \cdot F$$

$$\frac{F}{S} = \frac{1 + I_x}{1 + I_y}$$

$$\frac{F}{S} - 1 = \frac{1 + I_x}{1 + I_y} - 1$$

$$\frac{F}{S} - 1 \approx I_x - I_y \qquad (10)$$

Equation (10) shows us that the forward discount or premium on currency Y relative to currency X is approximately equal to the difference in the two countries' interest rates. The transaction that produces this relationship is called "covered interest arbitrage."

What happens when we compare the stock markets of the two countries? We should be willing to invest in market Y on a currency-hedged basis if:

$$[1 + E(R_y)] \cdot \frac{F}{S} > 1 + E(R_x)$$

$$\frac{F}{S} > \frac{1 + E(R_x)}{1 + E(R_y)}$$

$$\frac{F}{S} - 1 > \frac{1 + E(R_x)}{1 + E(R_y)} - 1$$

$$I_x - I_y > E(R_x) - E(R_y)$$

$$E(R_y - I_y) > E(R_x - I_x) \qquad (11)$$

Equation (11) shows that we should prefer to invest in the equity market with the highest expected *excess* return. This insight becomes more powerful in combination with equations (7) through (9). When we model local asset returns net of their risk-free component, as in equations (7) and (8), we produce forecasts of expected excess return directly. By comparing the output from models of stock–cash or bond–cash returns in the countries of interest, we can readily make currency-hedged cross-border allocations.

BUILDING LOCAL MODELS

Construction of asset allocation models for various national markets requires both theoretical and empirical investigation to identify variables that are predictive of relative returns in each country. Although our models evolve as we continually seek to improve our forecasting ability, our research methodology has always been based on two key elements. First, we require that explanatory variables be theoretically sound, as well as empirically significant. Correlation does not imply causation. If there is no economic rationale for a variable's influencing asset class returns, it is better to omit it from a forecasting model. Loss of historical explanatory power is a small price to pay for avoiding potentially spurious predictive factors.

A second key element in our approach is to rely on objective, rather than forecast, data as input. In this way, we can backtest our forecasting models with a high degree of confidence. Objective independent variables also eliminate the potential additional forecasting error introduced by inaccurate or fuzzy subjective inputs.

Our work proceeds not only country-by-country but, within each country, "pairwise" by asset classes. In other words, we predict differences in returns between stocks and cash, bonds and cash, and stocks and bonds via a multiple regression model of historical data. Our explanatory variables generally are classified as fundamental, economic, or technical.

In our U.S. stock–cash model, for example, the fundamental variable is the U.S. equity risk premium—that is, a measure of the expected return on the stock market minus short-term interest rates. Economic variables include measures of interest rate changes and inflation; a technical variable measures the volatility of the U.S. stock market. All of these variables are theoretically appropriate, and all meet the test of statistical significance.

When we shift our attention outside the United States, our work on U.S. markets is helpful but by no means a complete guide. For example, in developing a stock–cash model for the U.K., we are able to make use of British adaptations of all of the variables that occur in our U.S. stock-cash model. We also discover some variables that help in our U.K. work but have little predictive power in the United States. For example, the weighted average change in U.K. import prices helps us to predict relative U.K. stock and cash returns. This is not a surprising result, given the import sensitivity of the U.K. economy relative to that of the United States. What is true of the stock-cash relationship is equally true of stock–bond and bond–cash models: U.S. analysis provides a base from which to begin, but the incorporation of specific local factors is critically important.

It is equally important that we weight these variables in keeping with local market sensitivities. Multiple regression analysis provides unbiased weights that measure each factor's historical influence. By grouping each country's variables into broad categories, we can compare their relative importance among countries, as illustrated in Table 17.1 for our four stock–cash models. As in the United States, fundamental variables include, for each country, a measure of the relative level of the expected return on the local stock market versus local cash equivalent rates. Economic measures relate to the broader macroeconomic picture, and technical measures describe the volatility and momentum of each country's equity market.

The U.S. market is dominated by economic and value measures, which, in total, comprise almost 90 percent of the weight in our U.S. stock–cash forecasting model. The U.K. and Germany are somewhat more balanced: technical measures amount to 27 percent and 18 percent, respectively. In Japan, however, technical measures are more dominant, accounting for more than 40 percent of the weight.

This result confirms that the Japanese market is more trend- and momentum-driven than are the U.S., U.K., or German markets. Moreover, the result gives us an important insight into why some investors have historically been skeptical about the possibility of successful tactical asset allocation in Japan. American investors in particular tend to think about tactical asset allocation systems in terms of fundamental value (i.e., risk premium) variables, even when other variables provide a substantial fraction of predictive power. If we had to rely only on fundamental measures

TABLE 17.1 Comparisons of Local Models: Stock–Cash Models

| | Historical Average Factor Contributions 1970–1992 | | | |
	United States	United Kingdom	Japan	Germany
Fundamental	38%	26%	21%	31%
Economic	50	47	38	51
Technical	12	27	41	18
	100%	100%	100%	100%

in Japan, we would do less well than we can by utilizing a more comprehensive set of variables. It is not true that value doesn't matter in Japan, but it is true that it matters less than do other variables.

The evidence of Table 17.1 also argues powerfully against both the complete segmentation and perfect integration paradigms of international capital market structure. If markets were completely segmented, for example, it would not be possible to identify factors that exert a powerful influence on returns in more than one market. Instead, we see that a simple measure of fundamental value has significant predictive power in each of the world's four largest equity markets. On the other hand, if world capital markets were fully integrated, we would not see the dramatic differences in variable weights across national borders that we observe in Table 17.1.

SIMULATED RESULTS: LOCAL MODELS

The differences in factor contributions across countries support our view that customized local models must be the core of any global asset allocation process. Table 17.2 shows the simulated performance of each set of local models (stated in its own currency). For each country, we utilize a portfolio construction rule that makes active bets away from a 50 percent stock/50 percent bond benchmark portfolio in proportion to the relative attractiveness of each asset class. In the United States, such an approach would have returned 18.4 percent per year between 1976 and 1992, versus 13.1 percent for a static 50 percent stock/50 percent bond benchmark portfolio. Value-added was positive in 52 percent of the quarters observed. Comparable results would have been obtained in the U.K., Japan, and Germany. Used independently by a local investor, therefore, each model would have

---

TABLE 17.2 Local Asset Allocation (1976–1992)

Benchmark portfolio: 50 percent stock, 50 percent bonds
Permissible exposure: 0 to 100 percent in stock, bonds, or cash equivalents

| | Annual Returns | | | |
Country	Active	Benchmark	Value Added	Quarterly Consistency
United States	18.4%	13.1%	5.3%	52%
United Kingdom	22.1	17.6	4.5	57
Japan	14.3	10.1	4.2	56
Germany	12.3	9.6	2.7	54

All returns are in local currencies.
Quarterly consistency = proportion of quarters when active portfolio outperforms or equals benchmark.

added substantial value during this period. Moreover, the models would have done so on a roughly consistent basis across national markets, although the tendency is for periods of underperformance in one country to be counteracted by periods of good performance in at least one of the others.

SIMULATED RESULTS: CROSS-BORDER MODELS

Our interest in global allocation is directed not so much toward developing local models for other countries as toward developing a way to make profitable cross-border decisions. In a currency-hedged context, this goal requires us to compare not simply expected returns on U.S. and Japanese stocks, for example, but rather each stock market's expected *excess* return. This is the point of equation (11): we accept foreign exposure only if the expected excess return on a foreign asset exceeds that of its domestic counterpart.

This gives rise to a two-step global portfolio construction algorithm. The first step, *asset selection*, requires us to solve for each market's recommended local asset allocation. If, for example, our recommendation for a British investor is to hold two-thirds of his assets in stock and the balance in bonds, it follows that whatever commitment we ultimately make to the U.K. markets will have a similar division of two-thirds stock, one-third bonds. The second step, *country selection*, uses a similar portfolio construction rule to allocate among countries. We measure country attractiveness by taking a weighted average of each country's individual asset attractiveness ratings. For this calculation, asset weights are dictated by the proportions that a local investor opts to hold.

We found this two-stage methodology to be effective in extensive tests. Table 17.3 shows how it would have operated for a U.S.-based

---

TABLE 17.3 Global Risk and Return

Currency: Dollar
Local benchmark: 50 percent stock/50 percent bonds
Country benchmark: 100 percent United States

	Annual Data, 1976–1992					
	Benchmark		Active		Value	Quarterly
Model	Mean	Std. Dev.	Mean	Std. Dev.	Added	Consistency
United States	13.1%	10.8%	18.4%	12.0%	5.3%	52%
Full global	13.1	10.8	22.0	13.5	8.9	60
Country						
selection	13.1	10.8	15.9	9.8	2.8	56

All non-U.S. exposure hedged to dollars.

investor. Simply holding a static balanced portfolio in the United States would have produced a return of 13.1 percent between 1976 and 1992, which could have been increased to 18.4 percent by our U.S. tactical asset allocation model. Using our full global capability, however, would have raised the average return to 22.0 percent.

Table 17.3 also raises an interesting question about global tactical asset allocation systems generally. It is possible that only some subcomponents of the full global process work well, while others do not. For example, it may be that all of the value-added comes from the success of the individual local models and not from the process of shifting among countries. To test this possibility, the row labeled "country selection" in Table 17.3 freezes all local asset positions at 50 percent stock/50 percent bonds. The only way for the active portfolio to outperform its benchmark, therefore, is to shift some portion of its assets from a static U.S. balanced portfolio to similar balanced portfolios in the U.K., Japan, or Germany. Table 17.3 shows that country selection, so defined, provides 2.8 percent value-added per year. Because asset selection, in this context, comes entirely from the U.S. asset allocation model, it contributes 5.3 percent per year. Interestingly, the annual value-added of the full global model (8.9 percent) exceeds the sum of the values of asset selection and country selection. This means that, in the full global process, asset selection and country selection are not independent; they are synergistic.

One possible objection to the conclusions we draw from Table 17.3 is that we have measured our results against a one-country benchmark. Some of the benefits of global asset allocation may be obtainable passively. Simply by redefining our benchmark portfolio to include foreign stocks and bonds, we can enhance returns and lower risks relative to a domestic benchmark. The exact degree to which we can achieve the passive benefits of global diversification depends importantly on how willing we are to shift our benchmark portfolio offshore. Few U.S. investors, for example, would be willing to hold 60 percent of their equity exposure abroad, even though the U.S. constitutes only about 40 percent of world equity capitalization. Table 17.4 therefore posits an extreme view by dividing our benchmark portfolio equally among the U.S., the U.K., Japan, and Germany.

Returns for the global benchmark are lower than for a domestic benchmark over this time period, although the volatility of those returns also falls. Value added is 10.7 percent per year, and quarterly consistency stands at 69 percent. As before, country selection and asset selection are important contributors to the active portfolio's performance.

In Table 17.4, country selection has the same meaning as before, but asset selection measures the impact of all four local models (weighted 1/4 each), not just the U.S. model. Asset selection and country selection

TABLE 17.4 Global Risk and Return

Currency: Dollar
Local benchmark: 50 percent stock/50 percent bonds
Country benchmark: ¼ each: United States, United Kingdom, Japan, Germany

	Annual Data, 1976–1992					
	Benchmark		Active		Value	Quarterly
Model	Mean	Std. Dev.	Mean	Std. Dev.	Added	Consistency
United States	13.1%	10.8%	18.4%	12.0%	5.3%	52%
Full global	12.1	9.0	22.8	15.5	10.7	69
Country						
selection	12.1	9.0	15.6	10.9	3.5	57
Asset selection	12.1	9.0	16.3	7.7	4.2	59

All non-U.S. exposure hedged to dollars.

each provide independent value added, but in the full global model they are once again synergistic. This point bears some elaboration. For each of our models, we calibrate attractiveness in terms of standard deviations away from neutral, and we know that larger signals are more reliable than smaller signals. For example, stocks typically outperform cash by a larger margin when the stock–cash signal is 1.5 rather than 0.5. This conclusion applies to each asset pair we have analyzed in each country. Suppose that the recommended mix for a local investor in each country is 100 percent equity, based on a stock–cash signal of 1.0 for the United States, 1.5 for the United Kingdom and for Germany, and 2.0 for Japan. The country selection part of our global balancing algorithm will, based on these signals, underweight the United States and overweight Japan. This causes assets to be drawn into the model that is most likely to be working well, that is, the country selection process tilts toward the asset models that are likely to be most reliable.

HOW MUCH IS ENOUGH?

Table 17.4 details results for a normal portfolio that is admittedly extreme. Most funds that utilize global asset allocation are likely to view it as an adjunct to their domestic portfolios. How large must their commitment outside their home country be to make a difference? Notice that we are asking about a *maximum* level of *active* foreign exposure, not a *normal* level of *passive* exposure.

Table 17.5 shows that the answer is, "Surprisingly little." For example, by permitting only 20 percent of a fund's assets to be invested outside the United States, we can generate an annual value added that is 110 basis points greater than by utilizing only a domestic tactical asset

TABLE 17.5 Impact of Increasing Non-U.S. Exposure

Currency: Dollar
Local benchmark: 50 percent stock/50 percent bonds
Country benchmark: 100 percent United States

| | Annual Data, 1976–1992 | | | |
| Maximum Exposure Outside United States | Return | | Annual Value Added | Quarterly Consistency |
	Mean	Std. Dev.		
Benchmark	13.1%	10.8%	—	—
0% (U.S. only)	18.4	12.0	5.3%	52%
10	18.6	11.6	5.5	55
20	19.5	12.0	6.4	59
30	20.2	12.3	7.1	59
40	20.7	12.6	7.6	59
50	21.2	12.9	8.1	60
100	22.0	13.5	8.9	60

All non-U.S. exposure hedged to dollars.

allocation approach. The benefits of permitting larger foreign exposures are commensurately greater. *Any* level of permissible foreign exposure (even 100 percent!) is less risky from a consistency standpoint than is a purely domestic approach.

CONCLUSION

Tactical asset allocation systems provide an important benefit to investors by shifting among assets in response to predictive signals. Applying these disciplines in an international context not only diversifies risk across assets, but also across countries and, importantly, across forecasting models.

Although not a panacea for the complexities of global asset allocation strategy, this approach avoids some of the more common pitfalls. World financial markets are becoming increasingly integrated, but local market movements are still dominated by local influences. It is imperative in any global market analysis that domestic considerations be given first priority. Only then can one see the larger picture clearly.

How to Beat Global Equity Indices with Low Risk Country Allocation Strategies Further to the CAPM Risk/Return Framework

Michael Keppler
President
Keppler Asset Management Inc.
New York, New York

INTRODUCTION

Capital asset pricing theory tells us that there is a positive relationship between expected risk and expected return and that investors may obtain a higher expected rate of return on their holdings only by incurring additional risk. Although espoused by most institutional investors, these assumptions have always been challenged by a minority of practitioners, including myself, who have maintained that it is possible to achieve risk-adjusted excess returns by exploiting the market inefficiencies pronounced nonexistent or, at best, anomalous by the academicians.

Although the strategies that have been devised to take advantage of these "anomalies" are as diverse as their architects, they all rest on the recognition that reality is different from the sophisticated models developed by the proponents of modern portfolio theory, who have perpetuated the myth of "efficient" markets in the face of abundant evidence that stock prices, far from being determined by rational processes, are the product of the all-too-often irrational behavior of investors, alternatively driven by fear and greed.

In my own work, which has focused on the global equity markets, I have found that, over the long term, investors can outperform global equity indices on a risk-adjusted basis by concentrating investments in undervalued markets selected on the basis of certain selection criteria with demonstrated predictive power regarding relative performance.[1]

HIGHER RISK DOES NOT NECESSARILY MEAN HIGHER RETURN

A careful risk–return analysis of a number of different global equity strategies tested over the years has shown that, contrary to the premise central to modern portfolio theory, the correlation between risk and return is *negative*. Investors are not rewarded for assuming higher risk. Instead, *high risk is associated with lower returns and vice versa.*

Illustrations of the negative relationship between risk and return also show that equally weighted market indices are more "efficient" than cap-weighted market indices, which is inconsistent with the capital asset pricing theory as well.

Figure 18.1 shows the results of global equity strategies based on cash earnings during the 20-year period from January 1970 to December 1989. The hypothetical investment vehicles were 18 Morgan Stanley

FIGURE 18.1 Cash Flow Strategies, Risk–Return Relationship (Local Currencies, 1970–1989)

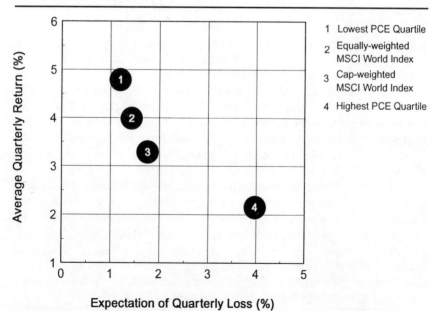

1 Lowest PCE Quartile

2 Equally-weighted MSCI World Index

3 Cap-weighted MSCI World Index

4 Highest PCE Quartile

SOURCE: Keppler Asset Management Inc., New York

Capital International (MSCI) country indices[2] sorted into four groups according to their respective cash earnings/corresponding index levels. The low-risk strategy of investing in the markets with the highest cash earnings in relation to price resulted in the highest returns (19.17 percent per year); the high-risk strategy of investing in the markets with the lowest cash earnings in relation to price resulted in the lowest returns (4.37 percent per year).[3]

VOLATILITY IS NOT ALWAYS THE BEST MEASURE OF RISK

Because the traditional variance (standard deviation) measure of risk is of very limited relevance in many investment situations, the risk-adjusted return shown in Figure 18.1 was calculated by using the Keppler Ratio, which indicates the return per unit of expectation of loss, rather than the Sharpe Ratio, which indicates the return per unit of variability.

If the assumption of a symmetric distribution of returns is violated, the reward–variability ratio is not exact. In cases where there is a positive skewness of returns, risk is assumed to be higher than it is in reality. Conversely, if returns are negatively skewed during the performance measurement period, the Sharpe Ratio shows risk to be lower than it actually is.

However, even if we were to accept price volatility as a legitimate measure of risk, the fact remains that there is a negative correlation between risk (as defined by the proponents of modern portfolio theory) and returns. Figure 18.2 shows that the low-volatility strategy of investing in the national equity markets with the highest cash earnings in relation to price resulted in significantly higher returns than the high-volatility strategy of investing in the markets with the lowest cash earnings in relation to price.

REDEFINING RISK

A similar negative correlation between risk and return can be established on the basis of other valuation criteria such as dividend yields or price–earnings ratios. The negative correlation is particularly obvious when standard deviation and beta are replaced by more realistic risk measures that focus on the downside, rather than on the ups and downs, based on the recognition that risk has to do with adversity rather than uncertainty.

Volatility may be a useful concept for futures traders who can easily switch from long to short positions, but it is of little relevance to most equity investors. The notion that portfolio risk is strictly a function of the volatility of portfolio returns rests on invalid assumptions

---

FIGURE 18.2 Cash Flow Strategies, Volatility–Return Relationship (Local Currencies, 1970–1989)

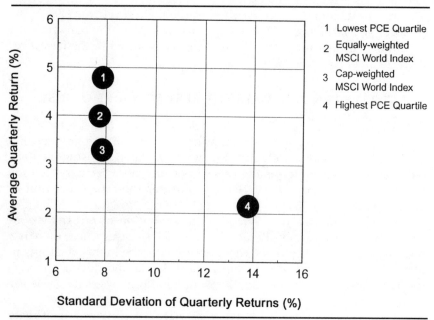

1 Lowest PCE Quartile

2 Equally-weighted MSCI World Index

3 Cap-weighted MSCI World Index

4 Highest PCE Quartile

SOURCE: Keppler Asset Management Inc., New York

---

and does not appeal to common sense. Volatility is very desirable in bull markets. With the exception of short sellers, I have never heard a market participant complain about positive deviations from the mean return. Few practitioners would equate that welcome occurrence with risk. Most investors intuitively feel that risk should have something to do with losing money, or, as Robert Jeffrey put it, with "having insufficient cash with which to make essential payments."[4]

Figure 18.3 shows that, contrary to one of the basic assumptions of modern portfolio theory, returns are not necessarily normally distributed. The frequency distribution of market returns is no classic bell curve. The shape is skewed rather than symmetric, and outliers are substantially different from those expected in a normal or log-normal distribution.

Given the limited relevance of volatility in most investment contexts, standard deviation and beta should be replaced by risk measures that are not based on the assumption of a symmetric distribution of returns, such as the largest drawdown from a previous high or the expectation of loss, which focuses on both the probability and the magnitude of negative results. Risk measures must be flexible enough to deal with

FIGURE 18.3 Examples of Skewed Distributions of Returns (December 1984–December 1989)

MSCI German Total Return Index

Average Quarterly Return: 5.2%
Standard Deviation of Quarterly Returns: 12.4%

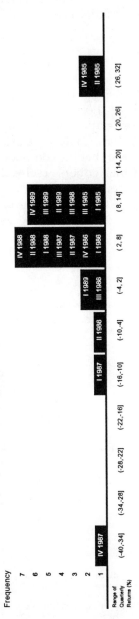

MSCI Hong Kong Total Return Index

Average Quarterly Return: 7.4%
Standard Deviation of Quarterly Returns: 16.1%

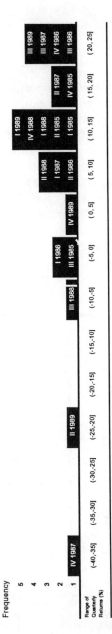

SOURCE: Keppler Asset Management Inc., New York

a broad range of portfolio objectives and constraints. The expectation of loss qualifies in this respect, because it allows us to define risk as the probability and magnitude of negative deviations from any required rate of return, depending on the liquidity needs of the investor.[5]

CONCLUSION

Why is it important to analyze risks realistically? As Charles D. Ellis has pointed out, money management has become a "loser's game" in which the ultimate winners will be those who make the fewest mistakes.[6] Minimizing risk is therefore critical to investment success.

If we are to reduce risk, we have to fully understand its main sources. Benjamin Graham suggested that the concept of risk should be applied "solely to a loss of value which either is realized through actual sale, or is caused by a significant deterioration in the company's position—or, more frequently perhaps, is the result of the payment of an excessive price in relation to the intrinsic worth of the security."[7] Robert Jeffrey correctly described risk as "a function of the characteristics of a portfolio's liabilities as well as of its assets and, in particular, of the cash flow relationship between the two over time."[8]

FIGURE 18.4 Range of Nominal Returns on U.S. Common Stocks (Various Holding Periods, 1926–1992)

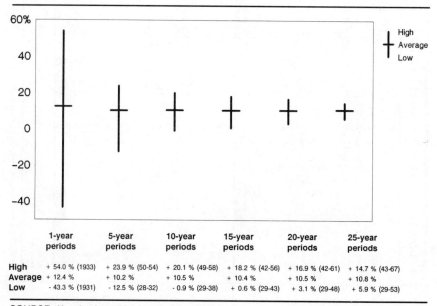

	1-year periods	5-year periods	10-year periods	15-year periods	20-year periods	25-year periods
High	+ 54.0 % (1933)	+ 23.9 % (50-54)	+ 20.1 % (49-58)	+ 18.2 % (42-56)	+ 16.9 % (42-61)	+ 14.7 % (43-67)
Average	+ 12.4 %	+ 10.2 %	+ 10.5 %	+ 10.4 %	+ 10.5 %	+ 10.8 %
Low	- 43.3 % (1931)	- 12.5 % (28-32)	- 0.9 % (29-38)	+ 0.6 % (29-43)	+ 3.1 % (29-48)	+ 5.9 % (29-53)

SOURCE: Keppler Asset Management Inc., New York

Thus, the two most important risk factors are overvaluation and dependence on short-term results. We know that the average rate of return of asset classes such as stocks and bonds is hardly affected by time, but the range of distributions of actual returns around the mean is greatly affected by the investor's time-horizon. Figure 18.4 shows the range of nominal returns on U.S. stocks for various holding periods from 1926 to 1992. The message is clear: Investments (such as stocks) that are highly risky in the short term become less risky as the investment horizon lengthens.

If risk, in the last analysis, is a function of price and time, and minimizing risk is the key to achieving superior returns in the domestic and international equity markets, the prescription for investment success can be condensed to the following simple formula: "Don't overpay, and invest for the long term!"

NOTES

1. See A. Michael Keppler, "The Importance of Dividend Yields in Country Selection," *Journal of Portfolio Management, 17* (Winter 1991): 24–29; "Further Evidence on the Predictability of International Equity Returns," *Journal of Portfolio Management, 18* (Fall 1991): 48–53.
2. The 18 MSCI country indices comprised the markets of:

1. Australia	7. Germany	13. Singapore/Malaysia
2. Austria	8. Hong Kong	14. Spain
3. Belgium	9. Italy	15. Sweden
4. Canada	10. Japan	16. Switzerland
5. Denmark	11. The Netherlands	17. United Kingdom
6. France	12. Norway	18. United States

3. This was true for both the local currency and U.S. Dollar analyses. Subperiod results, which confirm the findings, suggest that the relationships are generic rather than time-specific. The analyses will be updated as of the end of 1994, to show 25-year results.
4. Robert H. Jeffrey, "A New Paradigm for Portfolio Risk," *Journal of Portfolio Management, 2* (Fall 1984): 39.
5. To evaluate the risk of a given investment program or strategy, I subject the portfolio to a thorough downside analysis:
   - Number of losing/underperforming periods;
   - Probability of loss/shortfall below the required rate of return;
   - Average loss/shortfall in losing/underperforming periods;
   - Expectation of loss/shortfall;
   - Longest losing/underperforming streak;
   - Largest drawdown from a previous high.
6. Charles D. Ellis, "The Loser's Game," *Financial Analysts Journal, 31* (July–August 1975): 19–26.
7. Benjamin Graham, *The Intelligent Investor,* 4th rev. ed. (New York: Harper & Row, 1973), 61.
8. Jeffrey, *op cit.,* 33.

19

Emerging Markets and Risk Reduction

Arjun Divecha
Managing Director
Grantham, Mayo, Van Otterloo & Company
Berkeley, California

Everyone knows that investing in emerging markets is risky, but only if you put all your money in emerging markets. Recent work[1] has shown that investments of up to 45 percent in emerging markets (in a well-diversified portfolio) would have reduced the overall volatility (and increased return) of a global investor's portfolio over a recent five-year period. This chapter proposes using a low-volatility approach to country allocation in the emerging markets, to further reduce the risk of a global portfolio.

RETURNS AND RISKS OF EMERGING MARKETS

Casual readers of the financial press know that there have been stories of incredible returns (high and low) in the emerging markets. The Venezuelan stock market was up about 450 percent in US$ terms during 1990. On the other hand, the Taiwanese Stock Exchange Index, in 1990, started at about the 5,000 level, went up to 12,600 during the first quarter, and collapsed to near 2,500 during the third quarter. What makes this sequence even more interesting is that the Taiwanese market ranks only fourth or fifth among the most risky emerging markets! During 1991, Latin American countries dominated all others; in US$ terms, they were up over 100 percent.

Overall, the emerging markets did better than the developed markets over the five years studied (January 1988–December 1992). During this period, the annualized total return (in US$) to the International Finance Corporation's (IFC) Emerging Markets Global

Composite Index was 21.53 percent, as compared to 7.69 percent for the Financial Times World Index.

Table 19.1 shows predicted risks, based on BARRA's risk model (in annual standard deviation percentage), of each of the emerging markets as well as a few developed markets. Emerging markets are extremely risky when compared with developed markets. Apart from the obvious threats (political instability, insider trading, and others), there are a number of possible reasons why these markets are extremely volatile. First, they tend to be fairly concentrated: the larger stocks have a high proportion of the overall market capitalization. As a result, there are fewer opportunities for diversification, and returns to these large

TABLE 19.1 Emerging Market Characteristics

Country	Annual Standard Deviation (%)[a]	Market Capitalization (Million US$)[b]	Turnover Ratio[c]
Argentina	108	$ 18,633	84%
Brazil	74	45,261	45
Chile	29	29,644	7
Colombia	21	5,681	10
Greece	56	9,489	17
Hong Kong	31	172,106	53
India	31	65,119	32
Indonesia	39	12,038	32
Japan OTC	20		N.A.
Jordan	19	3,365	39
Korea	29	107,448	108
Malaysia	30	94,004	23
Mexico	56	139,061	32
Nigeria	13	1,243	2
Pakistan	10	8,028	12
Philippines	46	13,794	23
Portugal	61	9,213	38
Singapore	33	48,818	29
Taiwan	63	101,124	238
Thailand	31	58,259	124
Turkey	84	9,931	82
Venezuela	44	7,600	35
Zimbabwe	20	628	3
Total		$960,487	
Developed Markets			
Japan	22	2,399,004	26
United Kingdom	19	838,579	46
United States	17	4,757,879	56

[a] Predicted annual standard deviation in %, based on BARRA's Emerging Markets Equity Model.
[b] As of December 31, 1992.
[c] This is defined as the ratio of annual trading volume (in US$) divided by beginning-of-year market capitalization (in US$), for 1992. SOURCE: International Finance Corporation.

stocks dominate the overall market return. Second, unlike the developed markets, which tend to have forces that affect diverse sectors of the economy differently, the emerging markets tend to have a strong market-related force that affects all stocks within a market. This widespread effect tends to accentuate volatility.

Some anomalies are apparent in these results. Colombia, Jordan, Nigeria, Pakistan, and Zimbabwe appear to have had relatively low risk over the five-year period. We believe that these low figures reflect a lack of liquidity in these markets; observed volatilities (and correlations with other markets) must therefore be viewed with caution. When we look at the turnover ratio (value traded/market capitalization) for each market, we find that these five markets rank among the bottom six (see Table 19.1). The real volatility is likely to be much higher, if and when these markets become more liquid.

When we look at the emerging markets as a group (using the BARRA Emerging World Universe of about 4,000 stocks), we find that the group has much lower volatility than most of the individual markets. This has occurred because of low correlations among these markets. The diversification that these low correlations offer the global investor is one of the biggest benefits of investing in the emerging markets. Later in the chapter, we will examine in greater detail the impact of these low correlations on a global portfolio. The volatility (over the five years studied) of the IFC Global Composite Index was about 23.39 percent, as compared to 15.58 percent for the Financial Times (FT) World Index.

The emerging markets have low correlations not only with each other, but also with the developed markets. The fact that the emerging markets (individually and as a group) have low correlations with the developed markets implies that there is an opportunity for diversification for the global investor.

Modest Investments in Emerging Markets Actually Reduce Risk

Figure 19.1 shows the effect of adding an emerging markets index fund (the IFC Global Composite Index) to a global portfolio (FT World Index). Putting 20 percent of the investment into emerging markets would have not only reduced risk from 15.5 percent to about 14.5 percent, but also would have increased overall annual portfolio return (over the five years studied from 7.69 percent to just over 10 percent). In fact, investments all the way up to 45 percent in the emerging markets would have reduced risk and increased return, relative to the FT World Index. This risk reduction (and return enhancement) is not simply an artifact of those five years; it would have been true during any five-year (or longer) period since 1985 (when the IFC Global Composite Index was created).

FIGURE 19.1 Effect of Adding an Emerging Markets Index Fund to FT World Index (January 1988–December 1992)

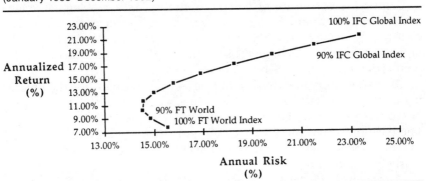

This analysis assumes that one was to buy an emerging markets index fund (i.e., weight countries in proportion to their market capitalization). The results are likely to be true for any well-diversified emerging markets portfolio. Putting all of one's emerging market's assets into one region (say, Latin America) would not constitute a well-diversified portfolio. But in the absence of any other information, how should one allocate money to different countries (or regions)? Is indexation, using market capitalization weights, the right answer?

Capitalization Weighting Requires Market Efficiency Assumptions

In order to weight countries in proportion to their market capitalization, one has to assume that markets are efficiently priced. If, in fact, markets are not efficiently priced, market weighting leads one to overweight "overvalued" countries (e.g., Japan in the late 1980s) and underweight "undervalued" countries.

In the emerging markets, where there are frequently severe restrictions on the investments global investors can make within each market, the definition of what constitutes market weighting depends on who you are (a local or a foreigner) and what is available to buy.

To determine each country's weight in such bipolar markets, would one use the total market capitalization (available to the locals) or just the float that is available to foreigners? Each of these leads to radically different weights for countries such as India, Korea, and Taiwan. Korea forms 14.9 percent of the IFC Global Composite Index but only 3.3 percent of the IFC Investable Composite Index (as of June 1, 1993). The difference between the two indexes is that the IFC Global Composite

Index uses total market capitalization and the IFC Investable Composite Index uses the float that is available to global investors.

Thus, the definition of market weighting is a problem. Furthermore, it would be hard to make the case that emerging markets are efficiently priced. No market that went from 5,000 to 12,500 in two months and back to 2,500 in three months (as Taiwan did in 1991) can be considered efficient, by any definition of efficiency.

If market capitalization weighting is inappropriate for the emerging markets, what is the right way to choose country weights? One proposed solution would be to use gross domestic product (GDP) weights. The reasoning behind this approach is that GDP is more directly tied to real economic activity and not subject to the whims of sentiment (as markets weights are).

However, the World Bank has recently redefined the GDP of countries, basing it on purchasing power parity (PPP) rather than current exchange rates. This causes the emerging markets (as a group) to increase from about 20 percent of world GDP to just under 50 percent. This new definition of GDP weighting would require global investors to immediately shift a large proportion of their investments from the developed markets to the emerging markets. In short, using GDP weights now requires investors to make a judgment about how GDP is compared across countries (PPP or current exchange rates) and would cause huge differences in relative weights, based on which choice was made. This approach has serious problems associated with it.

If Not Market or GDP Weights, Then What?

One proposed solution to this problem is to use "low-volatility" (LV) weighting. The concept is simple and well understood (in the context of the U.S. equity market). We pick the weights of each country that would create a minimum variance portfolio, viewed from the investor's numeral currency. Thus, each country would be weighted according to how much it contributed to *lowering* the risk of the overall portfolio, rather than according to its market capitalization. Countries that had the lowest predicted volatility coupled with low correlation with other markets would have the highest weight; those with high predicted volatility or high correlation with other countries would have the lowest weight.

The theoretical basis for using such a low-volatility strategy is that the LV portfolio is likely to be close to the efficient frontier. The reason is that one can forecast future volatility with a fair amount of accuracy. A portfolio that is forecast to have low volatility ex ante is highly likely to have low volatility ex post. If we visualize an efficient frontier chart, we can be reasonably sure that the ex-ante LV portfolio is likely to be close to the ex-post minimum variance point, even if we know nothing about what its return might be. On the other hand, one can make no such assertion about market-weighted portfolios. One can only discover ex post whether they were close to the frontier or not. As a result, the LV portfolio is likely to be more mean-variance (MV) efficient than the market portfolio.

Thus, although we would expect the LV portfolio to have lower volatility than the market portfolio, we have no ex-ante forecast to the relative return of one vis-à-vis the other. If, in fact, the market portfolio is highly inefficient (i.e., it is a deep interior point within the frontier), there is a possibility that the return to the LV portfolio will be as high as or higher than the market portfolio. Numerous researchers[2] have investigated this phenomenon within the U.S. market. Their work indicates that, in the U.S. market, an LV portfolio would have in fact outperformed the market portfolio while having considerably lower risk.

Therefore, this weighting scheme has the multiple benefits of making sense (from an efficiency point of view), lowering risk (for an asset class whose image is synonymous with high risk), and having the possibility of doing as well as the market portfolio (if the U.S. precedent holds).

If one uses such a methodology without any constraints on the weights of each country, one ends up with weights that are either unpalatable or uninvestable from a global investor's point of view. With any unconstrained optimization, one needs to be wary that resulting country weights reflect true diversification, rather than data errors in the estimation and optimization process. Thus, it makes sense to set constraints on country weights based on the true investability of each country and the "prudent person" test (i.e., no matter how low-risk India may seem to the optimizer, no prudent person would put 80 percent of his or her money there).

A Nice Idea, but Does it Work?

We tested this idea to see how it would have worked over a five-year period (1988–1992). To make this a realistic strategy, we used a simple constraint: each country's weight could range only from 50 percent to 200 percent of its market capitalization weight. Thus, if a country constitutes 10 percent of the IFC Global Composite Index, its weight in the LV portfolio had to be in the range of 5 percent to 20 percent. This ensured that each country would have a weight that is reasonable and investable by the global investor. The numbers 50 percent and 200 percent were chosen quite arbitrarily; for an actual investment, the range should probably be tailored to the investability of each country and the risk aversion of the investor.

To construct the portfolios, we used the following methodology.

1. We chose from all the countries listed in the IFC Global Composite Index, except Colombia, Indonesia, Jordan, Nigeria, Pakistan, Venezuela, and Zimbabwe. All of these (except Indonesia, for which adequate data were not available) were deemed to be uninvestable and/or uninteresting to the global investor. Additionally, they cumulatively constitute less than 5 percent of the IFC Global Composite Index.

2. We used the monthly total return (in US$) to each market (the corresponding IFC Global Index for that country) from January 1985 to December 1987 (36 months) to form the first variance–covariance matrix. Using this matrix, we computed the LV portfolio for January 1988 that met our constraint (50 percent to 200 percent market weight for each country) using quadratic optimization.

3. We held this portfolio for 12 months, until the end of 1988.

4. We then repeated steps 2 and 3 for 1989 through 1992. At each year-end, we used the previous five years' data to compute the variance–covariance matrix (except in 1988, when only four years' data were available).

5. We computed the return (in US$) to the LV strategy and the IFC Global Composite Index over the period from January 1988 to December 1992.

And the Winner Is . . .

The results of the simulation are shown in Figure 19.2. A visual inspection reveals that the LV portfolio did indeed have lower volatility (as

FIGURE 19.2 Cumulative Return to LV Portfolio and IFC Global Composite Index (January 1988–December 1992)

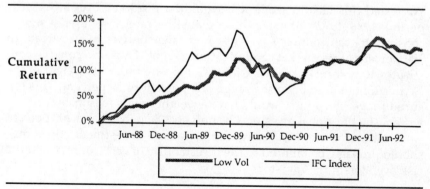

expected) than the IFC Global Composite Index. Somewhat surprising (but not wholly unexpected) is the finding that the LV portfolio outperformed the IFC Global Composite Index over the same time period. This would imply that the IFC Global Composite Index was almost certainly not MV-efficient over this period.

We find that the realized volatility (annualized standard deviation of monthly returns) of the LV portfolio over this five-year period was 16.54 percent as compared to 23.39 percent for the IFC Global Composite Index. Figure 19.3 shows the 24-month rolling volatility over this time period; the LV portfolio had lower realized volatility than the IFC Global Composite Index over the entire time span.

These results show that such an LV strategy would indeed have worked over the five years studied. In our opinion, a case can be made to think of the LV weights as the basis for country weighting in passive investments, or as the baseline for performance evaluation of active managers.

More Is Better

Thus far, the analysis has focused on how to weight the emerging markets among themselves. We now look at the impact of adding the LV portfolio to a global investor's portfolio, that is, what would happen if we were to blend the LV portfolio with the global market.

Figure 19.4 shows the impact of adding the LV portfolio to the FT World Index. Up to weights of 10 percent in the emerging markets, it doesn't seem to make much difference whether one uses capitalization weights or LV weights; but beyond 10 percent, the impact is quite dramatic. The strategy clearly leads to much greater risk reduction than the capitalization-weighted IFC Global Composite Index.

FIGURE 19.3 Realized Volatility of IFC Global Composite Index and Low-Volatility Portfolios (January 1990–December 1992)

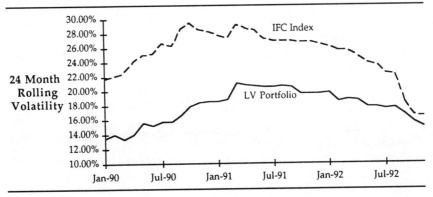

FIGURE 19.4   Adding LV Portfolio and Emerging Markets Index to FT World Index (January 1988–December 1992)

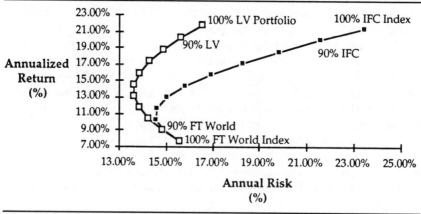

Additionally, whereas the lowest volatility of the IFC–FT mix is about 20 percent invested in emerging markets, the lowest risk point of the LV–FT mix is between 40 percent and 50 percent in the emerging markets. Thus, using this methodology strengthens an already strong case for investments in the emerging markets.

The Early Bird Gets the Worm

The main reason for this significant risk reduction is the fact that emerging markets are uncorrelated to each other and to developed markets. As their economic and trade links with each other and with developed markets increase, these correlations will undoubtedly rise. When this happens, the "diversification free lunch" that is currently being served will diminish. Investors should indulge while the opportunity exists!

In conclusion, modest investments in an emerging markets index fund would reduce overall portfolio risk of a global investor; larger investments in an LV emerging market portfolio would lead to further risk reduction.

NOTES

1. Divecha, Drach, and Stefek, "Emerging Markets: A Quantitative Perspective," *Journal of Portfolio Management* (Fall 1992): 41–56.
2. R. A. Haugen, "Building a Better Index," *Pensions and Investment Age*, October 1, 1990, p. 56.

20

Global Passive Management

Brian R. Bruce
Vice President

Heydon D. Traub
Senior Vice President

Larry L. Martin
Principal

Jennifer Hargreaves
Investment Officer
State Street Global Advisors
Boston, MA

We begin this chapter by asking what global passive management is and what makes it different from other forms of management.[1] We will analyze the performance of passive strategies versus active strategies. We will also explore different passive approaches, highlighting the most commonly used strategy: market capitalization weighting.

PASSIVE MANAGEMENT

What is passive management? How is it different from active or quantitative management? Investment management styles can be defined in terms of risk and judgment. Table 20.1 shows the taxonomy of investment management styles and asset classes. It shows how judgment and risk increase when one moves from strictly passive products (no judgment and low risk as defined by variation from the accepted asset-class benchmark) to active products (significant judgments and higher risk because of potentially large variation from the benchmark). The asset classes are the horizontal component. Bruce[2] points out that nontraditional asset classes (real estate, venture capital) can fit in this framework along with the more traditional equities and fixed income.

TABLE 20.1 Investment Management

	Portfolio Level			
	Passive Level	Enhanced Passive Level	Quantitative Level	Active
Asset Allocation Portfolio Restructuring				
Equity:				
U.S. Large Cap	S&P 500	Enhanced S&P 500	Tilts	Income
U.S. Small Cap	Russell 2000		Tilts	Growth
Venture Cap				
International	EAFE		Country Allocator	Growth
Fixed:				
U.S.	Shearson-Lehman	Enhanced Shearson	Dedicated/ Immunized sector allocators	Duration
International	Goldman			
Cash	T bills	Enhanced Cash		Yield Curve
Real Estate	Frank Russell			
Monetary Metals	Gold			

Table entries are widely followed indexes or examples of a style that exemplifies the category.

Active management relies on human judgment to determine portfolio holdings on an ongoing basis. Active funds take two forms: (1) "traditional" management, which relies on a manager's ability to look at all the relevant information and judge a stock's value, or (2) quantitative management, which relies on human judgment to build a model and then apply this model in an objective manner. These funds may also make country and currency bets based on macroeconomic data. Other types of funds that are becoming popular are country allocation funds and active/ passive funds. Country funds involve holding the security selection within a country passive and making an active country bet based on a quantitative model and/or a manager's judgment.

Passive funds use little judgment. Traditionally, the funds under management use capitalization to weight both countries and stocks, thereby minimizing turnover costs and the related drag on returns. Recently, in response to concerns regarding the huge capitalization of Japan relative to the rest of the world, funds have sprung up that weight the countries based on the gross national domestic product or other somewhat arbitrary means to reduce the Japanese exposure.

Today, over 30 percent of the domestic equity assets of the largest 200 U.S. pension funds are indexed. InterSec estimates that 15 percent of the international funds are indexed. Currently, there are three major indexes: (1) Morgan Stanley Capital International (MSCI) Europe Asia Far East (EAFE); (2) Financial Times Europe–Pacific Basin; and (3) Salomon–Frank Russell PMI. All three use market capitalization weighting. They differ in the number of securities included and the number of countries covered. Table 20.2 compares the three.

REASONS FOR PASSIVE MANAGEMENT

Why invest in global passive funds? There are four primary reasons:

1. Diversification;
2. Cost;
3. Fees;
4. Performance.

Each is discussed in the following subsections.

Diversification

The first justification for global indexing is diversification. Because international equities have a low correlation with the S&P 500, they help lower the risk for a given level of return (or, conversely, they help raise the return for a given level of risk). Figure 20.1 shows the efficient frontier of the S&P 500 versus EAFE over the period from 1979 to 1989. The figure shows that because of the low correlations between markets, a mixture of domestic and international securities outperforms a 100 percent domestic portfolio.

TABLE 20.2 International Indexes

	MSCI-EAFE	FT-A	SR-PMI
Countries	18	20	20
Securities	1,023	1,690	724
Market value	$3,500 billion	$4,400 billion	$2,600 billion
Other	Longest performance record	Broadest	Large capitalization; most liquid
Correlations with MSCI	1.00	.99	.99
Annualized returns 1987–1989	20.9%	21.5%	20.5%

SOURCE: State Street Global Advisors.

FIGURE 20.1 Efficient Frontier S&P 500 with EAFE (1979–1989)

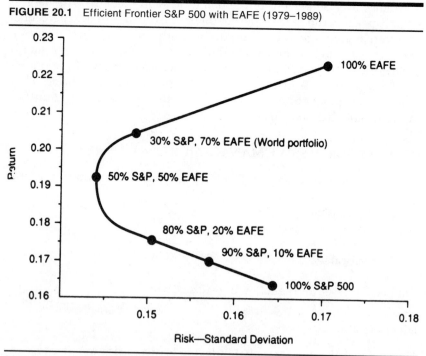

SOURCE: State Street Global Advisors.

Cost

Passive management, a less expensive way to operate in the investment business, is very system-intensive. Remi Browne[3] states:

> Once systems are in place there is no need to hire large numbers of highly compensated investment analysts to seek out new ideas. This is quite the opposite of what is required in active management. Since active managers are marketing their services on a basis of adding more alpha than their competitors, it is essential for active managers to attract and retain highly compensated personnel who can convince the marketplace of their superiority. Passive management firms need not be managed on this "star" system, nor is there generally a need for as many professionals per unit of assets managed. While the construction of complex systems can pose a formidable "barrier to entry," once the systems are in place great economies can be passed on to the client in the form of lower fees.

Systems and personnel costs are fixed costs that are lower with passive management. In addition, passive managers are more likely to retain assets because they almost always meet their objectives. Passive managers can therefore operate with lower fees. A variable cost is also lower: transactions cost. As Traub pointed out,[4] transactions cost can be broken down into: commissions, taxes, bid–offer spreads, and market impact.

Commissions are a major reason that passive strategies are less costly to implement than active strategies. The saving stems from the use of program trading. Active managers trade with the block desk at a brokerage firm. Most trades involve a large number of shares in a single name. These trades are done because the active manager has a reason for wishing to either buy or sell a particular security. This type of trade is called an information trade (i.e., the person who is making the trade has some information that brought about the trading decision). Because of this information, the broker must price the offer or guarantee to reflect the possibility that this information may cause adverse movement of the security before the position can be purchased/liquidated.

A program trade, a purchase or sale of a large number of securities at one time, is utilized by passive managers who need either liquidity or a rebalancing of current holdings. This type of trade is considered informationless because the person making the trade has no hidden information about the securities involved. The effect this difference can have in the price of commission bids from brokers is amazing. State Street Bank estimates that international program desks average 25 basis points for agency program bids versus 50 basis points for international block desks trading the same securities.

Taxes is the next transaction cost. In the United States, there are no exchange taxes, with the exception of minimal SEC fees on the sell side. Overseas, taxes are as high as 1 percent for both buys and sells. Sweden has the highest tax structure of the EAFE markets. Taxes are a major reason that global active managers trail their benchmark by more than domestic managers. Active strategies have a higher turnover than passive strategies. If traders must pay up to 100 basis points to the local exchange every time they wish to trade, high turnover can significantly impact returns.

Bid–offer spreads also contribute to the cost of transacting. Spreads can be very high, especially in some small-capitalization issues. In the United States, over 4 percent of all companies in the second and third thousand-largest-names groups have bid–ask spreads larger than 4 percent. These spreads typically represent the largest part of the transaction cost, yet managers often overlook them when moving from one security to another because the spreads cannot be easily measured. As with other costs, they are typically higher overseas. Based on data compiled at State Street Bank's Asset Management Group, the weighted average bid–ask is estimated to be at least 1.2 percent, which translates to a cost of 60 basis points each way. Realistically, we would expect an active manager to face higher bid–ask spreads because many active managers equally weight the holdings in their portfolios. This means that a larger proportion of their dollars traded will involve smaller-capitalization stocks (as compared to an index fund), which have above-average bid–ask spreads.

Market impact is the last component of transactions cost and the most difficult part to measure. Because of the difficulty involved, we will not add market impact to the transaction cost calculation given later in the chapter. However, based on our experience managing both passive and active portfolios, market impact exists and is typically greater for active portfolios. The latter is true because active managers often take large positions relative to the size (capitalization) of a company. Capitalization correlates highly with trading volume, so we should expect smaller positions offered at a given price for small-cap stocks. This means that the offer price is more likely to be "impacted" up for a small stock if a manager tries to accumulate a sizable position in a short amount of time. We would expect that most active managers would not be willing to wait very long; before they have bought all the desired shares, other investors might discover the "bullish" information that led them to want the stock.

Fees

Management fees make it difficult to beat the index. According to a recent SEI survey, international manager fees average 68 basis points versus approximately 25 basis points for an EAFE index fund. SEI also found that the average domestic active fee was 58 basis points. (An average fee for an S&P 500 index fund is 5 basis points.) Management fees alone constitute a drag in performance of over 40 basis points.

TOTAL COST FOR AN INTERNATIONAL TRADE

How this translates into total cost can be seen in Figure 20.2. The first cost is management fees. We conservatively estimate an active management fee of 60 basis points. Next, we figure the brokerage commission at 50 percent turnover and estimate a commission of 50 basis points (each way). This is equal to a total cost of 50 basis points.

Finally, we estimate the weighted-average tax to trade (Australia, Germany, Hong Kong, Italy, Japan, Singapore, Sweden, Switzerland, and the U.K. tax trades) to be 25 basis points. Ignoring contributions and withdrawals, and assuming 50 percent turnover each way for an active manager, this causes a drag of 25 basis points for an active portfolio.

FIGURE 20.2 Annual Cost Comparison: Indexing versus Active Management

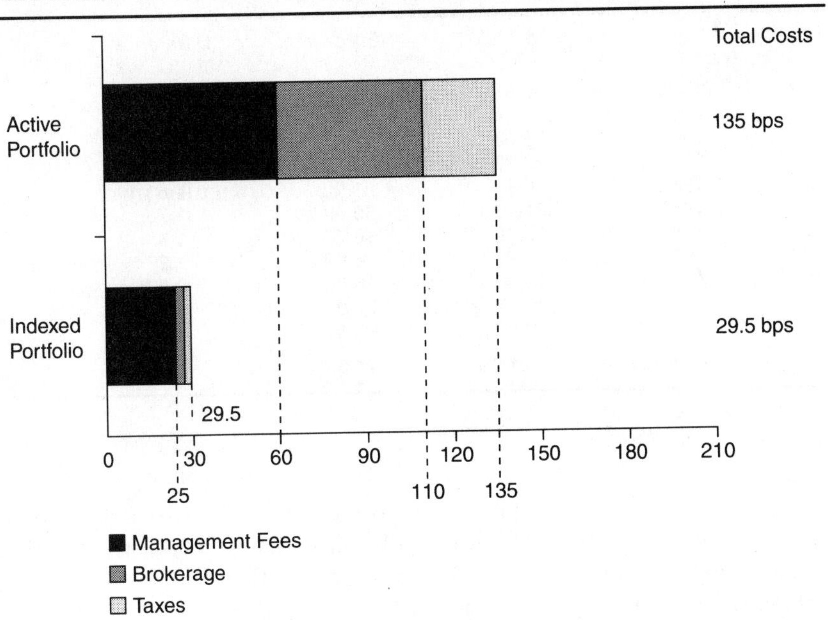

SOURCE: State Street Global Advisors.

The total for the active portfolio is 135 basis points, ignoring the important (but harder to quantify) market impact.

In analyzing costs for an EAFE indexed portfolio, we first look at turnover. The average percentage of change in the composition of the EAFE index is about 3 percent. This translates to turnover for an index fund of 6 percent. At a cost of 50 basis points for commission and 25 basis points for taxes, the total cost is 4.5 basis points. Add on the management fee (25 basis points) for a total of 29.5.

Even assuming no market impact costs, an active portfolio must select stocks that outperform by 1.05 percent just to match a passive portfolio's returns. This is a large hurdle to overcome.

Performance

Perhaps the most convincing argument in favor of index funds is their results. An index fund manager seeks to achieve returns identical to a specific benchmark. This objective is achieved by holding a basket of securities designed to track the index.

TABLE 20.3 S&P 500 Index Performance versus SEI Median

Year	S&P 500	SEI Median	Difference
1980	32.57%	30.60%	1.97%
1981	−5.34	−2.20	−3.14
1982	21.08	22.40	−1.32
1983	22.39	19.60	2.79
1984	6.11	1.50	4.61
1985	31.73	30.00	1.73
1986	18.55	16.70	1.85
1987	5.23	4.00	1.23
1988	16.83	16.80	0.03
1989	31.52	27.30	4.22
1990	−3.07	−3.50	0.43
Average	16.15%	14.84%	1.31%

According to data from 1980 through 1990, the two best known global indexes, the S&P 500 and EAFE, have easily beaten the median manager performance. Table 20.3 shows that the S&P 500 has beaten the SEI median manager by an average of 131 basis points per year. Table 20.4 shows that the EAFE index has beaten the InterSec median manager by 136 basis points per year. In addition, from 1983 to 1987, the EAFE index was in the top 1 percent of the InterSec rankings of all investment managers.

TABLE 20.4 EAFE Index Performance versus InterSec Median

Year	EAFE	InterSec Median	Difference
1980	23.50%	28.80%	−5.30%
1981	−1.60	−1.90	0.30
1982	−1.20	3.90	−5.10
1983	24.20	28.70	−4.50
1984	7.60	−2.90	10.50
1985	56.20	55.90	0.30
1986	69.40	60.00	9.40
1987	24.60	11.30	13.30
1988	28.30	16.40	11.90
1989	10.50	21.60	−11.10
1990	−23.40	−18.60	−4.80
Average	19.83%	18.47%	1.36%

SOURCE: State Street Global Advisors.

EMERGING MARKETS: THE NEWEST GLOBAL INDEX FUNDS

Based on its small market capitalization in 1970, few could have predicted Japan's phenomenal growth. Opportunities similar to Japan in 1970 are often obscured by the tendency to aggregate countries into two groups: (1) developed and (2) underdeveloped. Among the countries in the latter group are the emerging countries, whose markets are growing faster than the mature markets and have experienced extraordinary returns. Three markets that have shown impressive returns in U.S. Dollar terms through May of this year are (1) Brazil (140 percent), (2) Argentina (86 percent), and (3) Mexico (67 percent). One influence driving this growth is a dramatic increase in foreign investment as legal restrictions have been reduced or removed. High returns, combined with the low correlation of these markets with the developed markets, make this relatively unexploited investment option an attractive addition to institutional portfolios.

An "emerging" market is one that is not included in one of the accepted, developed indexes. It has an established stock market and reliable data that can be obtained and updated on a reasonably accurate and frequent basis. Emerging markets comprise approximately 4 percent of the world's capitalization, as represented in the MSCI World indexes. Fourteen markets are included in the MSCI Emerging Market Index, which has been calculated since 1987. The countries in this benchmark are:

1. Argentina
2. Brazil
3. Chile
4. Greece
5. Indonesia
6. Jordan
7. Korea*

8. Malaysia
9. Mexico
10. Philippines
11. Portugal
12. Taiwan
13. Thailand
14. Turkey

*Open only to local investors

When investing in emerging markets, volatility, liquidity, and transactions costs are major concerns. The volatility of the individual markets may be high, but the aggregate Emerging Market Free Index has a volatility comparable to that of the MSCI EAFE and S&P 500 indexes. Liquidity is controlled by MSCI's use of a liquidity screen when selecting securities for index inclusion. The high transaction costs and active management fees associated with investing in emerging markets are even higher than in EAFE markets and make more compelling the argument that passive management is the most cost-effective way to gain exposure to these countries.

Market Volatilities in US$
(December 31, 1987–December 31, 1993)

MSCI EAFE	16.1
MSCI Emerging Market (Free)	15.4
S&P 500	12.4
MSCI Japan	24.0
MSCI U.K.	17.1
MSCI Brazil	53.6
MSCI Mexico (Free)	25.6

(Free) indexes include only securities that may be held by foreign investors.

CONCLUSION

A strong argument can be made for the use of passive funds in any investment strategy, because of the lower costs compared to other styles of management. Passive funds should be considered as the core portfolio for any global equity portfolio.

NOTES

1. Parts of this chapter are adapted from an earlier version that appeared in Business One Irwin's "Global Portfolios" in 1991.
2. Brian Bruce, "Tactical Asset Allocation: Trends and Prospects," *Investment Management Review* (September–October 1988).
3. Remi Browne, "The Theoretical Basis for Indexing," *Investing* (Fall 1990).
4. Heydon Traub, "The Outlook for International Passive Management," *Investment Management Review* (July–August 1988).

Appendix

U.S. and Global Asset Allocation Statistics

FIGURE A.1 Wealth Indexes of Investments in U.S. Capital Markets (1925–1992)

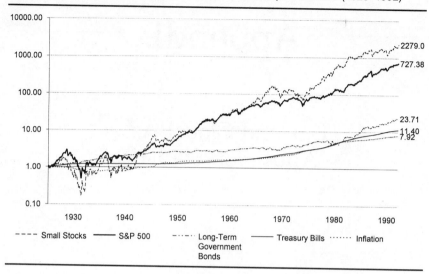

FIGURE A.2 Investable World Wealth by U.S. Investors (Year-End 1991)

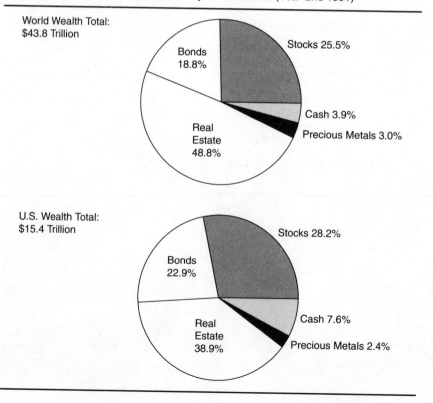

FIGURE A.3   Total Equity Market Capitalizations (January 1993)

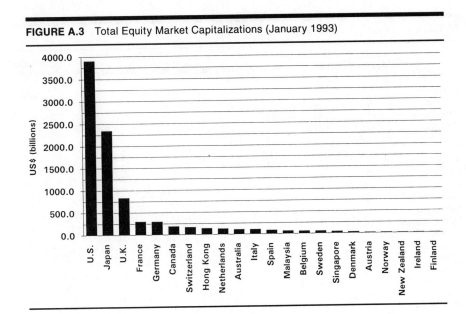

TABLE A.1   U.S. Stocks, Bonds, Bills, and Inflation: Summary Statistics of Annual Returns (1926–1992)

	Geometric Mean	Arithmetic Mean	Standard Deviation	Serial Correlation
S&P 500	10.3%	12.4%	20.6%	−0.01
Small stock	12.2	17.6	35.0	0.09
Long-term goverment bonds	4.8	5.2	8.6	0.11
Treasury bills	3.7	3.8	3.3	0.92
Inflation	3.1	3.2	4.7	0.64

SOURCE: *Stocks, Bonds, Bills, and Inflation 1993 Yearbook™,* Ibbotson Associates, Inc., Chicago (annually updates work by Roger G. Ibbotson and Rex A. Sinquefield).

TABLE A.2 World Equity Markets Correlation Matrix (1970–1991)

	Australia	Austria	Belgium	Canada	Denmark	France	Germany	Hong Kong
Austria	.07							
Belgium	.43	.59						
Canada	.71	.21	.37					
Denmark	.43	.37	.38	.50				
France	.64	.55	.84	.50	.36			
Germany	.24	.83	.68	.14	.43	.69		
Hong Kong	.50	.12	.31	.60	.39	.36	.14	
Ireland	.70	.79	.89	.68	.63	.93	.88	.55
Italy	.51	.61	.68	.32	.26	.75	.62	.31
Japan	.40	.17	.61	.37	.54	.47	.30	.58
Netherlands	.66	.56	.69	.55	.49	.81	.72	.46
New Zealand	.64	.29	.36	.76	.38	.64	.61	.54
Norway	.37	.33	.28	.57	.14	.28	.10	.09
South Africa	.37	.35	.43	.36	.10	.59	.38	.23
Spain	.31	.35	.72	.14	.15	.54	.29	.33
Sweden	.44	.34	.61	.29	.52	.57	.58	.09
Switzerland	.40	.76	.74	.34	.48	.75	.93	.37
U.K.	.56	.14	.27	.36	.16	.44	.36	.48
USA	.61	.28	.36	.63	.42	.49	.40	.57

TABLE A.2 *(Continued)*

Ireland	Italy	Japan	Nthrlnds	New Zealand	Norway	So. Africa	Spain	Sweden	Swtzrlnd	U.K.
.87										
.60	.46									
.92	.61	.46								
.70	.63	.50	.82							
.72	.20	−.19	.15	.00						
.44	.44	.28	.57	.79	.00					
.55	.67	.61	.34	.86	.10	.32				
.72	.57	.50	.51	.51	.06	.47	.47			
.91	.62	.42	.82	.91	.17	.40	.33	.52		
.79	.27	.25	.64	.69	−.08	.27	.11	.18	.57	
.67	.42	.32	.77	.99	.05	.64	.13	.46	.52	.58

TABLE A.3 Summary Statistics for Developed Equity Markets

	Compound Annual Return ($US)	Annualized Monthly Standard Deviation ($US)	Period Covered
Australia	9.0%	26.9%	1971–1992
Austria	12.7	21.9	1970–1992
Belgium	15.0	20.0	1970–1992
Canada	9.1	19.3	1970–1992
Denmark	13.7	19.2	1970–1992
France	12.3	24.5	1970–1992
Germany	10.9	21.2	1970–1992
Hong Kong	20.9	41.5	1970–1992
Ireland	14.5	26.5	1981–1992
Italy	4.7	26.1	1970–1992
Japan	16.5	22.8	1970–1992
Netherlands	15.0	18.6	1970–1992
Norway	11.5	28.2	1970–1992
South Africa	1.9	34.6	1981–1992
Spain	7.4	22.7	1970–1992
Sweden	14.0	22.2	1970–1992
Switzerland	12.1	19.6	1970–1992
United Kingdom	12.8	26.6	1970–1992
United States	10.8	15.9	1970–1992
World	11.2%	17.7%	1970–1992

TABLE A.4 Summary Statistics for Emerging Equity Markets

Region/Country	Compound Annual Return (US$)	Annualized Standard Deviation	Period
Asia			
India	18.0%	27.3%	1/76–11/92
Korea	21.6	32.3	1/76–11/92
Malaysia	14.1	25.5	1/85–11/92
Pakistan	21.7	24.0	1/85–11/92
Philippines	48.9	37.8	1/85–11/92
Taiwan	21.0	53.6	1/85–11/92
Thailand	24.5	26.4	1/76–11/92
Americas			
Argentina	28.9	93.2	11/77–11/92
Brazil	4.3	63.9	1/76–11/92
Chile	33.2	39.5	1/76–11/92
Colombia	52.3	33.0	1/85–11/92
Mexico	21.1	44.0	1/76–11/92
Venezuela	22.8	49.4	1/85–11/92
Europe—Middle East—Africa			
Greece	1.6	36.4	1/76–11/92
Jordan	10.3	20.5	1/79–11/92
Nigeria	1.7	35.1	1/85–11/92
Portugal	14.2	50.4	2/86–11/92
Turkey	59.5	98.9	1/87–11/92
Zimbabwe	2.4	34.2	1/76–11/92
World	13.9	14.4	1/76–11/92

SOURCE: From the IFC Emerging Markets database, provided by the International Financial Corporation, an affiliate of the World Bank.

TABLE A.5 International Bond Market Performance

	Compound Annual Return ($US)	Standard Deviation	Period Covered
Australia	6.6%	13.1%	1961–1992
Austria	12.3	15.3	1972–1992
Belgium	9.9	15.9	1961–1992
Canada	7.3	9.0	1961–1992
France	7.8	14.9	1961–1992
Germany	10.5	13.5	1961–1992
Ireland	8.8	22.0	1965–1992
Italy	7.2	21.2	1961–1992
Japan	12.1	17.2	1967–1992
Netherlands	10.1	14.2	1965–1992
New Zealand	5.2	18.3	1965–1992
South Africa	1.9	18.7	1961–1992
Sweden	6.3	12.2	1965–1992
Switzerland	8.6	16.2	1965–1992
United Kingdom	7.1	20.6	1961–1992
United States	6.6	10.9	1961–1992

TABLE A.6 World Bond Markets Correlation Matrix (1961–1991)

	Australia	Austria	Belgium	Canada	France	Germany	Ireland
Austria	.07						
Belgium	.22	.88					
Canada	.21	.10	.11				
France	.32	.74	.85	.21			
Germany	.13	.90	.87	.15	.69		
Ireland	.39	.52	.64	.18	.62	.59	
Italy	.44	.47	.65	.18	.74	.44	.41
Japan	.41	.50	.68	−.05	.56	.58	.63
Netherlands	.15	.95	.89	.28	.77	.93	.60
New Zealand	.42	.46	.52	.15	.41	.34	.47
South Africa	.25	.32	.26	.06	.22	.28	.01
Sweden	.14	.77	.84	.13	.70	.64	.28
Switzerland	.14	.89	.85	−.10	.67	.88	.53
U.K.	.42	.34	.47	.11	.40	.41	.90
USA	.11	.26	.31	.82	.45	.35	.28

TABLE A.6 *(Continued)*

Italy	Japan	Nthrlnds	New Zealand	So. Africa	Sweden	Swtzrlnd	U.K.
.47							
.49	.53						
.32	.51	.40					
.40	.03	.27	.30				
.57	.45	.70	.58	.31			
.35	.65	.86	.41	.24	.65		
.32	.60	.42	.46	.02	.15	.41	
.37	.07	.49	.00	.11	.21	.12	.16

Index